THE DEATH OF
MARIA CHAVARRIA

One Man's Journey from Doctor to Damnation

John G. Deaton, MD

iUniverse, Inc.
Bloomington

The Death of Maria Chavarria
One Man's Journey from Doctor to Damnation
A Memoir of Growing Up to be a Doctor

Copyright © 2011 John G. Deaton, MD

iUniverse books may be ordered through booksellers or by contacting:

iUniverse
1663 Liberty Drive
Bloomington, IN 47403
www.iuniverse.com
1-800-Authors (1-800-288-4677)

ISBN: 978-1-4620-5525-8 (sc)
ISBN: 978-1-4620-5526-5 (hc)
ISBN: 978-1-4620-5527-2 (e)

Library of Congress Control Number: 2011918447

Printed in the United States of America

iUniverse rev. date: 2/13/2012

Parts of this book appeared previously, in much different form, in *Texas Monthly*, *The New Physician*, *Hospital Physician*, and *Alumni News (UTMB)*

With great pride I dedicate this book to my son Steve.

When a doctor does go wrong he is the first of criminals. He has nerve and he has knowledge.

—Sherlock Holmes

Contents

Introduction

If your character is your fate, your honor is its mate. And honor, its presence, lives in fear of its absence. But the only person who can take honor from you is yourself. It is an easy theft. Pickpockets abound. I've stolen and sold my honor too many times to count. Sometimes you have to steal something to understand that you cannot steal what is already yours, not without losing more of yourself than you had thought possible. Because honor is priceless. Without it, you are a pauper. Lose it and the rest of your life will consist of begging.

I have been the physician of begging. I've begged and nibbled on the small things at the edges of medicine. I've learned roofing and car maintenance, worn concrete beneath my nails. I've built a cabin, mowed yards, and done as many kitchen suture jobs on kinfolk and friends as one might want. I've done things at the house.

Once, in 1995, a chinaberry tree blew down but was stopped by a wooden fence I had erected. I needed to cut it in two and relieve the pressure on the fence. It was a big tree, and I attacked it with a carpenter's saw. But the saw wasn't enough. I went for my double-bit ax, the one Graydon Adkins had taught me to use and, while standing on a ladder, chopped at the tree trunk until I was almost through. Needing the saw again, I propped the ax on the top rung of the ladder, level with my chest. In reaching for the saw, however, I knocked the ax off its perch. Its blade glanced off my right ankle on the way down. I continued with the saw, managed to get the tree severed, and finally noticed drops of blood on the ladder. The ax had cut a gash several inches long in my right instep. I made my way upstairs, hauled out my stuff, and sutured myself at the lavatory without anesthetic (I had run out). Then I went downstairs again and got the rest of the tree off the fence and repaired same.

Can I repair my damaged reputation? Because I am truly ashamed of some of the things I've done. All I ask is a place at the banquet of redemption, should there be one. Life has taught me that a thing lost can only be recovered by the one who lost it.

People ask why I left medicine. Students, mainly, ask with a serious tone of dismay how something so wonderful as the practice of medicine could be left behind by one who had gone to school all those years. I've answered in various ways, none satisfactory. To them or to me. Were I to try again to explain, I could do a lot worse than to write this book, the first in a planned trilogy about my decade in medicine, roughly the years 1960, when I entered medical school, to 1971, when I quit my last medical position and Mimi and I moved to Austin with our four children. Here we found employment, raised those children, and grew old together. Here we have known exceeding joy, bottomless grief, and blessings from kind people and kindred spirits, Austinites who shared their lives with us and gave freely of themselves in this most congenial of cities.

As to being damned, it was my own doing. Deep down, my secret is that I should not have gone into medicine. But I was deep inside it before I acquired that knowledge, and from Plan B I slid all the way down through the alphabet before coming to a stop. And this: my deepest secret is that I am privileged to have become a doctor. Besides family, it is, was, and always will be the greatest accomplishment of my life. I know firsthand how hard that job is to perform, how much doctors mean to their patients, and how inseparable medicine is from our society. Yes, along the way a few doctors counted me out of their lives, but as Frank Sinatra put it, "Too few to mention."

The drug addiction I blame on no one but myself. And I got over it. I've said things in print revealing a side of me that former friends hadn't known existed, and I have exposed things they might have preferred went unsaid. Still, a few good friends from my medical days have remained my friends. Some have been my physicians for various ailments, and all have been true friends. The same for those I had in Pittsburg, Texas, while growing up. Troubled for sure, but mine has been a good life. To my wife and my children I owe the credit. For them and for me, and for one other person, it has all come down to this: I've spent my life writing this book. This book is my career in medicine.

Part I.

An Undeliverable Lie

The phone rang at exactly five thirty in the morning on Monday, July 1, 1963, my first day on the job. I slept on the side of the bed nearest the phone and reached for it. We had taken the master bedroom down the hall past the kitchen and bath, and Roger, who would be a year old in September, slept in the smaller bedroom that was level with ours. He was prevented from escapades by his baby crib, still enjoyed interacting with his mobiles, and was mature enough to sleep through the night.

I knew, of course, who was calling. I had spent the last few days learning the layout of the hospital and meeting some of the people I would be working with on my first rotation, Obstetrics and Gynecology (OB/Gyn), so I had expected the call. Closer to the truth: I had eagerly awaited it. But things are never as anticipated; the phone had jangled in a special way, like the siren of an ambulance, and I stiffened to consciousness in an instant, feeling like a buffoon who had crossed paths with a porcupine. I felt the stinging in every nerve in my body.

I was frightened shitless.

Then it was okay. I heard those sweetest of words, *Dr. Deaton*, telling me I was urgently needed at the hospital and how quickly could I get there? The nurse spoke in hurried tones, telling me of the emergency, and there was a frightful screaming audible in the background, the shattering kind you feel inside your belly rather than through the ears. No time for breakfast, in answer to Mimi's question, who always heard the phone and wondered whether she could help.

I had laid out my clothes on a chair beside the bed and dressed quickly, white shirt and white pants supplied by the hospital, and my regular black shoes, but no tie or clinical jacket or preprinted nametag. Instead, my last name was stitched modestly in black thread over the breast pocket of the shirt. I said good-bye to my wife and departed for internship, telling her that I would see her again in about a year.

*   *   *

Things like that were fun to say because I was having fun. That phone call was the most exciting thing that had ever happened to me. Although I had been a doctor for all of three weeks, today was the actual start of my career. It was my first day on the job. I had a woman in labor who was having great difficulties, the hospital requiring the newly minted intern's services. They had taught me that if the patient wasn't still alive when you got there, rushing would have made no difference, and that was as good a reason as any to explain why I was racing like a demon through the empty streets south of the hospital at daybreak. No one could stop me; I was a doctor! It was not the first day of the rest of my life, it was the first day of my life.

Five minutes after setting out, I swerved onto Morgan Avenue and then Hospital Boulevard and there it was, the sprawling, one-story concrete oddity that was Corpus Christi's original Memorial Hospital, opening in 1944, splaying across a hectare of land upon these South Texas plains, and resembling the crash-landing of an oversized World War II bomber—albeit one made of concrete and having way too many sets of wings. Indeed, the parallel wings of concrete appeared to have been flung down upon a gluey sea of asphalt with such force that they were half-submerged. The asphalt, white-capped with parking spaces, lapped all the way out, save for a thin row of palm trees, to Hospital Boulevard, and I sped toward the west end of the hospital—the nose of the plane. Its cockpit consisted of two delivery rooms and, as of today, I was the pilot, or at least the copilot. The brakes screeched, the Dodge Dart skidded, and I killed the engine and bolted inside, the slamming of the door behind me lost in the tumult.

*   *   *

"Me duele! Me duele mucho! Por que no me sueltas?"
Her birth part exposed, she was strapped into the stirrups of the delivery table in the delivery room nearest the street and screaming at the top of her lungs because it hurt. A lot! Having the baby was the cure, and people waved frantically at me. At a glance I took in the table, the people, the stark dashes of

color: white and green and yellow and silver. A spotlight of the kind found in the operating room was suspended above the table, which was handily placed in the exact center of the spacious room. The beam of the light was directed at the most public of places in that most private of parts, and five or six nurses were bustling around the delivery table as though they were playing musical chairs at a church social. The patient's face, I saw, was twisted in agony. The very air quivered with fright.

My chief of medicine in Galveston, upon learning that I was going to Corpus for internship, had called Memorial "a shithole." But it was a shithole with character, I decided in that moment. There was life in this shithole, and the best nurses in town, and the most eager doctors, and, not incidentally, the most babies delivered in the city. Memorable things were bound to happen because it was *Memorial* Hospital.

My scrub consisted of a splashing of hands and arms at one of the double faucets in the hallway between the two rooms. I turned, hands dripping, and stepped into a white operating gown they held for me, and shortly I took my place at the foot of the table even as a nurse finished tying at the back the two or three strings that held the gown in place. The silver stool was not quite right, and a nurse adjusted it for my height. I glanced at the patient and then turned to my left so a nurse could help me with the tight-fitting surgical gloves.

Haste makes waste. My dripping hands made it difficult for the gloves to go on, and the contact of water with the powder they used to make the gloves more accessible to dry hands left my hands caked, as if I had dipped them in flour. A towel was found, but the nurse still had to fit the gloves on one sticky finger at a time, while another nurse had me dip my head for a mask and a cap to be tied in place, the patient screaming all the while.

"*Me duele mucho!*"

"*Senora,*" I tried, demonstrating rudimentary Spanish but nada beyond it.

"*Senora,*" a nurse in white scrubs said smilingly, "*necesita   relajar su estomago, por favor. Y respire por la boca. Entonces, ahorito, el doctor va a decirle lo que es usted necessita hacer!*"

Yeah, I thought, *that's it.*

That was the charge nurse, Linda Gomez*,[1] RN, with her beautiful face and lilting voice, as though life were a series of rooms, each more rapturous than the one before, so that even her questions were gleeful utterances: *Can this really be? And isn't he nice? And aren't we lucky to have him*? I had learned from the outgoing intern that she was the best obstetrician in Corpus, but

---

1   An asterisk at its first appearance means that the name given is a pseudonym.

I withheld judgment for now. Since she worked the night shift that ended at seven a.m., I knew that I would be spending time with her later on. Then again, I already liked her. She was shapely but plump, instantly lovable, a dainty woman careful to add pounds in proportion. I couldn't tell whether she was twenty-five or forty-five but would learn quickly enough that the previous intern was right—she was more skilled in attending term pregnancy than I would ever be.

Obeying her instructions, a circulating nurse opened an obstetrical pack. Another nurse tinkered with an anesthetic machine and, in between screams, reassured the patient in brisk Spanish. Gomez, meanwhile, asked whether I wanted a certain type of forceps, and was it all right if they gave oxytocin before the placenta and Syntocinon after the placenta? And did I mind if they gave this patient some nitrous oxide for pain, since it had already been, she said, over four hours since the last injection of Demerol?

Disagreement with any of her suggestions seemed foolhardy, and I had concerns of my own. The patient was definitely in trouble.

"Me duele mucho!"

Her body contracted in a heaving tumult, as though she were gripping barbells in an attempt to lift the entire world, not caring whether it killed her. Yet fetal progress was nil. No, that was wrong.

As she bore down with excruciating effort, the baby's chin appeared briefly at the introitus. I palpated it to make sure, found the kid's mouth, and flinched as most of the face came bulging into view. I took a hit to the pit of my stomach. Was this a brow presentation? Infants born headfirst, as almost all of them are, find easiest passage through the bony pelvis with the head bowed, a courteous greeting to the life ahead. With its neck flexed, the baby's chin fits against its breastbone, and the back of the head becomes the bullet-like presenting part. But this kid's head was not positioned like that. This kid's head was extended the opposite way, the back of it wedged against its spine, its chin the protruding part. Wrong, all wrong, because the more the mother pushed, the more likely it was that the descent of the baby's head, the largest part of its body, would become wedged in her pelvis like a kidney stone that wouldn't come out. Stymied. Stuck.

An undeliverable lie.

A nightmare. Won't go out, won't go in. It of course explained the woman's excruciating pain, her slow progress in labor, her inability to have this baby like the ones before.

With a desperate ache of futility, I realized that I must call out the staff man, obstetrician Dr. Marvin "Sam" Hastings*, on this, my first day of internship. In this, my first hour of internship. Hastings was surely at home at this hour, eating an early breakfast or still asleep. In fact, Gomez would make the call; all I had to do was give the word. But what if I had Gomez call Dr. Sam and he refused to come out, telling me to perform a C-section? I'd scrubbed in on one, with geysers of blood spurting higher than my head, but I was far from qualified to do a cesarean operation by myself. Sure, I had delivered eight babies during medical school, but those were normal deliveries with a den mother standing by. Now, alone with my first complicated delivery, the piercing screams trivialized everything that had come before, and I was like a man standing before an abyss. The uproar came at me without cease, electrifyingly, maddeningly, and everyone in attendance to this delivery braced as for a crash. As my mother used to say, it was so loud I couldn't hear myself think.

That conversation never ended, the one I had with myself, and it often took turns I didn't particularly like. Such as now, when my composure was in the balance: *Help!* it screamed. *I'm not qualified! Shouldn't be here! I'm twelve years old and scared! Me duele mucho!*

More nurses appeared. Voices that had been praising the new doctor suddenly expressed their concern. Gomez asked whether I wanted her to put on gloves. I said nothing while staring at my future, which was staring right back at me in the person of a baby who deserved better. From somewhere: *It doesn't take a doctor to do nothing.* Superseded by: *First, do no harm.*

It occurred to me to push the head back into the pelvis a distance, possibly a way to try and flex it. It didn't work, or I gave up too easily in trying. While I watched, the kid's eyes blinked open, and blinked again, as of someone drowning and signaling it by the only available communication. The kid was appealing personally to me for help. Then the mother unleashed the loudest scream so far. In pushing down, would she break its neck? Should I call Hastings immediately?

Tiny but growing was the possibility of being sued. *A doctor is a professional who puts the patient first*, a statement grilled into me from day one. You recognize the need for consultation and get it. Yet to overreact by calling too quickly for help would end the masquerade and possibly bid rigor mortis to my fledgling career. *Hey, did you hear? That new intern on OB/Gyn has not a scintilla of experience, up to his ass in alligators on day one and lost his nerve!*

I responded in kind, *No matter! Surrender to the obvious! Be the idiot you are!* Delay put the patient in peril—a crucial, terrifying event thrusting me into a legally untenable position. *Why me and why this on my very first morning and what is to become of me?*

Do something!

Now!

People continued screaming at me, drowning out the patient. Wrong. Her wailing had risen to an inhuman pitch, bellowing beyond the decibel range and into the earsplitting canon of doom, as though she were being murdered in front of everyone. At the absolute bursting point, the kid's eyes grew into enormous, sightless globes, and then his entire face exploded in the unbelievable fury of a righteous deity, for the mother had decapitated him!

Or at least I thought so, until the entire kid spurted into my hands, wet and squalling, a teeming mass tethered to a lavender rope, not a *him* but a *her*, six pounds of squirming baby that I adeptly deposited upon its mother's belly. I applied two clamps a little way back from the baby's body and several inches apart, cut the cord precisely between the clamps, and basked in the shimmering waves of silence lapping through the room. Nothing to it. In the faint distance I heard Gomez yelling her congratulations.

For what? My incompetence? Then she was asking me again about oxytocin and so forth, but we were on automatic pilot so far as I was concerned, and the bawling baby proved it. I had done no episiotomy, used no forceps, applied no manipulations, made no decision, and yet life had renewed itself in my neophyte presence, demonstrating to me how closely entwined are death and birth, and expertise and idiocy, and I was more humbled than enthralled, more reverential than proud. The free end of the umbilical cord, weighted by the clamp, danced toward the floor. At the other end, which was still hidden in the birth tract, things were not yet concluded. A nurse handed me a saucepan without a handle. Shortly the placenta popped out—the meaty pancake at the other end of the cord—and I caught it in the pan and passed it to the nurse. Blood loss was minimal. There was nothing but to examine the infant—a perfect 10 on the Apgar[2] scale—write a note, and yield the floor to the nurses.

In her mother's arms, the baby went contentedly to sleep. The raucous sounds of the near calamity were erased by the purring of women and the hum of the air-conditioning. Peeling off the gloves, I discovered that I was trembling. I wished to be alone but was instead ushered to the side of the delivery table.

Gomez beamed. "She wants to say something to you."

The mother smiled gloriously, and I waited, as she took my hand in hers and squeezed it, for the litany of Spanish that was bound to follow. Not at all.

"Thank you, Doctor," she said in perfect English.

"You are welcome," I told her, and I made a mental note to read up on brow presentations and to learn, perhaps, not to panic in an emergency.

---

2   Virginia Apgar, 1909–1974, was an anesthesiologist who standardized evaluation of the newborn.

(Upon reflection, it was most likely the baby's size—on the small side of normal—that had facilitated delivery, even with a brow presentation.)

*   *   *

Were life's ultimate goal to have the world kiss your ass, I had allowed myself the entertaining thought that I was almost there. A few weeks earlier, as a "clinical clerk" in Galveston, I had awakened one day to the real possibility that my days as a medical student were numbered. That bit of amusement was almost over. Were one to have ventured a thought as to what I found most tantalizing about my immediate future, one would not go wrong in predicting that it had to do with the rapid approach of my internship, that fabled odyssey to which every infant doctor is born, and this by way of what might or might not turn out to be an undeliverable lie.

Internship for us—Mimi sharing everything—meant moving to Corpus, but Corpus couldn't possibly be less accommodating than Galveston had been to us during my tenure as a student at the University of Texas Medical Branch. Galveston was the pits, its merchants in cahoots with the pirates dating back to the infamous Jean Laffite, near whose harbor hideout in Galveston Bay the nine-story John Sealy Hospital stood, flagship of the Medical Branch. Of the barrier islands sheltering the Texas Gulf Coast, Galveston was the biggest and earliest settled, and UTMB had long been its pride, its darling, its mistress. It bragged of being the oldest medical school in Texas and of counting the great majority of Texas physicians as its alumnae. And this was true, at the time.

Executives at UTMB knew how to entice funds from the state legislature, and the campus itself offered a flamboyant spaciousness more suited to a palatial estate than to the setting for dire human illnesses and their dreadful consequences. Somehow, in Galveston, the irony seemed appropriate. The setting was lush, rapturous, tropical. Lazy oleanders graced the grounds and their bright plumage, along with roses, lapped at the sidewalks. The thick carpet of St. Augustine grass that covered the hospital grounds, when mowed, as it was weekly, imbued the air with the sweet smell of fresh-cut watermelon. Palm trees swayed like belly dancers beside every accompanying street the mile or so to Seawall Boulevard, and the whitecaps of the Gulf of Mexico seemed to splash against every glass surface on the south side of the yellow-brick hospital.

So it was that in May and early June of 1963, with Corpus on the horizon, I had spent my last days of dashing madly through the sleek, green corridors of the John Sealy Hospital, seeing patients and drawing blood and starting IVs and performing whatever other bedside maneuvers were asked of me by the medical school. Studentship owned me but I was slipping its bonds, and the excitement burgeoned into a giddy, throbbing ecstasy, like my first time on a bike or like the first day of spring, when I was let to run barefooted upon the earth. I teetered on the threshold of an exultation that built upon itself by the day—days that could be agonizingly, unendurably long or that might (if one weren't looking) sneak past like minutes. John Sealy Hospital had become so much a part of my persona that I no longer thought of myself as separate from it.

Have I said bad things about it? Have I lashed out at the greedy Galveston merchants? It was a pique of momentary duration. Many of the merchants were nice, the medical school was excellent, and Galveston, whored by legions of Texans past and spat upon by Houstonians as when a pipsqueak outgrows the bully next door, did the only thing it could do: attempt to survive in a world that had basically passed it by. As for me, I was proud to be a UTMB graduate and never changed my mind about that.

*   *   *

The blessed event took place on June 10, 1963.

It would become another birthday, my academic name day. The ceremonies at the Moody Center on Seawall Boulevard loomed, and occurred, and stayed. I was Rip van Winkle, awakening every day to the sensational news of an astounding new discovery in my life, having slept through the part that no longer mattered. Everything in the world was deliciously changed. Everything was mine because, on that date, I became entitled to wear two indelible letters after my name: *MD*. It was as though I had been favored of all people, a surprise so lovely I could barely believe it. The diploma itself, of bold white sheepskin stretching the enormous distance of two-thirds of a yard, and very nearly that high, ordained me in enthralling officialdom: *Johnny Graydon Deaton ... has been, by the authority of the State of Texas, declared a Doctor of Medicine and is entitled to all the rights and privileges appertaining to that Degree.* It was signed by no less than Harry Ransom, chancellor of the UT system, and by John B. Truslow, the last executive dean and director of the Medical Branch, since those who followed him as its leaders would hold the title president.

Still again, there was a downside to graduation. A certain inexplicable twilight had begun to reproach my sunny days as a student. It began to seem to me, and this well before the graduation date, that I had benefitted from blind luck. It began to seem to me that I was undeserving. It began to seem to me that the riches awarded from the podium the night of graduation were for the parents, not the students. Thrilling as it was, I still thought doctorhood beyond my attainment. If I had achieved good marks, it was merely that I had followed directions and worked indefatigably toward my goal. I had conquered cadavers, learned materia medica, could evaluate and treat. In consequence, I had allowed myself to become intoxicated on the self-worship that is practiced unceasingly in every medical center. I had dined on arrogance and found it rather tasty, had drunkenly swilled the wine of pomposity, had learned to interrupt people, keep them waiting out of a sense of my own importance, to issue orders and command a ward and grapple with that common enemy, *disease*.

Somewhere back when, medicine had honed in on all of the things causing people to feel *dis-at-ease*, and medicine and disease had been interlinked ever since. But now that I was graduating, something felt wrong. Behind the White Curtain sealing the medics and the nurses and such from patients and their families, I had gathered the terrible knowledge of the possible. The inevitable. It had disabused me of the simple belief that life was fair. It was fair only in its indifference. Which was frightening. I had seen things I was supposed not to tell, sworn not to tell. In certain ways, I was a renter who had discovered one day, quite by accident, that his landlady was a hooker. An expensive one. A ballsy one who had invited me into her boudoir and had had her way with me and sworn me never to tell, ever. To reveal that she was a whore would be to confess to being a whoremonger, and that was that.

I consoled myself that the next phase of my training would be different. As a doctor, I could make my own way. Yes, there were restraints, but that was not what I meant by making my own way. Exactly what I did mean, I didn't know, but I would recognize it when I found it. Or it sounded good to say so. Selected for internship at Memorial Hospital, I knew that by July 1, 1963, I had damned well better be a confident doctor and not a kid six years out of high school, and only twenty-three years of age at that.

GRADUATION CEREMONY

The Seventy-Third Commencement Exercises of the
University of Texas Medical Branch. <u>Monday, June the
Tenth, Nineteen–Hundred and Sixty-Three</u>.

An Organ Prelude by MM Nichols, MD

PROCESSIONAL *(Audience please remain seated)*

MUSIC—"The Star-Spangled Banner"

INVOCATION; Introduction of Guests

GREETING FROM THE BOARD OF REGENTS
INTRODUCTION OF SPEAKER; ADDRESS;
CONFERRING OF DEGREES AND DIPLOMAS
NURSES' PLEDGE; HIPPOCRATIC OATH

MUSIC—"The Eyes of Texas"; BENEDICTION

RECESSIONAL *(Audience please remain standing)*

I took the oath. I felt as though I had vowed to be different in the presence of others, even as I was the same in the presence of myself. Your presence in someone else's mind. Someone else's presence in your mind. Nobility replacing what had come before. They all talked of nobility and seemed to mean it. And honor, yes, whatever that was. I decided that honor was … nobility.

Applause! The clapping was endless, seeming as it did to define the new world we had entered, human fanfare to a symphony of importance. But what it actually felt like was falling off of a mountain into an unknown void. The 150 of us, my ranking that of seventh or eighth in the class, broke into applause and sang out a lusty cheer when they told us that there would be no more examinations. The laughter gave way to a stunned silence when the speaker, a physician, quickly corrected himself. The real tests, he warned, were just beginning. Every patient we examined was exactly that: an examination.

This called up something they had told us in the first days of medical school. "Half of everything we are going to teach you is wrong. It's just that we don't know which half." Forewarned, I had attempted to learn both halves and by the time of graduation was startled to realize that half of my doctorly knowledge was, or could be, wrong.

*   *   *

Mimi and I, the two of us, were photographed. My beanpole frame was wrapped in a dark robe and topped by a matching mortarboard angled over my head, which plateau was enlivened by a sash of orange intermingled with white that dangled into my visual field. Mimi was in her Sunday best, blonde, beautiful, blue of eye and shapely of thigh, of whom, it could be said, I had known since seventh grade but was just now, three years into our marriage, getting to know her. In other words, there in Galveston, Texas, commitment was no longer just an intention: the world awaited its fulfillment by our happy band. I had a wife I did not deserve and a son we loved dearly, cutest son in the world, and the smartest, and the noblesse oblige of our future awaited us. People kept asking me things. Wanted to know what it was like to be a doctor. I told them in truth that I also wanted to know what it was like to be a doctor. Was looking forward to that very thing.

First thing the next day, I swaggered into a drugstore in Galveston and wrote myself a prescription for the eye drops I had been using since college: wonderful! Later, I wrote the drug company for a free supply, which they promptly sent. Amazing! The prescription was from an ophthalmologist, Dr. Calvin Payton of Longview, and called for two drops in both eyes four times a day. Often I had needed more drops than that but couldn't afford them, the prescription costing two or three dollars. I'd learned to husband the drops like the coins of a skinflint. But with my new bounty, I'd be able to flop on the bed and turn my eyes to the ceiling and *pour* the drops onto my face until they soothed my aching eyes and went joyously sliding down my cheeks like ski tracks on a mountain slope in wintertime. I rejoiced in my newfound powers.

In mid-June, along with everyone else in the UTMB Class of 1963, I appeared in Fort Worth and presented my framed medical degree and my ID before being admitted to take the examination for certification to practice medicine in the State of Texas, given by the Texas State Board of Medical Examiners. We wore smiles that day as big as the one on Big Tex, the giant cowboy that graced the fairgrounds in Dallas where, each year in the Cotton Bowl, the Texas Longhorns engaged the Oklahoma Sooners in a football game. The fact of the matter was that my knowledge of the beaux arts at the time was limited to football. Beside it, *Beowulf* was a blocked punt. My following of UT football had begun in earnest in 1958, when Coach Darrell K. Royal became my hero, and in the fall of 1963 the Texas Longhorns would vie for the NCAA national championship in football.

*   *   *

As for Corpus Christi, were cities jewels, it would be the Hope Diamond of the Texas Gulf Coast. Indeed, it had a glittering quality to it, a splendor, an engulfing radiance, as though to proclaim that here, at the mouth of Corpus Christi Bay and the estuary of the Nueces River, shadow had been obliterated and light penetrated into every corner and cove; the happy people gliding across the Yacht Basin fronting the "downtown" section of the city, as opposed to the adjacent and elevated "uptown," constituted all of the evidence needed to prove it. The population that summer of 1963 was 170,000, making it the largest city south of San Antonio, although it was dwarfed by that city as well as by Houston and Dallas–Fort Worth. It was a city of wealth, Corpus, but also one of poverty. A city of sprawling, oil-built homes provocatively confronting the sapphire-blue water just beyond Ocean Drive, a winding promenade past five-car garages and accompanying tennis courts and ridiculously manicured expanses of roses in a choreography that of course included azure swimming pools the size of miniature oceans.

Yet elsewhere in Corpus, like shadows cast by an eclipsed sun, were teeming barrios of crowded white-frame dwellings with too many cars, too many pink flamingos decorating those yards, too many tots toddling across those yards in diapers. Constituting the majority of its citizens, the Hispanic population of Corpus lived back from the coast, some of them on streets with names that resonated in state history: Goliad Drive, San Jacinto Drive, Alamo Drive. For the most part they worked for hourly wages and lived from paycheck to paycheck and called themselves United States citizens because that is what they were. The sun glittered just as brilliantly on them as on Ocean Drive but with far less fanfare, hardly any reflection. Sunlight is funny that way. It gleams upon the gleaming, but less so across paned windows and broken tricycles and possibly the shiny twin shoots comprising the antlers of a doctor's stethoscope. Even the Hope Diamond, to a certain light, emits a red luminescence that lingers well after the light is withdrawn, a refulgence no less bright for its limited scope. This had meaning well beyond what was immediately apparent to me. Indeed, 1963 was important not only in my life; it would mark a turning point in American history, the beginning of a new era.

Perhaps this was evident in the reckless anger that shoved aside convention that summer of 1963, a volatility sprung from a disquieting winter and spring, a tumult that brought massive arrests of demonstrators in Birmingham in May and the slaying of Medgar Evers—shot from ambush in the driveway of his Mississippi home—in June. And this was not to mention a burgeoning war in Southeast Asia that was already claiming American lives and that, like all wars, was proving harder to end than to start. There was talk of Martin Luther King Jr. enjoining a march on Washington in August of that summer. Under threat of federal intervention, Governor George Wallace had opened the doors of the University of Alabama to two students of color on June 11. But if 1963 were a scrapbook to the capricious winds of change, this surely meant that not everything going down that year was hopelessly unpleasant, which was true.

That spring, for example, Winston Churchill had been made an honorary US citizen—not as unlikely as it may have seemed, his mother having been an American. On June 20, the United States and the Soviet Union set up a hotline to avoid nuclear war, and a James Bond movie, *From Russia with Love*, became so wildly popular that year that Sean Connery became a household name and set the tone for an entire new generation of celluloid heroes.

What was more, new leadership had come to Washington, marking this as a time of "vigor," a word that was popularized by the new president and seemed to fit him. John Fitzgerald Kennedy, forty-six as of May 29, had brought youth and freshness to Washington after the stolid Eisenhower fifties, a rebirth embodied in the word that was on everyone's lips to depict his presidency: *Camelot*. Jacqueline Kennedy—Jackie!—radiated a magnificence that mesmerized the world. Thirty-four and pregnant with her third child, she extended her style-setting cachet even to maternity garments, and when her newborn died a few days after his birth in August, the entire nation stopped to mourn.

At the 1963 Academy Awards, *Lawrence of Arabia* had been chosen as the best picture of the previous year. The best actor award went to Sidney Poitier for *Lilies of the Field*, and the best actress award to Patricia Neal for *Hud*. But Doris Day was still the leading box office star among women and John Wayne the leading male star. Wayne himself had no peer among actors, as he embodied the American myth of one man against all odds and all others, succeeding because he was right. A man who would test that myth was Cassius Marcellus Clay, an American boxer out of Louisville, Kentucky, who was beginning to make a name for himself after winning a gold medal as the light heavyweight champion at the 1960 summer Olympics. Some of the leading songs in 1963 were "Blue Velvet," by Bobby Vinton; "He's So Fine," by the Chiffons; "The End of the World," by Skeeter Davis; and "Surfin' USA," by the Beach Boys. All of these things I was aware of, but distantly, my attention having been enshrouded by a dream. What I could not deny: the convergence of dream and reality.

*   *   *

We rented the two-bedroom home at 2030 Seventeenth Street in Corpus in a prim neighborhood of older houses between Staples Street and Morgan Avenue. The house suited us perfectly. It was not that far south of Memorial Hospital, it had a fenced backyard and a detached one-car garage, and it was convenient to shopping centers. The paint was white and the roof was green and the driveway was of chalk-colored caliche, though there was a nice concrete sidewalk extending from the front porch out to the street.

After renting the house, we coaxed Mimi's mother into babysitting Roger for a week and whisked ourselves away for a short vacation. The Grand Canyon looked exactly like it did on postcards. Durango, Colorado, was fun, and it was cold enough on Pike's Peak in June to make hot chocolate taste delicious. Then we did what made Coloradans happy: we turned around and came home. It was time to go to work. Time to learn doctoring.

*   *   *

That first morning of the internship, after delivering the little girl, a nurse handed me a cup of coffee and a spoonful of it spilled and began to soak in. Was I a physician yet? Was it real, did it count, could I continue my first-hour momentum? The questions, the concept, the grappling for meaning continued for the next several days and then were lost in the swirl of my duties, a buyer overwhelmed by the calls of an auctioneer rattling off things too fast and too numerous to keep up with.

Somewhere in there I fused into the layout of my new workplace. The fuselage of that putative aircraft extended straight east in the opposite direction from the delivery rooms. Its aisle, a wide ribbon of waxed concrete, lived on light reflected from the adjacent wards and other powers along its length: the cafeteria, the operating rooms, the emergency room, the interns' lounge, the outpatient clinic, the Record Room, and so forth. Old Memorial wasn't as big, as new, or as pretty as John Sealy Hospital. It hadn't Sealy's prestige, and it was a sad groundling in comparison to the New Memorial Hospital, built next door in 1953, eight stories tall, serving private patients only, and connected to the east end of its ancestor by a roofed walkway.

Old Memorial served staff, or "charity," patients. They knew it and the doctors knew it and that was how it was. To be sure, some private patients, such as for obstetrics, or those requiring surgery, or those visiting the ER, shared the Old Memorial's facilities. Well-to-do Hispanic patients were treated like other private patients, and Anglos who did not have medical insurance were treated like other charity patients. In 1963 in Corpus Christi, Texas, however, the hocus-pocus at Memorial Hospital sent "Mexicans" to one place, and Anglos to another. I learned quickly enough that I had no business in the new hospital and was glad for it. I stalked the Old Memorial with a fierce sense of pride and ownership: these were my people. The old hospital made up in enthusiasm what it lacked by way of a physical plant. Within a week I had been in and out of Labor and Delivery more times than

I could count, including seven deliveries during those first twenty-four hours. Nursery, the Obstetrics Ward directly across the corridor from it, and the nearby cafeteria were my domain. Time consolidated into action and the one canceled out the other.

At the corridor entrance to Labor and Delivery were swinging double doors, like saloon doors in the Old West, and I burst back and forth through them like a gunslinger. In time, as had been true in Galveston during medical school, I stopped being able to tell where the hospital ended and my personal life began. I was not even sure, bounding from one end to the other of the central corridor, that I had a life apart from this.

A big part of that new existence was pretense, of course, at least on my part. But by the second or third day, hurtling here and there with a burgeoning sense of confidence, I allowed myself to begin to believe in the new fiction. I didn't feel any different on the inside, but people saw me as different, and I hesitated to disabuse them of that.

And it worried me. Even as I began molting into the person they believed me to be, which brought an untold joy, I looked the same to myself in the mirror at home. Yet they saw me differently, and that was more frightening than I had expected it to be. The days passed in a whirlwind of activity that was so much fun I dared not let it show. The eight of us who had come to this internship from UTMB passed one another in Memorial's busy thoroughfare and shared grins of pleasure at our newfound powers as we hurried on to the next surprise. I strolled onto a ward at Memorial Hospital and the nurses, by God, stood up! That didn't happen in Galveston. The nurses were nice enough in Galveston, but a medical student was just another face. Back then we had a vague idea that things would get better, but not this much better, not this quickly. At Memorial Hospital in Corpus, things were happening too fast to reconcile.

One doesn't see patients who are in dire straits without buying into what they have to offer: a cold sweat, an internal hemorrhage, a pain so severe that it threatens to burst open when you touch it. Blood from their wounds found its way beneath my nails and into my shoes, I carried them home with me, they gnawed their way into my soul. *This*, I shouted to myself, *this is what it's like to practice medicine?* I had had no idea! It was far more personal and far more gripping than I had imagined. Women spread their legs for me, men gushed out their secrets to me, I wore their lives around my shoulders. They shared solitary hurts nursed since childhood, bruises just now exposed to a gawking world, pustules from a plagued marriage. The examining room was a basin; I the stopper in their bowl of misery. It was too great a responsibility, and yet that made it all the more enticing, and it filled my world with magic and moxie and made me so glad I was there that I dared not break the spell.

In the quietest whisper of ego, I began to feel ennobled. I began to feel worthy of an honor I may not have earned. I had stepped onto a high scaffolding, erected before the world, for the sole purpose of convincing the world—and maybe myself—that I was deserving of it, that everything I claimed to be and that they thought me to be was true, that I had been victorious over everything life had put in my way, and in my exultation I was granted to see that everything in my life had happened for just this sublime purpose. It was one of those rare times in life where the patchwork of happenstance knitted together not only expectations but dreams, and I knew a happiness I had not known existed. My ego would not let it go at that. I envisioned a future for myself in medicine approaching the divine, torrents of pleasure rushing past in the tinkling grandeur, the certainty of a career that would be the envy of the world, wherein the art and science of medicine would be wedded as they had not been since the sovereignty of Sir William Osler, and the first person I would honor at the awards ceremony, of course, was my wife.

*   *   *

We were married on August 26, 1960, just before I entered medical school and she returned for her last semester at Baylor University in Waco. It was an impulsive act, to elope, but not a rash decision. We had been high-school sweethearts, had been engaged since the previous Valentine's Day, and had known each other since grade school. She and her folks were steady churchgoers at the First Baptist, true also for myself, and year to year those of that affiliation got to know one another rather well.

Mimi's family had moved to town the year she started seventh grade, 1951. For a town with a population of three-thousand, five-hundred people, Pittsburg, Texas, was able to house most of its Caucasian students in one big school building. But after an elementary school opened in 1950, the big building held only junior high and high school students, and in seventh grade, my classmates were split into separate rooms on the bottom floor. As it happened, my girlfriend was in the other section and I went most of the day without seeing her. This was unacceptable to me.

What I did was to make acquaintance with the new girl in town, who was in my room and who saw my girlfriend at physical education every day. It became my habit to let the new girl convey my love notes, written in pig Latin, to my girlfriend each day. In the throbbing tickle of such things, a fragrance relevant to all, my future wife being the courier rather than the recipient of these missives of undying devotion, a puzzling transfer of affection occurred that was personal, relevant, and about three-quarters eternal.

We did not date until junior year in high school, when hearts are most fragile, and when one of us had suffered a broken heart. This affliction was visited upon the other during the first year of college—wherein I learned something. Faint at first, like the hope that reposes in songs that suddenly begin to have meaning, it meant that self-pity is fine, but healing begins on the other side of that in a venture that moves joyously beyond "The Great Pretender," by The Platters, the piano slip notes of a Floyd Cramer, and the fever and thunder incumbent to Patsy Cline's "I Fall To Pieces." One did not have to heal without scarring, only survive. That bright twinkle of hope led to the best music of all, of two ultimately attuned to one.

Fortunate to put myself through college by door-to-door sales during the summers of 1957 to 1960, I had by the summer of 1960 accumulated a bit over $2,000, enough to see me through the first year of medical school. Enough to get married? It was because of my financial shakiness that I had shortened the years of study. Having taken the prescribed slate of courses in college, allowing me to enter medical school in three years, I was informally accepted pending successful completion of my third year of college, and I never interviewed anywhere else but Galveston. A big plus of Galveston medical: it was two hundred miles farther from Pittsburg than the Dallas medical school. So it was that during that torrid summer of 1960 I mentioned to Mimi that if she was willing to teach and provide a paycheck, why didn't we go ahead and get married? She seemed to have thought of the same thing, and so we did.

Her family had moved to Crystal City, in South Texas, and I was visiting there in late August of 1960. We had an event to attend in Waco, and Mimi and I left Crystal City that Friday morning, August 26, 1960, having secretly obtained a marriage license a few days before in Carrizo Springs, county seat of Dimmit County. I belonged to the University Baptist Church in Austin, adjacent to the campus of UT–Austin, and we arrived there in midafternoon. We parked in the street beside the church. Mimi remained in the car, and I went inside with the blunderbuss idea of asking the pastor, Dr. Blake Smith, whether he would as a special favor marry us on such short notice. We were both twenty-one, had the license, and wanted to get married.

But Dr. Smith was out of town, and the associate pastor refused to marry us because we were not going to be living together! She was returning to Baylor for her last semester, and I'd be starting medical school in a few days in Galveston, where she would join me next January. The refusal was a great shock to me. I thought of the church as love and service, even though I'd stopped believing in some of its tenets. From my meager daily funds, I had given to this church regularly for the last two years. But by the time I got outside and walked to the car to tell Mimi, I was glad the man's name was not going on our marriage license, happy that the associate had at least named a Baptist minister who might officiate.

I had been to quite a few weddings at the First Baptist Church in Pittsburg. Somehow each always seemed a staged event, pretty as strawberry shortcake, but a public ceremony all the same, bringing together two people to recite their lines and disappear up the aisle in the direction of that dessert. So it was that I had thought that when the time came, someone else would show up for the ceremony, not me. At the very least, the groom would be some idealized version of me, dusted and slicked and bedecked with aplomb. Startlingly, it was me. That was the shock. In selfish truth, I had also been thinking more about the dessert than the hors d'oeuvres. In my inner soul, I heard one voice. *Give of me your troth and I will give of you my crutch, so that we may both be free.* I did not know what Mimi was thinking, only that she was willing, and then suddenly the two of us were standing in the front room of the parsonage of the Hyde Park Baptist Church in Austin.

Mimi was beautiful. As well, her beauty was not lessened by her total lack of awareness of it. More than that, like all great beauty, it rescued time to still the moment. Blonde, stunning, with lavish blue eyes and a stupendous smile, she bespoke the winsome ideal of young womanhood: happy but sensible, strong but vulnerable, impulsive but careful. And promises to fill… She was a windup maiden in a windup world, but not a world where one and all wound up the same. I was the one who had broken her heart our last year in high school, and the one I had broken it for waited a year and returned the favor. Yet that had made this possible. Here we were in happy obeisance to the divine chalice that one marries the person one was meant to marry.

Having called Dr. Ralph M. Smith—no relation to Dr. Blake Smith— from Zales Jewelers on the drag, and him having consented, we drove to the parsonage, which was off of Speedway and Thirty-Eighth Street, not that far north of the UT campus. The pastor greeted us warmly, as did his wife, who would serve as witness. First we slipped away to change clothes, and when we returned to the front room, it was so astounding that the pastor and his wife were actually doing this for us. A tumbler spilled, lavishing its riches upon us.

Your life is your only possession, but you don't own it until you share it.

Dr. Smith asked whether we were Christians. Yes. Mimi wore a green blouse of chiffon. Its beguiling polka dots were stars to a timeless green skirt, as though her beauty were grown from all of the loveliness in all of its divine inspiration, the way happiness is the easiest garment of all to wear but also the most delicate. The person who had come here with me for this service had been in a disguise now revealed. Where had the girl gone to create the woman? That was the abiding mystery, I the gumshoe in the cheap gray suit and tie. Dr. Smith asked of our plans, and we answered cautiously. He held the marriage license we had brought and asked whether we were ready to be married. Yes.

And then all of a sudden everything changed. All of a sudden the outside world vanished. There were merely four people gathered together indoors in all of the world for a ceremony that had been planned by God. And then there were only two people. Forgotten were the bad experience at University Baptist and also Mimi's phone call to her best friend as we'd passed through San Antonio. She had thought to ask whether she knew a preacher who might marry us. The lengthy conversation had grown dangerous, as the phone booth was situated on the shoulder of a busy highway. When I asked what her friend was saying, Mimi allowed that she was trying to talk her out of it.

"Hang up the phone!" I said, and possibly assisted her in the task. That was gone too. Gone were the broken hearts, the broken promises, the brokenness of life in general, every hurt and disappointment, every failed dream and its sequel. For that one swelling instant, everything was as perfect as could be and all of the dreams came true, all of the songs their cue, the deepest yearnings and the highest bliss and the heartbeat of the two of us, because the best person in the world was about to commit herself to a worm such as I, and she stood and faced me and voiced a smile that rose to meet me, rose to meet my own.

> Do you take this woman, Mimi, to be your wife?
> To have and to hold, forsaking all others,
> For better, for worse,
> For richer, for poorer,
> In sickness and in health,
> To love and to cherish, from this day forward
> As long as you both shall live?

I affirmed, and then it was her turn, and surely enough she said the words, this most endearing person ever, and in a very few moments the deed was done. She had been wearing the engagement ring, and now I added the wedding ring. She gave me one as well, a simple gold band we had purchased for eighteen dollars at Zales. I had tucked a five-dollar bill into an envelope, which I slipped to the pastor as we were leaving. Ralph Smith made a comment like, "Oh, my wife gets these." She was very nice, he was very nice. What a wonderful favor that grouchy associate pastor had done us! Now that it was over, it felt perfect. I had done the most important thing of my life. Marrying Mimi was the smartest, luckiest thing I ever did, though I was much too much of a dumbass to know it at the time.

Our first night was spent at a motel in Temple, halfway to Waco. We attended our scheduled event the next day without telling anyone we had eloped, spent another night in a motel, and arrived at the bus terminal in Waco late Sunday morning, August 28. Mimi was returning to Crystal City to get ready for her last semester at Baylor, and I was leaving in our car for Galveston. It was how we had planned it.

As for the bus station, it was large and boxy and smelled of stale popcorn, like a movie theater after a busy Saturday night. Because bus stations had them, we slipped into a photo booth, pulled the drawstring curtain, and had four different poses made for the grand sum of twenty-five cents. And we would not trade those black-and-white pictures for the glossiest of commercial wedding portraits! The bus station pictures, stunning, innocent, and treasured, caught the bubbling happiness of two youngsters wonderfully in love, blessed to be one. I loved Mimi because she loved me, but more than that because she was so special, so strangely frightened of things that one wished to protect her. Years later I came across a passage that summed it up better than I could. "The man wants to rescue the woman; an illusion will do. But more often than not it is the woman who rescues him by letting him find out what has lain hidden and subversive within him for too long, making trouble."[3]

It was exactly that. The man I might or might not be had the effrontery to love with all his heart one who had brought to him what had been irretrievable by himself: a reassurance that life can be rich and quiet, shiny as new coins, and quadruple the fun of two people bouncing together on a magical trampoline.

The secrecy of our marriage lasted only a week. Mimi found out that she would be kicked out of Baylor were the secret discovered while she was sharing a suite with unmarried girls. I drove back to the bride's home in Crystal City after the first week of medical school. Her parents, Gilbert and Helen, who lived in a small rental house a block from downtown, were surprisingly good about it. The only people genuinely disappointed were the calendar counters who, upon learning of the hush-hush wedding, surely had their day. Would there or would there not be a healthy eight-pounder born three months prematurely? Roger Stuart Deaton was born two years later, an eight-pounder who arrived in Galveston on September 28, 1962, but for the rest of their lives, bless their hearts, Mimi's parents had him as one year older than he was. Suspicions die hard to hard-shell Baptists, but then again, they

---

3   Gloria Emerson, *Some American Men* (New York: Simon and Schuster, 1985), 243.

could not have been nicer. The people in Pittsburg even gave Mimi a bridal shower—thanks to Bob and Mary Pendergrass—and the two plates Mimi received of her chinaware selection became our first and our only, workhorse family heirlooms too pretty not to use.

*   *   *

Pictures survive of me in those first few days of internship. Mrs. Hargrove, who taught drama and speech in high school, said I had an honest smile and suggested I use it more often. At least that was free. Money had always been a problem with me. Friends had told me, when we were on trips to and from college, that I always wanted to eat in the "sorriest-looking café in town." They laughed about it, never understanding that the worst-looking cafés also had the lowest prices. I had taken with me from home to college a yellow towel so thin I could read through it and had made it last three years. I wore glasses of the cheapest kind sold by Texas State Optical, and had been told by an eye doctor during medical school that I must remember to have my prescription for myopia changed more often. "I don't see how you could see the board from the front row," the surprised ophthalmologist said, charging me not a dime for seeing him. But the glasses cost twelve or fifteen bucks, an enormous amount to me. Still, I had done well enough to marry the girl who played clarinet in the front row beside me, and we had tooted along well enough these three years since.

*   *   *

People tended to be surprised when I admitted that I had accepted the internship in Corpus sight unseen. I'd entertained no other offers and was surprised that the other graduates of 1963 could discuss the merits and so forth of internships around the country. I simply had my mind on other things. Galveston had voiced interest in me staying there for internship, but that would have put me in the awkward position of having to be the boss over the same students who had taken gross anatomy with me, and even worse, having to give them a grade. One of the others in the group talked me into choosing Corpus. George Trader, the hospital administrator, had driven to Galveston to meet me, was super nice, and seemed to genuinely want me to accept his offer. Trader carried upon his person a certain honesty, the way with some people you can just tell, and I liked him immediately—liked him explaining that the hospital drew all of its interns from the same graduating class at UTMB on the theory that, knowing one another, they would work well together, work better than would interns from separate medical schools. I signed the papers and was duly accepted.

Mimi and I had moved from Galveston to Corpus the day after my graduation, found the house we would live in for the year, and rented it on the spot. One of the things Mimi and I loved about it was its proximity to a Butter Krust Bakery that always smelled of good things when we drove past. (Rent should go up for those living near a bakery.) Our landlord, P. E. Clark, showed us through his former residence and let it to us for fifty dollars a month, utilities paid. After he was gone we laughed at how he had kept telling us to "put your one unit *he-ah*" (being from the Midwest, that was how he said *here*), indicating a window in the front room, "and your other unit *they-ah*," indicating a window in the master bedroom—referring to our two nonexistent air-conditioners. We laughed because we didn't need them. We laughed because we were young and dumb and happy as daffodils, crazy in love, and slyly between the two of us put his units *he-ah* and *they-ah* to a usage that would have surprised him and about which more need not be said. This lovely man turned out to be the best landlord we ever had.

We joined the First Baptist Church, Mimi in a Sunday school class with the daughter of Herbert E. Butt, whose H-E-B grocery stores were just then beginning to take off. Since we would only be there for the year, Mimi could not get a teaching job and would have that time with Roger; we would live on the $300 a month paid to interns, though her parents occasionally brought us groceries from the store her father managed and my mother visited and bought us a new refrigerator that we used forever. In addition, the eight interns had a fund consisting of fees earned in the ER from those who could pay, and we split it eight ways for a much-appreciated $25 or $30 extra each month.

*   *   *

From that very first day of internship, it was as though the hospital were on fire, I the only firefighter. I answered calls, putting out flames here and there, responding to the blazes and the flickering embers while everyone else seemed to be standing still and watching me. It was probably a dream, but I lived it. A week or two into July, someone flagged me down and handed me the phone. The page operator said I was wanted by Surgical Annex, the pharmacy, and the hospital administrator (because there was an interns' meeting), and that my wife had called twice, and so had the OB/Gyn clinic, where I was needed to see fifteen or sixteen patients.

The operator laughed and said, "Now what are you going to do?"

I did what I was trained to do. As I was also doing duty that day for the ER, I called my backup and he agreed to do the OB/Gyn clinic. I ignored the calls from the pharmacy and the hospital administrator, but like an ambassador to hell, I knew that I could not ignore the one from Surgical Annex. This last was a ward on the north side of the hospital that seemed to exist in another dimension, like the smoldering ruins of a city in a Stephen King novel. But it was really just an extra wing of the hospital, matching the one on the south side of the hospital serving the clinic. For the convenience of patients, the latter extended toward Hospital Boulevard and was home to the various clinics held on specific days each week. The clinic was easy. They didn't have emergencies in the clinic. Emergencies were all they had in Surgical Annex, and it was convenient to no one. One reached it by stint of traversing the entire thoroughfare of that inflexible concrete corridor, waxed and waxing, and getting there was as much fun as going through the belt line in Boy Scouts. The entrance was past the breezeway between the old and new hospitals and that was probably why they called it an annex. Perhaps it was the tailpipe of the aircraft, *to expire* being the terminus of so much of what transpired on Surgical Annex.

*   *   *

I was astounded that first time to discover that it was as big as the Obstetrics Ward. A call had come midmorning, well after I'd finished that first delivery. I had made quick rounds on the Obstetrics Ward and had just finished delivering a second baby. While resting, as they would say in East Texas, I was getting acquainted with the nursery. I took the phone and was instantly frozen in horror. *Surgical Annex?* A ward I hadn't heard of wanted me? I was responsible for most of its patients? It was outrageous! I arrived there out of breath, having listened to directions and then raced through the morning crowds that thronged Memorial's hallway. Seeing it, my first thought was that it was the scene of an accident. Some of its victims were responsive, but most of them were unconscious and receiving IV fluids and buckets of blood. It looked like Custer's Last Stand, except all the patients were women.

My patient, a young woman, had been admitted the previous night with a diagnosis of "septic AB," yet no treatment had been ordered. Back in 1963, before the word became so volatile, *abortion* was the term used by doctors to define a pregnancy that ended short of delivery by whatever means, and *AB* was its abbreviation. The *A* and the *B*, pronounced separately, were capitalized when written on a patient's chart. By the same token, diagnosis of a septic AB implied that the woman herself had done something to terminate her pregnancy or had hired someone to do it—and, sterile conditions not having been met, infection had ensued. Common knowledge among doctors: every such patient was critically ill, and even with the best of treatment, the mortality rate was staggering.

It was like apoplexy of the pelvis. Tubes, one on either side, connect the womb to the ovaries, but indirectly. The open end of each tube is a vacuum cleaner sweeping the surface of the ovary in search of an ovum, but also serving as a conduit for infection to reach the interior of the abdomen should pelvic contamination occur. In its fulminant phase, the virulence of my new patient's infection had led to vascular collapse—septic shock. She had no blood pressure and only the faintest pulse.

I found her halfway back on the ward, her bed surrounded by nurses and aides, who parted to let me in. She was in her early twenties, a Hispanic woman who was every bit as sick as septic shock could make her. She was unconscious and unresponsive to touch, and for a moment I thought she'd had a seizure. Her teeth were clenched so tightly it was as if she had just told you the worst secret of her life and was grimacing in agony pending your expected outrage. Indeed, her lips were bleeding, and by way of explanation, one of the nurses lifted a padded tongue blade that was soaked in blood. Malpractice had already been committed, no stranger to this ward, in that she had the bad luck to arrive in the wee hours of the last day of internship for the doctor on duty and the first day of my training. The outgoing intern had "saved her" for me, and since my term of duty had theoretically begun five and a half hours before that call from Labor and Delivery, I was as negligent as he. That thought came later. The patient's heart was failing and I saw at a glance that she might die in the next few minutes.

I felt once again the fright, that unpleasant tickle.

I confirmed that her blood pressure was unattainable. I brushed the stethoscope across her throbbing chest and heard what sounded like horses racing through a distant field. Then I did what I was trained to do. She already had an intravenous drip, and I ordered Levophed, a vasoconstrictor, to elevate her blood pressure. I started a cut-down in one of her ankles to access her veins in case the first IV infiltrated. Continuing to give verbal orders, I named heroic doses of the various antibiotics that could be added to an IV drip and that I thought might save her. And I did something I had not planned to do. It could truthfully be stated that I surprised myself by doing it. Dr. Leslie Garrett was an older general practitioner who had retired to Corpus and taken a part-time job as director of the clinic. Dr. Garrett saw patients in the clinic until noon every day. I told the nurses to page him stat—on the run—for

Surgical Annex. He arrived at bedside a few minutes later, and I presented this critically ill patient to him, asking whether he had any further suggestions.

A man of modest height and great humility who dressed in a suit and a bowtie that may have dated back to the Roaring Twenties, Dr. Garrett listened and then hesitated before saying that what I was doing sounded fine to him. Unstated was that this was a first for him. He may not have ever set foot in Surgical Annex before.

I felt the fool, but all the same, with another first-day emergency, I craved all of the help I could get. Doctoring wasn't turning out as I had expected. I simply did not want to take the responsibility for a patient's life. My desperate urge was to explore every avenue I had by way of giving my patients the benefit of the best of medical expertise. I was not incapable of calling on anyone anywhere in the world for help, I needed it that badly. Were an orderly to have offered a solution, I would have awarded him the Memorial Medal of Honor. I was more than willing to race out onto Morgan Avenue and stop traffic and search every vehicle for someone to relieve me of having to take the full responsibility for a patient's life, that awesome burden.

A nursing supervisor came up while Dr. Garrett was still there, and I also asked her advice, which drew from her a tight smile of the kind I had seen on the face of a coach whose team had just been unfairly penalized. During our conversation, I glanced and caught Dr. Garrett looking at me as though I were very strange. Well, I'd never been in combat before! At this late date I am reminded of a couple who took their first baby home from the hospital and actually, really, tellingly, stood there at a loss, waiting for its parents to show up. Medicine is, was, and always will be about responsibility. Maturation of a doctor is nothing less than the conscientious acceptance of that mantle, sweat and hard-won knowledge and no little bit of heart having earned one that right. And luck perhaps, a bit of that too.

By contrast, cowardly me, that first day had brought me all of the spinelessness I had ever known, terror being the flipside of the heroic impulse. Scaffolding? I stood upon it in full knowledge of the trapdoor beneath my feet, cringing in the expectation of someone yanking the lever with the greatest of joy. I felt that I had been compelled to remove my clothing and walk naked among strangers, naked in all my misery. I stood to my feet in a grand auditorium, shouting to interrupt a reverential silence, drawing a stunned rebuke from all because I lacked the courage Hemingway defined as grace under pressure. All I needed was everything I didn't have.

*   *   *

Miraculously, that patient did not die. For reasons unknown to me, she responded to the medications I ordered and left the hospital a week and a half later. Other patients did die on that ward, including a woman suffering from gestational diabetes; she was in acidosis and had been put on Surgical Annex because her "hyperventilation" was bothering the other patients on Obstetrics! By then I was on another rotation and noticed the woman after I had seen a surgical patient on the Annex. I helped only to the extent of suggesting that they draw a sample of her blood to test for glucose and check her urine for whatever might be there. I still kick myself for not dropping everything and participating in her care, but it simply wasn't possible. Firefighters take it a blaze at a time.

What I did see that first day, beginning in Labor and Delivery and continuing on Surgical Annex, was the construct I shall call PAYA syndrome. The letters stand for peek-at-your-ass, and it is a syndrome of recent medical graduates cured only by experience. Allow yourself to look bad to others if this helps you to look truthfully at yourself. Doctoring is the art of exhibiting your ass to the world and not caring who sees it. The dynamics of timidity must be brushed aside by conscious effort until this becomes as easy as a reflex. I had played the coward to cover up my inexperience. I could liken how I felt on Surgical Annex to a young man on a first date with the school beauty, afraid to ask her for a first kiss out of fear that her refusal would fatally embarrass him. I already had on board all the medical training I needed to treat the patient in shock. But I squealed like a trapped animal because I didn't want to appear inadequate to people already at the emergency, people who were years and years more experienced than I and might by word or gesture demolish the new intern.

But do you need to prove to others what you yourself already know? Don't be too quick to answer; it is an open-ended question. You have hoisted your PAYA into view by showing up at the emergency. The syndrome is both inevitable and unavoidable. The only way past it, my discovery, was to find one's self in an emergency. Forget about everything else and look to the self that already exists apart from whatever niceties you may owe to anyone else at the time and you are halfway home. It's bad enough each of us is flawed. A flash of the ass beats fatal self-effacement, especially when the fatality is of both the patient *and* the doctor.

But isn't that awfully arrogant?

Yes, but it is the humility beneath arrogance, the face behind the façade, the character behind the caricature, waiting there to be discovered. What, then, of responsibility? You cannot accept responsibility for others until you accept responsibility for yourself. Then, those who come to you, the real, absolute, truthful you, do you the greatest honor imaginable in seeking you out, and what you owe them in turn is responsibility for them. Not accepting responsibility turns you into something else entirely: hustler, lackey, fraud, swindler. Call it what you like, choose any name other than *doctor*.

So when the operator asked me on that other busy day what I was going to do, I knew not to slight Surgical Annex and did not. I saw the patient there and drove home so that Mimi could bring me back and keep the car. I was learning that an intern's life could be exemplary one moment, hopeless the next. Was that any different from anyone else's life?

*   *   *

There it is, touch it. Test its strength. Push. Push harder. Push until it yields and there they are, the same two rooms and those double doors to the bereaved highway, waxed to give off light but absorbing everything instead, including ideals and dreams, silent the executioner. One had thought of an aircraft with its fuselage, its wings of concrete. It was still there, but what had become of the clamor, the chaos, the cacophony of voices, the crackling blazes of a fire with ten-thousand tongues?

It was the eighties, and we had returned to Corpus for the first time in two decades, the first time since I had ended my inglorious career as one of eight interns at Memorial Hospital. We had not returned to see the hospital but to a city we remembered with fondness, returned for a weekend trip. We found our way out of curiosity to our former house and, one thing leading to another, retraced the route to Morgan Avenue and Hospital Boulevard. Traffic was heavier than it had been, the city seemed to be thriving, but one had the idea of it being a different epoch from before.

I hadn't known that the old hospital was closed, though the reason was clear enough. Just in front of what had been the new hospital was a much newer hospital, many stories high, and I rather imagined it held private patients, while the staff patients were treated in the 1953 hospital, with Medicare and Medicaid helping, certainly an improvement from '63 and '64. I remembered that they had been working on the latest hospital when I'd left in '64. So they had vacated Old Memorial but in baffling consequence left its framework intact, boarded up and nailed shut, the frame bleached and shrunken in the way that a thing abandoned loses not only its life but its precedence, a graveyard of broken dreams. Where do old buildings go when they have served their purpose? What becomes of old houses seen from the highway, the ones with flaking paint and broken panes and sagging porches with splotches of grass poking through? Had they held happiness for their occupants? Or did they come to reek of death, like the smell of putrid flesh before the dressing is removed, or like the fluttering wings of lost angels searching among the dust bunnies for the children's hour? Was theirs the vacancy of a child gone to sleep, never to awaken?

We parked outside Labor and Delivery, and I forced my way inside, Mimi following. We were guilty of breaking and entering but didn't care, previous crimes committed there belittling the very notion of an arrest for B&E. Besides, no one was around to report us. It was the middle of the afternoon and bright and humid in Corpus, but inside Old Memorial—so different from the structure I had known and yet so much the same—it was as though we had broken through a wall into a tomb that had been silent for thousands of years.

What had I expected? The familiar landmarks were still there: the double doors, the entrance to the Obstetrics Ward, the cafeteria just there and, of course, that room. There it was, as I had known it would be, stripped of its misery and pathos, that walk-in closet across from Obstetrics. Could it have been that small? I went farther down the esplanade, but not much. The beds had been removed, and all of the equipment, the cabinets and the counters and the sinks and the lavatories. So what? There were still places in there too forbidding for the faint of heart. I knew they were there: the interns' lounge, the emergency room, the OR. And that little room way down at the other end of the hallway—turn right and it was across from the pharmacy, and so relentlessly inconspicuous as to be invisible, where the bed was apt to be uncomfortable were it not for the reason patients were placed there. It was one of the rooms I had wanted to see, but I changed my mind about that. Instead, I rejoined Mimi and the two of us skated out of that waxy pestilence, fleeing the simultaneously nonexistent and the hauntingly ineradicable.

*   *   *

Rosa Ramos* was in her midforties but looked a generation older than that, having already had seven or eight children, a thin woman with dark skin, a toothless smile, and an unassuming demeanor. She was not on the Obstetrics Ward because her presence there, as was my understanding, would have upset the other patients. Her room in Old Memorial was the one I would revisit in the eighties, a walk-in broom closet off the main corridor situated across the hallway from the entrance to OB and just west of the cafeteria entrance. It did have a lavatory, but not much else. The bed fit—just (dissembled and reassembled, I was told, to get it inside). The door to her room was kept closed so it was possible to dash past it dozens of times a day and never think of her. But that was not an option for me. She was one of my patients, the departing intern had informed me, and I knew immediately upon entering that room for the first time why she was sequestered there.

It was the smell. It hit with the power of a blow and left a coating as thick as molasses. There is in animal physiology a thing known as sensory adaptation, and because of it she was possibly spared the stench. She never said and I never asked.

The room itself, awful. She did have an overhead light but preferred it off. She had no TV or bathroom or air vent, preferring to lie in the darkness accompanied only by her thoughts until interrupted by the routines of the hospital or by the vicissitudes of her disease. Sometime about a month previously, late May or early June of 1963, she had been passing through the city when she'd experienced a searing abdominal pain, followed by a seeming miscarriage. Her husband accompanied her to the emergency room, where the intern on call determined that yes, she was pregnant, and yes, she had expelled a sizeable mass from her birth tract. But something was wrong. The mass had not detached like a fetus, a newborn. That was bad enough, but the protruding item was not a fetus. The protruding item was not even a part of a fetus. The protruding item, thick as pot roast and wide as a dinner plate, was a fungating, mushroom-shaped cancer of the cervix, a meaty excrescence resembling a propeller, albeit one situated at the wrong end of her body and susceptible to being thrust through the slipstream of her introitus, as from coughing, whereupon it took up its messy and painful residence between her thighs.

As she could not herself maneuver it back inside of her body, the medical staff had to find someone who could. That would be the intern on Obstetrics since, by the way, she *was* also pregnant—a woman with two uterine growths going in opposite directions like competing armies, the one mocking the audacity of the other. It was as though she'd been parasitized twice, one growth excitedly anticipated—the Spanish word for pregnancy means *hoping*—the other an opportunistic bloodsucker leeching her of her very life.

On the last day of June, the day before my internship officially began, I made rounds with the previous intern and was introduced to Rosa. Her pregnancy meant everything to her. Judging by the growth of her uterus, it was doing well. The cancer, meanwhile, was inoperable only in the sense that removing it would terminate the pregnancy, which she did not want. Thus the intention was to keep her in her closet on bed rest until term or until she went into labor, then to deliver her by cesarean section. Dr. Hastings, in his role as staff obstetrician, loved to ask me whether it would be best to let her deliver through that cancerous cervix or to go with the planned C-section. He couldn't get much argument from me. I had no idea. But Rosa's presence reinforced a subtle truth about Memorial. It was closer to a third-world country than was San Antonio, Houston, or Dallas, which made it unique. "Only at Memorial," was the time-honored saying. "If it exists, you'll see it here."

Strangers in a public place, Mrs. Ramos and I became, in those first few days, as familiar with each other in private as we might wish. Because the cancerous mass inside the lower portion of her abdomen was prone to repeated herniation, daily or more often, it was a part of my day to visit her in that room. She smiled deferentially, each time, and tried to apologize for herself in Spanish, but I waved it off, feigning an indifference I did not feel. Too late, I saw one morning that she had caught the involuntary look of revulsion on my face. I suspected she knew that look well. Did I dread coming to her bedside? You bet I did. It seemed a thankless task, but when I thought about it, I realized that was not it at all. The patient was always courteous and thankful. It seemed a thankless task to me because I got no public adulation for it. My responding to her amounted to doing a good deed without receiving one's due acclaim from the world at large. Why do it unless rewarded? Nurses didn't accompany me, I figured, because they also received no public acknowledgment for it. It kept coming back to this. The patient was in distress because of the protrusion of an unwanted thing from inside her, an interloper knocking on the doorway to the world, and I was the reluctant gatekeeper.

I would be the world's biggest dolt should I not mention that something inside her had slipped out, in contradistinction to her having something slipped in her that had come from without. The amazing thing was the two were so much alike. It was merely a matter of direction. That, and heft, and a challenge to the idea that blessings are bestowed that way.

However embarrassing it might be to her, however unwanted, it was unbearably painful to her when the mass slipped out. Shifting it back inside her vagina relieved the pain, and that in itself was a good thing and gave me a tickle of pleasure. Was that reward enough? It was not. Each day there I was again at that dreaded site, her bedside, my attitude befouled at having to do it again, staring at that herniated mass between her legs, captivated by its staggering size, overwhelmed by its olfactory assault, the stench hitting me long before I reached for the sterile gloves wrapped in crinkly white paper that the nurse had left on the bedside table, the patient's eyes following my every twitch.

Interaction with her allowed me to practice my rudimentary Spanish, but she didn't respond. What if I were to gag and rush vomiting from the room? How rewarding that? Odor punished me. The mass weighed seven or eight pounds, but the poundage of the odor was off the scale, this leviathan washed up from the deep, rotten and getting more so, impossibly bigger today than the day before. It was as if some dark mammalian thing had burrowed its way into her overnight and was being expressed at the expense of her very life. It grew unevenly, outstripping its blood supply, and bled a thin, rusty fluid from its ulcerated surfaces, like skin flailed with a cat-o'-nine-tails or like a conglomeration of spoiled meat, a purgative cork from the bottle of herself.

Despite blood transfusions, the patient was anemic. She was gravely ill and had that gaunt, cancerous look. The cancer itself, in all its blustery swagger, was beyond the scope of heroic medicine; it was a part of the secrets never told. It summoned forth the smothering possibility that life was lost well before death, and no matter how courageously one might meet the threat, the battle in this instance was nearing the point of not being worth the goddamned effort. But it wasn't for me to decide.

Each person had to decide when that time was, but for Rosa, not yet. Fever, pain, defilement; violation, trepidation, abomination: tumor, dolor, rubor, calor. She wanted to have her baby. With both hands and straining to keep my face neutral, I refolded the cancer as one might grip the upper surfaces of a giant mushroom, gently bending its edges down and around its stem, getting it into more and more the shape of a bullet, the shape it had upon being expressed from the vagina, the patient assisting me with one of her hands in keeping the folds of it together. Awkwardly I began to work it back inside her. It seemed impossible for it to fit, extravagantly more impossible each time I attempted it, yet fit it finally did, with a *swish!* And I looked quickly into her eyes and away, *Be still my heart*, slave that I was to the ancient embarrassment—that wink at eternity—imparting its perennial shame.

And yet, invariably, she broke into a genuine smile.

"*Gracias*, Doctor."

I loved the tilt at the end of *doctor*, the Spanish accent falling on the second syllable.

"*De nada, Señora. No es difícil.*"

Clean sheets having been placed on her bedside table earlier, now these were exchanged for the old. Holding one hand over her introitus to prevent another herniation, Rosa gingerly removed the bottom sheet, the bad one, from beneath her, and I gave her the new one in exchange. I also helped in straightening the new one under her, until she was functional.

Something was going on at Memorial, in that particular room. Dizzily, I was searching for and trying to reinsert the person I had thought I was before the most recent herniation. It came to me totally unexpected, for an effort undignified, unlovely, and unapplauded. *So this is what it is to be a doctor.* The initial rush over, the enthusiasm having waned, I was learning that doctoring was not in the big things one equates it with, one who has not dwelled behind the White Curtain. Inside, the fame and prestige were erased in a commonality with others, and what ruled, what remained, was competence and a lovely self-awareness of it, the simple fact of worth. One can aspire to no more than that.

Medicine repaid itself that way and it had practically nothing to do with a Stradivarius stethoscope. It had very little to do with the supposed splendor of saving someone's life. It was a little like those high school plays where everyone had a part and you showed up that night and put on makeup and a fake mustache that made you look older, which was funny, but you were replete with the comforting knowledge that it was only temporary. Underneath, you were the same. You could be less than what you were, but you could never be more than that. Happiness came, I supposed, from being as much as that. Doctoring was in the little things: the music in the nurse's voice waking you up, the way patients looked at you with such hope, the way you were witness to the bravery shown by every patient, bar none. Saw people at their worst, and it was not so bad. Or saw them at their best, and it was sensational. Cynic you were not. Pleasure came as the valet to open the door to the next patient, with a commitment to do your best for them, and the majesty therein was enough. Interacting with them in a doctor suit? It was an unending delight.

The old hospital echoed with the silence of those who had discovered that humanity was humility. As for Rosa Ramos, yes, she was sequestered in her cave away from those on the Obstetrics Ward. There were no amenities, was no one to visit her. Doing for her had no prestige. But the hospital had agreed to keep her there until she had her baby, she was fed three times a day, and people saw to her needs. Of course the treatment and hospitalization were courtesy of Nueces County for a person not a citizen except in the most fundamental of ways: she was sick and we were there.

Something else, a valid part of the sinew—one tended to treat others according to one's estimate of their worth. Was this true even for professionals? It was true most of all for professionals. Initially, Rosa Ramos did not score very high on that scale, not with me. Yet I knew that she had not chosen to have cancer any more than she had chosen to be born in one country or another, or one century or another, and I was just as sure that she did not choose to live in ignorance and survive by meager circumstances rather than to dine at a table draped with linen with settings of sterling silver. She was a citizen of existence. Mother to a pregnancy that mattered more to her than her own life, she was maybe the bravest woman I had ever met, and I grew fond of the stench of her, and consequently my estimation of her worth soared valiantly. She made me into a human being and a doctor, and we were both spectators at that unexpected thrill.

As for that ghastly smell, what of it? So far as I knew, no one had ever put down a good description of such olfactory sensations as her cancer emitted—

or the ones offered in the birthing room, for that matter, that raw essence of seawater seeping over an estuary bounded by jungle on one side and a barnyard the other. Rosa Ramos reeked of the perfume of life, and maybe the measure of a doctor was to reach a point where every patient smelled the same. Hide your nose and open your heart.

*　　*　　*

Corpus was situated two-thirds of the way down to Mexico along the Texas Gulf Coast and visibly marked by a notch in the bowed skeleton of the coast, the sharply sculptured notch corresponding to where the Nueces River—which lent its name to the county, Corpus being the county seat of Nueces County—met its destination by way of a salty answer to its freshwater question. The bay could be entered from the gulf or the Yacht Basin, which was south of it and directly in front of the city.

Indeed, one of my favorite doctors in Corpus that year, Walter Lemke, would take weekend calls for his patients on his yacht out in Corpus Christi Bay, by way of an onboard short-wave radio. Often the communication itself was sufficient, Dr. Lemke ordering a medication for the patient over the phone, but when his physical presence was needed, he could return to the hospital within an hour. He was a colorful character, much loved by his patients and admired by the clutch of interns, and I had many interactions with him through the year, often assisting him in surgery. To me Dr. Lemke might have been a stand-up comedian delivering his lines onstage. It was said that the true test of a pro was to make 'em laugh even when they weren't drunk, the problem being that everyone in the nightclub was drunk, period. But he made the sober laugh; he could steal every scene. One reason was that he was his own worst critic.

I once assisted him on a right inguinal hernia repair on a young man aged ten or eleven. The hernia repair required a small incision in the boy's groin, with access to the peritoneal cavity on that side, and Lemke, cursing himself for the risk he was taking, decided on the spur of the moment during the surgery to perform an incidental appendectomy. He had been telling of the biggest hernia he had ever seen, which had required a truss the size of a hammock, when he instantly grew genuinely serious.

Using two fingers to locate the appendix and tweezer it down and out through the hernia incision, he began lustily berating himself for his stupidity, thinking out loud about the folly of a fool for what he was doing and the price he would pay. Having delivered the appendix through the groin incision, he sealed and cut the appendiceal artery, mentioning that a patient could bleed to death if that weren't done—and how that would probably be the fate of this young man for his stupidity in doing an extemporaneous appendectomy, and so forth. Of course, the incidental appendectomy went perfectly, as did the hernia repair, the man's potshots at himself notwithstanding.

One time it became my job, newly appointed by Walter Lemke, to perform an appendectomy on a teenager with appendicitis. I had, when asked, volunteered to assist but not to perform the surgery on that young man from the world of private patients. It was frightening. While we scrubbed, Lemke lamented that he would probably regret his decision in perpetuity, how reckless of him to turn the surgery over to a raw intern! Gowned, masked, capped, and scrubbed, the two of us entered one of the operating rooms at Memorial, the patient having been placed on the table, prepped, and anesthetized. We took our positions, with me—for the first time—standing on the patient's right.

The first challenge was the incision. Unlike many of my patients at Memorial, I had never cut human flesh (beyond the occasional cut-down on a vein). There, in that moment, I found that taking a blade to the human body was as easy as beheading angels.

"Cut!" Lemke said, suddenly serious.

I drew a pink line with the scalpel.

"Cut!" came the order again, stronger and more impatient. The patient was thin, he was nineteen years old, he was the ideal surgical candidate, and all eyes were on me. But I had just discovered that I was a heathen among parishioners.

Finally Walter Lemke reached across the table and placed his large hand around mine, which in turn held the scalpel, and in this piggyback way the incision was made, subsequently exposing the lining of the peritoneum and then the interior of the abdominal cavity. To sever the wormlike organ within was an easier task than cutting into the skin. But first, find it. The inflamed appendix must come out to cure appendicitis, but the organ proved elusive to my grasp.

A three-inch transverse incision was not exactly roomy, and in that silent enslavement crowded with the liver, the spleen, the stomach, the small intestine, the large intestine, and the meeting of the two at the cecum, to which the appendix was appended, one searched among the imprisoned for the subversive. Wearing gloves, it was like reaching into a barrel filled with formaldehyde and bringing out the small shark that you had been dissecting in the comparative anatomy lab, the trick being that one shark looked like every other shark, and felt the same.

Lemke waited for me to retrieve the appendix so that it might be amputated. While I searched unsuccessfully, he began recounting the number of lawsuits he would have to reply to because of this botched surgery, naming the various law firms in Corpus that he might call upon to represent him. Every now and then, though, he would nudge my hand aside, reach in, and deliver the appendix into the wound with the effort it might take to switch on a light, only to greet my sudden kick of joy by releasing the escapee to roam freely all over again within the enclosure, a frustrated novice in pursuit. Somehow the operation was completed, the patient did not die, and I learned to do an appendectomy while understanding that doing them as a way of practicing medicine was not in my future.

Dr. Lemke died in 1991, missed by all.

*   *   *

Maybe it was the physical beauty of Corpus and its environs that evoked exhilaration among its inhabitants and the tourists who visited it, or maybe it was the coastal city's rich history. The first European explorer of the region was Cabeza de Vaca, to whom generations of Texas schoolchildren attributed a head like a cow's. Poor Cabeza. His actual name was Alvar Nunez, the *Cabeza de Vaca* an honorary title he had inherited because someone in his family had once placed the skull of a cow in a mountain pass as a signal that helped to prevent defeat by warring invaders. For that matter, before old Cabeza, Nueces County was explored by that swashbuckling but deluded Frenchman with a long fancy name who was known forever to Texas schoolchildren as simply *La Salle.*

Corpus had been fired upon by federal gunboats during the Civil War, had once served as a way station for travelers on their way to California during the gold rush, and before that, in the summer and fall of 1845, had served as the assembly area for US troops that in the next year moved south to fight the Mexican War, its outcome assuring the United States of possession in perpetuity of territories including Texas, New Mexico, and California.

I found Corpus such a pleasant contrast to Galveston—both in having more beauty and friendlier people—that it was a shock to see the city's underside. Prejudice against Hispanic people was boilerplate and instinctive. I will speak to this in some detail later, but suffice it to say that the ongoing balance between the majority Hispanic population and the controlling Caucasian population was tense, at best. What happened in consequence was a reflection of what had happened, was happening, and would continue to happen in Corpus and everywhere else in a world of haves and have-nots. Those who were the victims of the system expended their rage upon one another.

Affluent whites used Spohn Hospital and comprised the city's social set. Spohn actually had an emergency room—for a well-heeled clientele. And although Memorial offered a new hospital for private patients, as I have said, Old Memorial served those who could not afford private care, and the emergency room at Memorial was the city and the county's Trauma Center, its catchment area consisting of the one hundred seventy thousand people in the city as well as an additional fifty thousand people in greater Nueces County, the fifth largest county in Texas. So it was that many of the ER patients came from Robstown, Port Aransas, and Agua Dulce, as well as a few other cities in the county.

Between the old and new hospitals, Memorial had 462 beds. It was a city-county hospital owned by the Nueces County Hospital District and governed by a seven-member board of managers. Memorial had an open medical staff representing every medical specialty and consisting of two hundred members. That allowed it to become a teaching hospital, and the intern program had begun in 1951, with plans to eventually include a residency program. Memorial was affiliated with Corpus Christi's Del Mar College for professional nursing and with Driscoll Children's Hospital for pediatric training. During my two months at Driscoll in the spring of 1964, I beheld an entire ward of babies—constantly replenished—with neonatal tetanus from midwives having cut the cord with rusty scissors. As the hospital had excellent pediatric residents, few of these infants died of their lockjaw.

The ER at Memorial was used by the various law enforcement agencies for citizens requiring emergency attention on their way to jail. These devoted patients, men and the occasional woman, whether blue-collar dockworkers and roughnecks or those doing day labor or who took their wages by the week, attended the ER Mass to celebrate a holy—holey?—trinity consisting of a brawling rage, the wide availability of switchblade knives, and a beverage known as beer. And, by the way, it met each Saturday night.

Memorial's interns came to know some of these parishioners well, repeat worshipers, because at Memorial interns served in the emergency room every eighth day for the entire year. This was different from most teaching hospitals, where the ER duty lasted a month or so, a block rotation that the intern completed and was finished with. For that matter, the ER at Memorial belonged to a time when a nurse might constitute the entire staff, his or her job being to alert the physician on call or the doctor the patient had asked for. It was hopelessly too small, too understaffed, too galling for Corpus Christi and Nueces County in 1963. But the ER at Memorial—its modern version having been where Selena was taken after being fatally wounded in 1995—did what it could with what it had.

The emergency room was located on the north side, toward the tail of the aircraft, but unlike Surgical Annex, it was in close proximity to the main corridor. Ambulances found it by following a caliche driveway that circled around past Labor and Delivery, past a large employees' parking lot, and, just short of the hulking Annex, led to the outside entrance of the ER. That consisted of a well-worn set of double doors, each of them with a once-shiny metal integument, guarding a short corridor leading to the ER. Or, rather, to an alcove just outside ER.

Serving in the alcove, a 24/7 clerk did paperwork and sought payment where possible, and beyond another set of swinging doors built to absorb the blows of stretchers pushed by strong young ambulance attendants was the single room comprising ER. It was shockingly small, hopelessly outdated, and teasingly sufficient. It was perhaps double the size of a patient's private room. As such, it had no triage area or restroom. No flashing monitors with LCDs and LEDs clicking like fireflies, no IV machines, no pulse oximeters to slip over the patient's index finger, no buttons to summon a nurse, and no beds, as such. Instead, seven or eight gurney stretchers arranged in two horizontal rows were its waiting features.

Each gurney offered the brittle privacy of draw curtains. The curtains didn't always get drawn (except when a patient was deceased). The gurneys were close enough together to provide a space between them barely sufficient to allow people to maneuver, but sometimes, often, always, chaos did not allow such delicacies. Patients sat on the floor or were sprawled half on and half off of a gurney. It was easier to do CPR on the floor, for example, and when the patient didn't respond, removing said patient took second seat to stopping bleeding or ministering to pain or trying to maintain order in what became a rabble of seekers and providers. I remember having to ask patients who were conscious and suffering only a heart attack to hold the IV bottle or the bottle of blood for an adjacent patient in much worse shape. Fill the ER with a couple dozen cops, doctors, ambulance drivers, nurses, and lab people and you get the idea. The head nurse did have a desk just inside the entrance, but the intern and the technician roamed freely and might freshen themselves at a lavatory at the back, beneath a glass medication cabinet to which the nurse held the only key.

There were a couple of telephones at oddly inconvenient places. There were sleek metal stands with bare surfaces on which to place suture packs or whatever. The overhead lights made the ER bright enough to see, but I required one of the standing goose-necked lamps for use in getting a better view of a laceration while suturing same.

The crowded room, where far too many people breathed their last, served on occasion as an adjunct to hell, when it was not warming up purgatory and serenading attendees, when it was not blaring forth in the fanfare of an ongoing war played out in syncopated evisceration. The drama never ended, and the choreography was precarious, with actors roaring out their harmonics in counterpoint to the shrill cries of the ailing young, and it taught the participants lessons their parents forgot to mention, the ones they themselves would spare their own children.

One morning, for example, a lady walked in and calmly assured me that she had just killed herself. She didn't have the gun, but she hiked her blouse to reveal the entrance wound in the left upper quadrant of her abdomen. There was no exit wound, and after I had patched up her insides in the OR—under the supervision of a hospital surgeon—I admitted her to the Med/Surg Ward, treated her depression with pills, and then dug out that .25-caliber slug from her hip. I even made the nurse bring me a metal pan so I could drop the bullet into the bucket with a *ping!* just like they did in cowboy movies.

Another time, a fetching young woman walked in and said that she, too, had just killed herself by swigging a bottle of a mercury-based solution used in pest control. She admitted to stomach pain and began having bloody stools right there in the ER, symptoms of the mercury poisoning. She differed from the first patient in that she actually did succeed in killing herself, by means of the worst possible method. Perhaps a visit to the ER before things got so bad?

One evening about suppertime, during a lull because it was a weekday, a young woman wearing a housecoat started across the ER toward me, and a mass fell from her and established its gelatinous presence upon the tiled floor. It looked, in color and form, like a jellyfish fresh from the ocean, only much, much larger. It was the size of a serving bowl that had been filled with clear, white Jell-O, except it was much stickier than that and seemed to consist of multiple parts, metaphorical maggots dining on something from another planet. I had absolutely no idea. The woman had been pregnant, she said, and was more startled, were that possible, than I. While the nurse scooped and saved the gelatinous whatever, I called a gynecologist, and he took one look at it and shrugged and said, "Got yourself a mole, huh?"[4] I not only had never seen one, I'd no idea that they were possible.

Here's one. A guy walks into a bar and ends up in the ER with his penis wedged into a longneck beer bottle, which he had covered with his shirt. Having a strong essence of beer about his person, he claimed to have done

---

4   Hydatidiform mole is a cancer-like growth of the placental tissue, and spontaneous expulsion is most likely to occur around the fourth month of gestation. Louis Hellman et al., *Williams Obstetrics*, Fourteenth Ed. (New York: Appleton-Century-Crofts, 1971), 564.

it on a dare, the head of the penis having ventured too far for subsequent removal. A surgeon took him to the OR to unloose same, the danger being that when the bottle was broken to free the penis, it might lacerate the organ, and without careful attention, the man could have bled to death. The patient said his friends had given him a hard time—no pun intended—and called him a sissy (or equivalent) for seeking emergency care, though in fact that was exactly what he should have done.

How many did we see a day? How many each night? What was it like? It was busier by night than by day, as one would expect, and busiest of all on weekends and holidays, when well north of a hundred people might join that bracing serenade. That might not sound like a lot, except to the trio on duty, these consisting of an intern, a nurse, and an ER tech.

The fourth day of internship, July 4, I arrived for my first rotation on ER at seven o'clock in the morning, knowing that the in-hospital duty lasted until seven o'clock the following day. Time permitting, one might nap on the sofa in the interns' lounge across the hall (and next to the telephone). But on the Fourth of July, 1963, time did not permit. On this July 4, the world seemed intent upon demonstrating to all observers its unflinching desire for self-destruction.

*   *   *

I was still introducing myself, the intern before me having already left, when a woman rushed in and deposited her limp four-year-old onto the nearest gurney, the one by the two windows on the north side of the ER, as she screamed that he had choked to death. The kid's color was poor. He wasn't breathing.

The thirty-eight-year-old ER tech, Johnny Cordova, jumped toward the little boy, holding the tube of a wall suction apparatus in his hands. I had no idea what to do but was thankful for instinct. I reached the kid a couple of seconds after Cordova began working on him and had had, in that brief eternity, enough time to think of something. The kid weighed about forty pounds, but I grabbed him by the heels with my left hand and swung him into the air, then hit him hard on his back with the side of my right fist. Immediately the kid dislodged a wad of bacon the size of a baseball, which went whistling across the room and bounced off the wall beyond the gurney. Next thing the kid did was to take in a long, deep breath and scream at the top of his lungs in a wail lusty enough to portray the terror he had certainly felt at being unable to breathe.

This set everyone in the ER to laughing, the ambulance attendants having joined us. The mother was crushing everyone in gratitude, and Cordova and the nurse seemed to relax from worrying about the competence of the youngest of the eight interns. On my part, it was a lucky swing by a rookie.

I was, in fact, the most dispensable of the four employees on ER. Firstly, they could not have run it without the clerk. And then, the technicians were better ER doctors than I was, at least at first. Rugged Hispanic men who had been combat medics during World War II, Cordova and Reyes had seen and done everything. They were smart, they were strong, and they were a godsend, a pleasure to have around, Cordova for days, Reyes for nights. The charge nurse was Mrs. Hulsey—Leesola "Lee" Hulsey—who was old enough to be my mother and wise enough to be my mentor and fair enough to be my champion. Lee was not too lofty, despite her seniority, to skip duty on holidays; she was there by my side that first ER call and I loved her for it, loved the experiences she shared with me and the way she did what good nurses instinctively do: protect the doctor. She would suggest things I hadn't thought of and handle the telephone, which in itself was a full-time task.

One time later that year I was seated at Lee's desk, tired through and through, having just finishing an ER rotation. It was a few minutes before seven that morning, the sun blazing in through those two apertures across from her desk. I hadn't heard a siren, but here came two ambulance workers conveying a person into the ER on a stretcher. I saw at a glance that he was DOA (dead on arrival), yet they had not covered him up.

"What's wrong with him?" I asked in a voice weak with supplication, the quavering voice of dread.

Lee Hulsey: "What do you think is wrong with him?"

Me: "What I think is wrong with him is that he is dead."

"Yes, but not until you say so."

It was one of those things that seemed just right, filling me with such an intense love for her that I would have followed her anywhere, would have killed for her. ER was a classroom, yes, but she was not the teacher. She was subtle that way. She was my angel.

Most of those we treated, of course, were AOAs (alive on admission), and almost all were AOD (alive on discharge), whether to home or to jail or to a bed in the hospital at large. The ones that became DOD (dead on discharge) were technically equivalent to DOAs, but they comprised a different category entirely. Most of the DODs—by definition patients who were alive on arrival—died at night, the cause being trauma by knife or GSW (gunshot wound) or car wreck, wherein we failed to save them. Most DOAs, by contrast, arrived during the day, before noon, the person having died during sleep and the body subsequently discovered the next morning.

My first DOA arrived on that Fourth of July, not long after the little boy who had choked on the wad of bacon. Wheeled in by ambulance drivers, this older man was stone dead, his unmarked body cold to the touch and showing definite signs of rigor mortis. I suspected that a heart attack or stroke had taken him overnight, and in advance of talking to the relatives, I was writing a note to that effect. Word somehow passed to the family as they began arriving outside the ER that the person was dead and, clamoring in grief and protesting to be admitted, they shoved their way inside and brazenly demanded to know what was being done to save the deceased. First the man's daughter, supported by a neighbor, then the elderly wife, supported by her sons, and then the dead man's brother, supported by the policeman who had been summoned when the body was discovered. I recognized their shock but was unprepared for their anger.

What history I was able to glean from the family was that the deceased slept in his own room and was found dead that morning after he did not come out for breakfast. They called the ambulance, and here he was. It was self-evident that the man had died hours ago, but to the family, he had been alive until he reached the ER. They were distraught at my "cavalier" manner, my unapologetic failure to do anything by way of resuscitation efforts for their loved one.

"How is he?" the daughter asked.

"Well, I'm sorry, but he passed away before reaching us."

"Oh no! That can't be! You must do something!"

She swayed and screamed and knocked down a tray, and in the scuffle others rushed to assist her. The enemy consisted of those on duty there, so that shouting at and heckling us was both warranted and expedient. More of the family arrived, equally enraged. Whatever the final total, they far outnumbered the trio on duty, and they did not intend to leave until they had met their objective. The idea, to them, was simple. The man, precariously in need of treatment, had died because the doctor had refused to give it.

"Why aren't you *helping* him?" was yelled again and again.

Or, "What's the *matter* with you?"

Or, "Who's in *charge* here?"

In part the problem was the setting, ER not lending itself to a good doctor–patient relationship. Far more often, it was adversarial. The trio of us on duty in the ER represented the government, you see, and the government never did give a shit. Corpus was big enough that stranger met stranger, with the perilous outcome always in doubt. Everyone knew that the doctor was nonjudgmental and at all times had to display courtesy, compassion, and professionalism, but people saw courtesy as weakness, compassion as idleness, and professionalism as slick evasiveness. As a public servant in the

ER, I was required to take their shit (and their assaults, to a point). It was my job. Policemen got it, but they had guns. Firemen got it, but they had hoses. Doctors and nurses and techs got it and had nothing but themselves to fall back on, and the cruel discovery I made that day was that the hardest thing about duty in the ER was to face the family of someone who had died overnight at home and was stone dead before being "admitted" as a DOA. Those were the ones I took home with me to remember for always. DOA *and* DOD.

That particular family, once I got them out of the ER and once the man's body was released to a funeral home, were so upset with me for not doing anything to save the deceased that they called to insult me and threaten lawsuits for the rest of the day. They were certainly not the only family that year that reacted so viciously to the news of a DOA.

Sometimes, of course, medical personnel put on a show of trying to resuscitate someone obviously dead, and I learned to do this. But it was a sham. It wasn't wrong for them to have brought their loved one to the emergency room. When a physician was not in attendance, death becomes a legal matter, and certain procedures must be followed. One's task was to examine the body, if only briefly, knowing that on the death certificate were three lines requiring the physician to put down the immediate and the two main contributing causes of death. When these were not obvious, the coroner had to be called and a forensic autopsy obtained in order to make sure a crime had not been committed. Understanding this and being a professional, I sucked it up and soaked it up, and DOAs continued to arrive each day I spent in ER.

Medical training, as did life itself, selected in favor of those who could hold their temper. Not holding it was a contagious disease made worse by any number of things. Those infected often found their way to our ER, where duty for an intern was less about medicine than about dealing with the general public and the general nastiness that goes on after dark in every American city. The ER was where you met what could go wrong with the human condition and learned how frail the flimsy tissue of civilization.

*   *   *

Lee Hulsey was likewise not enamored with dealing with the problems presented by DOAs. In fact, she was often the first one to see the body.

One time during the tenure of the previous set of interns, they took a gurney stretcher that had been left in the hallway, and one of them climbed onto it and was covered with a mortuary sheet. While having lunch in the cafeteria, Hulsey was notified of the arrival of a DOA, and since an intern wasn't available, she had to cut short her meal to return to ER, where the "corpse" awaited her on the gurney beside her desk.

She perfunctorily ripped back the sheet.

The intern sat up, grinning at her.

Hulsey screamed, "Oh my goodness! Don't do that to me!"

But she did not object too much. Silly as it was, it was the highest of honors to a nurse who was respected and loved by all.

*　　*　　*

Activity in the ER was cyclical. Afternoon brought accident victims, drug addicts looking for a quick fix, or people who had become ill and needed a doctor. Then there was the bizarre.

The fire department brought in a man at about lunchtime that July 4, a Caucasian male, twenty-one years old. He had been found unconscious at the bottom of the public swimming pool where he also happened to be the lifeguard. Seems he had challenged a buddy to see who could swim the length of the pool the most times underwater. It was the standard public swimming pool, filled with blue water and the white splashes of its happy occupants, with people diving off the boards and climbing out of the water at those steel ladders built into the wall. The lifeguard, to allow himself more time underwater, had hyperventilated before diving in. This was a dangerous practice. A series of long, deep inhalations and exhalations before submersion lowers the body's level of carbon dioxide by "blowing it off."

This is dangerous because the level of carbon dioxide in the blood is what drives respiration. It is the rise in carbon dioxide in the blood that eventually forces one to surface and breathe. Consequently, as the lifeguard swam underwater, he felt little urge to quit the race and surface, though his muscles were voraciously consuming the oxygen in his blood. Catastrophe occurred when he lost consciousness from hypoxia, took a deep breath of water, and, well, drowned.

The guy competing with him climbed out and sat on the side of the pool, catching his breath, while the Fourth of July crowd, unaware of the contest, splashed and frolicked in glee. Eventually, walking to the diving board, the friend spotted a blur on the bottom of the deepest part of the pool. He dove in and pulled the lifeguard out.

The fire department, with a resuscitator, had done a superb job on the young man en route to the ER, and consequently the lifeguard escaped fatality. I watched while Cordova participated in finishing the rescue of what we called "near-drowning," the adjective having been attained by way of the person's resuscitation. But that was not all. Apparently the lifeguard must have sensed his peril just before he lost consciousness in the pool, because as he regained consciousness in the reverse process of how he had lost it, he became manically hyperactive, thrashing about on the gurney like a man fighting for his life. It was as though we were his mortal enemies. He went at us with hands, arms, and legs, snapping at us and emitting screams of inhuman intensity, screams that were an earsplitting weapon. I grabbed a leg but needed help, and all in all it took firemen, cops, doctors, nurses, and volunteers working like wildcatters on an oil rig to subdue him, a dozen or more, and not without suffering blows themselves from this strong young Poseidon. The lifeguard left the hospital a week later, his brain apparently intact after the ordeal—the luckiest man in Corpus.

*   *   *

Three teenagers were critically wounded in an accident: two young women and a young man from the same high school, all of them in the front seat in a collision with a telephone pole out on the Kingsville Highway. The three were surprisingly bloodless. The young man's feet had gone through the soles of his shoes. One of the women had broken both thighs and tibias, possibly dying from massive internal hemorrhage.

The third person had been driving. Her face suffered the windshield, her chest the steering wheel. Moving from looking at the broken leg of a child who had fallen out of a tree, and freeing myself of a patient suffering a boisterous drug reaction, I moved over to see this person, whose body was still warm. She alone might possibly be saved.

It was midafternoon, and another intern, Dr. Dale Brannom, had stepped in to help. Dale was ten years older than I. He was a head taller and a hundred pounds heavier, a gentle giant with hair the color of a pumpkin that he wore in a crew cut, the latter resonating to the other aspects of his persona.

"Let's tube her," Dale said. "Why don't we?"

I pushed the gurney out enough to make room for myself between it and the two windows in ER. It was the second gurney from the left, the one where the lady had deposited her four-year-old son that morning ages ago, who had choked. It was next to the one by the wall, where the lifeguard had regained consciousness and required a small army to restrain him.

The young woman from the car wreck had no heartbeat or respiration, but Dale handed me an endotracheal tube. I measured it and determined very quickly that it was too big for the young woman's windpipe and asked for a smaller one. While Dale went for it, I pulled the patient by her shoulders until her head dangled off the end of the gurney, as if she were trying to look at me upside down (though her eyes were closed).

She had long blonde hair tied with a red ribbon into a ponytail that reached almost to the floor. Without enthusiasm, a female nurse who had come in to help was pumping her chest in the vicinity of the heart. Supporting the girl's head in this hyperextended position, I reached for the smaller tube Dale brought, checked the landmarks in her mouth and throat, and by the light of the laryngoscope inserted the endotracheal tube into her trachea on the first try. With a syringe, Dale quickly inflated the cuff that held the tube in place by an air seal. While Dale went for the Bird respirator, I took a deep breath and blew all of it into the tube. I was ill-prepared for what happened next.

The patient's bare chest expanded with the infusion of air, and as the elasticity of her tissues caused expiration, I was hit in the face with a spray of broken glass and other debris that stung like BBs, birdshot fired point-blank. The spray of detritus from her lungs meant she had inhaled those shards of glass, had carried the wreck from there to here to share with me.

One doesn't stop and think of such things, perhaps even notice them. But I remember her and my reaction, awaiting me all these years, save for the words to describe it—each word a shard of glass in the image of the broken physician I would become, my imperfections too numerous to count. But no. Drop it, leave it, prop up the dignity that invests the moment. One dare not mention the misshapen reality, the messy contours of the picture as it was punctured, the sickening crunch of ribs beneath the pumping hands during CPR on an elderly patient whom you hope was dead to start with, because you are sure hell killing him otherwise. One doesn't mention the vomit that is more likely than not to boil from the face of a person requiring mouth-to-mouth resuscitation, or the stolen pleasure of the bewildering sexual attraction one may feel toward a dead stranger.

I continued breathing for this deceased patient through the tube, remembering each time she exhaled that she had lived long enough to take in those particles of crushed windshield glass, and I must turn aside or be taken with her to the place where she had died and be ensnared by the screeching tires and the lurching vehicle and the brawny telephone pole in its bed of hard, brown earth and creosote awaiting anyone and everyone who wished to be a part of it, were accidentally a part of it, or were involuntarily a part of it, or were dead in at least some part of it, the way this person was.

So I gave her my breath through a tube, and lifelessly, she returned it to me. Was it resuscitation or the ostentatious theater I had so derided in others? I didn't know and Dale didn't say. He brought the Bird respirator but did not hook it to the endotracheal tube. What Dale did was to touch my arm and gesture.

It was a strange thing. Who decided that, and when?

Dale patted my shoulder and said, "Way to go," like a coach to a player for a good catch. Damndest thing was, it felt so good to be so magnanimously rewarded that I experienced a frisson of happiness. Limited praise in a limited martyrdom seemed exactly right for our abrupt withdrawal from the deceased patient, and I felt very glad that we had made the effort on this person even though we both knew that she was dead before we started. Maybe the young blonde beauty, DOA, wasn't the one being resuscitated. Maybe the thing they didn't teach you to expect on ER, the biggest surprise of all, was that the resuscitation was going on inside yourself.

*   *   *

Meanwhile, the phone did not stop ringing and Lee Hulsey kept up with it, calling private practitioners who could only be summoned by the magic words, "The patient has medical insurance." I prayed for medical insurance. Late that afternoon in the Memorial ER, several interns and private doctors were toiling like football players in a hard-fought game, colliding in the walkway while getting people ready for surgery and knowing that more victims were en route. I looked up at nine p.m., saw that the ER was still full. Lunch and supper were opportunities long gone. By then, my first day of emergency medicine, I was suturing lacerations I had no business suturing. Cuts involving the eyelids, the lining of the eye socket. These were jagged cuts, deep lacerations that penetrated all the way to the bone.

I learned something that we had never discussed in human anatomy. The skin over the forehead feels like a very thin layer, with the skull lying just beneath it. But stick your finger into a cut to the skull and it sinks as beneath the crust of a pudding, with all manner of layers comprising tissue that is the better part of an inch deep. Such a wound required several layers of stitches beneath the ones sealing the skin. Instant plastic surgeon, I pleated together noses and ears and lips, toggled faces into facsimiles. Often I didn't bother with local anesthetic on patients who were so drunk they felt no pain. Much has been made of secondary smoke; secondary beer was my menace.

Toward midnight, the ER was filled with cops and mean drunks. The vicious drunks would bite or shit on the stretcher out of spite. Having started the day an idealist, a callow intern who desperately wanted to help others, I had discovered the awful truth: that the American dream was in serious trouble.

*   *   *

The most embarrassing thing about weekly duty in the ER was to have weaknesses in one's training exposed. As an alternate student—completing medical school in three years—I'd received an alternate education. I spent all of two and a half weeks on orthopedic surgery at UTMB but failed to learn nearly as much as I should, the reason being that Orthopedic Service had no place for students. I was never assigned a resident or given a reading assignment or directed to do this or that. I spent some of those two and a half weeks in ER, but the ER in Galveston was far less busy than the one at Memorial, and no one seemed to care. I also studied the orthopedics section in my surgery text, and I followed the orthopedic residents on rounds but received no encouragement from them.

I went to the bookstore and looked over a couple of volumes on orthopedic surgery, but the books were expensive, like twenty-five or thirty dollars, and seemed far too difficult for my level of knowledge. I checked in the library, but all of the recent acquisitions on the topic were checked out to professors.

Yet when I took the oral examinations at the end of my three years of medical school, I went before a person on the Orthopedics faculty that I had never seen and who immediately began quizzing me on the different types of fractures known to occur. It was a long list and I knew but a few, the Colles' fracture for one, from the surgery text. But I did not know nearly all of the ones I was asked. The professor was disappointed, and I dared not give my comeback: Where the hell were you when I needed you?[5]

The Surgery rotation at UTMB consisted of general surgery and each of the specialty surgeries, including oral examinations for each service. Along with those in my class, I also had to pass National Board exams in everything from medicine to pediatrics to psychiatry. Dr. Truman Blocker, an internationally known plastic surgeon, and head of the Department of Surgery, called me in after the orals and went over the results with me, laughing in his feisty way at the various professors' comments about me. He ended by awarding me the grade of A for Surgery because of my making one of the higher scores in our class on the surgical portion of the Board exams.

That was nice, but an A amounts to an impaled derriere in the ER, and later that month I was there when a patient came in with a broken hip. She was an elderly woman who had fallen while getting out of bed. As she was a private patient with medical insurance, it was my job to contact the physician of her

---

5   Mea culpa. My duty as a medical student was to ascertain what was required
     of me, not to sulk away in silence because no one had happened to step
     forward and hold my hand.

choice. The man I happened to call was an older orthopedic surgeon, and the call woke him up. He was a tad crusty to begin with, and who wouldn't be when awakened like that? The orthopedist listened to a recitation of the physical findings and X-rays.

He said, "Put her in five pounds of Buck's traction and I'll see her first thing in the morning."

I paused. I took a breath. I said, "What is Buck's traction?"

"Ask the goddamned nurse!" the orthopedist yelled, and slammed the phone down with enough force to leave my ear ringing.

Traction was the application of a weight to an extremity by way of pulling on it in a longitudinal direction, bringing the bones into proper alignment and, not incidentally, immobilizing the limb. Of course I knew this but was unfamiliar with Buck's traction. It turned out to be the simplest form of traction: adhesive tape was used to attach a cord to the lower limb; the cord was led through a pulley in an apparatus at the foot of the bed, where a counterweight was attached to it. (Sometimes the foot of the bed was also elevated.) I wrote the order and the nurse, as predicted, put the patient into five pounds of Buck's traction.

Still another time a teenage boy came in with a fracture of the right radius and ulna at the level of the mid-forearm. The famous Colles' fracture, already mentioned, was named for Abraham Colles, a nineteenth-century Irish surgeon. This type of fracture was of the lower radius in its classic form, or of the lower ulna as well, basically just above the wrist, incurred when a person fell and caught the body weight on a hand extended in reflex against the floor or ground.

I might have called for help had this teenager had that fracture, but he didn't, and I had become rather timid about seeking help from orthopedists at night. The patient, thirteen or fourteen, was otherwise in good health. His fractures seemed straightforward enough, and I elected to set the arm myself and send the boy home in a cast, the latter applied by an orthopedic technician, one of several employed by Memorial.

The tech came out, I showed him the closed fractures and the good alignment obtained by manual traction applied to the patient's hand, and he took the patient to a treatment room and applied a plaster of paris cast. An X-ray was routine after the cast. When I saw it, I was flabbergasted; the bones were out of alignment! The only thing I knew to do was to remove the cast on the kid's arm, manipulate the bones into place again, take a confirmative X-ray, then reapply the cast and take yet another X-ray to check. Each time I did this, however, the same thing happened. When viewed beneath the cast, the bones were no longer in good enough alignment to heal correctly. This went on far too long that night, with multiple casts applied and removed. The orthopedic technician and I, to say nothing of the patient and his mother, grew tired of it, and finally I just put on another cast, x-rayed it, and gave up, the bones still out of alignment.

Discharged home, the patient was given an appointment to be seen for follow-up in Orthopedics in six weeks. My bad luck: by then I would have rotated onto the Orthopedic Service and would have to confront patient and mother in front of the orthopedic surgeon who supervised the clinic.

And that is what happened. I knew the youth was coming to that clinic, having remembered his name, and I had practiced my mea culpa ad infinitum, expecting and deserving to be blamed for the bad outcome. Not at all. An X-ray showed that the broken bones in the kid's forearm had mended perfectly. I removed the cast and discharged him, learning in the process what I should have already known—that in children the bones remodel like crazy, and perfect alignment beneath the cast is unnecessary. I spent a bit of time wondering why the orthopedic technician, who surely knew this, hadn't told me, but maybe he needed the overtime.

*   *   *

One evening, Mimi mentioned that she had received a traffic ticket and that it was going to cost twenty-five dollars, a huge sum for us. It amounted to a week's groceries lost. There was nothing but to pay, and I mentioned it as a humorous item to the night nurse in ER, Mrs. Chapa. Stunningly, Mrs. Chapa made a call, and the next morning I was summoned to the ER. Standing there among the gurneys, backlit from the sunlight streaming through those two windows, was the policeman who had given Mimi the ticket. He was in his policeman's uniform, and his calf-length black boots seemed to have cleats on them from the sounds they made on the tile floor of the ER. He smiled, introduced himself. He held up the ticket, apologized for giving it to Mimi, and tore it up. He tossed it into the trash can.

It was a rush, a high, a narcotic that scared the hell out of me. Petrified me, because the ER could be such a strange and worshipful place, wherein unearned deference was as common as the plotted anger of the trivializing few, and one might too easily succumb to the notion that it was his due.

Man came in with a heart attack, a myocardial infarction. He was writhing in the severity of his chest pain and bathed in a cold sweat—meaning sweat without his body feeling warm—and one of the best things one did, besides the diagnosis, was to relieve the pain. I injected a quarter of a grain of morphine into a vein in the man's arm; as the narcotic took hold, the patient relaxed under its spell and looked up at me. His face changed, as when death has been kicked in the ass. He spoke.

He said, "I love you, Doctor."

He said it as though not to a stranger, not to an intern, not to a surprised pilgrim on the road to the unforeseeable, but to a god. In those days I spent a lot of my time being stunned, and I was flabbergasted because what I had done for him was so simple, so easy. He wasn't the last patient to say that, he was the first, and I counted it the nicest thing I had ever had said to me—certainly by a stranger, which he no longer was. He was my patient. It was like the explosion of particles in a snow globe, a happy surprise for the enraptured toddler, and it aroused in me once again the disconnect, the breach between the dissected, disembodied creatures I had studied and the living examples of the real thing, the latter so dissimilar from what I had expected that the one could not easily be reconciled with the other. I had not expected that. I was not prepared for that. One had to earn that, which I hadn't done. Yet the naked sense of power, the omnipotence, the celestial stirrings of the god game—one could get used to that. Very used to it.

It was like the time, though of a lesser magnitude, when several of us had formed an ensemble from the band and played hymns and Christmas carols on the podium in front of the choir on a Sunday night service at the First Baptist in Pittsburg, circa 1955. That was in the old building, parts of it reaching back to the nineteenth century, its façade designed in the Victorian manner of a European cathedral.

The congregation was dressed up; the members of the choir were too, in their pretty purple gowns, each with a white sash trimming it, the women smiling and beautiful and at their best. The fragrance was of them and of the sweet, piney smell of decorations strewn about the church, and it was so nice and so wonderful that to me it had seemed unearned; the music of the songs we played was so disgustingly easy. Yet the people went on and on, praising us and praising God for us, and I had wanted to say, "Look, if you knew how easy this stuff was compared to what we play in the high school band, in technique and rhythms and octaves, you would know how little effort it took!" But I couldn't bring myself to say it because I was so painfully aware that they did not want to hear it. To have people fawning over you like that, I did not overlook, could be fun. For about two seconds. Then it became dangerous, a punch bowl filled with hemlock, pleasantness at the expense of character. It had the potential of mustering from the depths of the soul a self-love both deceitful and cunning, a bright trinket blinding out the simple and utter truth that nothing in life is free, everything has to be paid for, and they only take cash.

Part I.   An Undeliverable Lie

*   *   *

Literal cash was no less easy to come by than its figurative counterpart. Under state law, Mimi and I shared things by halves, but at the time of our marriage, by good luck, I had more than she. I owned the '54 Plymouth sedan, paid for, and had saved up some money from working that summer. It seemed adequate, with her paycheck as a schoolteacher, to support the two of us. After she joined me in Galveston in January of 1961, we opened a joint checking account at the First State Bank in Pittsburg. The arrangement the two of us had was for me to pay the bills that came in by mail and for her to tell me each check she wrote, so that we might keep the account in balance, but it didn't work out that way.

Blame it on the poverty inculcated into the medical education, which consisted of grown men yelling at other grown men, who actually paid them for the privilege. Blame it on the value of one's skills. I had married above myself, a fact I well knew, but upon which Mimi never commented. She had both parents, Helen and Gilbert Garrett—solid, middle-class citizens in Pittsburg. Gilbert managed Kimball's Wholesale Grocery operation in the city, and Helen did its books and served, as well, as a homemaker and mother of the two girls. Mimi, born in 1939, was elder to Vicki, born in 1945, her treasured sister. The family lived in the Pecan Grove neighborhood of Pittsburg, had two good cars, and was prosperous enough to send both daughters to Baylor University. It was the fulfillment of a dream. Raised in the Depression, neither Gilbert nor Helen had attended college. They wanted for their daughters what they had not had.

After graduating as valedictorian of her high school class, Helen was particularly sensitive of things that had not been possible in the 1930s, when a riptide had toppled the American economy and sucked into its vortex what was left of middle-class existence. It was brutal and humiliating to everyone who lived through it, but most especially the children of the Depression. Still, in some ways farm children were luckier than those in the city, and both Gilbert and Helen were born and raised on farms in Hunt County, Texas, which had the city of Greenville as its county seat.

Helen Ann Laxton was born at a settlement known as McFarland Ridge on September 1, 1916. She grew up loving to tell people, "I must have been a puny baby—I only weighed ten pounds." Woodrow Wilson was the president and the United States was on the verge of entering World War I, known then as "the war to end all wars."

Helen was the middle of three daughters among the sibs surviving childhood; Bonnie was the eldest and Bobbie the youngest. Together the three of them followed many a row of unending cotton that had to be planted, weeded, picked, and taken to the gin to be sold for whatever money they got, a sum that would have to do them until the following year. The soil itself, a waxy, black sod described in schoolbooks as part of the blackland prairie, was unrelentingly stubborn. When dry, it cracked. When wet, it turned into a mud that was like stepping through molasses, and it had been overplanted so many times that working it amounted to going at a stump with a hacksaw, or plowing with a milk cow, or attaching an outboard motor to an outhouse and fertilizing it while laying it by.

Hunt County was not a picturesque hinterland. Trees in this region a few dozen miles east of Dallas seemed to have given up and gone bust, and though rainfall was adequate, it was no more than that and sometimes much less, though the county did contain the headwaters of the Sabine River. It was a hard soil in hard times, a mean land, a cruel one.

The county had slavery in its earliest years of growing cotton, and it knew well the racism that followed the liberation of slavery into the twentieth century. "The Burning of the Negro" was a story that had been passed locally since the time, in 1908, that "Negro Ted Smith," accused of raping a white girl, was taken from the jail by a mob and dragged by a rope to the south side of the courthouse, where he and a pile of wood were doused with kerosene and a lighted match was applied. The victim was said to have managed a brief yell as the immolation began. It was a sign of the times that the black community of Greenville subsequently released a statement to the effect that the accused Ted Smith, "… did not in any sense represent our race in this community. … We respectfully ask that the public do not judge our race by the act of one culprit for whose conduct we are in no sense responsible. No two races of people ever lived in the same community with a more friendly or cordial relation existing than exists in this community, and we ask that the same relation continue that we have always had."[6]

Despite this, a bold downtown sign proclaimed:

THE BLACKEST LAND	GREENVILLE WELCOME	THE WHITEST PEOPLE[7]

The sign's tenure lasted well into the fifties. Other signs, more brisk in their threat, had appeared at one time or other: "Nigger, Don't Let the Sun Set on You!" To an extent that is closer to the truth than not, the same overt

---

6   W. Walworth Harrison, *History of Greenville and Hunt County Texas* (Waco, Texas: Texian Press, 1977), 384.

7   *History of Greenville*, 335–36.

racism and history of lynching infested most other places in rural Texas during the first half of the twentieth century.

And Hunt County had also nourished the famous, none more so than Audie Murphy, who was the most decorated American soldier in World War II. Murphy, born in a farmhouse north of Greenville in 1924, grew up poor in a family like so many others in the county and the state, a family that existed by hardscrabble. Helen and Gilbert would relate that they knew him and his people, and how their families, at one time or another, had often picked up the young Murphy, hitchhiking into Greenville, or had taken him back home after his errand was completed.

Helen's grandparents, Linsey and Emily Sandusky Laxton, had left Mount Pisgah, Kentucky, in 1897 and with eight of their nine children boarded a train that took them west and south to Caddo Mills, Texas, a small community a few miles west of Greenville that served people who lived on the surrounding farms. Helen's father, William Laxton, was four years old at the time of the move and grew up at the farm the family bought, the same one that Helen grew up on, consisting of land owned and rented or leased, with the unpainted farmhouse set back from the road. Bill Laxton met and wooed Laura Mary Dees. Like him, she had been born in 1894. But her family lived in Black Cat Thicket, a settlement near Ladonia in Fannin County, which borders Hunt County to the south. Laura was the fifth of ten children, and Laura's father was half Choctaw Indian, which was a nice conversation piece for her son-in-law in future years.

For reasons never made entirely clear, the man who was to become Helen's father—and Helen's mother did not dispute the story—drove his buggy under Laura's second-floor room one day. She jumped out the window, went the tale, and he caught her and they went to Squire Hulsey's house. He married the couple in the buggy that same day.

Of the portraits of the newly married of the day, the man was often depicted seated in a chair with his bride standing beside or behind him, and Bill Laxton, who spoke in a voice filled with a quiet laughter, was known to explain this as follows: "He's too tired to stand and she's too sore to sit."

September 1 of 1916 was Labor Day in addition to being the date of Helen's birth, and it also marked the day that the US Congress enacted a law barring from interstate commerce any item made by child labor. In those days children were sometimes forced to work twelve and fourteen hours a day, without a chance of going to school or having anything like the bright prospects of a better tomorrow. The Child Labor Act did not apply to farm children, who continued to work "from can to can't," as it was known. And so growing up, Helen helped her mother around the house and helped her father in the fields, and she reminisced in later years how much fun it was to find one of the plentiful Indian arrowheads turned up by the plow and to throw this bright trinket into the air as far as she could, because of the neat way it had of flashing through the sky like a comet. (The Caddo Indians, of the Caddo Confederacies of East Texas, had settled the land and sustained themselves by farming for centuries, if not millennia, before the advent of Anglo-American settlers in 1839.)

The Laxton farm was known to the family as the Home Place, but Helen Laxton determined early on that she wanted more than that. Having graduated at the top of her class of sixteen at Caddo Mills High School in 1933, she earned a business school scholarship at a trade school in Dallas.

She moved to Dallas immediately and learned how the Depression had affected people there. Two bits—twenty-five cents—was a lot of money. You could do things with a penny, light up a penny arcade; buy a good hamburger for a nickel. Men stood on street corners selling apples to try and make fifty cents a day. That or a dollar was a good wage for a day's work. There were soup lines, the homeless, multitudes of people desperate for work. Many of them, including children, left home and just wandered.

Helen saw this and realized how fortunate she was to earn her scholarship, wherein she learned secretarial work and bookkeeping. Afterward, she got a job with a construction company in Dallas and lived there as a single woman for several years. This was the first time in her life that she had money to buy nice clothes and to dress in style, and even with glamour, as a picture taken by a photographer on a downtown street in Dallas attested.

One night in 1938, she and her roommate dressed up in their "formals" and went with their dates to a dance at the old Jefferson Hotel in Dallas. It was a landmark in the city at the time, with a large ballroom that catered to such events, but Helen and her friend did not have a good time. Taken home, they went inside until the two boys left then changed clothes and got into the car Helen by then owned, and they began driving.

Her friend mentioned that she had heard of a cute guy who worked nights at Pete's Café on East Grand Street in Dallas. She had heard that he was breezy, slang in those days for someone "with a line." No sooner had they parked at Pete's than out he came, and he went on and on about how pretty the girls were and how their boyfriends were so lucky, that sort of thing, and it turned Helen off completely. She remarked to her roommate on the way home that she didn't care whether she ever saw him again and had no intention of returning to Pete's Café. Helen didn't even remember his name, but her roommate did. The young man's name was Gilbert Garrett.

*   *   *

At the time of that meeting, Gilbert was nearing the age of thirty, having been born on June 8, 1909, in Celeste. (Audie Murphy attended grade school in Celeste, beginning a generation later, in 1933.)[8] Celeste was in northeast Hunt County, half an hour above Caddo Mills and half that town's size. Gilbert's family, like that of so many other Texans, including the Laxtons, was Scotch-Irish. His father owned a cotton gin but did not prosper as so many who ginned cotton did. There was the possibility of the bottle, which soothed one's problems as quickly as it drowned one's future. Gilbert grew up with a younger brother, Herbert, and an older half-sister, Geneva, known thereafter as "Pete," or "Aunt Pete." He became familiar, Gilbert, with the ways of a small town and with moving here and there restlessly, as he would continue to do into adulthood.

He attended eighth grade in Collin County, immediately east of Hunt County. That was 1922, and the young man, though attending only sporadically, did average work in rhetoric and composition, in arithmetic earned a final grade of B-, and made an A in history. He had trouble with algebra, final grade of D, and deportment, with no final grade given. The thing in which Gilbert Garrett would excel, however, was in making a way for himself in the world.

Literally turned out by his folks at the age of fourteen, he never went to high school. He had no opportunity in his setting of becoming a Boy Scout and going on camping trips.

He never learned to swim. He missed out on football, band practice, pep rallies, drama, and all of the rest of the gentle idiocy that calls itself high school. He did play baseball, somehow, somewhere, and was said to be a fair country player. He saw, in one of these games, a young man at the plate who was hit in the head by a pitch and died right there in the ballpark in front of everyone, Gilbert being the catcher at the time. This was not his only witness of tragedy.

The year he hit the road, 1923, was seven years before the onset of the Great Depression, but even so, many young men were roaming the country in search of work, a better life, a steady job, a place to take roots, maybe to marry and have a family. The teenager made his way by any work he could get, did whatever he could for a meal and a bed. Sometime in there he settled on a ranch in West Texas and lived with the other hands in a bunkhouse. It was a good opportunity for him, and he was happy to be earning his way at that early an age. It seemed to him good enough that he might eventually come to call this ranch home. But something happened that left him shaken to the

---

8   Don Graham, *No Name on the Bullet: A Biography of Audie Murphy* (New York: Viking, 1989), 9.

core, left him startled at the possibility that he would die unknown out there and be forgotten by the world.

Ranch hands looked forward to being chosen to drive into the nearest town, fifteen or twenty miles distant, on Saturdays for supplies. They all had the opportunity to go into town once a month, but the weekly supply run was a special treat. As one of the younger workers at the ranch, Gilbert did not yet drive, but he sometimes got to ride with someone else. Young men bunking together formed into twos, but at his age, he did not have a best friend. But one of the older bunkmates looked out for him, gave him advice, and loaned him money when he needed it. This man, in his twenties, was a favorite at the ranch and drew the straw to go into town and back on a particular Saturday. Gilbert was set to go in with him, but something came up, and the friend left without him.

The ranch hand was driving the pickup back from town. Among other things he had bought was a supply of coal oil in a five-gallon can. He had been told not to set it in the back with the other supplies out of fear of it turning over with a bump and dousing everything in kerosene. He'd elected to place the five-gallon can on the floor in front of the empty passenger seat beside him in the cab of the truck, and he'd thought it safe to smoke.

Like all smokers, this man's hands had grown used to the task. They did without being asked what he had trained them to do out of habit. He carefully held the cigarette near his window and lit it with a cardboard match from a packet he carried. But when through, he forgot his right hand, and it went through the functions it habitually did, consisting of swinging the match to the right, perhaps a way of shaking it out in the air. At any rate, it ignited fumes from the five gallons of kerosene, and right there in the truck the can burst into a firebomb. He attempted to seize it and toss it out the passenger window but only ended up horribly burned instead.

Taken by a passerby to the bunkhouse, the man was diagnosed by a summoned doctor with burns far too severe to even think that he might survive. A burn that bad was a ghastly thing. Great patches of black skin held the eye. These were interspersed with splotches of blood-red skin and its weeping surfaces, and the smell of burned flesh was both overpowering and unforgettable, the suffering of the victim pitiable and shattering. The worst of his burns were to his head, face, and chest, and also to his arms and belly and of course to his hands. The man lingered for several days in the bunkhouse, Gilbert and the others sickened by his bloodcurdling screams, screams that were born of a pain so severe its only voice was a scream. It was an unforgettable experience, one the young man would carry to his own grave. It became the horror story of his life, to learn early what it meant to have someone he idolized die, and in such a tragic way.

*   *   *

Pete's Café in Dallas in the thirties was a flashy diner with booths, tables, and stools along a bar, typical for cafés back then in Texas, an inviting place but of no pretense. It had room for a couple dozen people. The cook, a man in his late twenties, had been given the job because of his experience in cooking, which he said had begun out in West Texas when he'd learned how to cook for ranch hands. To have lived the life he had—his smoking and drinking and his having learned to chase women and to distinguish between the good ones and the not so good—to have done all of that in being on his own for the past fifteen years, Gilbert Garrett was in surprisingly good health. He had not lost his faith in the American dream, and he had something else going for him too. He was ecstatically good-looking. His was the face of a Hollywood crooner. His teeth were even and good, his smile both sincere and somehow mocking of itself. He had blue eyes and light-brown hair. He stood six feet tall and had the build of a natural athlete. He was a man who found himself in others, loved to have a good time, and was truthful and decent in his ways.

One evening Helen, who had a date with another young man, suggested after they had seen a movie that they drop by Pete's Café. Her second dose of Gilbert Evert Garrett proving much better than the first, a phone number found its way into Gilbert's possession, and she consented to a date with him.

The two went on that date, and then on more, to movies and sometimes to eat at the Pig Stand, a California-style eatery where winsome young ladies came out to wait on you in your car. Then one Sunday afternoon the two of them drove to White Rock Lake, drove around the scenic lake, parked, and began sparking, as it was called. Somehow the subject of marriage came up, it being a bet on an unknown horse—a filly, they say. They made the wager and never looked back.

They were married a few weeks later, June 27, 1938, in the parsonage of a church in Greenville. Helen wore a pastel blue lace frock with white accessories and had a shoulder bouquet of white orchids. The groom dressed in his white suit of clothing with white shoes and a modest tie, and pictures afterward showed him holding in his hand his white boater. The bride was attended by her friend Ethel, and best man for Gilbert was his friend W. M. Barney. The couple took a wedding trip to San Antonio and Corpus and kept as a souvenir the card of the man who took them "deep-sea fishing." The card mentions red snapper—found in warm seas and valued in sport fishing—and the vessel, *Boat Ann*, was undoubtedly named for the wife of Captain J. P. Mitchell, whose address was Edgewater Beach Pier, Phone 5537W, Corpus Christi, Texas. This card contained a small calendar for the year 1938, like a timeline, with room on the back of the card to record the names and addresses of a few friends they apparently knew in Corpus.

Among the newly married in Texas, family Bibles were a cherished heirloom. Young couples were imbued with a sense of time both vertical and horizontal, and they either began a Bible or accepted one from their parents, recording in it the dates of marriages, their own in particular, and births and deaths, an informal genealogy. As a keepsake, people also sent off to have baby shoes bronzed and then displayed these mementos in their living rooms. It was a time of doilies on the arms and the backrests of overstuffed living room chairs. People drank iced tea in glasses so ruby red they matched Dorothy's slippers, and married couples entertained themselves by listening to the radio or by playing dominos and cards with other couples. A proud new couple might also celebrate their marriage by way of an imprinted ceramic plate. The Garretts' depicted a couple of hitched horses seen from behind in matching leather collars and individual girths, but close enough to suggest a doubletree, and before it was fired, the words "Helen & Gilbert Garrett // Hitched June 27, 1938," were emblazoned on it in gold.[9]

At the time, Helen was the bookkeeper for a department store in Dallas, and Gilbert continued his job at Pete's Café after the couple made their home in Dallas. Both Mimi and Vicki were born in Dallas. Gilbert, having served honorably from 1924 to 1927 in the 144th Infantry of the Texas National Guard, was unable to enlist during World War II. He had slipped in the bathtub and broken his back and was medically exempted. Instead, he served as a guard at a defense plant. After the war he worked for a Ford assembly plant.

Mimi started first grade in Dallas in 1945, but the family moved to Garland during that same year, and in 1946 to Greenville, where Mimi entered her third first-grade class. The family resided in Greenville through Mimi's time in sixth grade and moved to Pittsburg just before she started seventh, where I shared a classroom with her.

Along the way, Helen, already a believer, saw to it that Gilbert accepted Christ, was baptized, and was welcomed into the faith, where he literally found himself, church being showbiz for the devoted. He gave up cigarettes and alcohol, cursing and philandering. Church finished his education, became his high school and college, his postgraduate. In the Protestant faith, where so many functions are handled by the laity, people found an outlet for their singing, their ability to teach, their organizational skills, their leadership.

---

9   The plate, having already been passed one generation, was in 2011 given to Gilbert and Helen's grandson, Bret Clark, upon his marriage to Casey, and the couple will pass it to their daughter, Garrett, in years to come.

Within a year of moving to Pittsburg, Gilbert Garrett was the president of the First Baptist Church's Sunday school programs where, as well as having fellowship with his fellow attendees, he exhorted them to bring others into the fold, to proselytize being the mantra of those who saw the way and knew that it was right, were but everyone else to agree.

God was on the other side of the river and the faithful boated toward Him but by grace were challenged to fill that boat with other souls, which made God very happy. (That it may have added to the coffers was never mentioned.)

Gilbert and Helen spent the rest of their lives in one First Baptist or the other, faithfully tithing 10 percent of their income. Having reached retirement and then old age, they found themselves without any other retirement income than a small Social Security check. One suspects that the college-educated pastors who conducted the services at those churches, members of the Southern Baptist Convention, did not have to depend only on Social Security for their retirement. It was just a thought, but what if Helen and Gilbert had put that tenth of every dollar into a savings account over the sixty years of their marriage? But the church did not encourage that. What the church encouraged was the taking of money by those who had more from those who had less. The Bible validated this blessed neglect of economics by the faithful, their loyalty in giving 10 percent to be repaid in spiritual riches, witness the Sermon on the Mount:

> And why take ye thought for raiment? Consider the lilies of the field, how they grow; they toil not, neither do they spin: And yet I say unto you, That even Solomon in all his glory was not arrayed like one of these … But seek ye first the kingdom of God, and his righteousness; and all these things shall be added unto you.
> —Matthew 6:28–29; 33 (King James version)

Or not. Gilbert and Helen were good people, if naïve. And according to their daughters, they were wonderful parents. Gilbert always worked hard and was grateful for what they had, Helen the same. She made the girls feel like they were the prettiest, smartest, best girls anywhere. And of course they were. Their parents loved them, saw to their physical and emotional needs, and they grew up in a loving home without exposure to alcohol or any of the other vices life might offer. As a junior and a senior in Pittsburg High School, Mimi drove a shiny green '51 Pontiac coupe that was their second car. Upon being asked what she did for gas money, she opened the glove compartment and withdrew a Texaco credit card supplied by her father.

*　　*　　*

So it was that Mimi took a giant step down in marriage, but the full extent of the break did not become apparent to her until the spring of 1961, when the First State Bank in Pittsburg notified us in Galveston, in a phone call, that we were overdrawn by $200 or $250. It was too much for me to comprehend. Mimi had continued to write checks for things she saw and wanted, and who could blame her? Well, her husband did. He never hit her, he never yelled at her (maybe once or twice), but he abused her time and again in the pocketbook, initiating in her a lifelong worry about money that no socioeconomic betterment in future years could possibly disavow. That young couple spent ten dollars a week on groceries during medical school, and she was time and again harassed by her husband to cut down on even that, it being the only variable in their budget.

It was simply not her way to worry about every dollar, and she was forgetful about keeping up with the checks she had written. She was, in other words, normal. I had just enough left in a savings account in Houston to cover the bank deficit in Pittsburg. I did that and then canceled the joint account in Pittsburg. (The people there knew us, of course, and had thought they were doing us a favor in continuing to accept all of our checks.) Thereafter, through the end of medical school, we banked locally in Galveston, moving the account to a bank in Corpus in the summer of 1963. The other draconian decision "we" made was that only I could write checks on the account. The plan, which usually worked, was for me to cash a check and give her grocery money each week. By internship, with Roger on board, our weekly grocery allotment had risen to twenty-five dollars.

Mimi had turned twenty-four in June of 1963. If anything, she had become more beautiful with motherhood. She was such a sound sleeper that during her pregnancy, I had worried whether I would have to get up at night every time the baby cried. Of course what happened was that the first time Roger cried at night, she was on her feet and headed that way before I was fully awake. It turned out that I would remain comfortably in bed while she got up with Roger every time he cried, a pattern that would continue for each of our other three children as well. She did Roger's diapers in the days when they were rinsed out in the potty and then washed in the washer, disposables being too expensive for us to afford. Still, the year in Corpus was an exciting time for her, and she was so creative that Roger never lacked for toys or books or things to do.

Part of their time together consisted of their weekly visit to the market. One particular day, Mimi, with Roger riding in the grocery cart, went happily along shopping as usual. It was a glorious fall day, full of color and hope, and she and Roger were carefree and very happy. Roger had learned to point to something when he wanted it, and often Mimi would get it. It was a spacious supermarket, probably the H-E-B nearest our house.

Mimi arrived at the line leading to the cashier, Roger alert and making the occasional surprising comment. The groceries were counted and amounted to about thirty dollars. She had only the twenty-five dollars I had given her and could not write a check for the rest. She glanced at the busy but sociable cashier and at the mothers and children waiting patiently behind her, as well as those in several busy checkout lines on either side of her. People had complimented Roger, telling his mother how cute he was, how bright. And she did not have enough money for what she had bought! It was the embarrassment, the humiliation, the flagrant unfairness of it. The problem was that we were the educated poor—that brittle façade—and too proud to ask for help from family or those who might have extended such help. At any rate, crushed in front of the others in the checkout line, and despite the pleas of the cashier, Mimi burst into tears and hauled up Roger in her arms who, frightened, began bawling himself. The two rushed out the door, leaving behind everything on the counter and weaving their way through the astonished people entering the market. Shortly they arrived home, devastated by the experience, and Mimi vowed never to go back to that store.

It was an indelible, awful experience, and afterward we went back to a joint checking account, which we should have kept all along. It was my fault, not hers. In 1963, all internships were like that. The supposedly best teaching programs of the day paid the least in salary, a mark of distinction, like paying in starvation for a crop you planted and attended but that would be harvested and sold by laughing others, who could always top you in their own tales of horror. It was bullshit then and remained bullshit, of the most humiliating kind, though things did improve for young doctors in training some years later.

*   *   *

Thursday, July 11, 1963, was my second rotation on ER, after I had traded my Friday call with another intern, who had asked the favor. It had not been a busy day in the ER, not even in the hospital, but I had been an intern for a week and a half and had learned a few things. One of them was that ER, when it was quiet, was as lovely and cozy as a hideout in the forest. Leaning against a gurney at twilight, the shift nurse behind me at the desk, the ER technician in the cafeteria, I watched out the two windows the delicate thinning of light beyond that caliche driveway and felt a strange, gaping happiness of the kind that startles you, as when they play the very song you have just been humming or somebody says something so incredibly nice that it brings tears to your eyes.

It was the time of day to live backward: a time to praise life—its blessings, its riches, its unfathomable depths, its presence no more understandable than its absence, the one blending so unflinchingly into the other, no one quite sure whether the reaction went in both directions or not. Perhaps the whole of life's experience was put into pursuit of that very thing. Perhaps we own the mind only to the extent that it owns us, and where did that come from? I decided that the alchemy resided in the discovery of a beauty heretofore unnoticed. Beauty was no more skin deep than it was elephant wide, but it had dimensions same as everything else, boundaries one employed to see the world, expanding and contracting in exact accordance with the beauty one found in going among others and taking their measure. The thing that made it so priceless was that it validated hope and peopled existence with the vulnerable and the beguiling, people who know all of this better than you ever will, and so you go on living. The best at it are gods and need be nothing else, no amount of trumpeted mischief can change that. Humans need gods and gods, it turns out, need humans. Beauty was finding it in others. When you are very lucky, as I was in that moment, it fetched a soft deference to unseen powers, a quiet way to defeat the twitching awful that one must conquer every day.

The phone rang and the nurse answered it. It was Labor and Delivery. They requested that I come see a young woman who might or might not be in labor. They wanted me to decide whether she needed to be admitted to the hospital, and I could do that. Food Service always saved a plate for the intern on call, and since Labor and Delivery was barely out of the way to the cafeteria, I told the nurse I'd be right down. Rosa Ramos popped into my mind, and I figured I'd surprise her with a visit before returning to ER.

*   *   *

The long dark corridor, granite quiet and verging on the seductive at that time of day, brought forth an image of someone I had noticed from day one. I could not help noticing people, having the gift of sight. I wasn't looking for an affair. Maybe I was looking for help, and there she was every day, entering the various nurses' stations along the way.

Starting from the Record Room, which was in the region of the tail of the aircraft, this person made her way down the long dark hallway every day at five o'clock, two hours ago on this day, dipping into each of the wards from east to west to bring the workups that had been dictated from a special telephone on each ward. Typed, the reports were returned by her so that they could be placed in the patients' charts. Someone doing this ought not to be so beautiful; I couldn't take my eyes off her willowy figure. I could no more keep from noticing her than I could be blind to her self-effacing ways. I adored the way she carried herself, the way she wore her clothes (which were better than my wife's). I liked the way her shoulder-length hair bounced so quietly in the air, like dueling pixies.

I did not know her name, her marital status, or anything else about her. I had never spoken a word to her and probably never would. I simply knew that she was a beauty who appeared five days a week for no other reason than to illuminate the dark, dreary corridor of the hospital, bringing to it a surge of hope. Possibly this was because she was a normal, a civilian, and not one of my constituents, not part of my consignment of the daily dreadful. She seemed above it somehow, representative of the haute, untaught things in life, the teetering undertone of flared possibilities, were one granted a person this nice. The beauty from the Record Room lived in the parallel woodland I had overlooked and could no longer reach, those boughs closing so quietly you don't hear them, yet there she was in the thicket of possibility, where wine from the vine is both vintage and corking new. She represented the newness that is and the irretrievable things that aren't, or weren't, or just might be.

*　　*　　*

On my right I passed Rosa's room—talk about contrasts—and strode through the saloon doors of Labor and Delivery. A nurse standing there pointed, and I entered the first room on the left. Since this was the stick-out end of the hospital, each of the labor rooms on the south side had a glaring view of the setting sun through the window, much different from the shadowy visage out the ER, on the north side of Memorial. The room was green, its stucco flecked white in places, and it had wooden venetian blinds. They made the sound of clacking geese when I quickly reached and closed them.

The light switch clicked on like a double slap to the face. It made the patient flinch, and just as quickly I turned it off. Adjusting the blinds, geese chattering, I obtained sufficient light for my purposes.

The patient on the bed, propped on her left elbow, was Maria Chavarria, a striking young woman. She was not looking at me. She might have been a teenager who had just picked up the phone but instead of a dial tone got a retching noise. While I watched, she tilted her head and vomited into the emesis basin held by her mother, Duvelia de La Torre, who was seated in a chair beside the bed. Mother and daughter bore a marked resemblance.

Duvelia gave Maria some Kleenex to wipe her face, and then the two of them assessed me even as I was taking in their smart appearance. Maria, term pregnant, was fully clothed in a blue Sunday dress, a maternity frock she wore with stockings and heels. She wore makeup on her face, and her hair had been done in that way that women have that makes it glow. She obviously hadn't dressed up for Memorial Hospital and, indeed, the covers of the bed had not been turned back. The nurses had not even prepared her for examination. I might have stumbled upon the two of them, mother and frail daughter, in the lobby of a hotel where they had stopped for the night.

As it turned out, the two had started for a party in a nearby city but came instead to Memorial when Maria became sick. Her blood pressure, I was pleased to note, was normal. She was a *primipara*—first pregnancy—and when I placed my hand on her abdomen (through the dress), I knew instantly that she was not in labor, although labor was imminent for one so pregnant, that whopping stowaway would see to that. No, Maria's pain was anterior. Everyone knows that labor pains commonly begin in the back, and she described the pain as more like a stomachache that occurred for a time and really hurt and then let up for a while before it started in again. The pain had begun that afternoon.

Mrs. La Torre, also formally attired, provided some details. They had started out at around five thirty for the birthday party of Duvelia's nephew in the nearby town of Mathis. Maria was staying with her mother for the time being, and I did not ask why. Maria broke in to state that she had eaten a banana and some ice cream before getting into the car and that they had stopped a few times and let her vomit on the side of the road. Mrs. La Torre worked for a judge in Corpus and had medical insurance. She used Spohn Hospital, the private Catholic-run facility overlooking Corpus Christi Bay, and had taken her daughter there before Maria's marriage two years ago, when the insurance plan dropped her from its coverage. Now Maria had a Memorial clinic card and had been followed in Memorial's OB Clinic. Looking through Maria's chart, which was thin because of its recent origin, I read several of the progress notes seeing that she had faithfully and uneventfully attended each appointment. She had gained the expected amount of weight and had showed none of the signs of toxemia of pregnancy, such as swelling of the ankles and elevation of the blood pressure. The pregnancy, in summary, had been perfectly normal, Maria never having reported so much as a single episode of morning sickness.

I had the nurse cover the patient with a sheet and stepped outside the room while they raised her dress above her abdomen so I could listen for fetal heart tones, the beating heart of that colossal spark, with that pronged stethoscope that made one into something between a jackass and a unicorn. I did hear a good fetal heartbeat, and that was a relief. Maria nodded when I asked about fetal movements.

The nurse left for a moment, and I found myself alone again with daughter and mother. They knew I was an intern and seemed to have made sure that I was not a teenaged ambulance driver masquerading as one. I wore the white trousers and short-sleeved white shirt, carried you-know-what, and flashed that honest smile. Immediately, Maria shook away any notions of doubt and accepted me. It was that obvious and that important. Her firm square jaw framed a wide pretty face that was traitor to her every thought, and I knew instantly that if medicine had meaning—and I had dedicated myself to that grail—this bond of trust between doctor and patient was its essence, two people united in the most insoluble wager this side of matrimony.

But medicine was matrimony of a kind, wasn't it? It was the wedding of science and humanity. Or was that wrong? What was medicine? I thought it a license to touch. Much was made of a doctor curing sometimes, relieving often, comforting always. But first came touch and everything went from there: see you, hear you, feel you. These first two belonged to anyone but the third was a pugnacious right, granted the one by the other in a godly risk, the creation of an instant deity—all you add is trust. It was a day for epiphanies, and I felt in that powerful instant the thrill of having earned that, or almost, which meant everything to me. Still, I existed in relation to her only in my ability to contend with the forces that had brought her to the hospital. One hoped not to forget that. Responsibility was love, respect, joy, happiness, and an eagerness to please, but the greatest of these was love.

Examining Maria more thoroughly, I checked for murmurs, for breath sounds, for tenderness on palpation. I did not do a pelvic examination because that would involve considerable manipulation in removing her to an examining room. Instead, I donned gloves and did a rectal examination, disappearing to test a stool sample for blood. I returned to report that it was normal. There I was and there she was and the sun had quit the sky.

Mother and daughter awaited my report.

The vomiting was an unusual problem late in pregnancy, I told them. Hers was abrupt in onset, which must mean something. While I spoke to them, Maria was sick again. I knew that the morning sickness of early pregnancy may actually have its onset late in pregnancy, but that was rare. And this wasn't morning sickness. I could not pretend it was trivial, but then I found myself doing just that. She had something wrong with her that was acute in onset and might be severe in nature, but I hoped not.

With my regular stethoscope, once she had stopped retching, I listened again over her abdomen in the slanted light of that shadowy room. Her symptoms were intestinal, and so her bowel sounds, hyperactive. That was such a nonspecific finding that it alone meant little. Normal bowel sounds, heard through a stethoscope, click and echo, ripple and sigh. They groan like staggering recruits in a phantom army. In Maria, with a sudden icy dread, I heard a whistle, a rumpus, a high-pitched pinging sound, like the upper register of a piano playing deep in a drainpipe, or like a xylophone banging away on the terrace of her viscera.

Perhaps, I hoped—and shared this with them—she had an old-fashioned stomachache. It was far less likely in the summer months than during winter and spring, but intestinal flu was also possible. There was also this. The uncommon features of a common disease are commoner than the common features of an uncommon disease. I didn't say that to them, but I was startled to realize it meant giving the disease the benefit of the doubt, the "disease," in this instance, being pregnancy. It was a normal event, yet I thought of it as a potential disease because that was how it was done. People had continued reminding me every day of my internship that I was still in training, and that was my training. Beyond that, a doctor has numerous opportunities to bail out along the way, and in all honesty, I did not want to do a complete workup on Maria right then. It would take an hour to do a full history and physical examination and to record these on the hospital chart they would make for her, and I hadn't the time. I wanted supper and a return to the ER, to catch up to that lingering epiphany.

The nurse returned and I ordered a rectal suppository to relieve the nausea. Then, outside the room while Maria was getting dressed, I answered questions from Mrs. La Torre. She was a warm, practical woman who was devoted to Maria, and she acquiesced to my idea of not admitting her daughter just yet. We rejoined Maria, who was seated in the chair beside the bed. The symptoms weren't serious, I said, but I wanted her to take it easy, stay at home. Should the vomiting persist or she feel the onset of hard labor, return immediately to the hospital. Should she rest in bed? Yes. Would it continue to hurt her, her stomach? I said maybe but to let me know. The call came just after midnight. The vomiting and pain having persisted, the two women had returned as ordered. I admitted Maria Chavarria to Memorial Hospital in the wee hours of Friday morning, July 12, 1963, her seventeenth birthday.

*   *   *

Later Friday morning, Dr. Hastings and I saw Maria on rounds. Though not in labor, she was in a room on Labor and Delivery and looked different from Thursday evening. It was the light that made the difference, daylight showing how young she was. She was not acutely ill at the time and smiled at us as though hoping for the best.

An hour later I passed Maria on my way to the delivery room. She was seated in a wheelchair across from the nurses' station, possibly to let them change her bed. Shortly I began scrubbing in at the sink between the two rooms but turned around to exchange a look with her. She was not looking at me. She was bent forward, looking at the floor, but not so much that I couldn't see her face. She might have just taken a burst of machine gun fire to the midsection. In her unguarded expression of naked, agonizing pain, she spoke with the subtlety of a lighting strike to how gravely ill she was. And it had nothing at all to do with her pregnancy—at least directly, meaning it might have everything to do with it on some indirect, dire basis. I hated to think what I was thinking. What I was thinking had to do with her appendectomy, the scar of which I had found during the admitting examination.

The appendicitis had been at age seven. At the time, covered by her mother's insurance, she had visited Dr. Hector Garcia, who had done the appendectomy at Spohn Hospital. Maybe the private hospital could help; I had asked Maria's mother to get a copy of the surgical record from Spohn, and she had promised to do so.

Surgery may leave internal scars, known as adhesions, attached here and there to the intestine and other structures as with gobs of glue. In time, a loop of intestine might be ensnared and trapped, the food passageway blocked. Could this be the case? Was my suspicion correct, that she had intestinal obstruction? Another cause of her pain might be a peptic ulcer, which in complicated instances can cause intestinal bleeding, perforation of the small intestine, or obstruction. Or she might have gallbladder disease or a tumor of the intestines or pancreas. The thing I no longer doubted was that she had intestinal obstruction. But making the diagnosis on a young pregnant woman was not going to be easy.

*   *   *

Strong people become doctors. You have to endure grueling hours of laboratory and the hated chemistry courses, then the intense clinical years, when a bedside oral examination can reduce you to a second grader—and this while delaying life's rewards, giving up a large chunk of personal comfort in expectation of a bright future, and then spending one's profession in differentiating between ostriches and kangaroos, between foxes and wolves, between, for the most part, wreath and wrath.

It takes a strong person, but doctors can be strong in different ways, and I had never met one who even remotely resembled the aforementioned Dr. Marvin "Sam" Hastings, my staff man on Obstetrics. Sam was a fine fellow and knew it. It was impossible not to like him and respect him. In the first place, he dressed the part. He sported an expensive suit with a red silk handkerchief lolling out of its breast pocket. He reeked of peppermint and cologne or aftershave. He was thirty-eight in 1963, muscular but quick, trim as a gymnast who might at any moment do a cartwheel. He wore expensive shoes. His hands bore rings, his wrist a gold watch. His voice was a melodious tenor, its lyrics announcing and delineating the perimeters of his influence. The man whisked in and out of hospital rooms and the open wards with the abandon of one who was completely at home. He was as smooth as silk, as effervescent as temptation. Insofar as it was legally permitted, he flirted with every woman he met. Holding eye contact, he touched arms, shoulders, backs, hands, and waists, and it did not take a special occasion for him to begin with a hug.

It was a well-worn cliché that patients fell in love with their obstetrician, and he was not above making a body fake in the direction of having sexual intercourse with them; in fact he often made this gesture, to the effect that the two of them should repair to the next room for more privacy. Of course it was done with gallons of goodwill and laughter; the man was a wellspring of laughter and fun, the flirting absolutely harmless because it was so out in the open, despite its occasional hint at being serious, and his patients seemed to love it and expect it of him. Flamboyant, charming, mischievous, and self-assured to a fault, he was Shakespearian, a Falstaff who enjoyed the practice of medicine more than any doctor I had ever met, whose pride was that medicine is a rhymed couplet and you won't be treated the way you expect to be treated until those who are treating you love you enough to dip into your sonnet.

On my part, I thought it wonderful. I loved Sam Hastings up close and from afar. I liked his exuberance, his ability to put the patient at ease. Should I ask him a question, it went something like this.

"Do you think I should do that?"

"Why not, Doctor, what's to stop you?"

"You think it's okay?"

"Of course it's okay! I'd do the same myself! It's what you came here for, isn't it?"

And he would laugh and the world was right. I thought him a master, his practice a masterpiece. I'd always modeled myself after men I admired, and to admire one who was also your supervisor was the best of luck. I wanted to please Sam Hastings, wanted, to an extent, to become him. The man sensed this, of course. People can tell whether you like them and we had hit it off from the start, a wonderful relationship. Dr. Sam and I made rounds together every weekday, me watching as Hastings reviewed his own work. Simultaneously the staff patients benefited from the same standard of care he gave to his private patients, and that made it even better.

*   *   *

As I have said, the Obstetrics Ward held both staff and private patients, the latter being a third or at times a half of the postpartum patients. A few of these patients I had delivered while the obstetrician was en route to the hospital. More often, I had started the role of the attending and then yielded the floor when the patient's physician arrived. As to that, I was scrubbing in on one of Dr. Hastings's private patients, him being en route back to Memorial, when I had turned and seen Maria in such obvious distress that Friday morning.

Earlier, I had timidly raised the possibility of intestinal obstruction with him, since it was on my workup. But when I mentioned it to Dr. Sam after his arrival and the delivery of his patient, stating that the obstruction might have been caused by adhesions from Maria's appendectomy ten years earlier, he laughed with a fine good humor, reassuring me that he had never seen *that* in a pregnant woman.

A bit later, when we emerged from the doctors' dressing room on Labor and Delivery and stood in the hallway near the nurses' station, Hastings ready for departure, he became unexpectedly silent. It was a part of him that I hadn't seen until then. There were nurses around, the routine tumult, but the obstetrician looked off into the distance for a long moment, almost as though gathering his thoughts before punishing a child. His words were uttered with the quiet certitude of granite truth. It was just possible, he said, that Maria had an infection in her pelvis and that was the problem. I listened for more but my superior did not elaborate. Maria didn't have fever and her blood count wasn't back yet, but that subject was finished, and Hastings whirled around and asked about Rosa Ramos. Next thing, we were on our way to see her, Sam at his jovial best, the patient responding warmly to him.

*   *   *

I had gynecology patients to see on Surgical Annex, and when I was through, I met with the staff pediatrician for rounds in the nursery, all the way back at the other end of the corridor. I had other things to do, always other things to do. The Record Room was on my case about a workup I had done and dictated but that hadn't come through. The woman who took care of seeing that birth certificates were registered in the official way caught up to me, and I signed a number of them, representing most of the babies I had delivered so far. I ate a late lunch in a cafeteria that was practically empty.

It was still Friday.

The Obstetrics Ward had a couple of private rooms between the entrance and the nurses' station, a door and a bed and a light, and they had moved Maria from Labor and Delivery into one of these, the one nearest the nurses' station. Perhaps that was after I saw her in the wheelchair. She didn't belong in Labor and Delivery, not being in labor, and she didn't really belong on the postpartum ward, not having had her baby. That she was still gripped by the unrelenting pain was written upon her face and her person. Her IV had infiltrated, knuckling its way out of the vein to balloon the surrounding tissues, like the blisters of a burn. I restarted it in the other arm and continued the dextrose and water. She asked what was wrong with her.

She had entered into a dark place for which she needed a guide, and I had been entrusted with that office. I told her she had a normal complication of pregnancy, though that was a lie. At Hastings's insistence, I had changed my admitting diagnosis to hyperemesis gravidarum—vomiting in pregnancy sufficient to require hospitalization. It was the medical model, as I have stated, and "we" were to look for the uncommon symptoms of a common disease, pregnancy, rather than the common symptoms of an uncommon disease, intestinal obstruction.

And it bothered me. To established doctors, those with less training than them were irrelevant. They considered themselves ventriloquists who trained dummies, medicine a blab school, outrage its seed. It could be intimidating, unnerving, and brutal. Toss aside the pompous bullshit, retain the rhetoric, and there it was, a gaping verbal incision slashed through those who still sat on hobbyhorses. You meet doctors and they are smart and they are strong and they are willing to kick ass, should it come to that, because they have had it done to them. In so many ways, like college, medical training was a revenge of the nerds. Doctors were the high priests of that faith: versatile, aggressive, and determined.

My problem was insubordination. I had a big mouth, a chip, an attitude. I could stop and ask directions and end up arguing with the person doing me the favor. In high school I thought I was smarter than some of the teachers, but that turned out not to be the case. Was I smarter than my fellow students in high school? Ask them; mostly in their inscriptions in my annuals they expressed that I probably wasn't as peerless as I thought. But does high school even count, beyond surviving the ordeal? At any rate, whatever notions I held about the student–teacher relationship were banished by medical training. Good-bye to the loving mentor. Medicine demonstrated that eventually you will yield, by the crack of your ass or the stifled scream of your receding derriere. The turnstile forms on the right, and take with you the shit that the teachers of medicine will not take.

*   *   *

Friday afternoon and all day Saturday I hovered between agreeing with Dr. Hastings and plotting against him. Maria was stricken with something outside the tenets of normal pregnancy, I believed. From the instant I had seen her doubled over in pain by the nurses' station, I knew I was on a collision course with my superior. Hers were not the uncommon symptoms of a normal pregnancy. Hers were the common symptoms of an intestinal obstruction. There was a very good reason why I must convince Dr. Hastings of it.

A blockage of the intestines—a clogged downstream pathway—was uncommon, but not in people who had it. In people who had it, its incidence was 100 percent. The outcome, if untreated, was an intestinal perforation. Few people survived that. On a sheet of paper, I began a list of potential causes, some of them already mentioned. Peptic ulcer, I knew from my surgical training. A spontaneous twisting of a part of the intestine might occur, blocking the works. Once again, that was also uncommon, but not in the people who had it. Cancer could not be ruled out. As a student, I had seen a teenager with colon cancer, a sixteen-year-old black woman who was taken to surgery. Maria's tumor might even be benign, albeit large enough to block the works. In medical school an obstetrician had brought down the house by running through a list of "tumors of the uterus," ending by listing the one that was not only the most common but also the most likely to cause problems—the fetus.

In fact, fetal size could not be disregarded as a contributing factor in Maria's intestinal obstruction; she was a small woman. Maybe I could talk Dr. Sam into a cesarean section on her. Deliver the baby and check the intestines. What else did that leave? It left everything else in the world by way of the most dangerous thing of all, the critical failure to make the diagnosis. The obstruction's rarity made it no less dangerous.

On Sunday Maria's symptoms persisted. I had written the order not to give her food or liquids, but she was still vomiting. It consisted of the copious stomach and intestinal secretions that go on despite a starvation diet, fluids that are secreted and reabsorbed in a continuous cycle. Nurses looked in on her, and I went by as many times as I could. The patient, the sort of person she was, apologized that she was no better. She made no demands, called me no names, wanted so much to respond, to have her baby and go home. That she was my patient, her condition complicated or not, was no more than I had asked, trust having been given, and upon graduation I had taken no oath to surrender my will to another's, not even that of a superior. And yet … one must be sure.

Sunday afternoon, two days after Maria was admitted, I called Dr. Hastings at home. Quite possibly, I said, Maria's pain and persistent vomiting pointed to intestinal obstruction. I built the case on her appendectomy scar. I presented the patient, trundling out that ageless skit of doctor-to-doctor contact about a patient—which, by the way, fills every doctor's life with the lives of others. Medicine, before it was a science, before it was an art, before it was even a discipline, was about story, the stories of others. Medicine was legend. It was chronicle. And it was narrative. And it had, or should have had, the responsibility of truth. Yet I had begun wondering about that very thing, whether each version of truth was fitted like a tailor-made suit to each narrator, and where did that sartorial splendor leave the patient? Quite possibly, better off than were they all in agreement. Truth, unless it is a taught truth that isn't, suffers least when it is contested between equals, or at least among those suffering the pretense of equals. I might be wrong, the staff man right. But no amount of philosophical gibberish could set aside our responsibility to the patient. She was sick, and I liked my story of it better than I liked Dr. Hastings's version of it.

To give the man credit, he did remember seeing Maria. He was courteous, he let me talk, he did not cut me off. And he was cordial. But just that cordially and just that inflexibly he again laughed off the idea of intestinal obstruction. He went back to his suspicions of a pelvic infection spread from her pregnant womb to the soft tissues of her abdomen. Due to her having tampered with the pregnancy, was his suggestion.

Knowing Maria, whose honesty was as clear as a songbird in the morning, I knew this charge was preposterous, but by Sunday she had developed a fever and her white count had become elevated. Hastings's excellent suggestion was to start her on intravenous penicillin. As he had no objection, I also ordered a flat plate of her abdomen. The radiologist came out Sunday evening to read the film, which showed a normal pregnancy surrounded by loops of dilated intestine. The findings were classic for intestinal obstruction. They were also, the radiologist quickly added, indistinguishable from the findings in an abdominal infection.

*   *   *

Monday morning, July 15, Maria went into hard labor. After examining her on rounds, Dr. Hastings invited me into the dark tunnel running through Memorial Hospital, that alimentary tract with its own troubling obstacles. An old yellow teacher's desk, shiny as a smile, had been parked just beyond the entrance to the Obstetrics Ward. We stood athwart it, directly across the hallway from Rosa Ramos's room, the door closed as usual.

I had assisted Rosa again first thing that morning. No one had left gloves for me, and I'd had to close the door and cross the hallway and find them for myself—and by the way, how come I never had a nurse assisting me with an act wherein I could actually use some help? Treating Mrs. Ramos, I had inevitably taken on a bit of what the nurses held against her, that vague fret elicited when unpleasantness turns out to be just that: unpleasant—again and again. For some reason, I wished to place blame on the nursing staff, but it was probably just obnoxious me. Thwarted, one obstructs. Unwittingly, one becomes a blockage, an obstacle, a clog. So we stood beside the yellow school desk in the footpath to daylight, or at least to candlelight, and Hastings announced that after examining her he was more convinced than ever that she had parametritis, a dire pelvic and abdominal infection brought on by her efforts to end her own pregnancy. Her disease, in other words, was of her own doing, which called for an entirely different approach than what I wanted. But he was the teacher and I was the student. Of that there was no doubt.

School desk, schooldays, schoolboy.

*   *   *

1946. Cooper's Chapel, Texas. On that first morning, having arrived the previous evening with my suitcase, I was awakened before sunup at the back of the farmhouse and was stumbling around in the dark when Choc came back to check on me. Sixteen, the oldest of the Anderson children still at home, Charles G. "Choc" Anderson was as tall as an end on a football team and had the sort of dark, wavy hair that glows with pomade. Handsome, a young man attracting notice by his natural leadership, he was looking out for me.

He said, "Okay, here's what you need to do."

He reached and took my hand and led me to a sagging wooden counter on the screened back porch. A big wooden bowl held water, a metal bucket of well water beside it. He pointed to a bar of lye soap and told me to wash my face. The water felt ice cold, but also good. Choc, whose head almost reached the slanted roof of the back porch, stood there until I was through and then loaned me a comb, showing me how to wet my hair and comb it into an arching cowlick on the right side, as I would wear it ever after. My shoelaces I knew how to tie, and I had already put on a white shirt and blue overalls—"unionalls"—which would be my garb for this school year in the country, 1946–47. They were blue overalls fitting so loosely I was afraid some girl might come up and yank them open from the top and see my goober, underwear being an unneeded luxury on the farm in the warm weather, which definitely persisted into these September days.

Dressed, fed, and supplied with my sack lunch consisting of a baked sweet potato from the potato cellar, a biscuit or two, and some sausage left over from breakfast, I was ready to leave for school. We kept the brown sacks, grease-spotted or not, day in and day out. After I finished lunch, the sack went into my back hip pocket to be ferried home and used for the next day's lunch. One sack lasted the year.

As the house faced south, the road ran east and west in front of it on the other side of the gate to the "bobbed-wire" fence, the house itself being a part of a cow pasture. One was required to establish the whereabouts of the honoree before opening said gate, but during my time there, she evidenced no urge at all to leave that pasture. The gate, consisting of four strands of barbed wire stapled to several fence posts, the way ribs on a big section of barbeque are so evenly spaced, stretched between the fencerow to the right and the gatepost to the left. The front fence extended forever to the east, along the path I would be taking to school, but it only went a short distance past the sycamore on the west. There it made a clean right turn, extending straight north behind me, past a cultivated field on its west and on its east the house, the well, the smokehouse, the privy, and the cowshed—a fence continuing on forever, for all I knew. The misaligned gate, when fully opened, was ample in size to drive the pickup through, but I didn't need that much room. Two loops of wire held the gatepost. Undo the post from the top loop, lift it out of the bottom loop, step through, and then replace the gatepost. It took all of my might to get that gatepost back under the top loop, which stretched the gate almost as tightly as the rest of the fence. Opening and closing it did get easier through the year, though I never figured out why.

Passing on your right that giant sycamore, with its lovely old black tire dangling from a frayed rope tied to a limb far above, one realizes, by the position of the tree, that the gate is set back from the road, which runs straight as a row under cultivation, one way and back the other, like the long brown ears of a jackrabbit.

The walk to school was pleasant enough, and usually there were other children to talk to along the way. One of these was Lula Faye, who was the youngest of the Anderson children and in third grade that year. She was taller than me and about as slender, a quiet girl who smiled as though she had discovered the secret of life but would never tell, a girl more cute than pretty and who rushed to do her mother's bidding whenever asked, though Lula Faye would predecease her by almost a decade.

As well, there were boys and girls from the farm across the road, their place situated a bit to the west. The youngest, Shelba Davis, was my age and also in second grade. Her mother and my maternal grandmother were sisters, making her first cousins with my mother and once removed from me. Shelba was the girl next door in summer's dreams. She had the blondest, happiest hair I had ever seen. It was the color of sweet gum leaves in autumn, the ones that turn an impossibly brilliant shade of yellow that is set off by brown and russet and all the lovely colors of the season. It caught and held the light as though it radiated sunshine. To see her coming from her house across the road was to put one in mind of rich grassland as far as the eye could see, with one slip of a flower giving it color, set right out in the open as a form of hope, a beacon resplendent in contradistinction to every reason in the world why it should not be. Shelba was also Lula Faye's best friend, and that made it even better.

Evenings before dark, Shelba, her brothers and older sister, Lula Faye, and Lula Faye's older sister Anna Beth, and Choc and I, would gather outside the Anderson house and play a game I heard as "Annie over" but was actually *Ant'ny*—for *Anthony*—*over*. The kids divided into two groups, one on either side of the unpainted farmhouse. One side threw a round ball up and over the corrugated tin roof—the undulating surfaces of which bore the brown stains of rust—letting the ball run down the other side, whereupon someone caught it. Once that happened, he or she and the others ran around the side of the house, and the person who'd caught the ball threw it at someone in the other group, not hard, but hard enough, kids running and laughing and shouting in good fun. We might start with Ant'ny over and go on to kick the can, a countrified version of hide and seek. The games might last till dark.

But on that first day of school in the autumn of 1946, I knew none of this. I did what I was told. The road to the school was sandy and warm, as it was surrounded not by trees and woods but by pastures and cultivated land. How far to school? Add sunshine to happiness. Divide by the distance required, as they put it, "to go a long way." Thing was, I never measured it except in barefooted feet and fidgeting yards, but I figured that the dirt road to the school at the very least ran through the panhandle of Texas and connected to Marco Polo's Silk Road; we were all Venetians exploring the unknown, the first stop being that dilapidated little store on the right just before you reached the school.

People who ran it were nice. They were Andersons too, Uncle Milt and Aunt Sweet Anderson. The shop offered soda water and various canned things on shelves that no one seemed to have the money to buy. The item I remember that I always bought when I had money, such as from picking cotton for a half a cent a pound, was a drum-shaped container of salted peanuts. It was small. The label was blue with red lettering, and supposedly there were buried treasures in the bottom of the containers. I thought that was just something they told the gullible until the day I bought one of the little boxes of peanuts for a nickel and found a quarter at the bottom, the fat coin just fitting the diameter of the peanut box. It was magical! I was the happiest I had ever been.

I waggled my way around that little store enriched by a delirious intoxication, as if I were the richest boy in the world. That quarter was worth picking fifty pounds of cotton! I knew that once I had it, more awaited me, but never again another quarter.

The school itself, one story tall and of white clapboard siding, was set back a distance from the dirt road and protected by a copse of tall shade trees, which made the most wonderful noises in the gentle wind, like giants tap dancing in joy because the children had returned. Three rooms comprised the T-shaped structure. The room to the right was for grades 1 to 4, the stick-out room to the left was the cafeteria, and the room for grades 5 to 8 was tacked on directly behind the cafeteria. Having been built near the turn of the century, the school sagged a bit on its redbrick piers, which were designed to keep it several feet off the ground. My favorite part was the front porch, long and sweeping and gently covered by the overhanging roof.

The porch was made of oak planks loosened a bit by the years and was attained by climbing the three moldering concrete steps leading up to it. First thing in the morning, however, students did not climb those front steps without permission. First thing in the morning, when it wasn't cold or raining, we lined up by grades in front of the school and marched in when the two teachers appeared on the porch and rang the bell. Before that, we were let to play among those trees, which meant joining whatever game was already in progress.

Officially it was the Cooper's Chapel Overland School, named for the settlement. For that matter, the church preceded the school and the cemetery preceded the church, both of which were a hundred yards south of the school, the church built in front of—west of—the cemetery. John Cooper started the cemetery on his parcel of land, his daughter being the first person buried there. Subsequently a chapel came into being. Like the cemetery, the chapel drew people in the region and came to be known as Cooper's Chapel, which lent its name to the settlement. The chapel subsequently became a church of Christ affiliated with one ten or so miles west, in Mount Pleasant, the county seat of Titus County.

The two holy places were connected by the present CR 1001, the drive consisting of innumerable right or left turns around sections of land, each followed by a long stretch as straight as a bobbed-wire fence, which I learned was built by stretching the wire before adding the posts. Mount Pleasant was where my mother lived and worked. Why I was in Cooper's Chapel and she was in Mount Pleasant had not been explained to me. But there I was, and it changed my point of reference. Everything was related to the farmhouse. East were the store, the church, and the school, and the only reason we ever turned west was to go into town on that shockingly irregular piece of roadway. The church had a service Sunday afternoon at two o'clock, a butt-numbing hour of sermon. But every so often there was a glorious dinner-on-the-grounds following the service, and I loved those.

Despite the place-names, the surname Cooper had disappeared from those living in the community. My schoolmates were named Anderson, Davis, Wofford, Gentry, Freeman, Vaught, Crabtree, Ellis, and Taylor, among others. They lived north and south on other dirt roads, but the families all farmed for a living and earned extra in whatever way they could. The lineage that had put them in Cooper's Chapel, the same as mine, was etched in red earth, in a genealogy consecrated in Mississippi, South Carolina, Alabama, and Arkansas before it ever reached Texas. Boatner, Egner, Baker, and McCauley were some of the early names. John T. Anderson met and married Lula E. McCauley, and they had eight surviving children including Alma Anderson, my maternal grandmother. (My uncle Raymond Anderson, once removed, was Alma's younger brother, and he was my host for the year.) Alma was fifteen when she married James T. "Jim" Kimberlin, eighteen, in that Cooper's Chapel Church of Christ on December 15, 1913. He was my grandfather.

Jim's father was William Thomas Kimberlin. This W. T. Kimberlin lived in a large farmhouse north of the church and school and had married Rhoda Cooper, John Cooper's daughter—and not, of course, the one who had died as a girl, prompting her father to found the cemetery. This was the second marriage for both, and Rhoda had previously had children with the surname Opry. She was also ten years the senior of W. T. Kimberlin. They had two children, Jim and his younger brother, Robert Kimberlin. Jim Kimberlin and Alma Anderson having married, Fannie Opal Kimberlin, my mother, was born February 11, 1915, their first child. It meant I was descended not only from the Andersons and the Kimberlins but from the same Coopers who had lent the place its features and name.

The markers in the Cooper's Chapel cemetery recorded the names, but that was not all they did. They bestowed a framework of individuals, their lives written in blood on an unseen wall in a house that wasn't yours, until you grew up and discovered that it was yours after all and always had been.

Cemeteries are about love and they contain much more than memories: they contain you, or at least your grounding, your start in life, your past, your present, and your future in some vertical way that no one could predict and yet no one dares forget. This rich history the beneficiaries repaid by knowing nothing of it and consequently very little of those who came before, their backbreaking work, their unending struggle, the storms, the sicknesses, the sleepless nights, the ocean voyages, the hunger, the pain, the persecution from which they had escaped, the bequeathing to the new generation of that most precious of gifts: life.

Precious it was, but as fragile as a puff of air on a frosty morning. Tragedy befell the young Kimberlin girl, "Little Bertha." Having been born in Cooper's Chapel in 1900, she was six years old in 1906, a first grader in the then-new Overland School. It was January and cold in northeast Texas and she had worn a wool flannel dress to school. It was a hand-me-down, a makeover from an aunt's wardrobe in days when many country girls still wore dresses stitched from dyed flour sacks. The skirt of the dress was full and the sleeves were bloused and hung loosely. Bertha and several of her friends were gathered around the cast-iron cookstove that heated the schoolroom. It had circular iron plates that could be removed with an iron wand for stoking the wood fire. As it happened, a plate had just been removed and the fire stoked. The plate was left off because the opening was the warmest place for hands to go.

But when Little Bertha put her hands there and then turned to say something to a friend, she did not see the flames catch the sleeve of her dress. While people stared in horror, fire leapt up the sleeve to her shoulder and head and breast. She seemed to catch fire instantly. The teacher reached for a heavy woolen coat to smother the flames, but the screaming child raced ahead of her out the door, running hysterically toward her home a half-mile away. It was brutally cold out, and windy, and the winds fanned the flames mercilessly. By the time the teacher caught up to her, she had fallen, and it was too late.

The story was still circulating among schoolchildren in all its chilling particulars the year I was there, a cautionary tale of the ills that befall children. It seemed to capture the theme of that country school, that learning was not something done to punish children but as an endeavor to acquaint them with the ways of the world, in all its fascination and danger. The Cooper's Chapel Overland School had opened its doors in 1904, under the aegis of the Titus County superintendent of schools and the Texas Education Agency, and it belonged to the community in a way that was quite different from modern urban schools. The physical distance between the church and the cemetery behind it, and the school itself, was said to be a hundred yards. But on reflection, the two were much closer than that. The school was an annex to the church and the cemetery in the same way that the house is an annex to the road and the road an annex to human need, each generation an annex to the one before. Students studied who they were, where they had come from, where they might go, and how they might get there.

It was different from the classic country school only in having three rooms instead of one, and it seemed big enough to me to accommodate every schoolchild in Texas. There was a grand feeling, shared by all, about its physical nature. Inside, we were one with all schoolchildren everywhere, and the physicality of our surroundings grew to a dimension defined only by one's dreams. One story tall? Ridiculous! There were more stories there than could be listed in any book. Those walls stood on girders supported by three-foot redbrick piers, walls as tall as the imagination and as sweet as wild honeycomb. The frame was held together with square nails and dovetail joints and by every split rail and halved timber that had gone into every log cabin along the way—every pitched roof, every ridge row placing people "in the dry" so that their people could go on, their heartbreaking letters written home proclaiming, "I don't think we are like to see you again."

School was let out at first frost, hog-killing time. It was known in Cooper's Chapel as Butchering Day and was a social event. First one farmer's hog was processed for the smokehouse and then another's, the children watching and running errands and having the delicious fun that comes from the interruption of a routine, especially one where the parents were in on it and didn't mind. The school cafeteria served as an auditorium when programs were held for the parents, but it could also be a huge kitchen on occasion, because meals were never fixed there otherwise. One day, two or three pickup trucks of men arrived at the school grounds and began unloading washtubs filled with buffalofish they had caught by the process of "grabbling" in the nearby White Oak River (later proclaimed a creek). After the giant fish fry, adults played a softball game with the children under those immense oak trees, celebrating the splendor of a life that was good.

*   *   *

The teachers that year were "Miss" Callie Cochran, who turned fifty in 1946 and taught grades 5 to 8, and her unmarried daughter, Miss Charlie, who was twenty years old and taught the first four grades. They came out on the porch a little before eight in the morning, in dresses and low-quarter shoes. Miss Callie was the principal, and she held the school bell and rang it by rapid up-and-down movements of her wrist, allowing the clapper to strike the bell multiple times until all of the students heard it—and it could be heard from well into the woods behind the school. It sounded like a fire alarm in the city.

The ringing brought kids running and as quick as they could they lined up by age groups and grades, perhaps a dozen students for the first four grades and another dozen for the upper grades. Many of them, boys and girls, came barefooted in the warm days. Boys wore the inevitable denim overalls, like mine, except more faded. Girls wore cotton dresses or a blouse and skirt, bright designs that caught the eye and seemed special to each of them—and was. Each girl's hair was brushed and held with hairpins or a ribbon, and a shy smile was stitched into place. It was as though in representing their parents and themselves, this also true of the boys, each student was also paying homage to a learning tradition that went all the way back to the Texas Revolution, a few years over a century ago, or to Texas becoming a state, exactly a century ago. What the state had done was to set increasingly tough rules for the accreditation of teachers who, as everyone knew, could begin teaching the primary grades after high school and achieve their teaching degree by attending college in the summer.

Callie Cochran had finished her degree at East Texas State Teachers College in Commerce, but Miss Charlie had only done a year and held an Emergency Teaching Certificate. Its use was to fill vacancies in rural Texas schools during and after the war. Both teachers had been hired by the trustees of the school board, who were elected.

*   *   *

Choc related how a prospective teacher in early fall had once come wading across rows in a cotton field seeking the approval of Raymond Anderson, a trustee that year, and so the interview was conducted.

Raymond Anderson had at a time been strikingly handsome, a Robert Taylor or a Cary Grant. But that was many years earlier, toil and illness and the fleeting years of raising children having taken their toll. Seeing the other coming, he rose up, literally, from picking two rows of cotton. First he stretched to get the sack off his back. That felt good. The cotton sack was the height of a man and made of coarse white denim that had long since turned brown. You wore it over only one shoulder so you could switch to the other side when that one got too tired and sore, the bag dragging the ground behind you. The cruelest thing about that cotton sack was that the more you picked, the heavier it got. Most labor begins hard and lightens up as you near completion. Picking cotton was exactly opposite.

The two meeting in the field, an introduction was made, standing between two rows. Need met needy. Raymond was said to be easy on would-be teachers, his cotton sack serving as a perfect example of why.

Raymond Anderson's life had been typical of rural Texas after the turn of the twentieth century. His wife, Randie, née Vaught, had lost her parents when she was twelve years old. She married Raymond when she was fifteen. They had worked as they could and with a growing family moved to Oklahoma to work in the oil fields for a time during the middle of the Great Depression. Choc and his brother, Donnie, were born to them in a tent on an Indian reservation, where the family lived while Raymond worked for the Carter Oil Company, owned by J. Paul Getty. The Indians were friendly enough, Choc was told, but probably resentful, having yielded inevitably but unwillingly to the advancing tide of settlers. Choc was told of a time, near or after his birth, when the Indians roasted an entire cow, just put it over the flames and cooked it until it was done.

The Anderson family had returned to Cooper's Chapel to farm, at first to sharecrop and rent land and then to own their own place, the one I lived in with them that year. It was part of the John T. Anderson farm, originally 140 acres. After his death in 1933, the property was divided among eight children. Some children sold their parts and some, like Raymond and Randie, lived on theirs and raised a family. Raymond Anderson supplemented his income by sometimes driving a school bus and also by operating a grocery truck that made rounds every week, selling canned goods, feed, flour, and so forth, and often trading groceries for chickens and eggs. He would haul the chickens in a wire cage at the bottom of the two-wheeled grocery trailer that was pulled behind an old army combat truck.

I begged, and they let me go on one of these excursions that year. Along the route, the grocery truck would stop at every house and honk the horn. Farm women wearing white bonnets to protect them from the bright sunshine came outside, drying their hands on their aprons and quieting the dogs, and with a pleasant expression each would begin sifting through the things that Choc, being the driver that day, would offer them from a cabinet that was stocked with cans on shelves. They liked that. They smiled like people at a picture show, going in and sitting down and enjoying it until one or the other would turn and say, "Oh, this is where we come in." It was a genuine heartiness back then, people cradling in their arms the treasures of freedom. It was unnecessary to state to another that they were honest and hardworking and appreciative of what others did for them. That was a given.

"And y'all come back now, hear?"

*　　*　　*

Once inside the schoolhouse, I settled into my seat at the back of the second row and tried to be inconspicuous. Miss Charlie began with an introduction to all of the students in her room then gave reading assignments for each grade except first. Her method was to begin by teaching first grade and to work her way up to fourth from there, though she went through this rotation several times each day. In teaching one class and then another, she might as well have been directing a band: piccolos in the first row, flutes in the second, oboes in the third, clarinets the fourth. They were the woodwinds, the kids in that room, and the brass was in the other room. The strings—well! There were no strings attached. The purity of the aesthetics was in learning to sit quietly; it was not a blab school. Every moment precious, and meant to praise the fabled stuff of the mind, the part that could only exercise when it was let out of its cage at such times as these.

In later years, I couldn't remember a single lesson Miss Charlie taught me that year, but I remembered that she cared. I remembered that she was nice. I remembered that she did what every good teacher has always done, made learning fun. And I could listen to those in the third and fourth grades doing their lessons, which was the most fun of all. Miss Charlie was a serious beauty in the sense that seriousness went with beauty in those days, as though young women like herself had to work twice as hard to be appreciated for what they knew and could do, rather than what those who might harass them thought they could or would do. Working from a yellow teacher's desk at the front, she moved tirelessly back and forth before the grades, windows to her right, blackboards behind her and to her left, issuing assignments and answering questions.

What stood out in all of this was the harmony that existed at Overland School. It was a feeling of mutual respect between teachers and students, a kind of awed appreciation of this opportunity, from which emanated an attitude that was almost worshipful, as though this thing they were doing was not only important, but priceless. Perhaps that explained why there were no discipline problems. There were no bullies, and if there had been, everyone knew everyone else and their parents. Good behavior was the expense each of them paid for staying in school. It was far too expensive a bracelet to wear in an idle manner—except some of it was wasted in a glorious idleness, a pageantry befitting the riotous energy of youngsters in their prime.

We had these enormous noon recesses and were set free to roam the schoolyard in front of and behind the schoolhouse. Back of the building, diverging trails led to the two privies, the boys' on the left, the girls' on the right, the side nearest the church. Each facility had been erected with board blinds at the entrance, rather than a door. They were set back about forty yards from the school itself and bordered on a woodland behind the school that belonged to anyone who wished to run and play in it, and that is what we did during noon recesses.

It sometimes seemed to last an hour or more, recess, and the woods back there became a part of the schooling, for boys mostly but sometimes the girls. I grew to know huckleberries and blackberries. We also gathered walnuts, but were called hickory nuts. I'd fill my pockets with them at recess, and upon returning to the school building, crush the entire supply between two bricks, as I had seen other boys do, and then pour the debris into my pockets. Then, seated at the country school desk, the brown ones that have an inkwell and are bolted to the wooden floor, and the writing element attaches to the back of the seat in front, and with a storage place for books and paper in the form of a shelf beneath the writing surface, I could spend my spare time in separating and eating the fruit of the nut while disposing of the bits of shell and so forth in whatever way I could. I probably did not brush my teeth that entire year. Toothbrushes were an inconvenient luxury, though some of the adults used toothpicks or a frayed willow sprout for dental hygiene.

After school I had chores, feeding chickens and gathering eggs in the henhouse, but they left plenty of time to explore the world. At night, we read or talked by kerosene lamp or the light of the fire in the fireplace, the Rural Electrification Administration's program not reaching Cooper's Chapel until the spring of 1947, just before I left.

There was a brown wall phone in the kitchen of the kind you had to hand crank to get it to work, and it was a party line, Aunt Randie frequently having to tell someone, "Get off the phone!"—who chronically listened in, people being as curious then as now. At night, not too long after dark, people went to bed. When it was cold, you stood in front of the fire until your nightgown was warm then rushed to the back and dived into the cold bed like a buzzing insect, swishing your feet and arms back and forth as gleefully and as rigorously as possible to warm a spot to sleep in. We were up before it was light outside, chores before breakfast, then back to school, precious school with our pretty teacher.

And even that school was coming to an end. A year or two later Overland School District #16 consolidated with the Argo Independent School District in nearby Argo, Texas. Trustees sold the school grounds to the Cooper's Chapel Cemetery in 1949, and the school building was purchased and its materials used to build a home. Argo was a bigger school with more students, and consolidation made sense. For that matter, by 1945 the Cooper's Chapel students in the ninth or tenth grade already rode a bus to Argo, and upon completing the tenth grade there, they were bused into Mount Pleasant for an additional two years to graduate from Mount Pleasant High School.

Choc Anderson was the only one of ten or twelve students in his class finishing tenth grade in Argo to continue to high school in Mount Pleasant, where he was sized up as a farm boy by some teachers, one of whom offered in class that he might one day be able "to read to himself while he plowed." Those who laughed never expected that Charles Anderson would finish high school, earn his college undergraduate and master's degrees, and became a teacher and a school principal in Snyder, Texas, as well as a respected author of more than half a dozen books on Texas history.

Later, Shelba Davis also attended Mount Pleasant High School, graduating as valedictorian of the MPHS Class of 1957. She would also earn her college and master's degrees, and her career as a teacher would be spent in Port Arthur, Texas. My own progress is herein related.

School desk, schooldays, schoolboy.

*   *   *

School wasn't out for a new intern in Corpus Christi, had in fact hardly begun. In that yellow school desk that Dr. Hastings and I stood beside were lesson books and grade books and personal things to fill the lives of others, such as kindness and understanding and encouragement and the gentle spoken words by which the days and the weeks and the months and the years turn into life itself, the taught life of diligence and striving, even the occasional pursuit of the surpassing, all lessons being a means and not an end.

If it were the most noble of arts, teaching—the oldest and the grandest even if also the most underpaid—it was to me, for now, my life. I listened as my superior blared out the lesson of the day: Maria's problem was caused, he had just said, by her own hand in trying to abort her pregnancy. Mentor and novice disagreed but I spoke by silence. Meanwhile, bobbing past us like soldiers on parade, the people who worked in the hospital. We stood as straight as trumpets playing a fanfare, proper pose for those who marvel at how much they know, how much they have learned. The patient was to blame—wasn't that often, even usually, the case? Conversation takes two: standing beside the school desk we became quiet, in contrast to the bonhomie of the people weaving their way around our obstruction. My mouth did not express what my head could not but address.

She did it? Okay. But by the way, why wait so long? Horse sense made horseshit of that affectation. Surely one wishing to end her own pregnancy, by herself, required less than nine months in making up her mind? An odious something reared into outrage. To Dr. Sam, every Hispanic woman with a pelvic infection had attempted to abort herself in those days before 1973's *Roe v. Wade*. He had a technique for eliciting a confession. Bluntly asking whether she had tampered with the pregnancy, he told the woman that if she had, she would die unless he gave her a certain medicine. Should the patient remain silent, he paused and articulated into reality the grave consequences.

"Okay, we won't give it," he would say, and this while walking slowly away, hoping but not expecting that the patient would babble out a confession in order to save her life.

I thanked the small gods, the ones with only a regional impact, that Hastings hadn't tried this on Maria. For one thing, it was just too farfetched that she would do that. For another, he did not know Maria Chavarria. Made no attempt to know her and never would, preferring to tinker with the fate of a stranger as though that were his function in medicine—to soak patients in that Sightless Sea, dipping Maria into his preconceptions about how other people lived their lives in a shameless world. How valiant, that? Maria's intestinal obstruction was a quarrel between her intestines and the unknown and at the worst possible time, late in pregnancy, with Dr. Timidity caring for her and Dr. Certitude the attending authority. It was a fragile alliance, and the bitter seeds of discord had just been planted—just past that fence to the other side of the sycamore tree.

Two weeks into internship, I drove back to the hospital on the Monday night of July 15 and delivered Maria's healthy baby boy at just before eleven p.m. Every baby grows to maturity inside a splashy sac of amniotic fluid, an anatomical nod to the evolutionary ocean, and the breaking of this bag of water (BOW) may signal—or precipitate—the onset of the hard labor that immediately precedes birth. Maria's BOW had not broken despite her hard labor, and upon arrival outside the back delivery room I scrubbed and put on gloves and gown and cap and used a special forceps designed for that purpose to puncture her BOW. The fluid itself was dark, turbid, malodorous, infected. Did this confirm to me that Dr. Hastings had been right after all and I had been wrong? Actually, it did. It certainly did, however hard that was to believe. What was no longer in doubt: she had an infection inside her abdomen. It didn't mean that she had caused it, however.

Her amniotic fluid was unlike any that I had ever seen. I took cultures of it and, after the delivery, manually explored the cavity of her uterus searching for perforations, but I found none. It was the first time I had done that, having read that it could be done, and in a few minutes I was through, whereupon I joined in the happiness that filled the room, that soared through the dominions of rejoicing as Maria basked in the glory of being given her newborn, that seaborne, that innocent, that potentate, and everyone was moved by the quiet pleasure of being in the vicinity of God.

*   *   *

Tuesday morning Maria's fever was higher, much higher, and she continued to vomit and have severe abdominal pain. To me, it meant that the infection hadn't ceased with delivery. I continued her penicillin, awaiting the culture and sensitivity studies from the amniotic fluid to select a more specific antibiotic, were that indicated. Now that Maria had graduated to the open ward, she was in the first bed to the left past the nurses' station. The ward, two long rows of beds, was a gentle meetinghouse of women celebrating their mutual happiness. These patients had joy in common, the future in mind. I saw breakfast trays on those odd stands that seemed to exist in hospitals and no place else in the world. I saw bouquets of flowers with their joyous greeting cards. The sun was bright, scampering through the room like a nursery child. Pregnancy, one was reminded, was a blessed event that brought new people into the commonwealth, and that was a good thing.

But Maria was still sick and that wasn't good. Postpartum, she resembled the slender twin of the woman who had given birth the previous night. As she held her own emesis basin, the hospital ID bracelet practically slipped off her wrist. *How unfair*, I thought. How totally unfair it was. At least the other women were sympathetic. They knew her problems and were worried about her; several of them had asked me about her and wanted to know what they could do to lift her spirits. Good people, all.

After Maria was through being sick, she greeted me with a hard look because of the needle and syringe I held.

"Do you have to put me that shot again?"

I explained that it was a necessity for fluids and antibiotics, her intravenous having infiltrated again. She asked about her baby and I said good things, having checked him in the nursery first thing that morning. Then it occurred to me.

"Haven't they brought him out?"

"No, no, and others already been here. I want to hold him again."

I put down the needle and syringe and stepped away to find a nurse.

"Can you bring her baby?"

The nurse whispered that there were rules against bringing babies to mothers who had a fever; they didn't want her infection spreading through the nursery. I maintained that Maria was not infectious, to the baby or to anyone else.

Shortly I was locked in a contest of wills with the head nurse on OB, one Josephine Crabb. I was in training, she was not. Once that was straight, I took stock of her. It was a feature of the field of nursing, especially in the days when it was 100 percent female, that each nurse wore the nursing uniform required by the hospital where she worked but was entitled to wear the cap of the nursing school from which she had graduated.

Women had perks about hats. They were permitted to wear them indoors, for one thing, and my take on the cap that festooned Josephine Crabb's superior region was that it was both austere and somehow hilarious, eliciting the reaction one might have to seeing a stagecoach-and-four, complete with someone riding shotgun, drive by on Morgan Avenue. I was as sure that I had never mentioned that cap as I was that I had probably snickered at it behind her back, which made its way into her repertoire of reasons not to like me. Crabb, I suspected, was behind the failure of a nurse to help me with Mrs. Ramos. Crabb, I suspected, thought me a nonentity too dense to know that one didn't intrude upon her domain. She held against me, I was sure, that I was young enough to be her grandson and what right had I to tell her anything? I didn't worship her gods, didn't hazard her whims, couldn't shimmy like her sister Kate. I had already begun to discharge patients a day or two after their delivery, if they wished, in contradistinction to the head nurse's thunderclap mandate that a week in hospital, awarded to the new mothers, was a much-needed rest before they went home. I had thought to relax strictures in a temporary incarceration, but the warden disagreed.

We spoke. She said to the effect and I said to the effect and she repeated herself to the effect and I did not back down. I would take responsibility, I told her.

What I failed to mention was that I was a lightweight in a heavyweight world and did not expect to win this or any other argument. People called me a doctor, but I wasn't. I was still the same person inside that I had always been, and one had to change, it seemed to me, to become a doctor. I was still the scared new kid, hustling up to make my side of the bed on those mornings that I wet it so that Lula Faye, who shared the bed and made it each morning, wouldn't discover my secret. How could I expect to overcome Florence Nightingale?

Regally the head nurse withdrew from the insufferable boor. She carried with her the court that she presided over, and I was left to my own miserable self. Or not. Reaching with her one good hand, Maria found mine and squeezed, then settled back, her hair spilling upon the pillow like a pool of dark ink. So it was that I was blindsided by her question.

"Dr. Deaton, am I here to die?"

"No!" I said too quickly, and the word revolved into motion those tiny little specks, bright as shellac, that are always there, in every shaft of sunlight, eavesdropping upon the unsuspecting.

I was thunderstruck. Is a hospital a place where people go to die, or is it a place where people go to live? What a terrible thought, on a day for them. As I watched, a bird flew over a placid lake, its call oddly close and shrill, like a ripple in a torrent, and along with my instant denial came forth a summons from my own lips to the numb racism that had generated it.

She seemed not to understand, and then she did. "Can you mean …? Oh, I am the good Catholic and never would harm my baby!"

"No, of course not! I'm sorry, I shouldn't have asked it."

With effort, she lowered herself onto the pillow again, a teenage mother unjustly accused, and for a queasy instant we were strangers to each other. The women, the others on the open ward, having ceased their visiting, were smothering us with attention. The ward could have been the deck of a great ship, every bed a lifeboat, two rows in perfect alignment. But are there enough lifeboats for all? Maria tried to speak but her voice broke, her virtue impacted by my stupidity. I apologized again for the hurtful question.

"What is wrong with me, Dr. Deaton?" she said. "Here is where I hurt," tapping her stomach, "and what do you think? I am sorry, but my baby I did not attempt to harm."

"No, of course you didn't."

Touching her hand in the awkward gesture of a fool, I was buoyed by what she said next. "I want give him. Give him …" Her voice went, and I died for causing this to a woman so sick, her tears flowing freely. "Give him a happy," she managed, "always."

"You can give him that."

"Not so very sure," she said, and her eyes darted past me.

I turned to find the head nurse leading a procession from the nursery. Two of the nurses handed Maria her little boy, whose tiny face and round mouth and abundance of hair were appealingly located inside a long white funnel of bedding. Coming as it did, getting her baby thrilled Maria. Thrilled me.

"Oh, *baby*," she cooed to the five pounds and ten ounces of Luis Eduardo Chavarria. "Oh, my little baby!"

I watched her glowing with motherhood and wheeled around to thank the head nurse with all my heart, informing Mrs. Josephine Crabb that few nurses in world history had broken the rules for a new mother and that she had my undying gratitude. I had been an ass, I told her, but no more. No patient would henceforth go home before she, the experienced one, allowed it. Furthermore, I was going to try very hard to do my very best during the rest of my time on OB to be respectful of her wishes. We had moved away from Maria's bed during this, and I whispered that she was a very sick patient and, if possible, should be moved back into that private room the other side of the nurses' station.

The head nurse, put on a pedestal and in the same instant presented with another request, did what anyone in her place would have done: she looked at me as though I were very strange. She and the others left, and I returned to Maria's side.

I wanted more than anything in the world to be granted to stand beside her there in perpetuity, Maria and her son, not in triumph but in homage, watching over her and her baby for eternity. But the fife played my note and I followed it like the obedient slave I was.

*   *   *

Dr. Hastings came out that Tuesday evening, July 16. He came at my request because that was the kind of doctor he was, who appeared when needed and did what he thought was correct. I knew that better than most. I may have disagreed with him but was glad for his guidance, more particularly in that he had been right about the pelvic infection. But Maria had taken a turn and was much worse than that morning, and I didn't know how to proceed. I stood by while Dr. Sam examined her, and afterward we retired to that yellow school desk on the road to Mandalay.

Supper was over. Cafeteria carts of shiny aluminum went trundling past on the dark surface, leaving incandescent sparks of the dawn that comes up like thunder out of China 'crost the Bay. Nurses and aides went quietly about their duties to the tinkle of passing bells, the ones that accompany the most serious of matters.

"Why," Hastings said quietly, "did you explore her uterus last night?"

"Because of the infected amniotic fluid and what you said."

"Did episiotomy? Used forceps?"

"Yes. I used outlet forceps."

Still, I did not see it coming any more than I had anticipated Maria's question that morning on the ward. "Are you real sure," the attending said, "you didn't perforate her uterus with the forceps?" He paused. "Because this girl has a perforated uterus and the classic picture of parametritis. That hole in her uterus, corruption spreads straight through to her belly, and she's more than likely going to die."

Distracting us, a hospital orderly slid by, riding a gurney like a wave, "Surfin' USA," but my thoughts bred verses memorized long ago and in another land. Book learning wasn't enough. That was today's lesson. Memorized poems were a cedar chest oh so sweet, until it was opened. Real learning took place outside the classroom. Nonacademic lessons, as it were. People ones. The dimple in the ass of the stricken, though they didn't tell you that because there was no way to tell you that. It was in the tickle at the trailhead of life: who lit the sun, who poured the sea? Who dug the chasm and who could say how deep it really was? The leery looked in vain.

"It's too bad," the obstetrician was saying as he began walking slowly away, as if inviting me to babble out a confession in order to save my life. He paused at the double doors of Labor and Delivery. "It could have happened to anybody."

*   *   *

Standing in the principal's office, called to account for my misdeeds, I am convicted by circumstantial evidence. Lucinda Thompson* has accused me of stealing her fifty-cent piece. I do not think of myself as a thief, but I am accused and I know why. We are students in Pittsburg High School, and Lucinda is one of my friends. She is a pleasant person, fun loving and accomplished, someone I admire. She is the daughter of a former teacher who had taken her to Dallas one summer years ago for a ballet tryout; though it is for her skills on the grand piano that she is best known. She excels at the recitals held each year in the auditorium, though she has the artist's tendency toward moodiness. What characterizes the rest of us at PHS is that we have the moodiness without the art, unless art is the indigestion of a force-fed shit sandwich.

What had happened was this. Some of us had been playing with Lucinda's purse upon the lawn before class, running back and forth with great glee around a couple of sycamore trees that guarded the three-story school building and its sidewalks and stairs. The sycamores had leaves the size of dinner plates, and we gorged ourselves with our feet. I assumed Lucinda liked the attention, since she was shrieking like people on a Ferris wheel as one or another of half a dozen boys played keep-away with her purse.

My incurable conniption was the need to go further, to do more than anyone else, and I had grasped her shiny black purse to my chest and, on an impulse, proceeded to run all of the way around the brown-brick school building with it before returning it to her.

It was a big school building, a blockhouse, an edifice big enough to contain the hundreds of students and faculty and administrators within its jurisdiction and the ideals and dreams that drove them, a schoolhouse at once too big for them and yet simultaneously too small, small as only a small town can be small. Small in a grandiose way. An architect had described it, many years later upon being presented with a picture of it, as a "functional school building of the time, styled in Gothic revival." (Photograph, pp. 298–299.)

John and Mimi Deaton, 1960. Celebrating our
nuptials at the bus station in Waco.[10]

---

10   All photographs not otherwise credited are from the author's collection.

Clockwise, from upper left. 1. An engagement on Valentine's Day, 1960.
2. The new doctor after having his degree framed. 3. Roger in our bedroom,
1963. 4. Roger and proud father in front of the house, July of 1963.

Christmas of 1963. Mimi, Roger, and John.

Helen and Gilbert Garrett, June 27, 1938

Memorial Hospital, 1964. New hospital, right; previous "new" hospital, middle; the sprawling "concrete airplane" of the old hospital, left, with four wings on the side nearest the street and three wings on its north side. The south wings, from left to right, are Obstetrics, Med/Surg, Medicine, and the Clinic Building. The two delivery rooms are in the part that pokes out to the west, the "nose" of the aircraft. Buildings in the foreground, between Hospital Boulevard (nearest the hospital) and Morgan Avenue, bottom, are doctors' offices. [From the files of the Corpus Christi Public Library, Local History Collection, used by permission of Margaret Rose, Special Collections Librarian, 1997.]

1. Maria during her pregnancy, with her in-laws. 2. Mr. and Mrs. Jose de La Torre, Maria's mother and stepfather. 3. Maria, a restoration of the top photo portraying her with a timeless quality. [Restoration by Jenn Downes-Twilla, T-Squared Studio, Austin, 1997.]

Ramiro Peña, MD, FACS. [Photograph by and courtesy of Dr. Peña.]

Fannie Opal Kimberlin hated her first two names and went by
Frances, but she wasn't crazy about her last name, either, seeing
fit to change it four times. Mount Pleasant, Texas, 1931.

First grade, the West Ward School in Mount Pleasant, Texas, 1946. I am in the back row, fifth from the right. Gerald Cox is to my right. Seated, to the far right, my friend Carolyn Cross. These kids were my first audience.

Charles Deaton, left, and Frances Kimberlin beside him on running board, with Minnie and Lacy Rogers, May 13, 1934. The vehicle is parked at the service station located at 204 Quitman Street in Pittsburg, Texas. Inset: Charles Favor Deaton, Machinist Mate First Class, World War II.

Anderson farmhouse, Cooper's Chapel, Texas, 1941. An outhouse, a well, a smokehouse, a chicken shed, and a cowshed were located in back, with a cow pond nearby. The white items are rocks shielding a small flower bed. [Photograph courtesy of Charles "Choc" Anderson.]

Raymond and Randie Anderson, 1953. [Photograph courtesy of Charles "Choc" Anderson.]

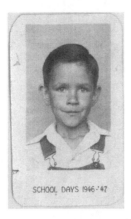

John G. Deaton, second grade, Cooper's Chapel Overland School, 1946–47.

Cooper's Chapel Overland School, 1944–45. Lula Faye Anderson is second from right in the front row, first grade. At the back, "Miss" Callie Cochran, left, and her daughter, Miss Charlie Cochran, right (later to be Mrs. Charlie Groom). In the top row, on Charlie's right, is Lula Faye's older sister, Anna Beth, finishing eighth grade that year. She was in high school the year I spent in Cooper's and became the angel who watched out for me. Not shown: Shelba Davis started first grade the next year in Cooper's, while I started first grade in Houston before completing it in Mount Pleasant. We met in the second grade at Cooper's, 1946–1947, when Lula Faye was in third. [Photograph courtesy of Shelba Davis Spears, who also helped with identities.]

Cooper's Chapel Overland School, taken on the same day as the photograph on the preceding page. Lula Faye is fourth from the left, front row. Shelba's brother, Jack Davis, is second from the right, back row. The girl seated in front is Zonetta Gentry, just visiting that day. The shy person third from the right in the back row is possibly Dovie Nell Taylor—shown barefooted on the first of the porch steps in the school photograph on the preceding page. [Photograph courtesy of Shelba Davis Spears, who also supplied the identities.]

Argo School, late 1940s, after the Cooper's Chapel School had consolidated. Midway in the back row, Miss Charlie Cochran, who by the time of this photograph probably had her teaching degree and had moved with the Cooper's students to the Argo school. Shelba Jean Davis is seated in the middle of the front row. Lula Faye is in the dark blouse, fifth from the right in the back row. Zonetta Gentry, now a bona fide student, is first from the right in the front row. [Photograph courtesy of Shelba Davis Spears, who also supplied the identities.]

Beyond its style, it confronted the world through glass. The four offset sections of PHS contained as many windows as could be built into its façade. One forgot until seeing a picture of it that the school offered three continuous rows of windows sweeping horizontally across its entire breadth, seventy-two windows in all, each with two dozen separate windowpanes. It was an incubator for the visionary. If you had a really good eye and looked closely enough, you could see in those windows the reflections of everyone who had ever passed through those heaving portals. There were windows on the sides and back as well, giving the interior of the building a spacious look, as if each part of it had been lifted and set down in an arboretum as lovely as any modern shopping mall.

Indeed, PHS had the feel of the out-of-doors. Hallways were wide, classrooms spacious, the concrete frame lending itself to floors cast in place concrete, with wooden floors in the classrooms and polished terrazzo for the hallways and interior stairs. I don't know about the rest of the student body, but I loved that building without reservation. I loved it almost as much as I hated it, and I hated it for no other reason than that serving there was like being in the Army, deadly as any other form of combat.

*   *   *

I had finished the tour around the building, including the various features of the physical plant at the back, in plenty of time to return Lucinda's purse to her, which she accepted without anger, and we went our separate ways to the first-period classes. Mine was band, my favorite class. The band hall was directly behind the school, on the other side of a small driveway that I had recently trod. And it was brand new that fall of 1953, lengthened and remodeled for us to enjoy upon return from summer vacation. The sixty or seventy of us were assembled in the hall at the back, in sections in front of the podium. I had finally gained the front row of clarinets, situated to the left of the band director, Jack England.

In the first chair of the front row was a young man who was a senior, a truly great musician and a gifted clarinetist. The second chair was Betty Sue Adams, a sophomore. An attractive brunette, Betty Sue was impossibly and hopelessly in love with the occupant of the first chair, unrequited as it was, and she and I often joked about the children she and the first chair would never have, those "little cotton-headed rascals," as Betty Sue put it.

Mr. England was highly popular, a great man and a great band leader. He had the band rehearsing our program for Friday night's football game when the intercom barked for attention, and he waved his arms in the way he did meaning *Stop!* Mr. Acker's voice filled the band hall, his message short but frightening. Everyone in the band stared—gaped—at the third clarinetist as the principal in a terse message summoned me to his office. Burning with embarrassment, I awaited Mr. England's instructions. He was as surprised as I, and made a signal of ready dismissal to the higher authority.

Still stricken with embarrassment, I fled to the adjacent instrument room, took apart my clarinet, and placed it in its case, which I left in its spot on one of the shelves provided for our instruments. Stepping into the sunlight, the agriculture and shop building down to my right, I took the short walk to the east side of the main building and climbed to the third, top, floor. The principal's office was on the other end of the third floor, past the library and the elongated study hall which, except for a classroom at either end, ran the entire length of the building. With room for everyone, we gathered there first thing each morning to be led in prayer by the principal, and I felt a shiver of dread when I saw the selfsame Mr. Acker awaiting me outside his office at the other end of the study hall. Having arrived, I was instructed to follow the man down to a smaller office situated on the west side of the building off the stairwell to the second floor, its window facing the stairs and allowing those climbing to the third or descending to the second to see inside. (And allowing those inside to see out, should they dare to look.)

O. E. Acker—for Ollis Elton—was forty-seven years old that year. He had BS and MS degrees from East Texas State Teacher's College, where he had played on the varsity football and basketball squads. He had served as a lieutenant junior grade in the United States Navy from 1942 to 1945, a drill instructor. He had accepted the position of principal in 1941, returned upon his discharge from the Navy, and was the only principal PHS students would know until the seventies. Taskmaster to a fault, he often taught classes in physics and chemistry, or world history and algebra, in addition to being principal.

He had a way to "raise the students' level of concern." The first day of classes, Mr. Acker would bring in a wooden pointer as tall as a man and lean it against the blackboard. Without saying a thing to the students, he would suddenly seize the pointer and turn and snap it in two on top of the teacher's desk or on an empty chair at the front of the room. As a means of demonstrating authority, it was matchless. But what it gained in that measure, I am afraid, it simultaneously lost in the two-way respect undergirding teaching excellence. Fear is one thing, trust another. Only in small jolts can people be forced, and the electric chair deterred crime only one individual at a time.

Even so, by the time I came under his authority, there was no need for him to break pointers. Everyone was frightened to death of O. E. Acker. There were tales of how, in that same small room off the staircase between the second and third floors, he had whipped male students in high school with a heavy leather strap, expending such force that he literally lifted them off the floor with each blow. That sort of thing gets around.

*   *   *

And it explains why I am scared stiff to be summoned to see him.

Mr. Acker has me wait in that glass office off the stairwell while he fetches my accuser, the same Lucinda Thompson. Only then do I learn of the alleged theft. I listen to Lucinda and readily admit taking her purse in fun and running around the school building with it. It had proved longer around than I'd thought, and I had worked up a sweat by that extemporaneous activity, but it would never have occurred to me to open her purse, I tell them, much less to take something from it. We had just been teasing her.

But, the theft having occurred, she reported me, and Mr. Acker intends to see justice done in whatever way is required. He dismisses Lucinda to return to her classes and has me take a seat in the tiny office beside his desk, my back to the window, and he begins to quietly draw the noose of circumstantial evidence tighter and tighter around my neck. At one point I stand and empty my pockets to show that I have no money, nothing but lunch tickets for the week (twenty-five or thirty-five cents each that year), purchased on Monday. The principal does not take that as proof of innocence. Instead, he grills me, mentioning again and again the incriminating nature of the circumstantial evidence, and I break into tears that add to my embarrassment as I glance around and confirm what I already know—that everyone in high school is witnessing my punishment while flocking up and down those stairs each time the bell rings.

There is also this. Mr. Acker has been put out by this. I am wasting his time. It takes him from the better things he has to do, such as police the hallways and check the restrooms for cigarette smoke. The quicker I confess, I gather, the better it will be for our beloved student body. What is better for me doesn't matter; I have lost that privilege by virtue of being arrested and convicted for what I have not done.

That I am a convicted criminal until proven otherwise is obvious. Unrepresented by counsel, I am detained in the glass holding cell all morning. My anger suddenly turns inward. Forgive me for living. What in the hell is good about living if it brings you this? My mind turns to eggbeater, scrambling my brains. I relive my life in all its punitive glory. I am ashamed beyond words. Again and again the entire high school passes by, and in my misery I cannot stop crying, that sickening release. In my anguish I collide with the real possibility that my honor has suffered irreparable harm and may never be regained, though I had come to regard it as my most valuable possession. Mr. Acker enters and leaves throughout the morning, awaiting my confession, and I expect that the leather strap is resident in one of the drawers of the desk and he is itching to get his hands on it and mete out a just punishment.

Meanwhile, I continue to cower in shame each time the bell rings. What bothers me most is that I am a Christian. Apparently that counts for nothing with a man who converses with God in front of the high school every morning. (I suppose I am but an eavesdropper on that conversation.) We do, in fact, attend the same church, First Baptist. It is the same church that Lucinda and her mother attend. They were there on the Sunday night I was baptized. I see them there every week as we honor the Ten Commandments; what would make me break one for a pennywhistle of a half-dollar? And add to the crime by lying?

But I know this: the school is preparing us for adulthood, and toward that end it might very well treat us like kindergarteners. Indeed, until the last diploma is handed out at the end of the 1956–57 school year and we file out in a compromised silence, what difference does it make how we are treated? Whether the system is unjust to one or two, does that matter? Tuition must be paid, revenge collected. Better to make sure that all are punished than to let one criminal escape unpunished! What was—to put it in the fifties patois—the big deal? There are others to take our places, always others to take our places. Method worked and method remained. Students must learn cause and effect. They must suffer now to save them from suffering later. They must learn here, and learn well, the first lesson of life: that it is unfair. That unruly thread wove its way through the linen of time with scarce a thought that the garment was made not all at once, but in pieces that fit a pattern, a pattern having as its goal the completion of the task. Except the task, of course, was never completed. The difference between the functional and the dysfunctional school building of the time was that the first knew it and the second did not.

David Copperfield, a century earlier, was forced to wear a sign on his back: "Take care of him. He bites." The six words on my back were, "From morning's scorn, are evenings borne."

By the time Lucinda's mother called and said that she had left her fifty-cent piece at home and that she was bringing it to her so that she could eat at the Pirate's Den across the street from the school instead of at the less-desirable school cafeteria, by the time of my exoneration and Lucinda's apology, whereupon I told her it was my fault for taking her purse, Mr. Acker has dismissed the matter. There being no fault on his part, he need not condescend to apologize to me. He was merely making sure that justice and fairness were applied to all.

Were the present-day me to attempt to put thoughts into that young man's head, expressing the misery of a fourteen-year-old disgraced in front of the high school by his detainment for four hours, they might go like this. "Mr. Acker, it was not Lucinda Thompson who kept me all morning. You had such an airtight case on me that my devaluation by you and by my peers was immediate. The leather would have been so much quicker and less painful."

Of course I speak from a distance of safely and protection. That morning, I was terrified. The only other memory of the event is that, unlike Lucinda, I lost my appetite, much too much the coward to appear in the school cafeteria. I went somewhere and hid.

*   *   *

Now, a fortnight into my internship, that feeling of deep humiliation had returned. After my accuser left, I stood there in that hallway in Memorial Hospital beside the yellow school desk and contemplated the fact that I had perforated Maria's uterus. What I had not grasped until then was that *I* did it. It was my fault. I had through gross negligence committed at the time of her delivery the very condition she had upon admission to the hospital three days earlier, a feat never before accomplished in the history of infamy. My thrashing was complete.

My accuser, Dr. Sam Hastings, had earlier in the month let me peek over his shoulder during several deliveries of his private patients. He had passed time with me in the dead of night, awaiting the full dilatation of the pregnant cervix in the first stage of labor. Sam Hastings was a raconteur. He loved to regale his audience with the things he had done during his training as a resident in OB/Gyn at the University of Texas (Southwestern) Medical School in Dallas. He spoke with braggadocio, in front of the nurses, as if he were proud of himself for being so daring. According to him, he and fellow residents had "played around" with the deliveries of staff patients at Dallas's Parkland Hospital. At the time, these patients were almost always black women who hadn't the money for a private doctor. The residents saw them through their pregnancies by following them in clinic, as did the interns at Memorial, and then delivered their babies. What they did during the hours leading up to delivery, on the other hand, was a stunning admission. Smiling wistfully, Dr. Hastings told of creating "sleepy babies" on purpose. What he and the other residents in Obstetrics had done in Dallas, he said with a naughty grin, was to give injections of morphine to relieve the labor pains of staff patients who were less than an hour from delivery. This caused sleepy babies—that is, ones with depressed respiration.

All physicians learn that morphine, which easily crosses the placenta to the fetus, has a depressant effect on respiration. It is true of humans at any age. Morphine can literally eradicate the robust breathing efforts that a newborn must initiate to survive on its own. Robust breathing efforts, coincident with the lusty crying of a newborn, constitute the universal signs of a healthy birth. When breathing doesn't occur, various maneuvers can help to stimulate it. These include giving an antidote to counteract the depressant effects of morphine or Demerol, although prevention is far more preferable.

Indeed, I had been taught, and vociferously so, that morphine and Demerol were never to be used when delivery was expected within the next four hours. (Giving a painkiller earlier in labor enabled mother and fetus an interval of time sufficient to break down and remove the depressant from the baby's system.) The egregiousness of purposefully inducing babies with depressed respiration was in the potential outcome. The baby's response to the antidote wasn't invariable. And even when a response occurred, it was often delayed. That sleepy babies might never take a first breath despite resuscitative efforts and be pronounced stillborn was well-known. Sleepy babies that were finally resuscitated after lengthy efforts might have hypoxic brain damage from the prolonged period of oxygen deprivation and go through life with cerebral palsy, a lifelong paralysis with or without accompanying mental disability.

But Dr. Hastings eschewed any idea of causing such problems. He basked in the glow of how the sleepy babies he induced in unsuspecting mothers at Parkland Hospital had allowed him to practice the resuscitation techniques he might need later on in his private patients—the ones that really mattered. It augmented his technique in using the antidote. It was a way to practice airway suction and the other modalities employed to jumpstart delayed fetal breathing. He said that it was such a common practice of residents at Parkland that no one thought a thing about it. For him to remember it seemed to call up a happier time in his life, which he celebrated by singing, "Oh, those sleepy babies!"

Sam Hastings equated it with the youthful pranks of adolescence, of high school boys stealing watermelons, possibly, the act permissible because one permitted it. I thought it an example of doctors dangerously testing the limits of possibility, were that their character. Eden was not lost, merely encircled by a White Curtain. It was even possible that Dr. Hastings's brazen recklessness may have affected him more than he dared admit. He may have wished to impugn the abilities of a young doctor under his tutorage by way of calming the heckling doubts he had about his own training. Perhaps it also explained his cynical attitude that all women of a certain group who had an infection in pregnancy had tried to abort themselves. I maintain that no doctor has the right to instill hurt. And the measure of a professional is one who does the right thing even when no one is looking. On some level I knew this but, for once, I kept my opinion to myself.

*   *   *

Tuesday night I did not sleep. Wednesday morning Maria's abdomen was so ballooned that she may as well have had another full-term baby inside her. She continued to vomit, her pain persistent. Seeing her like that was a terrible thing. A portable flat plate of the abdomen again showed multiple loops of dilated bowel, but incredibly the radiologist still could not tell between mechanical obstruction and intestinal dilation from infection.

Clinically, the differentiation between the two is easy. Bowel dilated from infection is silent, while obstructed bowel howls in protest, like captured animals inveigling the world for their release, and Maria still had those same high-pitched bowel sounds that I had heard that first time I examined her. I relayed this to my staff man, who had not stopped by for rounds. I informed him, as well, that she was much worse. Over the phone he told me that he had called the surgeon on the Surgery Service that month, who suggested that we should pass a nasogastric tube. I was glad to do it, should have thought of it myself. I explained the procedure to Maria and poked the plastic tube through her nose into her throat, then fed it in as she swallowed it with the help of some ice in her mouth. I hooked my end of it to a portable suction machine that ran from an outlet in the wall of her room. Draining fluids and air from the stomach helped to reduce her abdominal distention and also relieved some of her pain and nausea.

Wednesday, July 17, at noon, Maria's mother took the baby home after giving me a copy of the operative note on the appendectomy done by Hector Garcia at Spohn Hospital when Maria was seven. I placed it unread at the back of her chart in the rush of things, for Maria's blood pressure had plummeted. She hovered in confusion for an hour or so and then fell into a deep coma. Diagnosing the complication as septic shock, I treated her with the same plethora of antibiotics that I had given to that poor woman on Surgical Annex the first day of internship.

Treating Maria, I inevitably began neglecting my other duties. Soon, other interns were delivering babies while I made flying trips back and forth between Maria's bed in one of the private rooms on OB and the interns' lounge at the other end of the hallway, where I thrashed madly through journal after journal, like a detective on a case, book after book touched and tossed, seeking what I could not find, attempting to cross-reference and still not locating the article, the paragraph, the single sentence that might save this patient, this precious patient.

Wednesday night I inserted an additional IV to sustain her feeble blood pressure. And I put her on corticosteroids, remembering the time outside the Medicine Ward in the shiny hallway of John Sealy Hospital that the intern on 4-B had asked me, a medical student on the service, the three indications for giving steroids, then answered himself: *When they are dying, dying, dying.* Now I was the intern proving him correct.

Doctors, being human, do say such things. We speak of a patient being a crock (full of shit), meaning the person's illness is an illusion. We speak of a patient being PPP (piss-poor protoplasm), but in truth, such things are said not as a reality but as a way of maintaining a healthy and even cynical distance from the suffering. Had I just accused Dr. Hastings of this? I had. Could I maintain my distance from Maria without doing that? It remained to be seen. Sick on admission and growing desperately ill thereafter, and having slipped into a coma from sepsis, she had little chance of recovery and I knew it.

As her coma deepened, her pupils became dilated and fixed. This meant that the opening at the front of the eye would not respond (by constricting) to the stimulus of a light shone directly into it. Watching "dead" people in a movie, I always noticed something. The pupil is a modest opening, compliant and receptive. The ingress of light is its nature. It is circular, controlled by a sphincter muscle, and relatively small in ordinary light. In a movie, the actor stops breathing and his face assumes a fixed position, like a mannequin. But the pupils are not dilated. Perhaps verisimilitude goes only so far.

Fully dilated and fixed, the eyeballs turn into two bunkers with their fronts blown away, and that amount of dilatation of the pupils speaks to death or its precursor. Pupils are supposed to be active and competent. Normal pupils are never dilated and fixed. They sense what is presented to them and retain it. They respond as readily to hate as to love, the one stinging like venom, the other smacking in bubblegum delight. Pupils learn this or they don't make it. According to all that I had been taught, it meant that even if by some miracle Maria were to survive, she'd have brain death and continue in a coma, becoming—flippantly—a vegetable (requiring only watering). Fixed and dilated pupils were no good. They were unseeing and unchangeable. Fixed and dilated meant death of that pupil because it or they or those could no longer distinguish between darkness and light, and what good is that to they or those or them?

*　　*　　*

A buzzing sounded and a nurse sallied forth. I jumped from the chair beside the bed. The nurse asked whether it was okay if the Father came in and gave Maria last rites? Of course, and I cleared out of her room, where I had become, in effect, a special-duty nurse.

At the nurses' station I wrote an order on Maria's chart placing her on the Critical list. Hospitals did not like it when patients died who were not on the Critical list. Via the Critical list accrued certain benefits to patient and hospital, by way of visiting hours and attention and expectations. In 1963 the Critical list was a writ granting, to the writer, the unappeasable knowledge of impending death, and in silent resignation I placed myself on the Critical list along with Maria and took my own last rites.

After the Padre left, there being no more drugs to give Maria, I went through the list, increasing to heroic doses all of them. With no warning at all, I experienced what amounted to a fury, a passion, an ultimatum twenty-three years in the making. I would have her live! That was all there was to it! I must have her survive! I focused on her to the exclusion of all else. I ceased knowing night or day; time lost its grip. I became movement and thought and nothing else, fixated on her. I wanted her to live because she had put her trust in me. I demanded her to live because I still believed in happy endings and the triumph of human virtue. I rescinded her sentence of death because I knew what a fine mother she would be. I had seen the love she had given Luis, and he deserved that care from his loving and lovable mother. I wanted her to live, finally, because I was a doctor and she my patient, explanation enough.

*　　*　　*

Thursday morning was as bright and lovely as any morning had ever been, and upon arrival at the hospital I stood, watching Mimi and Roger drive away. She had gotten together with some neighborhood women and was taking Roger to the birthday party of a two-year-old who lived down the street. The party was that afternoon, July 18, and another of the interns' wives was going with her. Mimi could move to a new neighborhood and have friends within a week. I watched her go and loved her so. I tried to remember last night away from the hospital, with her, but it wasn't easy. I could only live in one place at a time. It was my allegiance as well as my curse, and the notion that a doctor must surrender his life left me feeling strangely depressed. Where was all of that applause and happiness upon graduation a little over a month ago?

At seven o'clock happy people were entering and leaving Memorial Hospital, people I did not know, though I suspected they knew me. I hated every last one of them. Having crossed to a place they couldn't, I felt simultaneously alienated from them and envious of those remaining behind. I ballooned with a seething, queasy anger directed at them, blaming them for a freedom I no longer had. Their happiness! Their dismissive calm, their scathing demeanor! How dare they enjoy a hospital that filled me with dread! Those leaving seemed so content in their happy careers, like the nurse just there pointing to a runner in her white stockings then jabbering something to her two companions that sent them into hysteria. They might as well have been leaving the hospital behind forever, they were that casual about it. And the ones arriving were happy to leave home for a few hours and be paid handsomely for it, looking forward in their happy pursuit of the day that lay ahead. Everyone was in a good mood, festive air. Uniforms crisp, gaits brisk. They smiled at me in the way of people trying to cheer one up, but only one person in the world could do that.

I swallowed my contempt and swept down the short hallway of Labor and Delivery, heard but did not respond to the sounds of a couple of women in labor, and went first to Maria's bedside near the entrance to the Obstetrics Ward. Mrs. Crabb and the other nurses, having just finished their meeting with the night shift, were planning the day. Stopped by the fife, I told the operator to notify the intern on call to cover in Labor and Delivery (which my fellow interns did not mind doing, since they had been asking me to deliver fewer babies so that they might deliver more).

Maria was the same.

I managed to do a few things, chart rounds on OB, rounds with the attending in the nursery. She was the world's tallest pediatrician and had emphysema, which was manifest in a low whistle as she slowly exhaled each breath. She also had a secret. She'd discovered in a baby I had delivered and failed to examine completely a cleft palate—more precisely, the nurses found it and told her—and she caught me in a lie when I said I had examined the kid. It reminded her of a story. "Doctor delivered this baby, everything fine, sent it home. The father brought the kid back a couple of days later saying, 'Hey, Doc, this kid ain't got no asshole!' Doctor looked, and looked back at the father, and said, 'Well he did when he left the hospital!'" I joined her in hearty laughter, accepting my mistake. An imperforate anus was the least of my problems; caudal virginity had its own rendezvous with destiny.

I devoted all day Thursday, a week after I had met Maria and her mother in Labor and Delivery, to taking care of Maria. Notes in her chart extolled the visit last night from the intern on duty, who was called to check her when she looked particularly bad, but he made no medication changes other than to increase the dosage of the Levophed that was supporting her blood pressure, the reason being to avert the kidney complications of shock. There was nothing more to do for her and everything to do for her. That afternoon I again took up my vigil in the chair beside her bed.

I could not leave; nothing bad could happen to her while I was there.

Mimi called and told me about the birthday party. Roger was a hit with the other women, and she related how he had, with maternal prodding, returned a toy to the birthday girl that he had begun playing with. The women were, "Oh, he's so good!" Then there was an abrupt thudding sound and when they turned, Roger had thrown himself prostrate with grief upon the floor. So much for selflessness among the young. Mimi asked when I might be home. I told her not to worry, I was treating Maria. Someone, probably me, had ordered that her blood pressure be taken every fifteen minutes and I did this myself, recording the readings on a lined piece of paper the nurses had taped to the nightstand. Her pressure was low, but stable. She continued to put out heroic volumes of urine corresponding to the amount of fluids she was receiving.

After due course of internal debate, I called Dr. Hastings again. He told me to be sure to get a "post" when she died. He didn't say he wanted a postmortem because I would have a tendency not to get one—in order to cover my mistake—but we both knew it was there, the way two people meet at a funeral and speak as pleasantly to each other as though they were unaware of the reason for their presence, that unspoken thing.

Putting down the phone and feeling belittled in the same way I had felt every time I had spoken with the man since our special conversation, I returned to Maria's room, lifted the transparent sheet of the oxygen tent, and shined my penlight into her eyes: both pupils remained fully dilated and fixed in the manner of one who is dead in everything but body. Pupils could be like that. But not all pupils! Visit the learning curve of someone still in *training*, staring at the truth in the lesson before him, and one might come to the conclusion that, beneath their exhilarating veneer, normal pupils sustain the world and fixed pupils betray it.

*　　*　　*

The private room was as austere as a naked cockroach but large enough for a conference and I spent hours deciding who to invite to that conference. Hoist the White Curtain: showbiz! Hear the faint whispers of Love, and Love Always, and Love Forever and oh! the special ones—those like Davie Box*, who stuck his hand under a power lawnmower and came out with a spurting red nub for his right index finger and seemed so valiantly happy about it, how special it made him in sixth grade, glad if nothing else for the attention and the limited fame. Davie had received new socks for Christmas and informed me of this on a Sunday morning in church the following summer, when he added that he had worn them every day since then without once changing them or washing them and, to prove it, exhibited them to me. The stench was bad enough to draw the attention, finally, of the pastor, who stopped the sermon, and Davie having seen his renown grow proportionately did put his shoes back on and possibly put the socks in the wash a few weeks later.

This was a conference as bold as a dream and almost as wacky, and after it was over I remained with Maria in that same room, its shades drawn over the one window, room for one chair, me in it, and I did not stop for supper or do any of the after-supper tokens of the normal normality of the normal world. Indeed, I would have very little memory of the night, beyond the conference, because my needs were forgotten, the night given over to my beseeching Any Gods There—AGT—that this person must live. Evening passed into the time when one's consciousness is eclipsed by one's fatigue.

My clothes were no longer crisp; my mind negotiated with wrinkled thoughts. At least Maria's blood pressure, on gargantuan doses of Levophed, had risen a bit. She was still putting out volumes of urine through the catheter, that golden stream, which the nurses had tapped after she'd lost consciousness. The urine bag was a nether appendage of the bed. The nurse looked in on us now and again, like a chaperone, taking Maria's temperature, checking her vitals, checking attendance for her pupils. I grew drowsy and dreamed of racing to a class for which I was late, and as usual everyone was already there and knew exactly what was going on and I knew nothing. They jeered with shrieks of laughter at my predicament; they were almost finished with the most important examination of my life, and the professor asked me a question I could not answer, being only a pupil, and I shouted angrily at all of them, all of them, that if they were willing to give me enough time, I would find an answer. Answers had unleashed me from the bonds of northeast Texas, granting me the opportunity to make something of myself. *You'll go a long way.* To where?

Phone, pay the fifer. Someone imitating me pretended to care as much as I, my problem being not that I didn't care, but that I cared too much. Care too much and you will be severely punished. I returned to her room. Her pupils were still dilated and fixed. The room itself was dilated and fixed. No, the window was constricted, its shades drawn, and the single chair had a single occupant, a pupil—dilated and fixed. I was unimportant—*Please, AGT, she must live. Forgive me, my boss has misjudged me.*

She must live because I willed her to live. The hospital, my abode, was a microcosm not of life but of the forces that yank and stretch and jostle the human soul. It was the place where people did not go to die, but to plead for their lives. The dynamic beat you there, of course, and was set in stone, and yet at the same time it was malleable enough to accept you, under certain strictures, and they were these: "We are historical, we have our ways, and we will outlast you and outlive you. Do what you will, but it will not change what's unchangeable by you. Quite simply, we own you."

All night the nurse looked in on us, as if we were teenagers seated in Ruth Collins dormitory, Baylor University, on a Waco Saturday night, engaged in twentieth-century pre-pantyhose courtship. But I may have already said that. The fact of the matter was that everything in life related to everything else in life except, of course, life itself.

That the eight interns were an intimidated group was obvious. We were used to being beaten up by our professors, emotionally, socially, physically, and by way of the fisticuffs of overwork and exhaustion. They wore you out by wearing you down. Interns were imprisoned by their expectations, mauled by their desires, belittled by their gods. I was expected to suck up and kiss down and crawl upon my belly like a reptile. It was *training*, don't you see, *training*. Novices in patient care, *trainees* grow to expect the overall belittlement that no intern can escape, a bemused intolerance of the species by their betters, who did not mind exhibiting it by way of proving their superiority. It had been just as true in Galveston, at John Sealy Hospital, as it was at Memorial in this coastal resort city of South Texas, where we ranked below nurses, nurse anesthetists, orderlies, ambulance drivers, and probably gurneys. We were under doctors of doctors, dedicated to civilizing the doctored few. Doctoring a coercive discipline in the lineage of Hippocrates, anagram the rot and sniff the cod, trust in the cod-damn over the cod-damn cod rot! At home each intern had a wife and one or more children, but at the hospital, under scrutiny, we were the children, offspring of the doctoring impulse. Render these children drowsy. Let them make their vows and own up to a dream of racing to a class for which one was late and everyone else was already there … can one have the same dream already dreamed the same night, same nightmare? The professor asked me a question I could not answer, and I shouted out for time. Give me enough time, and all answers would be questioned, all statements unstated, leaving only the thing I dreaded most, which was no longer the dream but its solemn absence.

*   *   *

I bolted awake in the chair beside Maria's oxygen tent. It was Friday morning, July 19. The floor stayed beneath my feet. The window delivered a harsh, numbing light through its curtains. Maria stirred beneath the oxygen tent, slapped at its crinkly folds. I was paralyzed. She beckoned to me, mumbled something about the tube in her nose, pointed to it. I stood to my feet. Impossibly, she still recognized me, asked for a glass of water. She might have been any other hospital patient, awakening after a refreshing night of sleep instead of forty-eight hours of coma. I made sure and then raced away to tell the nurses, who rejoiced with me, an exhilarating thunderbolt piercing through Memorial Hospital: *Maria is awake! Maria is awake!*

It was like being reborn.

It was like nothing I had ever known.

I felt special, not because of myself but because of her! Too excited to stay, I called Mimi and told her the news, asked her to come get me, *Maria is awake!* As depressed as I had been, I was double that in happiness. Triple it! It was like entering another room in heaven, the highest level of ecstasy, eminence granted. It was happiness redundant and I relished every surplus second of it. I had not known it was possible to feel that good.

I had not known that level of happiness existed. Hadn't known that I could be rich beyond measure, own the world and everything in it, feel so good that I must stop and share it with everyone in this incredibly beautiful world, share with them the riches aplenty sent in answer to my prayers. Truly, my newfound nobility ennobled me. At home, I took a bath and had something to eat, gave Roger a hug and was driven back to the hospital. As soon as they left, I sprang atop the hospital and beat my chest in gilded paradise. *Maria is awake!* I wished to strike a bargain with God that would keep me always like this. I wished to trade my befuddled past for this perfection, this payback in scores and multiples for every hour of that sorry, ass-weary chemistry laboratory, cookbooking my way through the snarling afternoons, one after the other in mocking rebuke. Now I was a doctor and this proved it! If I'd had doubts, they were gone! If I'd had discouragement, it was past! I felt the certitude of when I had held the sheepskin in that very first instant and took the Hippocratic Oath on that stage in Galveston. It was my finest hour.

All day Friday the triumph continued, Maria awake and alert, having suffered only minor memory loss, being unable to remember anything after her son was born. Otherwise, she was fine. On neurological examination her pupils were no longer dilated. They were no longer fixed. They responded normally to light by constricting as they were supposed to do. My training had taught me that this was impossible. My heart had taught me to give it my all and I had. Maria's thin body, having been wracked with infection and the broiling inferno of fever, was, on Friday morning when I examined her, without a sign of disease. Her abdominal distention was gone. Her nausea, her vomiting—gone. Her appetite was back, and she was asking for her baby. She left the Critical list and so did I, and it was wonderful.

I went through the rest of the workday in a magnificence I felt I deserved. Mimi, having sampled cafeteria cuisine, preferred for us to eat at home, but I coaxed her to Memorial that evening with the idea of introducing her to Maria. We parked in one of the lots fed by Hospital Boulevard and, with Mimi tending Roger, entered the hospital through a side door between Postpartum and Med/Surg; in fact, we passed Maria's window, though I did not see her. The other interns in the cafeteria shared in the magic of her recovery, and one of our friends offered to keep Roger while Mimi and I slipped in to see Maria, but Mimi wouldn't. No amount of persuasion worked, and after supper we returned to the car and drove home. Somehow, inevitably, it seemed anticlimactic. Then I thought of Maria again and the elation returned, that meteor orbiting the heavens!

*　　*　　*

I knew, even then, that it got no better than that. The miracle of Maria's recovery was such that it changed my life. I had not prayed for it, believing as I did at the time that the silent gods were the most powerful of all, the ones who did not need reminding of this and that, of what is wanted to the exclusion of others. It was instead an awakening to what lies out there just beyond the possible. In subsequent years, many years subsequent, I could feel that same tenor of joy only through music, that skilled peddler of richly exalted dreams, transporting, as it did, one to the zeal of limitless boundaries. Roger, dear son Roger, died in 1989 of Lou Gehrig's disease, died just before his twenty-seventh birthday. He left no children. But he left his music, and what a gift that was! At his secular memorial we played the songs he loved, including John Denver's rendition of "Today." One hears in it, who listens closely, echoes of the majesty that blesses one in all parts and in all ways and for always. Rapture we humans may attain, it, but only temporarily. Gods don't take boarders.

But they do take music and, as people in church find their loved ones through the singing of hymns they used to sing together, I find Roger in "Today" and the other songs he left us on a tape we listened to after his death. He exists in the music! It opens up what wants opening, its alchemy changing sad longing into a rare extract almost too sweet to taste. Can you touch your soul? Can you vault through forever? Can you stretch apart your dreams and make room for many more? I did and discovered a part that only exists for dreamers and fools who are very lucky indeed.

*   *   *

Saturday I was again on call for ER but broke away to see Maria. Upon entering her room midmorning, I discovered a new person from the one I had admitted to the hospital on her seventeenth birthday. She was seated on the bed by the window, wearing a robe over her hospital pajamas, smiling at me like any other patient on the Obstetrics Ward.

To be sure, she had lost weight. A few mementos of her struggle were still evident, the details written on her forearms and hands, but beyond these, she was totally different. It was some other person who had become critically ill, it seemed to me, but this one had miraculously recovered, and it moved me to exultation, though I am being redundant. Permit it! It was the most profound experience of my life. Seeing her there on Saturday morning proved it, and I knew that she saw in my person the delicious morsels of joy bursting out—we fed each other. She cut the bondages of exile, releasing me. Words coined by others were too blooming laughable to apply. I laughed anyway, in joy, even as an angel stilled my voice, and I understood in the moment why we have gods, why we must trust in the beyond, why we must leap from the mundane to the exquisite on the sorry crutch of words, rather like reaching for manna from heaven and coming up with a lop-eared jackrabbit instead. Let it gnaw! Let it rise above the plains to snip at the gnats of the unwavering tedium, that distant façade. Gnomes tend rainbows, because they know what is on the other side. I had a peep, myself, and it was well worth it.

"Dr. Deaton," she said, "I saw you last night! I saw your wife, she is so beautiful! She is so beauty magazine! And your little boy? Oh, so cute! You lucky, you have the fine family, you have everything!"

It was too much. Make of me grateful, make of me humble before it. We reached and touched in the way of two people brimming with love and unable not to share it. Her person spoke to that, the brave bent of her shoulders in courage against the foes that would ravage the vulnerable. Her eyes shone, and brightly, as though a rare eminence had settled upon her and she was incapable of deflecting it. Playing in the band, one had to learn technique. That took practice, lots and lots of practice, until one became aware of a point finally reached where technique and tone stopped mattering and it was just about the music—not how to play it but how to enjoy it, how to rise to its miracles in a thrill of happiness. But it was not about me, I kept reminding myself; it was about her—and her son. I asked whether she had seen him again.

"Yes, my mother bring him see me, he is so big! I am so happy! Isn't it wonderful?"

She mentioned making arrangements for the baby while Duvelia was at work, and the subject of her anxiously awaited homecoming came up. I reassured her that she would go home as soon as it was feasible.

"But you!" Maria said again. "She is so beauty magazine, your wife, you have everything. And your little boy, so beautiful!"

It was easy, good as I felt, to give in to the happy notion that when you save someone, you are responsible for them forever. I had just learned why: you love them so much. Love them because they represent the best in you, a part of you that you discovered in them, a part that could not exist without them. What it was, she had given me the greatest honor one human can grant to another: redemption by responding not to what I was but to what I might become. Everything was secondary to that, though a good secondary. She admired me for doing what I had been trained to do, and I admired her for teaching me truth, staying my doubts. I sensed between us the trouncing of a winged predator that had threatened one of us. I sensed that we were sworn forever against that foe but, looming just there, this side of Mandalay, a tribute was due, and I began by offering a quiet thanks that our lives had intersected.

*   *   *

Maria Sylvia Mares was born July 12, 1946, at Spohn Hospital in Corpus, to Duvelia Gonzales Mares and Martin Mares. Her two older brothers were born in 1943 and 1944. To be the youngest child with two older brothers was, in her life, good. They were kind to her in a brotherly way, and if not, they had to answer to Duvelia, five feet tall and eighty-five pounds of concentrated womanhood. In 1949, when Maria was three, her mother and Martin Mares were divorced, the problem being a woman that Duvelia accused of "breaking up our marriage."

Duvelia had a good job working as a secretary, but raising three young children as a single mother was difficult. Through friends she met Jose de La Torre, who worked at a local zinc plant in Corpus. They were together for a year or two and on January 15, 1953, were married. The family of five moved into a house northwest of Memorial Hospital, on Hidalgo Street, one of the wooden two-bedroom homes, most of them painted white to protect from the heat. There were also shade trees, sidewalks, and two concrete strips leading to a detached garage that was almost never used as such. The yards were set off by a chain-link fence, cars parked in front or in the driveway. It was a lived-in neighborhood of people who knew one another. They knew the days of the workweek, Monday to Saturday, but Sunday was good. It began formally, with attendance at Mass, but afterward there were ballgames on TV, visits to relatives, a time for the family to eat out. Time to talk with neighbors and friends, then Monday again and the week repeated itself, the days dragging, the years flying.

In 1954, Rosie de La Torre was born. As Maria was eight years older than the baby, she delighted in doing for her half-sister and became Rosie's second mother. To Rosie, Maria was the most important person in her life: "She was a part of me." Rosie loved and trusted her older sister, depended on her. It was Maria, when Rosie was old enough, who got her off to school and picked her up afterward, Maria's schedule permitting. Through the years, despite their age differences, the two became dear friends. They shared secrets, spending hours giggling about things that were funny to them, boys, and boys, and boys. They watched TV together, did the housework while listening to songs on the radio, tried out dance steps, cut ads from magazines, and with a new catalog tore through it in excitement, becoming fascinated by it. They loved pretending how exquisite it would be to own this or that, to live a life of luxury and have others work for them, rather than the opposite.

Maria attended Stephen F. Austin Elementary, Ella Barnes Junior High, and Roy Miller High School, all in Corpus. She was a good student, pleasant and well behaved, but formal education was not important to her in the sense of her wanting to become a professional with a career. That was fine for many people. But there were other worthy things to do, exciting things to do, so much that life had to offer. Maria loved discussing these things with Rosie, who learned from Maria how to do her hair and nails, to sew and cook and clean the house.

The cultural tradition among many of the young Mexican American women they knew was to marry early, soon after their *quinceañera*, a traditional and joyous coming-out party for a girl coinciding with her fifteenth birthday—and besides, Maria had fallen in love.

Luis Chavarria grew up in the same neighborhood as Maria, a couple of blocks away, and they had attended the same schools. Maria saw him every day. He was older and did not know she existed, at least like that, but the world has its ways. If she went out in the evening, just to get a Coke, he was there too. (Do kids ever really go out for just a Coke?) It turned out that he did know her, had noticed her. But that was not all.

Teenagers formed groups, then as now, and Luis was with that same group of joking guys that flirted with Maria's group. As it happened, perhaps, the boys were in one car, the girls the other. Then the crowds thinned, and so the cars, and eventually it was just Maria and Luis, the one she had thought all along was the cutest. He was not a "clunk head" like the boys in her own class. He was three years older, an eternity! He was charming. He had money. He knew how to be nice to a girl, knew how to treat a young woman with the respect she deserved. He bought her things and protected her, and when she was with him he was the handsomest and bravest man she had ever known. Luis swept her away.

He was eighteen at the time of their marriage in August of 1961. Married, Maria quit high school to become a homemaker, and she and Luis moved into a small apartment close to Duvelia and Jose. Luis continued working for a furniture company and Maria made a home for them, but from the start, all was not bliss.

Maria did not get along well with her in-laws because they weren't nice to her. This was hardly a new event in family matters, but there may have been something extra in the mix for Maria. The elder Luis Chavarria had been in the merchant marines and was a large man with a scowling face and a contentious, contemptuous manner. His wife, Lupita, cleaned rooms in a local motel. Perhaps their new daughter-in-law was not good enough for their Luisito.

Both of the elder Chavarrias were abusive. Maria, physically small and not in the least threatening, was the kind of person that bullies might be inclined to pick on. Maybe the elder Chavarrias faulted her for reasons of their own. According to Duvelia, Lupita began saying bad things about her daughter-in-law, things that reached Maria and had the expected hurtful effect on a young woman who was roundly loved by everyone else. It hurt in a special way, this betrayal, because it was so cruel and intentional. There was more. Luis the elder and Lupita had fights. They had real fights. And they resented a daughter-in-law who knew nothing of that and wanted only to get along.

Maria's husband also became abusive to Maria after they were married, because that is the way it may happen, and when he hit her or beat her up, she would phone and talk to Rosie. The two would cry in commiseration, one in emotional and physical pain, the other out of her deep love for a person who had always been there for her.

As the first to hear about the abuse, Rosie tried to console Maria. But Rosie also told Duvelia, even though Maria had sworn her to secrecy, and Duvelia was not one to remain impassive. Duvelia La Torre vented her anger on her son-in-law and he knew why. He knew. An abused person never wants it out, from embarrassment or from the threat that it will become worse if they tell, or out of the victim's natural feelings that knowledge of the abuse will lessen the opinion others hold of them. At any rate Maria still loved Luis, and even though he "did to her," she knew that when he wasn't drinking it almost never occurred, and in those times he could still be the same sweet, considerate man she had married. Perhaps a baby would make it better. But a man who is worried about money and how they are going to support a baby is not always a happy man. And a man tied to a wife and an approaching baby may begin to wonder whether he has given up too much of his freedom.

*   *   *

Despite these developments, Maria went into pregnancy with the innocent joy of expectant motherhood. She loved to dress up and go downtown, to Corpus Christi's "uptown." She looked forward to having her own baby and carrying him to town on her shoulder. She anticipated taking her place among the other smart young women parading their new children. She had intended to name her baby after her husband, but she tentatively changed her mind because of his parents.

During Maria's pregnancy, Luis began staying out late, very late. His trouble with the law, Maria and Duvelia contended, could be explained by him getting in with the wrong crowd (another thing that is not new). Eventually it led to a charge of breaking and entering. Arrested, he was found guilty and jailed in the spring of 1963.

Duvelia drove to Maria's apartment that same day. "You can't be here by yourself," she said. "You have this date for a baby; you must live with us." Maria gladly obliged, and in May of 1963 mother and daughter were together again in the same house.

On July 11, 1963, as soon as Duvelia got home from work as a secretary to a local judge, she, Maria, and Rosie immediately began getting ready to attend, in Mathis, the birthday party of Duvelia's nephew and Maria's cousin. The three had been wishing for something to do together all summer. It had been so hot and tiresome. Maria felt cooped up by her pregnancy and was depressed that her husband was in jail. The thought of going to a party had not at first appealed to her when they were invited a couple of weeks prior, but after all it was something to look forward to, first to shop for a present and then a nice time to be had by all, and it could count as a day-early celebration of her own looming birthday. She had finally agreed with some enthusiasm to go with her mother and sister to the party. It was a chance to show off how pregnant she was and maybe even to bring on the labor she was gladly awaiting.

The three had a snack of bananas and ice cream while they finished dressing. Maria lifted herself from the table and without saying anything went into the bathroom. She had been somewhat constipated, a frequent finding late in pregnancy, and felt the need to have a bowel movement. But she didn't. When she came back, she stood in the doorway.

Duvelia and Rosie noted the odd expression on her face.

"My stomach hurts," Maria said, and she slipped into her room.

Duvelia, thinking immediately of labor, followed her into the room and told her to lie down on the bed until it was time to leave—since Maria was already dressed—and Maria of course complied. Hers was a queasy feeling, a slight nausea, but she did not vomit. After a few minutes, Duvelia went to check on her, and Maria said that her pain was a steady discomfort around her belly button. She had no pain in the back? None. Duvelia then asked whether she had eaten anything else. Yes, some meat in the refrigerator a few minutes before Duvelia had gotten home. Anything else? No. Except, Maria had been chewing a stick of gum, which she now gave to Duvelia to discard. A quarter of an hour later Maria felt better, and the three of them started the trip to Mathis in Duvelia's car.

Mathis, a small city located in the northeast corner of Nueces County, is about twenty miles north of Corpus on the main highway to San Antonio. Traffic was heavy, the afternoon traffic rush not having completely abated.

Duvelia kept glancing at her watch. They were going to be late, but perhaps not too late to make the trip worthwhile. Then, and before they were all of the way out of Corpus, Maria felt the onset of something very like pain, except it wasn't pain so much as it was … but it *was* pain. It was pain and again that feeling of nausea, and when Duvelia found a gas station where she could pull over, Maria opened the passenger door and began vomiting. Then she wanted to continue to the birthday party. Duvelia, the engine still running for the air-conditioning, thought it over. It was well past six o'clock.

When Maria soon vomited again, greenish material, Duvelia made a decision. She had several relatives in Corpus and drove nine-year-old Rosie to her aunt's house, having to stop several times along the way for Maria to be sick.

Maria apologized. She wanted, she said, to go home and rest.

Duvelia turned instead in the direction of Memorial Hospital.

*   *   *

While in Maria's room Saturday morning, July 20, I examined her again, pronounced her normal, and discontinued her nasogastric tube. I put her on a clear liquid diet and answered her question, already stated, that she should be able to go home in a few days. Back at the nurses' station I wrote an explanatory note on her chart to the effect that she had recovered from septic shock. On the order sheet, I stopped the more toxic of the antibiotics, tapered the dosages of the others, and removed her from the Critical list.

I returned to the ER and found that I could not stop thinking about Maria Chavarria and her miraculous recovery. George Trader, the hospital administrator, sought me out to say that people were praising me, that I was going to be a wonderful doctor. Much as I liked hearing it, I knew Kipling's caution to the unwary, to treat those two imposters—triumph and disaster— just the same. But maybe, just a little bit, I forgot this on that good day.

*   *   *

That afternoon I debated whether to tell Dr. Hastings about Maria's recovery. Our last conversation had had him stressing the need to get an autopsy when she died. Not if, *when*. Well, guess what? Ultimately I did not call him, losing myself instead in the bustle of the ER.

*   *   *

Sunday morning, Mimi, Roger, and I were getting ready for church when the phone rang. Next thing Sam Hastings was bawling me out for pulling Maria's nasogastric tube. He informed me that when someone else orders a nasogastric tube—a surgeon, in this case—one does not pull it without the professional etiquette of calling the consulting doctor first and asking permission to remove it. I did not know this and was yelled at, my flawed life divvied up and flung to the fiery depths of hell. First opportunity, I asked why it mattered.

"Because they couldn't get hold of you and she's vomiting again!"

Now I was stricken. I had no idea why they couldn't reach me, unless it was because I had left the phone off the hook for an hour or so to take a nap after returning from duty in ER. I assured the attending that I would see Maria immediately. I changed back into my monkey suit and had Mimi drop me off at the hospital before she and Roger continued on to Sunday school. All the while the crippling insurmountable made its way again and again through my mind. *What could have happened to her?*

We passed other people on their way to church, radiantly happy in that tranquil paradise that I would never again know, having fallen so far since yesterday. But I did not hate them. I envied them while directing my hatred at myself, the bungling Neanderthal paying the penalty for creation. Mimi was nice. She understood. We made plans to have lunch at the hospital and, as I watched the others disappear into the distance, I jostled through my dreams seeking that mislaid pedestal.

It was as Dr. Hastings had said. Maria was vomiting again. Overnight, her abdominal distention had returned to the size of a term pregnancy. She had looked so well, completely recovered. Standing in her room and watching her, my humiliation gave rise to a more powerful and sickening emotion, that of fright. In Dr. Hastings's voice I had detected a growl of nastiness new to our relationship—a savage nastiness that hadn't been there before, even when the man had accused me of rupturing Maria's uterus. It was the nastiness of the blade slicing into the gristle, burrowing its way into the bone and the sepsis at its core.

On examination, I found Maria had the high-pitched bowel sounds of intestinal obstruction. I ordered another X-ray of the abdomen, and this time there was no doubt. The radiologist came out that afternoon, compared new films with old, and diagnosed her with intestinal obstruction. Not only that. Maria, he warned, had a high-grade mechanical obstruction of the small intestine. The peril was inherent. Loops of small intestine were dilated to five or six inches wide (several times normal). It meant that perforation was imminent, from which emerged two thoughts. The first was that she had already had a perforation, manifested in that infected amniotic fluid and subsequently in the coma and septic shock from which she had recovered. The second related to the surgical report on Maria's chart, which I suddenly remembered.

With all of the things pulling at me, I had neglected to read it, and for the first time I learned that although he had removed her inflamed appendix, Dr. Hector Garcia had also discovered and *not* removed from seven-year-old Maria a Meckel's diverticulum. This was a rare developmental remnant consisting of a short cord connecting the underside of the navel to a point on the small intestine. It wasn't rare for those who had it. I phoned the radiologist, who had just reached home. In desperation I asked whether a Meckel's could trap and pinch off a loop of small intestine, causing intestinal obstruction.

"Hell yes! Get her to surgery immediately!"

*   *   *

The intern on surgery, my friend Dr. Ramiro Peña, lived next to the hospital in rooms provided by Memorial to four or five interns and their families. He arrived five minutes after being called. Together we looked at the X-rays and examined Maria, both of us noting the same high *pings* that I had heard that evening I first examined her. Now that the diagnosis was made, the sounds were much clearer and more obviously symptoms of intestinal obstruction than could ever have been the case when they were merely the auscultatory findings of a raw intern on a patient at term pregnancy, who had been admitted to the hospital for vomiting and abdominal pain, which happened to be the unflinching antics of intestinal obstruction.

Within a few minutes of arriving at the hospital, Ramiro transferred Maria to the Surgery Service. All it required was for him to write it on the order sheet above his signature. In the instant, she became Surgery's responsibility.

But it was not as simple as that.

In the sobering interlude of pushing Maria down the corridor to Med/Surg, a group of nurses and orderlies helping us with the unwieldy iron bed, I experienced a strange flash of regret. I was like a man who had sold something to another without realizing that it contained too much of himself to let it go. I had just surrendered my right to be her doctor. Maria, at this most crucial point in her hospitalization, was no longer my patient. Something between jealousy and a strange sense of foreboding overtook me. But the diagnosis was finally made! It was what I had wanted for her! She would be cured and released from the hospital! My sense of relief returned. It was how things worked. Everything would be fine.

*   *   *

The entrance to the Med/Surg Ward was just across from the spacious, lighted thoroughfare to OR. The reason for the foyer resided in the group of idle gurney stretchers parked on that side of the corridor—not them so much as room to permit one to guide them from the hallway into the suite containing the several operating rooms. Entering Med/Surg, we lost the light. It was like going into a sickroom.

We pushed Maria's bed around to a private room behind the nurses' station.

People made sure she was okay and then the crowd dispersed. No one seemed to want anything of me. I watched the nurses leave to attend to their own protocol of papers to sign, summaries to give, medications to record, and I followed and hovered nearby in case they needed me. But they didn't. I returned to Maria's room, but Ramiro was doing an admitting history and physical examination, and they were speaking in Spanish. I wanted more, a ceremony. I wanted deference, even praise: *Wow! You did a hell of a job, and now we will all work together to get Maria into the best shape possible for her immediate surgery!* I wished them fawning over her and also myself. I felt as if they owed me that.

Instead, unnoticed on an idle Sunday afternoon, I turned away and moved restlessly through the ward, a ward darkened by the need to protect the many window air-conditioners that provided a cooling that wasn't present on any other ward. The number of beds was the same as for OB, two rows horizontal to my vertical, patients who may as well have been lifeless attachments to a beleaguered reality, cadavers living a dream for all I cared, which was a horrible thought. How could I be a doctor and not care the same for every patient? But I didn't. I had indicted Hastings for the same detachment, but at least the attending had been honest enough to admit it. What a profound shock to understand that if I felt that way about patients on Med/Surg, what was to keep those on Med/Surg from feeling that way about patients transferred from OB?

An elemental veracity articulated itself to me, bristling like an aroused snake. Equality of care for all patients by all curtain-hangers was a dream seen through a pinhole. It was an ideal. In reality it was more often a fabrication, a window display, the bait and switch of the fraudulent reality that was as flat as a mortarboard and as fanciful as an effacing coquette. Behind the White Curtain, decorum to the contrary, nurses and medics were mortals, mere mortals. Did responsibility to his patient mean a selfishness akin to ownership on the part of the physician? It did. It belonged to the doctor on a patient-by-patient basis in the same way that a person's doctors related to them on a doctor-by-doctor basis. It didn't mean you liked the patients who were your patients any better than you liked the patients who were not your patients, except that was exactly what it meant. It had to exist that way for the system to work.

Responsibility is ownership. Doctors constantly ask about this very thing. *"Is this your patient or my patient? Will you accept this patient or should I call someone else? She is on your service and therefore your patient, isn't she?"*

As for Med/Surg, I was on the other team. I had not worked these patients up, as making a diagnosis was called. I hadn't delivered their babies, scrubbed in on their surgery, made daily rounds on them, sat up with them through the night. I did not *know* them. And they did not know me. I felt toward them none of the responsibility I had for Maria. Yes, responsibility is made of elastic and can be stretched without breaking—a patient at a time. Fitted into the pattern of other doctors doing the same, it worked, didn't it?

*　　*　　*

Still on that strange ward, I found myself back at the nurses' station. No one so much as looked at me. Then I saw another reason. Had I gotten along with nurses on OB? I had not. Did word get around? It did. Could I ever get along with nurses? Doubtful.

One of the outgoing interns had suggested I not take any shit off of nurses. "They hate my guts," he had said proudly, smiling with satisfaction, "but they take good care of my patients." I pictured old Ed Bayouth at the Nu Sigma Nu house in Galveston, wearing his smock around the game room with the flap down to reveal his hairy chest, a man with a natural charisma and an instant likeability, that flap down like Ben Casey's to billboard the notion that he was no more than 75 to 80 percent involved in the current bullshit, whatever it happened to be. To hear him say that about nurses had, at the time, seemed exactly right, the fraternal order of doctors having as their first duty to kick nurses' butts. One gripped the concept of absolute dominion over Florence Nightingale. Rub it in. Make the nurses hate you and they will love your patients all the more. On reflection it sounded like horseshit and undoubtedly was, all apologies to Ed, who was nothing if not a good and caring doctor, RIP.

One good thing about the transfer, however, was Ramiro himself, an admirable man. Though he never spoke of it, Ramiro Peña had graduated from the Southwestern Baptist Theological Seminary in Fort Worth before attending medical school. Three years older than Maria's previous doctor, Dr. Ramiro Peña was both a physician and an ordained Baptist minister. He was a kind man, tall and graceful, and one rooting for Maria could only be happy for her sake that he was now in charge.

After Dr. Peña returned to the nurses' station to write orders on the chart, I found Maria alone in her room and stepped in for a visit.

"Are you still see me while I am here?" she asked before I could speak.

I couldn't help noticing that her voice betrayed the excitement she felt at finally having her problem diagnosed. In the two and a half weeks of her illness, it was a first, and I shared that happiness with her.

"Of course I'll still see you," I said, "but you're going to be well! Everything will be fine. You'll see. They'll operate on you and you'll be as good as new."

*   *   *

When I called him about Maria's diagnosis and transfer, Dr. Hastings apologized for accusing me of perforating her womb. It was nice of him and totally unexpected by me, and instantly our friendship returned to what it had been before. Or at least I hoped so. I was sufficiently impressed with his skills that, when Mimi became pregnant, I asked him to follow her through her second pregnancy, which began later that year, and the obstetrician delivered Mimi of Stephen Craig Deaton on June 23, 1964. That birth occurred in the middle of the night, and there was never a mention of charging a penny for it. I thought then and would always think of Dr. Hastings as a superior obstetrician. In our conversation about Maria that evening, we shared the relief of doctors who, having been baffled, are able to look back and understand a patient's illness. What mattered most, of course, was that Maria was going to have the surgery she needed; we ended our conversation on that positive note.

Before I left the ward I asked Ramiro when they would do surgery, and he said something I found troubling. He sometimes had trouble, he said, getting the staff surgeon, Dr. Carl Broderick*, to come out to Memorial and help him with his surgical patients.

But Maria was critically ill, and surgical intervention was necessary to cure her, and any surgeon would recognize that. Proximal to the obstruction, her small intestine was distended like a balloon, its walls strained to the absolute bursting point. Balloons pop, and so do intestines—and hers already had, once, and that put us in a race against time to save her life. I had expected them to call people out and perform the surgery that same Sunday evening, July 21. As a corollary, neither Ramiro nor I was competent to do abdominal surgery. By hospital rules, we were not permitted to take a patient to OR. It would have to be done by the surgeon rotating on the Surgery Service, the same Dr. Carl Broderick. Ramiro, before calling him, promised that if they didn't do the surgery that evening, they would most certainly do it first thing Monday morning. I thought that even that much of a delay was risking her life.

*   *   *

Busy with deliveries and rounds, I did not reach the Med/Surg Ward until Monday at noon, and I was shocked by what I found. Maria was not postoperative. She was in the same room we had transferred her to, and the only change was that her nasogastric tube was gone and in its place was something called a Miller-Abbott tube, a brown tubing snaking around and around in loops almost a foot high on her bedside table. The advancing end of it was in her nose, the enormous diameter of the thing seeming to make that impossible. It was as though somebody had swiped the air hoses from several gas stations and spliced them together end-to-end in an attempt to see if they might fit the human intestinal tract. I had never even heard of the device, much less seen it in use or read about it as an assignment in medical school.

I found Ramiro and asked what had happened.

"Dr. Broderick likes to see whether a Miller-Abbott tube will decompress an obstruction," he said, and left it at that.

"Did he see her X-rays? How serious it is?"

He nodded and swallowed. "I think he knows what he's doing. He said he'd give it forty-eight hours."

"Operate Wednesday? What if she perforates?"

"He doesn't think she will."

My anger was immediate and blinding, as if I had just been slapped in the face by a stranger. The outrage wasn't directed at Ramiro, who had no more control over his Dr. Broderick than I had over my staff man. It was anger on behalf of Maria, anger that quickly turned to fright. The radiologist called the obstruction an emergency on Sunday, surgery lifesaving. I had already spent a night beside her bed while she recovered from a perforation of the intestine the previous week. That had healed, but would another? Not likely. And by the way, why become a surgeon if you don't plan to use that career to its intended purpose? That the Miller-Abbott tube was supposed to decompress the alimentary tract meant that it was a holdover from the time before anesthesia and antibiotics made surgery a relatively safe procedure. Why go back to horse-and-buggy medicine in a modern hospital? Why use it at all in a patient obstructed by a Meckel's diverticulum? I simply didn't get it.

The Surgery Service at John Sealy Hospital during my time as a student had been the worst department in the medical school. Even so, the surgeons at least knew how and when to operate. My image had been of excited UTMB surgical residents surrounding Maria's bed and hurrying her down the hallway to OR, the bed itself a wedge that jarringly knocked open the swinging double doors leading into the operating suite on the second floor of John Sealy. By contrast, the absence of residents at Memorial Hospital was suddenly no longer so attractive as it had seemed. Sure, we got to "do a lot," but I hadn't counted on having to stand by like a knickknack while a patient died of malpractice. Was the surgeon aware? Was he aware of the unforgiving nature of an intestinal obstruction? I was the student, I was the intern, I was in *training*, yet I knew that if he didn't operate and operate quickly, Maria would die.

Then something else began niggling at me. Was it the matter of a surgeon's fee? Of course Dr. Broderick would not be paid for her surgery, but it was a teaching hospital where pro bono work was pro forma, the quid pro quo of being on the staff of the hospital and using its facilities. Surely it wasn't something as obvious as that.

When I spoke to Maria, I felt like a liar.

I was a liar. I had promised they were going to operate on her and cure her of the intestinal obstruction. But one can't make that assumption, I was learning, when the action requires the cooperation of another human being, even a doctor. No doubt the surgeon considered me a rank amateur, a brainless nonentity. I had removed Maria's nasogastric tube on Saturday, thinking her well, and been bawled out for same. Maybe a Miller-Abbott tube was exactly what should be done for her. It was just possible, I decided, that I was totally wrong and overreacting. On my part, I merged into the part of the White Curtain that is always opaque to the patient, and not very pretty at all.

The critical eye, its bearing, merges to sightless. A chameleon appears; *they* become *we*. It amounted to cowardice, but—no! It amounted to common sense. It amounted to good sense. We had been taught that it is a big part of being a doctor not to disagree openly in front of a patient and especially not to badmouth another doctor in front of a patient. It was also plain courtesy by a gentleman, should I grow wings and glide.

Lying in shame, I told Maria that the new tube was to get her ready for surgery and might even relieve the obstruction without the need for surgery. She didn't believe me, of course. By now, we could read each other's thoughts. But she didn't protest. In the nurses' station I pulled her chart and read Carl Broderick's short, noncommittal note. I had written long, detailed notes about her when she was on Obstetrics. Again, none of the nurses paid any attention to me. Why should a gourd care who uses it for a dipper? Maria's surgery, her lifesaving surgery, would take no more than an hour or so to perform.

*　　*　　*

I continued to see Rosa Ramos every day. That fungating cancer of hers had begun prolapsing when she used the bedpan, which accentuated the problem in certain ways that did not improve the smell in her room. Thenceforth I required gloves and gown to attend to her and it, and replacing it to its previous position came to resemble the exact opposite of removing a fecal impaction, the world's largest, though in fact I was able to wipe it as clean as the sheets would allow before its reinsertion. And she was always grateful.

But one day I got in trouble. For some reason I dropped gloves and gown on the floor of the corridor outside the door to her room, and someone from Housekeeping looked me up to complain. It was the stench! And complaints about same! I hadn't understood until then, in my total ignorance, that even Housekeeping employees were permitted to yell at me. So I listened. One does not introduce stench into that dark channel. Stench, people needed to understand, is not shared with others; stench is no more implicit than it is exquisite, and by confining it one will obviate the need to castigate the violator's genitals by way of punishment, this being perfectly obvious to anyone not suffering under the afflictions of cerebral anemia. On a worldwide scale, my deed was commensurate with the grisly appalling. Then the person softened. Merely this: "Stop what you are doing, forget you are in a hurry, and find a phone and call Housekeeping! Do not mess up our good hospital! Okay? Those of us who work here to provide your training are deserving of your respect. Do not squander your rite of passage."

*   *   *

Duvelia was busy with Maria's baby, with her other children, and with keeping her job at the judge's office. She could only visit Maria evenings and came out Monday night to discover that her daughter had still not been taken to surgery.

"Why don't they operate me?" Maria asked her.

*   *   *

It was in my mind that they would go ahead with surgery on Tuesday. Midmorning I found my way to Med/Surg, its environs still darkened except—no! The surgeon, though not in scrubs, was making rounds and had opened the tapestry sufficiently that a single beam of light followed him around.

First I looked in on Maria, peeked at her chart. Dr. Broderick had ordered the Miller-Abbott tube advanced more rapidly than the day before. (It had been almost forty-eight hours since emergency surgery was hoped for.) Beyond that, nothing had changed.

I was undecided whether to challenge him or to sulk away in anonymity. But Doctor did not know or notice me as I fell into line behind the retinue of fawning nurses, worship being Doctor's due, and by this I mean those real, have-been-initiated, out-of-training Doctors we all admired. A current of excitement crackled from him as from static electricity, everyone wishing to plug into that magnetism, and I admitted it: I, too, was sucked into the unguent, the noble balm. I wanted Doctor to like me, was fearful lest Doctor look upon me with other than pleasure. Power being entwined with it, it instilled a certain dread. It was as though, having seen the worst, Doctor could look straight through you and know you were dying and yet simultaneously, at his discretion, commute your sentence to life on Earth. Doctor made sycophants of all of us.

What was Doctor? Perhaps he was a reflection of others, a mirror of society—no stranger to human frailty, no stranger to deceit, passion, lust, greed, and prejudice. Perhaps Doctor was a prisoner of his time. If it was loose, so was he. If it was stringent, Doctor was that most of all. If it was a time of sense, Doctor was sensible, and if a time of humility, Doctor was humble. In a time of fervor, Doctor was fervent, and in a time of hatred, Doctor was adversarial. If the times were troubled, Doctor felt the trouble but did not necessarily return it. The only given about Doctor was his position at the exact center of the hagiography of healing, the sanctum sanctorum, the swiveling scimitar. As such, he moved gracefully through time, confident as one walking property that had been in his family forever.

His suit and his tie stood out in bold contrast to the white uniforms of interns and nurses. One recognized and admired the attaining of that status that required no iconic reminder of its limitations. Yet he was not without the apparel befitting his attire, that coiled covenant. I wore mine in the back pocket of my white pants, a Littman's stethoscope, small and blue and offering a fresh dynamic. Doctor's was different. It was glorious. It bulged out the side pocket of his suit coat, as noticeably unobtrusive as the sidearm of a lawman. His was larger than that, a loose confederacy of thick, dark tubing and silver fixtures gleaming like flashy coins to the ostentatious effect of silver rattling in a gentleman's pockets right out of Dickens, or of a shiny timepiece in a nineteenth-century watch pocket, its gleaming fob suitably expensive and worn smooth from use, an heirloom imparting by its elegance that here was something that had been passed down again and again, conferring upon its possessor all of the rights and privileges appertaining thereunto, such rights and privileges appertaining thereunto far greater than could be easily enumerated but encompassing at the very minimum certain secrets and accords as would suitably guide his hand in the great things that he did. The apparatus was his vindication that no matter his actions, they were for the good of all.

It was his gear, his talisman, his sustenance, and for a profession steeped in icons and a tendency to worship its forbearers as well as itself, it was the best of the best, granting unto him the enthralling canon of absolute power, the moxie and the clout and the distinction—the Father, the Son, and the Holy Ghost—of a doxology amounting to hymn praised, his worshipful call to whip into shape the access of the human race. Yet he was fashioned as neither Unitarian nor Trinity. Instead, he was the paradox between the ideal and its reality. He was the pilgrim strutting across the relief map of human geography. If worship is the vindication of hope, sickness is the daredevil of imperfection, and he razed devils aplenty. *Hallelujah!* His White Curtain, mopped clean daily, went into your throat like wadded gauze, capable of asphyxiating you in a pagan ritual so highly regarded and desperately sought that it commanded you to yield, and yield you did, its endpoint occurring only when you were dead or Doctor was, and then we had the incontrovertible doctor–patient relationship. (Take another bite.) Seek the high ground. Side with rifts unnoticed, subjects unseen, truths unsaid, plights unnerving. Doctor was ordained in the fictive church of life, a patient at a time, communion forthcoming after they passed the plate, but only to those who adhered to Doctor's conjured ideal. Was the investiture renewable or absolute? Probably neither, but what was any of it except the silly nonsense of a young doctor still in training, which by definition means to teach so as to make fit? And to make fit, of course, means to adhere to decorum, this being Doctor's annoying but ultimately supreme source of power.

*   *   *

Maria did not have surgery on Wednesday.

By then the piles of the Miller-Abbott tube had turned into a brown python coiling itself around her body, strangling her with her every breath. She was frightened.

"Dr. Deaton, why don't they operate me?"

I loved the way she said my name, as I loved her. In the almost three weeks since she was admitted, she had become an obsession with me. She had come to me for help, but I was the one who truly needed help, and she had given it to me by awarding me her life. I loved her as one loves a person with a shared past. We had, as doctor and patient, a history. It was of two humans searching for affirmation and finding it in a kindred spirit. She was seventeen and I was three and twenty, and we flirted innocently in Poe's kingdom by the sea, loving with a love that was greater than love because it was how two humans should be. Especially a doctor and a patient. Earlier, a few years ago, there had been light moments between us. One was when she had seen me pass her room that Friday evening after she had regained consciousness. There were other times as well, earlier than that. *West Side Story* had come out a year or two before, starring Natalie Wood as Maria, the modern-day Juliet, and I had sung the bars of the person dubbing Natalie's "I Feel Pretty" to Maria, who had not seen the movie but had heard of it. Sick as she was, Maria had smiled. I had thought to cheer her up by rewarding her with a taste of the outside world she would soon rejoin.

Besides Duvelia, whom I knew pretty well by now, the rest of Maria's family came in the evenings, including her stepfather, Jose de La Torre. The entire Chavarria family visited, were there every evening. Walk the corridors of a hospital and you will see them. They are still there, these people to whom family is so very important. They have not been blessed by education or elevated by money or made precious by society. They are out of their element and know it. Yet they come because one of them is sick, they wait outside the room because they feel awkward and in the way, and they do not speak, except for some of the women. They hold their hats in their hands and keep their thoughts to themselves.

*   *   *

Maria had no surgery on Thursday. Her surgeon in waiting, Carleton C. Broderick—"Dr. Carl" to those who knew and loved him—had impeccable credentials. He was on the surgical staffs of Spohn Hospital, Driscoll Children's Hospital, and Memorial Hospital. He was a part of the American Medical Association and had some years before met the criteria and passed the rigorous evaluations required for board-certification in General Surgery, making him eligible for what in fact had occurred: he was a Fellow of the American College of Surgeons. As to age, he was in his prime that summer of 1963. From all appearances, Maria was fortunate that he was the attending surgeon rotating at Memorial that July and August, as he was an exemplar of all that a skilled surgeon should be. He occupied that high office wherein specialists supervise trainees and set the example that they should follow.

*   *   *

Maria had no surgery on Friday.

I tore into Ramiro, but in fairness the guy was already in agony and said that he would insist they do the operation. Maria, upon seeing me that afternoon, asked her question—*Why don't they operate me?*—and I told her for the first time that I didn't know and that I was very sorry they hadn't. What I did not tell her, could not tell her, was that the deep knot of fear in my belly that had begun on Sunday had not only never gone away, it had grown bigger each day. I desperately hoped she still had a chance to have surgery, but when I spoke to her about it, what I said was not believable even to me. I experienced in myself a repugnance that sickened me to my fraudulent soul.

I did not know what to do. I examined her because it was the only thing I could do. Her distention was much worse. She looked worse, much weaker than when she had been transferred. She looked as bad as she had before lapsing into a coma after her baby was born. Did she know? Yes, but she was not self-pitying. She never spoke in any voice but that of courtesy. She never asked anything for herself except the obvious. All she wanted was a question answered that she had been asking for six days, almost as long as it took God for the Creation: *Why don't they operate me?*

It was a question demanding an answer. An answer I demanded of myself. Leaving her bedside, I threw myself at the nurses' station intent on kicking ass, brazen as I thought I should be. Three nurses were on duty there, justifying their existence.

And I was a coward and knew it.

I had been an intern for a month. I did not know it, but my license to practice medicine in the state would not even be issued to me until August 18, a day before I turned twenty-four. The women did not look up, the nurses, much less notice me. A charge nurse, a medications nurse, and a nurse to supervise the various treatments required by the thirty patients on the ward went on about their business. Ordinarily the nurses would either rise as a show of respect to the doctor or they would look up and engage themselves in helping to serve the doctor's needs. Maria was not my patient, and no matter what, they ignored me. Then, in one crushing instant, I understood why. It was the most devastating thing of all.

*   *   *

You think your own experience is exclusive, but it isn't. The perfunctory greeting of two people, one by the other, consists of sleepwalking past the other's pain and despair, their hidden commitment to courage of the most basic kind: the bravado to go on living even among killers who call themselves healers. The nurses were angry because they knew. And nurses know a hell of a lot.

Afflicted with the same emotion as an intern, they deflected it through anger, the very anger I felt bristling from them, an anger I shared. They were fawning to those in power out of fear of losing their jobs. Upon that investment: this dividend. People are smarter than we think, more knowledgeable than we give them credit for, and much closer one to the other than we can possibly grasp. I stood in the nurses' station as though seeing it for the first time because that was the case.

All around me, the mundane maneuvers in the care of the sick. The care that is never enough. Somewhere a potty flushed, a gurney squealed, a door banged shut. Syncopated foot traffic shuffled by in its oh-so-harmonious way upon that causeway to hell. The nurses' station greeted and processed it. The nurses' station was the heartbeat of every ward and the patients its pulse. It was called a station because it was not a complete room closed off to others. Instead, it was an open office for nurses and such hospital employees as had business there. It was usually painted white, and the floor was tiled in the same professional manner as the rest of the ward. Sometimes it was less than pristine, and in the overhead fluorescent light I sighted an errant something that had been dropped to the floor. I reached for it and had the aberrant thought that memory requires place, and people and things do not exist out of place.

In nurses' stations I had found on the floor various items, including pens, pencils, and wadded bits of paper, along with paper clips, clothespins, chewing gum, and the occasional broken heart. The nurses' station had that counter everyone recognizes and is for relatives and others to approach and lean on, with a built-in desk on the other side of it. The desk drawers held forms and spare parts, and on its top was a Rolodex listing the medications each patient was taking. Opposite the desk were glass cabinets, built high. Some of these could only be opened by a key, because they held controlled medications. It was possible that they hailed medications. It was equally possible that the toll road to hell was paid for with medications that had more to do with the mortuary arts than with the healing ones.

The repugnance I felt went searing through the nurses' station inside me, the one that sponsors beating hearts and the flagellating self. I was once removed from Maria, and whatever happened to her, I would go on living. It was the blessing and the curse of a physician, his revulsion. A death to those who deal in death initiates the machinery of death, which is both internal and external. They had faced the great foe and fought it to the end, even were it the death of another. This could not help but be reassuring. It was more than that. Death could bring to the physician an improbable and magnanimous relief, a blithe pleasure replacing the worry, fear, and dread that had preceded it. Death made you sad but could also make you glad, something physicians knew but did not say. Death measured your power but did not subtract from it. To tinker with death, someone else's, and survive it, how many people could say that? Wasn't that the pinnacle, the anointment, the spectacular? Wasn't it the one thing in life deserving to be revered? Hadn't lesser mortals rather see a sermon any day than to hear it?

Alive, I stood in the nurses' station. The freestanding rack for charts was to one side, holding metal charts that clinked like garden tools whenever one was removed or when the entire cart, loaded with them, was shifted and rolled on its wheels out onto the ward and down the aisle between the two rows of beds, accompanying rounds. Every patient had a chart, every chart a workup and progress notes and a top sheet containing all of the vital information about a patient and, unnoticed at the bottom, a place for the date and cause of death, in the event. Whereupon the chart would pass to the Record Room, where they typed the information onto the death certificate, and it would subsequently be signed by the doctor with a ballpoint pen so that the three carbons would all reflect the fact of its certification by the physician attending (i.e., pronouncing) the death.

Friday afternoon, July 26, 1963, having undergone a revolting mutation, I approached the most important object in the nurses' station, the telephone, that dark noose. The nurses' station also held a couple of those convenient little stools on rollers, for people to slide from one side to the other of the nurses' station without having to stand up. I didn't need one. If I sat down now, I'd never be able to get up.

I stood there, inhabiting the preamble of myself, taking constitutional measure. The hero of the hospital wasn't a hero at all. He was merely a self-loathing coward. The public adoration during the recent graduation ceremonies, the kind words Dr. Gregory had whispered to me while assisting in my investiture, the wonderful, thrilling credentials granted by study and by law, the idealism and its certain culmination in helping the sick and feeling blessed by it, were receding faster than the drying of that splotch of water on the floor over by the sink, where a nurse in white shoes had scurried away so briskly that she spilled from the cup of water she held. All of it mundane, all of it striking, a shithole as I had been promised, and I felt that I would always be in a shithole because nothing was ever as it was supposed to be and almost anything could turn into a shithole. I still had a lot to learn in this shithole, but first came a purgative for all of the ingested lies. Medicine is teamwork? Soldiers on a battlefield fight a common enemy? Nobility is honor? These lessons I had learned with great difficulty over time, as others had learned them before me and forgotten them just as quickly and necessarily as would be the case for me.

*   *   *

Saturday, July 27, was my fourth rotation on ER. Corpus was brighter than seemed possible that day and as hot as can be described without using curse words. Yet it was also the kind of day that brings camaraderie with one's fellows, a smile acknowledging one's effort toward that very thing. We were busy in the ER, very, and I could not sneak out of there until noon to check on Maria.

As it happened, I remember well.

Even as I crept up that unseemly corridor, that dark charnel, here came sounds, voices, things, as of the sliding of feet and the banging of objects against the clanging reality of dissonance. A group appeared, pulling a bed from the confines of Med/Surg. Nurses, including OR nurses, and Drs. Broderick and Peña, all in surgical scrubs. I already knew. They were guiding her bed to the OR for the emergency abdominal surgery she should have had a week ago. The people in the hospital corridor had stopped to allow their egress. This particular part of the corridor was swollen like a balloon. Then I saw Maria. Her head was flung backward, her eyes open and roiling in their sockets, lost in agonal submission to a coma from a perforated intestine. It had happened overnight.

A few minutes later, in a natty suit and tie, Dr. Carleton Broderick strode out of OR and exited stage left, without a word to me or Mrs. La Torre or anyone else, and all of the family members were there, whom this Fellow of the American College of Surgeons had never met and had no intention of meeting, having already spoken to them in his own way.

Shortly Ramiro appeared, still in surgical scrubs.

Tenderly he approached Duvelia. I was standing beside her.

"I'm very sorry. She died before we could get started."

*   *   *

Early Sunday morning Mimi picked me up at the hospital, my ER duty having ended at seven a.m. I took a bath and ate breakfast and she drove me back to the hospital on her way with Roger to attend Sunday school. I spoke to the nurses in Labor and Delivery, which was quiet, and made quick rounds on the Obstetrics Ward. Then I made my way down the long, dark passageway of Memorial Hospital to the end nearest the new building. But instead of continuing toward it, I turned right. Across from the pharmacy was a small room on the right, Pathology. It was about the size of Rosa Ramos's room, but unlike her room, it was built for a specific purpose. Two people were already there, and one was Maria.

Each time you see death, you have never seen it before. Death is the never-before. It blinds us to past and future yet dips us into both, and we come out bereft of that casual certainty that stays insanity. Or not. What it does, it leaves an aching void one wishes to express with words, like a climber reaching for a hold that isn't there, or like a band deprived of its music and blasting forth in silence, or like a forgotten recitation before an auditorium of giggly students who know very well about earth and air and fire and water, but know nothing at all of the institution of death. In that sanatorium, for those in training, feelings are inadequate, much less words. The struggle is with the very idea of the survival of what had been a part of you. Maybe the best part. I could not but conclude that there was not enough love in all of eternity to undo this instance of hatred and its blind expression, that I had witnessed, participated in, shared. It became a part of me, what follows, and throughout eternity will remain in present tense, as I experienced it.

*   *   *

She is naked, one final insult, and lying on a slanted aluminum table with her hands at her sides, as though she had been told to lie very still. Why would she not? She has done everything else we asked of her, but what of the question she had asked of us? Borrow a set of eyes—but you already have, haven't you? Do you know how to use them? What do you see? A young woman, seventeen years old, a new mother. She was born to what the world calls a Hispanic family, the founders of Western civilization in the New World, a family unit at once respectful and fiercely proud, diverse but united, a family known for its history and its sentiment and its sensitivity, its strength and its forbearance, and maybe most of all its lovely language that trills off the tongue, lending itself to expressions from the heart in the whispery sibilance of *amor*, and as well to double negatives, so that *Que paso?* elicits, *No paso nada*. Which brings a smile of familiarity and, yes, love from men too proud to say it but feeling it all the more—fiercely devoted men and their equally devoted women in a culture shaped by the church and molded by realities, double negatives to avert misunderstanding and provide an emphasis lacking in other languages, or at least in English, and double negatives are symbolic as well, standing for the timeless oppression and shameless hatred shown them by the tall ones with blue eyes.

As for Maria, she did not hate in return. She had come to the hospital on our terms, knocking respectfully at the back door, waiting patiently for the only thing that would save her, abdominal surgery. Well, now she will have her surgery on this slanted aluminum table, by Dr. John Pilcher, one of the two pathologists employed by Memorial Hospital.

The joke is that a surgeon knows nothing and does everything, an internist knows everything and does nothing, a psychiatrist knows nothing and does nothing, and a pathologist knows everything and does everything, but too late. Ha-ha. Today, the joke is on Maria and verbiage cannot save her. She has been dipped beneath that faucet of human indignities that calls itself life, and the people in white have had their way with her in a dark burlesque that was as obvious as it was unspoken, and now here she lies.

Dr. Pilcher, a man of small build who is in his sixties, reminds me of the sneaky ways of the aging process, that gleaming trombone in harmony with its lulling tuba, before time wilts trombone to piccolo and its residue, its antics, barely add up to a wheezing melody. The table is perpendicular to Hospital Boulevard, and Maria's feet point that way. A southpaw, the pathologist stands on Maria's left and lets me stand on her right. Pilcher is a quiet man, six years from his own appointment, and has lowered the table sufficiently that I have to stoop to see things clearly.

Were this real, were I to be a real doctor in a real hospital with real nurses and real nurses' stations and real telephones and real thrills and real operating rooms, with me holding a retractor, which was the limit of my undergraduate training in surgery, I might take more of an interest. But nothing is real. Maria will open her eyes any moment and tell me how beautiful are my wife and son, Mimi so "beauty magazine," how I have everything. Well, guess what? I don't. The hospital administrator will stop by and tell me what a wonderful doctor I am going to be, but guess what? That is also a part of the bullshit.

I have no future beyond this because I am in uncharted territory. I have just met myself and become a stranger to the imposter I had been. A genuflection in deference to the pathologist, an apostle to the mirage, I am the rubble left of my own life. I must get through this; the rest of my life must be rebuilt on the other side of it. It is what I tell myself as the doomed have always told themselves, apprentices to extinction.

For now, Dr. Pilcher is the most important person in that world. Were one to need an autopsy, I'd highly recommend him. He works with infinite care, like a person setting out to climb Everest and bewildered to studiousness by its every crevasse. He only sees patients on Sunday mornings in this little room, but he might be able to finagle an appointment for one who really needs it. His is the practice of a man not given to opinions. His is the manner, besides caution, that bespeaks a self-effacing gentleness, like a grandfather holding a newborn. I have seen him once or twice in the clinical lab, where he is in charge, and he seemed nice enough. Personality is not the strong suit of a pathologist any more than hilarity is a bloodsport.

As Pilcher makes the usual cuts, I seek the names of those unnamed, written upon air's wall and held up by pride's swagger and interwoven into the stitchery of a certain curtain lurking beyond a marquee emblazoned with these words: *Give me your tired, your poor, your huddled masses yearning to breathe ...*

The words rebound in a room no bigger than the broom closet where … but that's already been stated. Actually the room is smaller, the ceiling lower. The cramped feeling owes in part to the things suspended from the ceiling. One is an expensive adjustable light of the kind that hovers over every delivery table and every operating table in the hospital. Of the three places in a hospital where it is always found, Maria has visited each, though only momentarily for the one. The light has a bulb as enormous as the headlamps on a new Cadillac, and its stalk is an indifferent appendage of metal with a knob that noiselessly allows the spotlight to be refocused at will.

Beside the spotlight, and also descended from the ceiling, is an aluminum scale of the kind one might find in the vegetable section of the local supermarket. But this scale is not so bright as those. It belongs to the things in life that are unbright. It goes with shadows and the cramped feeling in an autopsy room where the weight of Maria's organs cannot be weighed on any but the metric scale. An autopsy is about numbers. It is about the bad math and foul geometry wrought by human disease, and more especially about the trigonometry of death at the hands of marksmen who are so good at it that they can bring down the quarry without firing a shot. It is about the tactics of contempt. It is about the probability of the improbable. It is filled with statistical nuance and the proprietary mean and possibly the vitriolic mean. The mean is the most important element in any medical or surgical set, an advantage, as it were, and the quarry must recognize this or else.

With a swift cut Pilcher lays open the abdomen and falls back with a sucking in of his breath. The dark liquid erupts, flows, encompasses. A perforated intestinal obstruction is not a pretty sight. The peritoneal contents, normally pristine and limited to glistening surfaces, have surrendered to the eruption of an inner volcano, its feculent ashes and soot owing their creation to the work of enzymes and stomach acid and stasis and obstruction—and possibly for the last two weeks the metallic sheen of a bacterial presence. Pilcher twirls on a faucet and gets a splashing of water from what seems a stubby garden hose and begins washing the effluvium from her abdomen. There is a lot of it. It flows forever, like an elliptical river, the slant of the table allowing it to slosh along the gutters beside her and into the opening at the foot of the table, where it will join the parade of things that flow into the depths of restless possibility and hide there until summoned by an invisible motion known as time and rekindled by the distillate of reality and spilled again in the ubiquitous seepage known as memory.

To have a perforated intestine is to imbibe the arsenical draught. The susceptible lining inside the belly, the peritoneum, absorbs the dreaded contents, which amount to a toxin far more deadly than any devised by human hands. It's my training. I understand such. I can name the epithelium on every bodily surface, outside and in, the sinew and sinuous and spectral, and I have come to see what I already know is present because I must see. It is a part of my job as a *trainee*, don't you see? I owe this to Maria; I am here out of my respect for her and the special person she was to me. I am in training for the reckoning to come, and this will be there waiting for me. She does not blame me, I'm sure of that. She was too gracious for that, too thankful to have a new son. Happy thoughts had sustained her, of her life with that son and their beckoning future, and she had maintained her grace until the end. *Why don't they operate me?* will go into that solemn repository of people begging for their lives and losing them because their pleas went unanswered.

It takes all of my courage to reach and touch her shoulder, all I can do not to scream. Her body is not the same. Medicine is a license to touch and to refrigerate. Is it also a license to kill? Such things are neither registered nor spoken. The very idea is reprehensible, terrifying. That a doctor could be a killer stuns, horrifies me. Still, I had come across the word *banality*. The equilibration was that a monster not only looks normal, he is likely more normal and more laudable than anyone else. The monster is worshiped because when people see him, they see themselves and are blinded by the reflection. No. Mad as I am, devastated, eviscerated, I cannot allow myself to think that this occurred on purpose.

The secretary of the Nueces County Medical Society, who has an office adjacent to the interns' lounge, has told me that the Society has no control over which hospital a doctor chooses for his patients. Many doctors, refusing to provide coverage in Memorial's teaching program, simply did not admit their patients to Memorial, and those that did were well aware that the hospital needed them more than they needed it. It was the same in Galveston. Those on the faculty of the medical school recognized that their own patients were going into private rooms while the staff patients, the "teaching patients," received a much less personal and a far more generic care provided by young doctors in training. It went with teaching rounds, wherein those in training were acquainted with how every failure to order the appropriate test can have dire consequences, beginning with the embarrassment of the doctor in training and ending, unfortunately, in the death of the patient, were the diagnosis missed or the wrong therapy given or the appropriate surgery withheld. It made one defensive, it could make one angry, but it sharpened the intellect and produced, when it worked and was accompanied by work, a physician. A good physician? Define that. And leave out Hippocrates and all that hoary bullshit.

The idea of training, its goal, is to acquaint the young doctor with the worst of diseases so that he or she can more easily handle the least of them. But where does that leave Maria? Where does that leave me? Ideas consume me. I remember being told that if I chose Memorial Hospital for internship, I'd lose patients I shouldn't lose. Fair warning! In my mind, I tumble backward into Sam Hastings, an obstetrician trained in cesarean section and gynecologic surgery. Could he have helped me get Maria to surgery? No. I had considered asking him, but the man had accused me of causing during delivery something she had had on admission—a neat trick. The next would be to correct what she had before she was admitted, which was actually possible.[11]

Pilcher locates the Meckel's diverticulum. Its fibrous exterior is no more than a couple of inches in length, and its diameter is somewhat less than that of a pencil. It courses from the inside wall of the navel to a place on Maria's small intestine a few inches from where the small intestine empties into the large intestine. During the week she was admitted, imperiled by the expanding size of her womb, a loop of small intestine had become ensnared by the Meckel's thick band. Thence, a compensatory but silent struggle. The loop twisted, its vessels and nerves the same, in an effort to free itself. But it could not. The hollow part inside the intestine, its lumen, was constricted by the pinching effect of its tight fit between the wall of the abdomen, the gravid uterus, and the attachment of the Meckel's.

Swelling of tissues occurred; blood supply was compromised. The opening in the intestine inevitably became completely blocked—obstructed. The pain, mild at first, became stronger. The vomiting represented the backward torque of the intestinal assault. Maria vomited anything she ate, and she also vomited the ample, nay, copious and unpleasant-tasting volume of intestinal

---

11   Dr. Hector Garcia, who died in 1996, had performed the appendectomy on Maria and discovered the Meckel's diverticulum. He had the obligation, upon identifying the Meckel's during surgery on seven-year-old Maria, to remove it at the time or to go back in and remove it later, as an elective procedure, or to refer her for its removal. Or maybe he had offered to do it and the removal was declined, though Duvelia would have remembered, and she knew nothing of such a rejection. A Meckel's malformation occurs in 2 percent of people as a remnant between the fetus and its nourishment by way of the umbilical cord, and as it can cause serious problems, including intestinal obstruction, it should be removed in every instance upon its recognition. It is possible that this wasn't widely known at the time of Maria's appendectomy, and in no way do I intend to detract from Dr. Hector, who rightfully became an important man as a civil rights leader and the founder of the American GI Forum. I met him many times in 1963, and he was unfailingly kind and helpful to me. He was the first Hispanic person to receive the Medal of Freedom, the nation's highest award to a civilian. A statue of him in Corpus celebrates the achievements of a man who was loved and respected by all. (Some of the information in this note is from the *Austin American-Statesman*, July 27, 1996, A1 & A12.)

secretions meant to aid normal digestion, secretions proximal to the point of obstruction. The obstruction spawned a torrent of consequences, perforation of the intestine being the last of these.

I suspected, as did Dr. Pilcher, that the advancing end of the Miller-Abbott tube had ripped the three-inch linear laceration in her intestine that was the site of perforation. The delaying tactic, the Miller-Abbott, was double death. It provided the excuse not to operate on Maria and was simultaneously the instrument of her death. By poking a hole through her intestine at the bottleneck site of obstruction, it had caused the release of her intestinal contents into the peritoneal cavity. This had occurred sometime after I saw Maria Friday afternoon, when she still might have been saved, and the events earlier described outside the OR on Saturday, when it was too late.

*   *   *

Voices rule us.

Ultimately each doctor is alone inside himself or herself. But there is always a voice, and it rarely takes a day off. I could not speak for anyone else's inner voice, not having heard it. But my own spent no small amount of time in justifying my actions to myself. I was imperfect and far from proud of things I had done, some of them bordering on the terrible. But I was *aware* of them. And the reason I was aware of them was that I also had a second voice, fainter, that was far more severe than the first. The two were intertwined, of course.

Forget Freud—one can live just as long and just as happy a life without him. The great struggle inside every human being is the quarrel between these two voices. And the fault, dear Brutus, is not only in ourselves but in how incrementally easy it is for the first voice to drown out the second. And everything that happens thereafter, the same as to anyone else, can also happen to a doctor. And somewhere along the way: game, set, match.

*   *   *

Pilcher finds a small, healed perforation. That would be the one she had at the time of delivery and that had responded to the antibiotics I gave her during several days of her first week in the hospital. A better way to put it: antibiotics had helped her system fight the infection, giving her body time to heal the perforation. It gave her the chance to have the definitive surgery that would have saved her life. Surgery that should have been done a week before she died from another perforation. In insane docility I loop around and

- 146 -

around the obstacle that has seized and obstructed my thoughts, blinding me to the great secret that none of us knows but all will eventually share.

Dr. Pilcher speaks.

"Why didn't you operate to relieve the obstruction?"

Ah! I wish I had thought of that! I could write a book, but what good would that do Maria? I feel like a lawyer in the death house having just witnessed an execution, that of my client, and being called to task by the judge. I must stand before that magistrate and publicly extricate this thing that cannot be extricated. I will, in fairness to all, seek that revelation that is a testament to the new heresy. I will solicit at the doors of demons, abort my birthright, relinquish noble thoughts. Does the pathologist speak of the unspoken confession between physicians? I sense that this is what he wants, but mine is maddeningly undisciplined just now. Should I yell it or whisper it or mail it by parcel post? I cannot slay the dragon and free the princess, isn't that enough? What I can do is to dredge up all of the graveyards along the way. Is that confession enough?

*   *   *

Mother used to say, when she was upset with me, that I had better "straighten up and fly right" or she was going to take me to the doctor. It was as if no greater punishment existed, no natural pain could ever be the equivalent of that meted out within the confines of a doctor's office. And she was right. A visit to the doctor did summon up an unfathomable dread. It was that pungent, horrible smell, crocodile breath and adder's venom, a suffocating, paralyzing cotton dipped deep in rubbing alcohol and smeared on the body before a big, long, gleaming needle plunged into the flesh without your permission or even your cooperation, and it hurt and it bled and the Band-Aid they put on it hurt too and kept reminding you of it, and strange people whisked past doing similarly strange things by way of bringing tears to other kids as well, and people stared in satisfaction at what they had done and even smiled as though it were a good thing. It wasn't. It was all of those bottles of stuff that no one bothered to hide and no one could possibly fail to notice. A visit to the doctor summoned up the idea of physicality, of birth and death and all of the enhanced horrors in between. The doctor reduced you to your shivering self. *Doctor* stood for the medieval sparks down the bristling spine of the awaiting bogeyman, a fleeting shadow that seizes you and gobbles you up in what is worse than a nightmare because it is real.

Why become one?

Quite possibly, the obvious: to confront that fear, to fight it to a standstill, to tell that bully I was afraid no more. But set a goal and achieve it, and when you get there, the person you are is not necessarily the person you were, although the person you once believed in, with nurturing, patience, and quite a good bit of luck, might become the person you will be.

*   *   *

Put LUCK in caps. I believe that everyone has lucky years, and mine were years ending in a seven. In 1947 we moved to the northeast Texas town of Pittsburg. That was in May, and I was seven. At my birthday in August, I became eight. My life up until then had been notable—at least, to me.

I was born in Houston to parents from northeast Texas. My father, Charles Favor Deaton, who had been born on October 31, 1907, was an auto mechanic. My mother, Fannie "Frances" Opal Kimberlin, was born on February 11, 1915, and although eleven is not seven, the two are linked in certain games. Mother was the eldest child of a couple who had begun their married life on a farm in Cooper's Chapel, ten miles northeast of Mount Pleasant.

For my father's parents it was the same, except their farming had taken place a few miles south in Camp County, of which Pittsburg is the county seat. Camp, the second smallest county in Texas, was carved out of the upper lip of Upshur County. There was a reason for this. People in north Upshur County, Gilmer its county seat, were having trouble, with delays lasting days and weeks at a time due to flooded creeks, reaching Gilmer, located some twenty miles south of Pittsburg. In 1874, Camp County was born out of desperation.

The Deaton line was not dissimilar to the Anderson line. Rufus Allen Deaton was born in 1825 in North Carolina. His first of two marriages was to Mary Ann Scott; their only child was James "Jim" Franklin Deaton, born in 1852 in Louisville, Mississippi. Ultimately he would relocate, along with his family, to Pittsburg, Texas, in 1892. Before that, he had married Mary Ellen Gulley of Stamps, Columbia County, Arkansas, and they had eight surviving children. One of them, Allen Deaton, would twice become sheriff of Camp County before dying in 1959. Another of them, Maude Ellen Deaton, born in 1889 in Stamps, would ultimately die in Little Rock, Arkansas, in 1983, having outlived all of her sibs and having survived long enough for me to have met her and spoken with her, long enough for me to admire her graciousness and spunk. Her elder brother, James Elmo Deaton, was born in 1879 and died in Pittsburg in 1961. Elmo had married Florence Faver in

Pittsburg at the turn of the century, and their second child, the said Charles Favor Deaton, was my father.

Elmo had a younger brother named Eugene Charles Deaton, probably the origin of my father's first name. However, the spelling of Charles Favor Deaton's middle name, from *Faver*, is problematical. It may have sneaked onto his birth certificate as *Favor* and is spelled that way in every Deaton genealogy.

But this is incorrect. Those delicious summer days I spent in the country with my Grandmother Deaton also had educational benefits. Toward sundown, she and I would climb down the hill behind their farmhouse for me to take a bath in the shallow creek. She sat on the bank and watched for snakes, and I abided the cold water by splashing in it and feeling special that she went to so much trouble for me. We shared watermelon, fried chicken, and motionless Southern days without radio, TV, electric lights, or a telephone. (A daily newspaper came by mail and was much anticipated. I believe Humphrey Pennyworth of the *Joe Palooka* strip was floating across the ocean on an inner tube that summer and taking his disappointing time.) My grandfather was alive but usually not around, and my grandmother became my playmate and friend, my conversationalist. Again and again she would say to me, so wistfully and so proudly, that she had been a *Favor*. She seemed to intend the word spelled that way, the metaphor speaking volumes toward the idea that she had not remained that. She was not bitter, merely accepting of what life had given her.

A letter survives from his courtship of her that Elmo Deaton wrote to *Miss Florence Favrr* of Pittsburg on April 28, 1901. Spelling in handwritten documents of the time was careless at best, at least in my family, but it does indicate that Florence was originally a *Favrr* rather than a *Faver* or a *Favor*. My aunt Mary Lou Adkins, Florence's daughter and Charles's older sister, did genealogical research on her mother's family after the excitement of *Roots* had gripped America, and she determined that *Favrr* was the Americanization of *Lefebvre*, or any of the numerous ways that that word of French origin may be spelled. Such is America, where the scholarly lags behind the rambunctious. Hence *Charles Favor Deaton*, as was, became the name recorded in his World War II service record.

*   *   *

Genealogy can seem a motionless pursuit, static as a cloudless sky, but that isn't always the case. Between the lines, moving from one place to another is the archway of change. Both Jim Kimberlin and Elmo Deaton moved into town, a monumental step for farmers in those days, the one to Mount Pleasant and the other to Pittsburg.

Elmo and Florence settled in a frame house on Hill Avenue, on the east side of Pittsburg. By the end of World War I, Elmo, who had not served because he was in his midthirties, had opened an auto garage in Pittsburg. It was located at 204 Quitman Street, on the south side of the street, sandwiched between the two sets of railroad tracks crossing Quitman. I have its card. The Eastern Auto Supply Company, with a phone number of *310*, offered "Tires—Tubes—Accessories" in addition to its auto repair.

I was told by my uncle, Graydon Adkins—the *G* in my name—that Elmo Deaton had a strange way of conducting business. If someone asked him a dumb question about a car, Graydon said, he would knock them down. How this could possibly have helped business is doubtful, but maybe it reflected a less genteel time among our forebears. Maybe people in Pittsburg could brag of going to Elmo's and not being knocked down. The man did have a temper, threatening once to "beat the piss out of" me, and he'd proceeded to do so with his belt while I ran around and around Florence and she pleaded with her husband to desist. But we did do one thing together. He drove into town each Saturday, usually alone, in a Model A pickup to wistfully visit that auto shop, and during my tenure of a week or two in the country, I went with him.

It was a strange experience. To save gas, he switched the engine off at the top of a hill and coasted down, whereupon ignition at the bottom took us up the next. It was kind of like a rollercoaster, the act repeated a few dozen times in the miles it took us to get to town.

Charles Deaton had two sisters. Mary Lou was born in 1906, and Blanche Deaton was born in 1916. Mary Lou called Charles "Brother" and wanted me to call her "Aunt Sister," which I tended to resist. At my request in 1979, Mary Lou supplied some facts about her brother. He was driving a car by age ten, she said. Florence had spoken to me of seeing a car "without a driver" going past their house on Hill Avenue. Turned out he was behind the wheel.

Mary Lou: "He had an unusually good mind and was very quick-witted."

Graydon: "He was as smart as a whip. He could figure things out and fix any type of anything."

Mary Lou didn't know when "Brother" had begun drinking, but she found out about it when he was seventeen and said, "It was really a blow to me." Charles did not finish high school because of a fight he had with the principal, or so I was told. One is inclined not to doubt it, Charles's being a pugnacious personality. But to document it is impossible, the PHS school records having been lost in a fire around 1929 or so. The school that I would attend on the edge of downtown Pittsburg was built subsequently.

My mother's folks, Jim and Alma Kimberlin, moved into town immediately after World War I and opened a café on the Square in downtown Mount Pleasant. Jim had not served in the war, though of age, because he'd been a farmer. They were exempted because of the vital need to maintain food supply during a national emergency. My cousin once removed, Pauline Anderson Slovak, described the café as "a little hamburger and chili eating place." In any event they did well enough to raise their four children. The family attended the Church of Christ, strict teetotalers, the children held to similar values. Mother helped out in the café, as a waitress and a cook, but she earned no salary.

She graduated from Mount Pleasant High School in 1932, at age seventeen, and for the next two and a half years continued to live at home and work in the café. She also made pies at the house and would then walk them, often one or two in each hand, to the café to be sold by the slice. Their house had utilities but not sewage. "The toilet—out," as she put it. Since her sibs were all younger than her and she worked six days a week at the café, it was not surprising that she grew tired of that life. The hard times of the Depression found her wishing for more.

*   *   *

Frances met Charles Deaton while still in high school and became good friends with Blanche Deaton, his younger sister. One might imagine that their first meeting occurred at the café on the Square in Mount Pleasant, though it is also possible that Frances met him while visiting his sister at their house on Hill Avenue in Pittsburg. As she put it, "He was eight years older than me, and I guess that made him more fascinating." He would have been the exact opposite of the man her parents craved for her.

At the time, he also still lived at home and worked for his father as a mechanic at the shop in Pittsburg, which was a Texaco filling station when I grew up. In the late forties, the gas it sold was fifteen cents a gallon and worth it, such a pretty red color. You could see it in the glass cylinder forming the upper part of each pump, lined with gallon markers, and each dispenser had a hand crank one worked up and down—hence "pumping gas"—to fill the cylinder before draining it by gravity into the hose that fed the gas tank. It was the same at all the gas stations in Pittsburg, and the price was rounded off to the nearest nickel.

One benefit of working with cars was a proximity to owning them, and Charles always seemed to have his own car. He took Frances to the movies in Pittsburg or Mount Pleasant or, occasionally, all the way to Gilmer.

Sometimes they double-dated with other couples or would get together with several couples on a Sunday afternoon. One year, in October, Charles and Frances and several other couples drove over and spent a day together at the Dallas Fair. As Mother put it, "That was a big deal then."

Correspondence survives from him to her. The original, on the business letterhead of Eastern Auto Supply in Pittsburg, is here edited for spelling and grammar. The envelope dates its mailing as February 10, 1932, ten a.m., a Wednesday, and from the contents of the letter it seems that the writer was off a day on his dates.

> Thurs. Morn, 1:00 [p.m.]
> Dearest: How do you feel this morning? As usual I am sleepy tired and in a bad humor. I have read all of the newspaper's advertisements and pictures. I am listening to Station W.E.N.R., Ben Burney's orchestra playing "Paradise Lost." Did you ever hear that? It is real good.
> I might go to Wills Point tomorrow if I am not too sleepy, to carry a boy over there. And again I might be over to Mt Pleasant 'cause I might catch you trifling. I just wish I could. Do you? I might catch you sometime if you ever trifle. I bet that I do. I guess it will be with Boots or whatever his moniker may be. Say I know this sleepy writing is getting old, so By,
> Lots of Love
> Charles

The letter, oil-stained then or later, is disturbing. It is less noble than one might wish and indicative of a troubled relationship, him attempting to exert control over her by way of threatening her. Given the eight-year difference in ages, and his fractious self, the implied threats against a young woman he was dating, who was a senior in high school, smack of emotional abuse and harassment. Her seventeenth birthday was Thursday, February 11, but instead of wishing her happiness and promising a present or flowers, he is thinking only of himself. As Frances put it later, "We had our problems when we were courting. He was very jealous and mean, especially when he was drinking. But my life would never have been complete had I not defied my parents and married him. So, I've no one to blame but me."

The trip he mentions to Wills Point, a distance of well over a hundred miles west of Pittsburg, and back again, was a substantial drive in those days. But Charles evidently enjoyed traveling and had friends in many places. Had he and his girl in Mount Pleasant spoken of marriage yet? In a letter to me in 1978, Mother said, "I don't think we could have afforded to get married then. It was Depression years."

Charles would have been twenty-four in February of 1932 and, as to that, he had been married before, to an "attractive young woman" from Cason, ten miles east of Pittsburg in Morris County, of which Daingerfield was county seat. Mildred Henderson was her name, and apparently they were married for only a short time and then divorced, having no children. No reason for the divorce was given, at least by him, but one wonders. And one also suspects that it added to his allure, a certain danger to his stature, an infatuation with the buccaneer by a person who, in her own quiet way, was also rebelling. This older man knew things and knew people and had everything that was lacking in boys her own age.

For that matter, the attraction a young person in Mount Pleasant might have had for someone from Pittsburg (or vice versa) was known to young people in both towns. The people who had been in your school with you forever, perhaps, became boring. A person from another small town carried an enticing aura of mystery, like found money, and Charles Deaton had all of that and more. He had a skill and he had a job and he had a car. He was as exciting as an exhilarating ride at the Dallas Fair, and Frances found him irresistible.

A picture of him when he was twenty-six years old shows someone who appeared older than that, but by an indeterminate amount. He was not a big man, Charles Deaton, did not look particularly ferocious. He was five feet and eight inches tall, weighed 138 pounds, and seemed to have unusually long arms and big hands, but his shoulders were narrow and his neck bore none of the heftiness one sees in bodybuilders or football linemen. His hands, in every picture, hold a lighted cigarette. It dangles like a surgical instrument, low and away, that he had been using before someone interrupted him by intruding on his space. His meanness excuses nothing. It is intense, unforgiving, even harrowing. "The next move is up to you," he seems to be saying, "and you had better think very carefully about it, Buster."

*   *   *

I saw him once in a fight. He had just come back from World War II, meaning it was 1945, and driven us to a place on the Gulf Freeway south of Houston. It was noon, and I was looking forward to a hamburger. Those from a café were better than homemade, by a lot. The place itself was probably what in Texas in those days was known as a honky-tonk, which the dictionary defines as a place where one should probably not go for family dining. It was low and dark except for the bar, offered a floor of sawdust, and had a postage-stamp dance floor on a slab of concrete over to the right, beside the brightly lit jukebox. The sounds were loud and exciting, and the people at half a dozen tables seemed to be having a good time. The bar offered a line of sandwiches on the menu, served with the beverage of choice, and my father seated us and promptly left as soon as we placed our order.

Like a skirl of pipes came the music from the jukebox, and a handsome man, a complete stranger, approached our table and asked Frances Deaton to dance with him. Young and dumb as I was, I knew that this was the last thing she should do. But, pleased as a girl at the prom, she scooted back her chair, stood, and left with him. Soon she and the new man in her life were whirling to the music, along with several other couples.

The hamburgers still hadn't come when Charles Deaton returned, saw his wife and a stranger on the dance floor, and reacted.

"That's my wife!" he snarled, heaving forward and jerking them apart.

He snatched Mother painfully by the wrists and she emitted a shriek of pain and anger as he jostled her through the crowd of people, all of whom were in shock. Despite her protests, he roughhoused her into a chair at our table. Then he turned his attention to the man who had insulted him by dancing with his wife.

First they began shouting at each other while the other customers backed away, sensing a fight. But the man did not back down. He was to the effect that it was an honest mistake and don't treat the lady like that, okay? Charles hit him first but did not knock the man down. The man retaliated, and Charles Deaton either fell or tripped. He came up with a chair in his hands and went at the man. It's been in a thousand movies, what happened next. The man took an empty long-necked beer bottle and broke it in two on the bar, flashing the jagged edges at my father. Here, all semblance to movie fights disappeared. The two roared at each other, savage as beasts in a jungle, and things became very messy indeed.

Mother was screaming and had my hand and started for the door. The man charged after us, Charles retreating in the zigzag way required of staying between the man and his family, turning over one table after another while paying no heed to the other customers, who were by now yelling for the police. Charles hurled glasses and bottles at the man, some of which hit him. By this means we reached the front door, which was only a few yards away, and Charles shouted for Mother to get into the car, which we did, and he hurried out and threw himself behind the wheel and off we sped.

I never did get that hamburger. Mother promised one someplace else, but I was to remain one hamburger behind forever. My parents were too busy battling each other to be concerned about me. That night they brandished kitchen knives at each other by way of threats of death, and finally Charles told her that Houston wasn't big enough for the two of them and *he* was staying.

That was how we came to leave Houston and I ended up in Mount Pleasant and Cooper's Chapel and Pittsburg. In that respect, it was a good thing for me, because I had not particularly liked the beginning of first grade in Houston.

In the fight in the honky-tonk, Charles Deaton had met a man who was better at it than he was, not that it would have made any difference to him. How many such fights were there in all? Or was his alcoholic life one continuous altercation? He blamed the event on his wife. And it was her fault. Had she been intentionally provoking him? She hadn't exactly remained chaste and faithful to him during the war, and maybe the event was her way of telling him that she was never again going to let him control her as he had. The event sketched upon a small canvas the life of a man, Charles Deaton, who thought to remake the world with his fists, the demon of Armageddon coursing through his veins, and it is sometimes said of such men that they expend their lives searching for the one who will kill them. For Charles Deaton, the search would end successfully.

The fight itself held no glory. It was ugly—frightening and repugnant. My memory of the event was of shame, humiliation, and sorrow. The only other thing I came to understand about it was the reason for our speedy retreat. Charles Deaton knew that if he was there when the cops came, he would have been thrown in jail.

*　　*　　*

It clarifies to a satisfactory degree why Jim and Alma Kimberlin were so adamantly opposed to a man the caliber of Charles Deaton. How many times had he been arrested? How many times had he awakened in jail with no idea how he got there? It only made him more attractive to Jim and Alma's best waitress, and she by then would have built up her own lists of grievances against her parents. For her, Charles Deaton represented a way out.

"We had no money and there was no chance for me to get a job in Mount Pleasant," she said, "and I was anxious to get away from home." As for his drinking, he told her that after she married him he would quit, and a lifetime later she shook her head in amusement. "I was so dumb I believed him." She would learn quickly enough that not only hadn't he stopped, his alcoholism was far worse than she had realized. She spoke of so many days when he had to have a drink, literally, before he could pry himself out of bed in the morning to go to work.

As it happened, he left Pittsburg and moved to Houston in 1934 to work for Olan Smith as an auto mechanic in a garage. Perhaps he heard of the job through connections they had at the Eastern Auto Supply in Pittsburg, or a salesman recommended him. Olan Smith's business card is extant. It was "System Garage," featuring "General Automobile Repairing," located at 3820 Main Street (Rear) in Houston. The phone number was *HAD-0451*.

In spite of his alcoholism, Charles did quite well as an employee. His salary was eighteen dollars a week, good money for the Depression, and he owned his own Model A Ford. Once he was established in the job, he and Frances finalized their plans. A letter survives with its three-cent stamp, mailed to *Miss Fanny Kimberlin, Mt. Pleasant, Texas*, on January 17, 1935. It was written Tuesday, January 15, 1935, and has here been edited for spelling and grammar:

> Dearest:
> I received your letter today wanting to know why I hadn't written. I have only missed one night and that was Saturday night. Hon, I have been looking for an apartment today. One lady told me she would let me know Friday night so I don't know yet. Smith went back bird-hunting today. He hasn't got back yet, [and] I had to buy some parts today and I only have 90¢ left. Ain't we got lots of money? I guess he will pay me back before Saturday, though you said you might call me. Hon, that costs $1.75 for three minutes and I could talk for 10 hours. Figure that up. No, Hon, I haven't trifled, not once, haven't even been to town at night or to a show. We will have to have dishes, linens, lights, and gas in the apartment I looked at tonight. I had rather have one with everything furnished, hadn't you? I will write Wednesday night, so be sweet. Hoping to see you Sunday.
> Lots of love,
> I love you.
> Cha'se
>
> P.S. No church wedding for me. Nobody along but us, don't even mention it to anybody, because I am not positive it will be this weekend. I hope so, though, don't you? C.

He did drive back to northeast Texas that Saturday in January of 1935, and they were married the next day at the home of Buck and Ruby Wilhite in Mount Pleasant, evidence that Frances met him there rather than in Pittsburg. The certificate of marriage is dated January 20, 1935, and signed by H. E. Wilhite, Justice of the Peace, Precinct 1, Titus County, Texas. If it wasn't an elopement, it was its equivalent. She was soon to be twenty and he was going on twenty-eight. Afterward they drove to Pittsburg to visit with his mother and father, Florence and Elmo, and on that same Sunday evening continued on to Houston in his Model A.

The weather was very cold, and they finally arrived at two thirty Monday morning at Olan and Mary Smith's home, where Charles had been living. This was where they spent their honeymoon, meaning he got up and went back to work the next day and she made herself handy around the house and set about sizing up the job market and locating a place where the two of them might live with a bit more privacy. No account of the anguish experienced by Jim and Alma Kimberlin over the elopement of their eldest has survived, but surely it left irrevocably bruised feelings.

Eventually I came to understand why my grandmother Alma Kimberlin hated me. I was the only Charles Deaton she could take it out on, and take it out on me she did. I grew to hate her in return, a terrible thing toward a grandmother whose contempt outdistanced only her ignorance, deadening her heart toward those whose major sin was to have been born. Once, when I was enjoying a banana in her home, she passed by and said, "Them's probably where polio comes from," said it frankly and wistfully, and then continued on her inimitable and loving way. Every child should have such a granny! She expressed similar curses of me many times in many ways, including sending me to hell for not belonging to her church. To her credit, she treated her other grandchildren somewhat better. But I was son of a man she detested; ergo, I was detestable.

By contrast, Jim Kimberlin was never anything but gracious. We met weekly, Mother desiring to see "Mama" that often, and Jim Kimberlin, a tall, shuffling man, would reach out his hand and greet me with, "Hey, here, Brother Deaton!" When I reached the age of thirteen, Jim propped me behind the wheel of his automobile and taught me how to drive. He bought me my first car in 1956 and let me pay him back as I could. While Alma brought unpleasantness, he brought the unspoken love that yields tears of joy to this old man in reflecting on those times. He was a decent man, and kind, a man that anyone would be proud to have as an ancestor.

I eventually made an interesting connection to my mother's maiden name. In the same way that *Faver* is the Americanization of the French *Lefebvre*; in the same way the surname of the man Jimmie Kimberlin

(Mother's sister) married, *Bice*, is an Americanization of the German *Weiss*, the name *Kimberlin* is the Americanization of *Chamberlin*, or *Chamberlen*. It is a surname steeped in obstetrical history, embedded as it is in Europe's storied past. One way or another, a physician named Dr. Chamberlen, in the sixteenth century, invented the modern obstetrical forceps. Such discoveries are usually trumpeted around the world, but not this one. It was kept a tightly guarded family secret for a hundred years.

I had been taught to use forceps in medical school, outlet forceps serving to facilitate the last part of childbirth. Although I hadn't employed them on that first delivery at Memorial, in most of my subsequent deliveries I did, because they worked like a greatly expanded set of hands, with smooth, rounded surfaces. When the baby's head, its largest part, reaches the pelvis, delivery can slow down while the head becomes a battering ram to the birth tract. Taking care to apply the two halves separately, one slides first one forceps blade to the left side of the fetal head, then the other blade to the right side (or vice versa). The curve in each forceps brings them together at their handles and, when they are correctly fixed in place, allows a locking device just above the handles to convert the two blades into a single instrument. With a very gentle pulling motion on the handle, down and out, the fetal head is guided through to the exterior, saving up to several hours of delivery time for the mother and also sparing the fetus from possible head injury.

The original Dr. Chamberlen was forced to flee to London in 1569 to escape religious persecution, adding to the enshrouded history of what he had discovered. Two of his sons became physicians in England and employed obstetrical forceps much like the ones I used at Memorial Hospital four hundred years later. These and other descendents of Chamberlen used their secret as a way of earning an edge over other physicians in obstetrics, and indeed they flaunted their ability to deliver the most difficult of births by their secret method (applying forceps much higher in the birth tract than I have described). It is a strange link through Jim Kimberlin to that dynasty, and if it is there, what else might be?

Earlier forceps, developed by 1100 AD, did not facilitate a live birth. Having teeth to penetrate the fetal head, they were used to expedite the removal of a stillborn.

*   *   *

Frequently during my childhood, when Mother and I had trouble, she would revisit for me an item she left facedown, warning that "all this other might come out." Hers was a knack for veiled threats. She lived as though secrets nourished salvation, were she to finally share them. In speaking of things "coming out," she'd raise her arm with the elbow cocked, as in debating or to deliver a blow, her gesture batting away even the merest suggestion that one might talk back, a gesture masking an obstetrical secret of her own, if somewhat different from the above and of much lesser duration and import, except to me.

Its origin in whatever she was withholding from me remained a secret until a few years before her death on August 11, 2000. It came by way of a letter. In it, she informed me of my father's decision not to have me. "He did not want to be bothered with me at that time. He could never really accept responsibility and didn't want to be a family man." Nevertheless, a flight of wooden stairs was climbed in Houston, to an abortionist's office, prior arrangements having been made by the paterfamilias.

Locating the office, she came to a stop with her hand on the doorknob.

I've thought some about that doorknob. I've imagined it of brass, long devoid of shine, worn and loose to the point of rattling at the touch, dwarfed by a rectangular glass window above it, the milky kind that contains a name etched in black letters, the translucency of that grainy surface forbidding a look inside. Did the noisy doorknob scare her away? Did that save my life? In a moment of tumult and excruciating sacrifice, she did not go in, did not have the pregnancy terminated, and in consequence the product of conception came to fruition. Was it merely a close call or a miracle that I survived? That I might eventually entertain a memory of wakeful awareness during that gestation, a comfortable hibernation abruptly terminated at the appropriate time and protested by me in a crying outrage at the top of my lungs, meant at the very least that mine was a presence that day, having whatever influence I had, conjecture measured against the silence that would have been mine had the appointed termination been inflicted upon me that day. Marshmallows on hemlock are no less sweet when not tasted.

Mother had written that this made me *special*. She used that exact word, though it did not necessarily follow that she had treated me that way, proxy at times existing both at the grandmotherly and the motherly levels. In truth, I could stake no claim to being any more special than any other product of an unaborted pregnancy, each usually feeling special in its own way, with no reason in the world why this should not be the case. I was prone to a contradictory notion: in her mind it made me doubly beholden to her. I finally understood why, throughout my childhood, she had taunted me about unknown tariffs, told me again and again I should be thankful to have a roof over my head, expecting in return for her neglect a ransom consisting of a sum not less than full payment of my enormous debt to her, a debt that cannot be repaid except to one's own children.

*   *   *

At the time of my birth, Charles Deaton was working nights, or such was the claim, and a friend drove Mother to Hermann Hospital in Houston, where the lucky young man appeared by way of a promissory note dated August 19, 1939, and made out payable to the bearer upon demand, at any time and any place and any distance for the rest of eternity.

She began leaving me with a black woman when I was three weeks old and took a job at the Houston Packing Company, the first step in her financial liberation from Charles Deaton. It was contract work with a preference for female workers. It paid thirty-seven cents an hour for stuffing sausages or other meat products on an assembly line. Frances Deaton: "It was work and it was a paycheck and for the first time in my life, I had an income. I was thrilled. The job lasted eight months and then I was able to draw unemployment." The company got another contract, and she returned to work at the same place and was making forty-six cents an hour when Pearl Harbor was bombed on December 7, 1941, bringing our country into the war.

Like so many Americans, Charles Deaton quit his job and enlisted. Was it patriotism or an opportunity to remove himself from a family he didn't want? Possibly, it was both. He joined the Coast Guard on April 22, 1942, at the age of thirty-five and, as Frances put it, "They sent his butt to Galveston." His service record identified him as a Motor Machinist Mate 2c and then 1c, and he served aboard a destroyer escort, a vessel with 10 officers and 150 men. His job was to keep the engines running on what was basically a submarine hunter—large groups of these vessels accompanied any naval convoy. A Western Union telegram dated July 15, 1942, survives. It is addressed to Mrs. Charles Deaton at the Houston Packing Company:

SAILING AT 12. DESTINATION UNKNOWN
CHARLES DEATON

It was a telegram sent automatically for each man on the ship, by way of notifying his family of the sailing. A letter from him during the war, dated November 19, 1944, survives. Unedited below, it was sent to *Mrs. Charles Deaton, 711 Irvinton [sic] Courts, Houston (9) Texas*. It was an example, in size and format, of the "WAR & NAVY DEPARTMENTS' V–MAIL SERVICE. OFFICIAL BUSINESS." The four-inch-by-five-inch letter was folded once and placed inside a small brown envelope, which required no stamp. But at the site of postage it stated, "PENALTY FOR PRIVATE USE TO AVOID PAYMENT OF POSTAGE, $300." That was interesting. At its top, instructions in bold letters advised the correspondent: "Use typewriter, dark ink, or pencil. Write plainly. Very small writing is not suitable."

> Dear Fannie, Jonnie … I hope this finds you well. I haven't heard from you since I wrote you last. We missed one day this month, so November will only have 29 days. It is Nov. 17 here and Nov. 16 there … We are really south of the border now but still have lots of miles to go. We were broke down one night on the way here (kind of a funny feeling) it could be slightly dangerous. We are at a small island somewhere. Haven't been ashore. Will tell you more later.
> Love,
> C. F. Deaton, MM1C, USCG
> US Army FS #189
> % Fleet PO San Francisco, CAL.

Two things merit comment. That the ship's engines had stopped, a condition that could be "slightly dangerous," implied that he and others had worked furiously to get them going again before the ship came under a submarine's periscope. The other thing of note about the letter involves one last feature. In the upper-left corner beside the handwritten address, which is enclosed in a box, was a circle labeled CENSOR'S STAMP. Within it is a stamped circle of approval carrying the words "PASSED BY NAVAL CENSOR," with the censor's individual initials handwritten in a space at the center of the circle. The initials appear to be NJM. That the mail was censored forbade servicemen from giving accounts of battles and certain other forbidden information. For that reason, the machinist mate's son came to wonder whether Charles Deaton's ship was involved in one of the most wrenchingly important battles in the retaking of the Philippines from the Japanese, the 1944 Battle of Leyte Gulf.

The battle occurred after Admiral Halsey had been lured north some 350 miles with the main part of the American Task Force, leaving behind in Leyte Gulf a group of escort carriers (troopships) and destroyers just off of MacArthur's beachhead, all of them vulnerable to a Japanese naval attack. The attack came on October 25, 1944. According to William Manchester in his book *American Caesar*, the only vessels that stood in their way were "destroyers and escorts, the latter being puny vessels used for antisubmarine work and manned mostly by married draftees. The destroyers counterattacked Kurita's battleships, and then their gallant little escorts sprang toward the huge Japanese armada, firing their small-bore guns and launching torpedoes."[12] The Japanese retreated, and Halsey and his task force returned in time to prevent another attack.

Who knows? Charles Deaton's letter, written several weeks after the battle, would have given him time to have been in one of those "gallant little escorts" at Leyte Gulf. In three years of service in the Coast Guard, he spent a total of only seven months and three days in "Foreign and/or Sea Service." Where was he the rest of the time?

He was in training for some of it, maybe quite a bit of it. Following to a point further back from most historical accounts of World War II invariably leads one to discover how very much time the United States spent training its young warriors before they were sent into harm's way. It wasn't always true, but it was the rule rather than the exception. As for the remainder of his three years and four months in the Coast Guard, part of his service had a darker hue. He spent a good bit of time in the hospital, especially in 1945, and his honorable discharge was "by reason of physical disability existing prior to enlistment." That would be alcoholism. He had, of course, sworn on entry that he was not addicted to drugs or alcohol. His son would make the same declaration a generation later.

One aspect of his time in the service was shameful, having to do with his allotment, the percentage of one's monthly paycheck sent directly to one's dependents when on duty away from home, even if only away at a place as close as Galveston. All servicemen would fill out the allotment with a sense of importance since it related to the support of their families. But Charles Deaton stated that he had no dependents. This left Frances receiving nothing from him, which infuriated her and did lead her to a justified retaliation. She boarded a bus to Galveston, bringing evidence, and went before his commanding officer to expose the lie. Charles Deaton got in trouble over it, and the allotment subsequently arrived each month for his dependents, for the next three and a half years. The nerve of the man! Surely he had redeeming features.

Frances wrote a nice letter about that in 1979. "In the recent letter I wrote you I really didn't mean to leave the impression that everything about your daddy was bad. He tried 3 or 4 times to quit alcohol, by taking a cure at a clinic in Houston. But his willpower just wouldn't hold out." She went on to say that he had taken friends there for the cure and one of these, Morris Thorsell of Pittsburg, was cured forever and remained eternally grateful to Charles Deaton. He, Thorsell, had written a letter of appreciation of this to my grandmother Florence Deaton, which Grandmother Deaton cherished

---

12   William Manchester, *American Caesar, Douglas MacArthur, 1880–1964*
      (Boston: Little, Brown and Company, 1978), 393.

and lovingly brought out to show me one day, a letter counting forever on the positive side for Charles Deaton.

Beyond that, Florence Deaton spoke of having had an alcoholic brother who had accidentally killed himself. The story was that he was drawing a loaded shotgun through a barbed wire fence and it had discharged accidentally. Yes, and no doubt a practiced woodsman at that. At any rate the family history was positive for alcoholism, a drug, a hand-me-down ornament that each generation was as free to accept as to refuse.

*   *   *

I don't remember much about World War II, but I do remember the place where we lived, 711 Irvington Courts in Houston, and my earliest memory is probably from 1943, when I was given a sailor suit like my daddy's and a picture was made of me in that costume. I knew there was a war somewhere, everywhere, and airplanes flew in the sky and automobiles throbbed along in their persnickety importance and I gallivanted here and there on my tricycle flaunting the lighthearted perspective of one who felt honored to be alive. Food appeared magically before me, and a bed and a roof and a smile, but the world I inhabited was limited to the yellow two-story brick apartment complex in Houston.

I held the enticing notion that ours, being on the first row, was the best. I was happily convinced that I would live there for the rest of my life and be as happy as I could be, under the circumstances. The highway ran perpendicular to the street in front of the Courts and carried an unceasing flow of traffic. I can remember lying awake in my bed on the second floor and watching shadows soar and roar continuously across the wall as cars swept by all night long. I was forbidden to play near the highway, but in the other direction our street ended in Buffalo Bayou, and it seemed to me a gorge the size of the Grand Canyon—however big that was, to eyes that had never seen the tourist attraction—and myself and other kids, approaching it, were watchful for the dreaded alligators said to swim down there and that could swish up the embankment and take a kid and wrestle him back down into the murky depths and that would be that.

Besides staring into the menacing bayou, children in Irvington Courts played baseball or softball and busied themselves in the spontaneity of childhood. The kids were nice, and so were our neighbors. A teenage girl next door took an interest in me. I never succeeded in getting my shoes tied in my own apartment of a morning, Mother always in such a hurry, and this kind young woman volunteered to do the chore. I gladly accepted. Thenceforth, part of my morning routine became to walk next door, to the side away from the highway, to have my shoes tied. One morning, the novelty having worn off, the girl took four or five minutes and taught me how to tie my own shoes, for which I have been eternally grateful. It was my first pedagogic lesson, other than toilet training, and how good it was!

Mother had a job as a welder's assistant at the Todd Shipyard in Houston, which built "Victory ships," and presumably our neighbors were also working there or somewhere near and could carpool. My mother was also seeing a man named Herbert, who came to the apartment regularly. He sold suits, but possibly not in a store. He carried a miniature pallet of fabrics, a sample book offering a bacchanalia of colors and materials, which he could ruffle through like a cardsharp dazzling a kid with a deck of cards. He may have squandered one of these sample books on me, but if so, it did not survive.

What did stick was a memorable bit of advice from Herbert. I had just taken a bath, probably in Mother's water (often the case in early years), and it was daytime, so probably a weekend. As I emerged from the tub and began to dry myself, Herbert noticed my antics with the towel and commented that I should be sure and dry the region between my legs. To make sure I understood, he pointed.

It seemed more important to him than to me. My thought was, "I didn't bother to wash it, so why the hell should I bother to dry it?" I wasn't even sure what it was that happened to be between my legs and was probably a teenager before I made the connection between table and toilet. I just thought one did certain things, without explanation, as though on the honor system.

At the proper age I attended kindergarten, where teachers were unusually snappy and once washed out my mouth with a bar of white soap for saying *darn.* What was interesting was how they all vied to be the one that got to do it, each seemingly eager for a chore that didn't make any difference to me one way or the other; I was glad for the attention. Still, distance informs memory: one of the teachers was meaner than the rest, and the others spared me by sending the kindest woman with me to the bathroom sink. I remember her because she had a gentle touch and a kind voice.

Outgrowing my tricycle, I began to explore behind the first row of buildings of Irvington Courts and discovered a group of kids from the second row of apartments that often assembled there. The courtyard was a dry, hot space broken up by clotheslines, trash cans, and such items as push lawnmowers, automobile tires, pet cats, and examples of the local wildlife. The kids paid no attention to the preceding. There were more important things to do. Our main topic of discussion was what we intended to do with Hitler and the other Axis leaders once the war was won and they were captured and turned over to our tribunal. We planned on dropping them from airplanes so they would land right there between the two rows of apartments, as I recall. One boy regaled us with the astounding feats he had accomplished when "he used to be a man." This Odysseus would begin these fantastic stories and hold us riveted, and I found a use for the device in a book that came along much later. Things could also turn serious back there.

Vividly I remember when an older boy from the next row of apartments was bitten on the thumb by a rat. Said rat had drawn the interest of this young man when he saw it scurrying into a hole in an area of red dirt like that of a pitcher's mound. He had made the decision to capture it. The aperture, smaller than a baseball but larger than a golf ball, was apparently the entry and exit to the rat's quarters, and the rat had made him pay in blood for his quest and then retreated deeper into the earth.

As there were no adults around to ask for help, he went into his apartment and came out holding an empty Mason fruit jar, into which he placed the wounded digit and took a seat in the sunshine beside the rat hole, bleeding in glassy transparency, drop by drop, the bite having opened the skin deeply. He covered the bottom of the jar in blood and then some. In my fascination, tucking it away for future reference, I understood that it was what you do for the bite of a rat. For hours, like the mutinous crew of a grounded ship, the group of us waited beside that rat hole, armed and dangerous, but fortunately for it the animal did not venture out again.

*   *   *

On a Saturday afternoon when I was five or six years old, Frances was entertaining Herbert, and they were having refreshments. She summoned me and dispatched me on an errand that required me to cross that dreaded highway beside Irvington Courts. Beyond it and to the left, a little diner took in customers. It was about the size of a streetcar, which it may once have been. It had room for a counter and bar stools and a small table or two. My mission was to buy a bottle of Canada Dry Water for a use I didn't know but that had seemed important to Mother.

Holding the money in my fist, a quarter and a dime, I entered the business and told the waitress what I wanted. She didn't have any on the shelf and led me to a towering refrigerator at the back of the diner. On top of it, balanced there, was a row of shiny, clear bottles of Canada Dry Water, each bottle as tight and innocent as sin. She reached, trying for one on tiptoes, and managed to dislodge the nearest bottle. It fell straight down and struck me in the forehead near the hairline and continued to the wooden floor, where it burst open and splashed everything within reach.

The place didn't hurt, but it filled me with embarrassment. I was shy to begin with, and now this had happened. My pants and shirt were drenched and blood-spattered. The apologetic waitress darted into action, kicking at the mess and attending the casualty as best she could, having drawn the attention of every other customer and of her gruff boss, who poked himself from behind the counter and stood, glaring at us. Possibly at a signal from him, the waitress became even more solicitous, terribly sorry, and I went home with an intact bottle and a Band-Aid on my head, which got me into trouble because I had to be taken for stitches. (I believe Herbert insisted on that part.) Mother was mad at the waitress for her carelessness, but the waitress wasn't there and I was, and she was put out with me in that way she had of filling her lungs and exhaling, as though to filter the world of that funnel of troubles visited upon her. She ended it, as always, in exasperation: *"Oh! My! God!"* It meant, couldn't anyone—for one single time!—do something right and make her happy?

Almost the worst of it was the dread I'd had of her as I crossed that highway on the way back, looking right and left and carrying that bottle of chaser. The fawning waitress had been a blessing by comparison, and I was practiced enough to know that very well.

Memory informs; does it also explain?

Touching that V-shaped scar that I have worn on my forehead ever since, I ask rhetorical questions. Would I send a small child across a busy highway and back to buy something to make a cocktail? Would I allow one of our children to go next door each morning to get his shoes tied? Eventually, long before the epiphanies of old age, I came to believe that my welfare wasn't particularly high on my mother's priority list—and as for my father, once he returned from the war and the divorce was granted, he never gave a nickel of child support or financial help of any kind. Meanwhile, *You ought to be thankful you have a roof over your head!*

Every doctor learns that sickness is both an event and a role. To some people the role becomes a welcome one, a cherished belonging attained by those who have sought and found it after a lifetime of searching. To them it is a precious thing, not to be interfered with by doctors or anyone else. Sickness is their gift, their calling, their potion. They imbibe it and wish not to be disturbed in their rapturous enjoyment of it. Those around them learn this soon enough, and their doctors learn to smile when they hear another physician speak of a patient who has "enjoyed poor health" for years.

Mother's emolument was her *nerves*. I was amazed during my medical education to learn that nerves were actual physical structures, some as big around as your thumb, serving as the wiring of the human body, with the brain in control. To me from my experience, *nerves* meant a stamping of the feet and a reddening of the face and a gritting of the teeth and a scowl aimed in the trajectory of that anger spilling straight down like a bottle of Canada Dry Water from a shelf up there that was brimming with it. "You get on my *nerves!*" was the mantra, everything following from that. And it was sad. Sad because even as a small child I could see and hear and feel the rejection inherent in that. I wasn't the cause of her valetudinarianism, but I was often made into one of its symptoms. Everything in life goes into one of two categories: *to* and *for*. She had, for me, given me the most precious of gifts. But she followed it up, to me, with so many other things that it canceled out. Ultimately I was unable to stanch the hemorrhage of my resentment about it, but then, back then, all I could do was to learn to calibrate it, to predict it, to dread it.

I learned to take it.

It was my most important accomplishment, and it taught me that the deepest of life's wounds receive no stitches and therefore never heal completely. That they can't be seen renders them no less hurtful, cruel, and ineradicable. That isn't all. Tragic but true, I held her accountable for things that happened to me that would not have happened to me had my father been anything but the deadbeat, alcoholic failure that he was, a man I paradoxically had better feelings toward than I did her. He was not around but she was, you see, and in the same way that she piled anger on me, I shoveled it right back at her in the opposite direction.

But in between those troubling and all-too-frequent episodes, which she would end by beating me with a big, black belt, I loved my mother truly. I loved her so much I gave her a present every Valentine's Day (which was a few days after her birthday, and I sometimes combined the two occasions into one gift). Taylor's Drugstore in Pittsburg always had stacks of chocolate-covered cherries in various valentine-shaped boxes that were a sumptuous red, like nail polish, only shinier. I loved the way they made a big wedge-shaped display of them right inside the door, each wrapped in shiny cellophane, and they smelled so good, like dipping your face into a bouquet of flowers. The smallest was the cutest and cost a quarter, and I saved in my grubby hands the pennies and nickels that might come my way until I had enough for that box, all pretty in its exquisite design, and I purchased it and ran home and proudly awarded it to her. As I grew older, I could afford bigger boxes of chocolate-covered cherries, or even other candy. I continued gifts to my mother on Valentine's Day even into my married life, and she seemed to appreciate it.

Yet one day, much like any other, I began to require it of myself to revaluate my values periodically, sometimes daily, even hourly. And I had a thought. Maybe I had four fathers—one real and three steps—not because men were hopeless rakes but because my mother was not as soft and cuddly as she may have appeared in public. That didn't account for two alcoholics stumbling through the distillery, but it answered an awful lot of questions nagging me for an awful long time.

*   *   *

We returned to Mount Pleasant the winter of 1946, during a January ice storm. At the time, cars came in two types, those with "R&H," which cost extra, and those like ours, with no radio or heater. (It did have a cigarette lighter and an ashtray for Mother's cigarettes.) I knew that a car radio was for rich folks, but I made up my mind during that long, cold trip from Houston straight up through three hundred miles of the frozen, piney woods of East Texas, wrapped in a thin blanket, to buy myself a car that had a heater when I grew up, and drive in comfort. We moved, of course, back in with her parents. My mother must have heard *I told you so* a time or two, but they were family, and that was what mattered. I lived there with them to finish first grade, before my exile for second grade to Cooper's Chapel.

The Kimberlins having quit the restaurant business, Jim worked at Riddle's Furniture Store on the east side of the Square. They lived downtown in a one-story rent house at 500 North Madison, current site of the Mount Pleasant City Hall Annex. The residence had clapboard siding, electric lights, city plumbing, and glass doorknobs. It occupied the corner across from what was then the Mount Pleasant Hospital and Clinic at 501 North Madison, current site of Mount Pleasant City Hall. It was a long way from Irvington Courts in Houston, an older house smelling of older things—mothballs and flowerpots and peeling linoleum, the yodeling troubadours of distant melodies.

To me it sprawled like a castle, having a covered front porch and a porch swing and two front doors. The one on the right opened into a bedroom that led to a hallway by which one found the bathroom or proceeded to the master bedroom. The door on the left led to a formal sitting room, brilliantly lit by tall glass windows that were adorned with yellow window shades that rolled up and down with a pull on a cloth ring attached to a brown string. The single low-wattage light bulb, devoid of a fixture but with switch attached, was suspended like a braided lariat from a bent nail on the ceiling, a ceiling that seemed high enough for them to build cave dwellings up there, should they wish. Past the dining room the kitchen was not only big, it opened to the backyard. First, a small landing, then a sagging wooden stairway down to a backyard so deep that it was like looking at the ocean from atop a ship's mast. The stairway had wobbly wooden two-by-four banisters on either side, but descending the steps one felt like a sailor walking the plank.

The most frightening part of the house, though, was the crawl space between the ground and the tall, brick piers that were the structure's foundation. It was as if they had erected the house with the idea of parking cars beneath it. This space was covered in front by what on a car would be fender skirts but on this house suggested tin underwear—painted pink. The crawl space on the side facing the house next door was open to one who might dare to venture in and confront such dark, loathsome creatures as surely dwelled there. The space was mostly just that, though a few dusty (padlocked) trunks had been stashed there.

And there was a trapdoor accessible by the crawl space: it opened right into the hallway beside the bathroom. It meant that they could come for me day or night, and I worried about that trapdoor the entire time I lived there. I would sneak into the bathroom with a quickstep past the trapdoor, waiting to see whether they would pop up and chase me, and then spend idle time locked inside the bathroom, seated on the rim of the claw-foot bathtub filling my lungs with the smell of women's toiletry and disinfectant and hair oil and tooth powder. I took the time to peep into the cabinets beneath the sink, which held red, rubbery, indifferent items with tubes and such as to enlighten the imagination of a child.

Off the enclosed back porch between the kitchen and the master bedroom was a closet packed with homemade quilts in sufficient quantity that they reached from floor to ceiling. When it was very cold, I thought of sneaking into that closet and tucking myself under a mile or so of those quilts for warmth. Would they suffocate me?

*   *   *

The rest of that school year I attended first grade at the old West Ward School no more than a block or two north of the Kimberlin house. It, too, was memorable. First grade convened in a converted brick residence. It had windows and a door like most residential doors in the forties, each containing a long pane of cut glass that creaked in the wind and made shrill, shivery sounds when the wind blew hard and rattled when the door was opened and closed. We had twenty-six students, spring of '46, as the surviving picture shows.

Four runts are seated on the ground. Behind them is a row of mostly girls seated on folding chairs. Behind them is a row of boys, a few of whose faces one might recognize, including myself, fifth over from the right, standing next to my best friend, Gerald Cox, the biggest guy in the class, who would later move to Pittsburg and then confound everyone by moving back to

Mount Pleasant to graduate. Gerald, gone now, was a blessing as a friend. I know not what became of the rest and of their pretty teacher, nameless but not forgotten.

Also memorable: the break each day at midmorning for a snack. They brought out the same wooden boxes used for soft drinks, but laden instead with bottles of plain or chocolate milk, fresh and cold and delicious. It only cost a nickel for a student to buy and devour said bottle, but somehow I always forgot my nickel, and what happened was interesting. Since it was a rest time, the children had to have something to do while they drank their milk, and my fellow students elected a young man who ever after had no idea why. But there it was, the chorus of, "Let Johnny tell us a story."

And there I was on my feet in front of the class, sorting out an instant story that amounted to a chase sequence or maybe a Hollywood caper movie. Startling to me was the transfixing power of the story. As I began to talk, I held the rapt attention of the two dozen students in the audience and even the teacher. For those few minutes, I owned them. They were like a chorus singing by candlelight and watching for the director's every cue; it was an enormous feeling of power and satisfaction, more especially because none of them could do what came so easily to me. I turn to memory wistfully, as that infamous charlatan, to see whether any of them remunerated the storyteller with a nickel bottle of chocolate milk. It must have happened, I want so for it to have happened, but I cannot remember that it ever did. Each day, after telling the continuation of the story, I'd return to my seat and silently admit to myself that it was over, that I could never again do it because I hadn't any story left inside me to share. Overnight, as it were, the vessel would fill, and there I was on my feet again up there in front of the room, regaling them with a story. That chocolate milk!

*   *   *

A first grader discovers story: why that warbling vigil? Story would become my life, sketched here in places, but told not nearly all. Story has a beginning, middle, and an end, which is what we expend our lives searching for. Mine was of tapestries, not all of which could be peeled back at once. Embroidered upon each were fibers of beautiful white cotton, ruffles and lace, rich in the riches of an indelible thread. But there were other fabrics, as well. Here, different colors and designs, a broadcloth of denim upon a darker drapery, its weave hidden by its threadbare appearance, commitment or not. Here again, a simple sheath of momentous import, stitched in pain. Finally and finely came the unsurpassable depths of Asiatic silk in a covenant written upon my palm by a person I had loved, a patient, and filed in that registry that reaffirms nothing except the growing list of grievous errors that sail off into the infinite, to be taken up by others, finite like myself, until that lace filament is finally mended, the thread uniting all.

Maria Chavarria's death certificate. Dr. Ramiro Peña requested the autopsy and signed the certificate. The three causes of death are: (1) vascular collapse and cardiac arrest; (2) peritonitis and septicemia; and (3) intestinal perforation and obstruction [with] Meckel's diverticulum obstructing loop [of] intestine.

PART II.

Doctor's Choice

The chief of staff was the highest-ranking doctor at Memorial Hospital and was selected by doctors who had privileges at the hospital. He was the one in charge of granting such privileges, taking into account whatever input his own experiences left him and simultaneously receiving input from the other doctors on the staff. The chief of staff was not the CEO of the hospital. Hospital Administrator George Trader was closest to that, and outranked the chief of staff, the hospital being under civilian control. But the chief of staff was the medical doctor who lent it prestige, signified its quality. He did this by way of accomplishments and renown, as it were, and he was deeply involved in the dramatics surrounding the standards of care given to patients at the hospital. The chief of staff had the power to remove a doctor from the hospital staff, thereby ending that doctor's association with the hospital, or to bar from the hospital any and all such physicians as might compromise the public health.

Maria died on Saturday, July 27, 1963. Dr. Pilcher saw her on Sunday, July 28, and on Monday, July 29, I reported Dr. Carl Broderick to the hospital administrator, George Trader. Mr. Trader seemed surprised, but he took the report seriously, and the next day I met with the chief of staff. The chief was a doctorly man in a doctorly setting, a patrician. He was smoothed by age and creased by smile and exuded the confidence of a man who had lived his life without regret. We met in George Trader's office and the administrator, after introducing us, left the office. It was about ten o'clock in the morning. The chief of staff was dressed well but not overdressed, a man who thought of such things. It was instantly obvious that he was a warm human being, and he quickly expressed sympathy for Maria.

He said, "It's too bad, but forget it. Things like this happen."

He seemed to expect that this would be sufficient for me.

Later that day I returned to Mr. Trader's office and, at my insistence, he referred me to the chief of surgery, Dr. Broderick's colleague, whom I met on Wednesday, July 31. We met in the same office, but I arrived first and had to wait for the surgeon. I was getting to know that office. It was in the new hospital near where the walkway from Old Memorial ended in a glass door that opened with a *swoosh*ing sound. The office, on the ground floor, was everything a hospital administrator's office should be. It was clean and plush and the leather of the chair squeaked in that soft, cool way as when one is deluged with air-conditioning—and the office was air-conditioned—and in consequence bumps formed on my skin below the short-sleeve arms of my white shirt. The office had plaques on the walls and documents on the desk and a brilliant, beguiling sunshine conveyed to it by way of two or three windows with their curtains open. A cubbyhole it was not. Enter the surgeon, who served as chief of staff to the Surgery Service but was subject to the hospital's chief of staff. His was not a graceful demeanor: he took a fixation on me. Having introduced us, Mr. Trader again exited and closed the door behind him.

Briefly I had taken the seat behind the desk just to see what life was like from a seat behind a desk, or because it was so frightening I was trembling and didn't want it to show, and somehow I ended up back in that seat with the chief of surgery towering over me like a heavyweight who had just floored his opponent and was waiting to see whether he would get up off the canvas and require another haymaker. He was in his forties, well-groomed, well-finished, his body adorned in the stylish way of a man who kept up with what suited him. He was less than happy at this inconvenience. That would be his mien, of course, the hierarchy of medicine very clear about that. Some people wrap buildings and flag parks as anodyne to a Band-Aid hurt. Others summon up foodstuffs purchased on the cheap from those who dance in loincloths, and still others bask in the refreshing glow of bloody combat. But none of this, none of it, compares to the lacerating anger of one doctor upset with another.

There would be no smiles of bonhomie between us.

The chief of surgery jumped in anger, awaiting an opening, his mouth so dry from being furious that he hissed his every word. But I did not back down. I told my version of what had happened and asked the doctor what he planned to do about it. Standing there, hearing this, the surgeon conveyed to me that he had already heard about Maria, certainly had, and this too: *troublemaker*. That would be the charge, of course. Real doctors don't act like that, don't make trouble. Real doctors shrink from that accounting. Someone dies, and what the hell difference does that make? Everybody dies, the hospital sits in the stream and is sometimes the gondola; what in the fallacious hell of a good goddamned difference does that make? People get sick and die! That is the way it is! Death is a twitch, a creaking of old leather in a saddle that fits all, and who in hell anointed you God? The mockery was there, seething, foaming, but the chief of surgery kept it under control.

Like hell he did. "There is omission and commission," he snapped.

He waited to see whether his words had been heard.

"Dr. Broderick didn't leave something inside her and did not perform the wrong surgery, commission. Dr. Broderick omitted to do surgery, choosing to wait and see whether the Miller-Abbott tube would relieve the obstruction. That's his judgment, and you don't question another doctor's judgment— especially not as an intern still in training!"

I chose my silence very carefully.

"Now," he sneered, "do you wish to continue with your training?"

Surgeons are the tough ones, of course. Spot them on the first day of medical school tossing paper wads, raising hell. Often they are the college athletes, maybe not in football but in track and field or swimming or tennis or golf. They are the pugilists of medicine and one crosses them at his own risk. Later, in another venue, a surgical resident and myself would stop just short of blows in an explosion of anger at the bedside of a stricken patient, and thereafter we lived in the deadweight of that mummified stupidity, frozen rampage. And that is what I left with that day. The chief of surgery pushed me against a wall studded with wonderful accolades that he heaped upon my person; he could not praise me enough in words and manners, ax and hammer, and ended by wishing me well during my short life. *I make the rules and you follow, see?* I thought it graceless on his part, but that wasn't the point. The point was that it satisfied him. Tyrants live by tirades.

*   *   *

Wound healing in surgical cases occurs by one of three methods:

1. *Primary intention*, healing at its best;

2. *Secondary intention*, where open wounds heal by matrimony, the union of two advancing rows of a granulation tissue formed on the hillside of health; and

3. *Tertiary intention*, where a delayed closure is a complication produced by all of the factors that impair healing, including murmurs, whispers, summons, censures, threats, anger, and that dreaded ambivalence that is its own decision.

*　　*　　*

Saturday, August 3, 1963, having completed a month of my internship, I sat before a meaningless baseball game eating from a TV tray a lunch of sandwiches and soup that Mimi had made me and brought to our bedroom, where the TV was located. Roger was in and out and having fun. I would be on ER again starting at seven a.m. Sunday, but Saturday I was covered and had a chance to organize my thoughts.

The TV was from Sears, and we had bought it for our first apartment, on that third floor in Galveston, and paid it out but vowed never to trade there again because of the way the store had treated us. But maybe that was just Galveston. It was a good black-and-white TV and worked fine with its forked antenna. Our back bedroom in Corpus was vintage modern antebellum, defined as built before World War II and furnished with garage-sale couture. It had windows on two sides, rusty window screens, and venetian blinds to shut out distractions. I was dressed in a white T-shirt and the dark trousers I wore around the house. I had learned to wear a T-shirt under my regular shirt during summers selling magazine subscriptions, because it soaked up the sweat and saved the regular shirt somewhat. But around the house it didn't matter because I took off the shirt for the sake of comfort and wore the T-shirt, a clean one each day, as if it were a second skin. Mimi and Roger were there, but I was alone as never before.

A cat had taken up with us, and Roger loved it. Mimi said not to feed it or it would stay. It stayed. But as it was a stray, it was not let inside and didn't seem to mind. There was an unused, unattached garage out behind the house at the end of the driveway, and I saw Cat making its way back there, where it lived. It had come begging to the kitchen door a bit before, had its milk, and then left to do whatever it did until the next time. It was the same for the would-be doctor. Just there, propped open, was *Christopher's Textbook of Surgery*, our textbook on general surgery at UTMB.

"Although intestinal decompression [by tube] is primarily a method for combating distention, the history of its development has been colored by constant attempts to substitute decompression for surgical operation in the definitive treatment of obstruction … In these patients, it is not unusual for the tardy laparotomy to reveal that an unrecognized strangulation [dead place in the bowel] has been present and that the delay which had been intended for the patient's benefit has actually been to his great harm. Thus, it is the unhappy paradox that intestinal decompression, a valuable form of supportive therapy, through misuse becomes responsible for many of the deaths which continue to occur."[13]

*   *   *

The textbook omitted the dynamics of the thing: The dynamics were that Doctor knows, Doctor does (or doesn't), and Doctor is not questioned, least of all by an intern. Whatever happened was up to Doctor and, specifically, Doctor's Choice. The choice was the act, and Doctor had no blame. Maria Chavarria had to die for Dr. Broderick to grudgingly accept that she had an obstruction serious enough for his attention, serious enough for him to take an hour of his time to restore her to health. It wasn't catch-22; it was Doctor's Choice, and it frightened the hell out of me because it was so obvious and yet so stealthy. It was the taking of a life, in my opinion, by a doctor who knew exactly what he was doing, a path chosen by a doctor of that character. I had come across what would haunt me for the rest of my life. Only after years—decades—could I work out the dynamics, and only then did I conclude that Doctor's Choice, for Dr. Broderick, was nothing less than *neglicide*, a combining term of *negligence* and *homicide* that I will define more fully later on.[14]

For now, the death of Maria Chavarria when she could so easily have been saved was, in my opinion, a dirty little murder that the bleached white of the whitest of White Curtains could never be cleansed sufficiently to eradicate, and little because it lessened the doctor or brought out the lessening already present in the doctor. How sweet it must be to have the power to commit neglicide and get away with it! Doctor may accomplish it by doing nothing, while hiding behind his sacrosanct judgment. In practice, all Doctor needed to do was to pretend to treat by fielding some rigged sham such as a Miller-Abbott tube for a patient diagnosed with critical intestinal obstruction and who had already had one episode of perforation. Do that and hide behind an investiture of professionalism that is backed up by one's colleagues, and instead of being malicious, Doctor's Choice can appear valiant, a failed but honorable effort to save a life.

In those who dealt in life and death, apparently, it was never a matter of doing less for one patient than another, so much as a collective and reassuring certainty that all patients would die were it not for them. It then became the task of the busy practitioner to give the appropriate treatment based on the

---

13   Loyal Davis, editor, *Christopher's Textbook of Surgery,* 7th ed. (Philadelphia: W.B. Saunders Company, 1960), 747.

14   See page 213.

overall interests of the field and its professionals, even should the occasional patient be sacrificed in the bargain. The feeling of certainty about this among physicians—at least to Maria's surgeon and those who protected him—was very strong. It was an item they hadn't taught in medical school because you can't teach it, it wouldn't be allowed. It had to be sampled, imbibed, bootlegged, this gulped liqueur of divinity. And it must be intoxicating. Chugalug enough of it and it blinded you. Chugalug enough of it and it set you free—to thrill to the power of holding a human life in one's palm, whose death could not but reinforce one's magnificence! Perhaps it worked like an addiction. Nothing else could match its thrill, a thing as compelling as one could ever want, to satisfy that craving.

And there is this.

In the rarest of instances, the tube does decompress the obstruction and the patient does recover. In someone with Maria's surgical emergency, it might occur once in a million times, the exception proving the rule, but that was evidence enough for the surgeon hiding behind it; it was all Doctor needed to justify his actions to himself, presuming justification were required.[15] Doctor's Choice was ingenious, if barbaric, in that it was done so out in the open, committed in a medical and surgical setting by a leading physician who—and this was the most confounding part—also practiced honorable medicine and saved people's lives and was warmly loved by them for that. The choice was his to make and, I suggest, a barter: *I save so many lives that this one—were she to happen to die—simply doesn't matter.* How better to prove to oneself those Godlike powers? But there is another thing going on here, at a much deeper level: that of the heart. Perhaps therein, one finds motivation.

We live, each of us, lives wrangled from the raw materials at hand. I think people, most of them, tend to get away with what they can. What *we* can. I do not contend that there are murderers and non-murderers among us. I contend that we are each capable—capable of killing to protect ourselves and our families. And with the method and opportunity, and a dark tug at the heart, capable of even more. That Saturday in Corpus, reading *Christopher*, I saw it without fully understanding all of its hideous dimensions. That came much later and it is this: those deaths cited in the textbook, of people who died when "misuse becomes responsible for many of the deaths which continue to occur," were other Marias in other cities, other states, dying not through

---

15   A good surgeon, I was taught, takes out a few normal appendices. This meant that the good surgeon erred on the side of operating even when a good suspicion of a surgical emergency appeared. It meant that the dedicated surgeon did this with such a sensitive mind-set that, to protect the patient, one erred on the side of surgical intervention instead of leaving the patient at risk for dire complications.

mishap, though malpractice for sure, but by design. I hold that what I saw in Corpus in 1963 could just as easily have been in Chicago or St. Louis, Seattle or Bangor, Houston or Philadelphia. I am not sure, but I wonder whether the date might just as easily be changed to today.

*   *   *

In writing of the motives and personalities of serial killers, John Douglas, recognized as one of the nation's leading experts on criminal-personality profiling, writes that serial killers "tend to depersonalize their victims."[16]

Serial killers? In the first place, the vast majority of doctors are not killers at all, much less repeat offenders. But those who are, might be, and they do depersonalize their patients. In fact, the history of medicine over the last century is replete with instances of this very thing. Unknowing patients, devalued by doctors, were infected with disease, or followed with a diagnosis of a supremely treatable condition but denied that treatment, or used as guinea pigs without their informed consent, often to their detriment. The chosen population tended to be—well, you understand who they were. And these are only the published instances of wrongdoing.

I expect that every doctor beyond a certain age knows what I mean, having had it modeled to him or her during medical training. These acts were committed by physicians. Not only that, they were often committed by the most prestigious of physicians, admired doctors in private practice or the celebrity masters worshiped in academia.

Doctors are human. It is not a blameless species. As humans, they have the capacity of judgment, and, as we all do, tend to value others according to a judgment of that person's worth. It is not unlike the difficulties encountered in organ transplants. Call it the Difference Gene. Each of us is genetically different from all others, except for identical twins, and this Difference Gene must be suppressed by powerful drugs in order that the recipient's body does not reject the donor organ. Same thing occurs, I suggest, instinctively in every human heart.

We are different one from the other and the mind, no less than the body, recognizes this. Instinctive feelings and judgments toward others are there for a reason, a fairly obvious one, yet these may give rise to actions that are the farthest thing from compassion toward others. We all possess the Difference Gene of the mind. Powerful forces are needed to suppress it, and, should they work successfully, the instinctual, negative urges are replaced by love, tolerance for all, and the widening of the mind that occurs only through

16   John Douglas, et al., *The Anatomy of Motive* (New York: Scribner, 1999), 114.

education and reflection. But this is not a once and done thing, it is ongoing, and perhaps that is the scariest thing of all.

Every doctor has the Gene, and I had assumed that its suppression was universal among physicians in the hallowed grounds of medical practice. And I was wrong. I saw Maria as a patient seeking my help, a lovely young woman and a new mother ready to take her place in the world, to raise her son in love and joy and to live to the better good of all. She was not only my patient; she was imbued with that precarious risk known as human life. Hers was the contour of the divine hope. But to another, Maria might just as easily have been a pebble in the riverbed of our separation, one of the unwanted from that teeming source. After all, Maria Chavarria had already had a child at seventeen; how many more would she pop out over a lifetime, little "pepper bellies" that any decent Anglo-Saxon might enjoy sending to the weed patch? Blame her for atrocities we Anglos know were committed. Blame her for Goliad where, on Santa Anna's order, four hundred men, badly led and poorly equipped, were executed after they had surrendered. Blame her for the Alamo! Blame her for that wound that is cut into the bedrock of state history and cannot be removed by anything so paltry as mere time. Blame her for the loss of the flag of the New Orleans Grays, still held at the Chapultepec Palace, as art in the museum of that sorry chapter in their history and our victory. Blame her for the land we stole from them, the time they made us draw black beans and be shot. Blame her for all the sins ever committed, for tamales and frijoles and tortillas and the way they invade our garage sales. Blame her for greasy hair and old scars and miles and miles of wetbacks. Blame her for living, breathing, inhaling more than her share of our air. Blame her for the Catholic Church and for looking different and being different. Blame her for being and doing without our express permission. Teach her to disappear, dear God, or in Your vengeance remove her from my person and my state! Amen, and God bless America, especially those in the best part of it, right here deep in the heart of Texas!

Dr. Robert Jay Lifton, in his book *The Nazi Doctors*, sets forth the idea of doubling, a psychological defense mechanism consisting of turning one's life into a twofold drama, the one of decency supporting the other, its opposite.[17] Similar in meaning to the classic duo of Dr. Jekyll and Mr. Hyde, it is much more subtle. One's "second character" need look no different than one's first. It explains how those Nazi killers in the death camps could go home at night and enjoy their own children after, in some cases, tossing live Jewish babies directly into the fires of the crematoria. Impossible as it sounds, it does

---

17   Robert Jay Lifton, *The Nazi Doctors, Medical Killing and the Psychology of Genocide* (New York: Basic Books, 1986), 418–29.

exist—maybe in each of us. We just learn to struggle with the process and try and shed the doppelganger. Thankfully, most of us manage to do that. Dr. Carl Broderick, in my opinion, had not.

He is not here to defend himself, and maybe I err by arraigning and convicting a man, a doctor, fifty years after the fact. Were he here, I'd have to prove his guilt by physician testimony—iffy at best, and impossible at the time. At least this would seem so from what his colleagues said to me after Maria died. In their eyes, no neglicide, but to me that is a self-serving testimony that doesn't exonerate him or them. As is true for homicide, the statute of limitations never runs out on neglicide. The passage of time cannot eradicate that stain.

*   *   *

After Maria died, I never again wanted to be a doctor.

My heart was no longer in it. Arrogant as it may sound, I did not want to belong to a profession that allowed Doctor's Choice to be practiced with impunity behind the White Curtain. Consequently my story in medicine became my story of getting out of medicine, which turned out to be every bit as difficult as getting into the field. So what? Many people, maybe most, toil at jobs they don't particularly like: why should I expect to have it any differently? It went deeper than that, of course.

I had thought of doctors as special citizens in a nation within a nation, practitioners of a noble art. It was a nation governed not by laws but by an integrity that was beyond reproach. Learning better, I thought it my duty as a patriot to report the traitor, only to discover that I was the traitor, the sniveling coward of yore, and I wanted out. Call it the timid strength of the bruised bold. Maria would not be forgotten! One cannot pronounce another immortal, but I would explore that exceptional possibility. Cannot immortality in one heart exist forever? And be momentous? In wishing to right the wrong, a yearning that has never left me, I came to see the possibility of doing one thing at the very least, of witnessing what had occurred. Can bouquets blossom twice?

*   *   *

As for my job, quitting medicine and leaving it were two different matters. I had promised the year, and my salary was all we had. I owed my life in medicine to Mimi, who had sacrificed to get us through, and I wanted terribly to become a rich doctor, respected by all, to live a fulfilling life in noble happiness. But neither of us had gone into it for the money or anything else except, perhaps, the prestige. Set in granite was that I was still under their purview; I still had eleven months left of call and grueling rotations on the various services. And I dared not admit what was dreadfully true: I would never again be a normal.

I could go among them, I could look like them, I could act like them, I might even at times enjoy doctorly things with them, like a round of golf or a party where we doctors would—surprise, surprise—tell our "patient" stories (and every doctor has them). But at the most basic of levels, I stopped being one of them. I doctored out. Although I didn't know it then, it was my first step on the road from doctor to damnation.

*　　*　　*

August. Blazing hot. The full blast of summer heat turned Corpus into a steam bath. At the hospital I buried myself in the work that might set me free. I saw Rosa Ramos daily; it was my privilege to perform the acrobatics in which I had become expert. She was doing well, but unless she delivered prematurely, she would have her baby after I left OB/Gyn at the end of the month. There that baby was, inside her, wedged against a cancer of equal size. Looking at her belly after I'd returned that groundhog to its position, I expected to see an indentation of some kind, a delineation mark between the two very different growths. Maybe like someone making balloon animals at a children's party, a cinched waist separating the upper from the lower parts. It never happened. Each time the herniation was reduced, it rejoined its normal counterpart with no dividing line between the two. It was as if the two masses were fused into one, the normal, healthy part abutting and inseparable from the deadly, cancerous part. On the exterior, it looked normal. Inside, demons were waiting.

*　　*　　*

One afternoon I was called to see a young woman who had just been admitted in hard labor and had a disastrously elevated blood pressure. Preeclampsia is a mysterious condition, its main feature an alarmingly elevated blood pressure—known as hypertension—in a young expectant mother, especially a primipara. It causes swelling of the body and the abnormal passage of serum proteins into the urine. At worst, it also causes convulsions, whereupon the name changes to eclampsia, the victim typically having coma thereafter. *Eclampsia* is an ancient Greek word for an acute fever, and one can intuit how it came to be used for these women. The victim has swollen features, her face distorted by a shimmering puffiness that makes it seem as if her skin had air beneath it and were about to burst. One who survives it might still lose her baby if it had not yet been delivered. Preeclampsia was an obstetrical emergency of the highest order.

My first glance at Bonita Sanchez* told me all I needed to know. She was in hard labor and had that toxic look I have just described, which gave rise to the familiar term for preeclampsia: toxemia of pregnancy. The main need was to get that blood pressure down to the normal range as soon as possible.

The nurses and I started two IV lines and rapidly infused drugs to lower her blood pressure. That Bonita was in hard labor spoke in her favor, delivery of the baby being the single best therapeutic "agent" for preventing the convulsions of eclampsia. I also infused magnesium sulfate intravenously and gave it intramuscularly, having been taught to use it as a sedative for the central nervous system in patients with preeclampsia, its action yet another way to reduce the likelihood of convulsions.

The problem was this. Bonita had never visited Prenatal Clinic. Her blood pressure had not been taken until her admission to the hospital that day, when it was deemed to be an emergency instance of malignant hypertension. Whispers had it that she was madly in love with the father, who had seduced her and left her pregnant out of wedlock. Apparently she had been abandoned by her parents and lived in a terribly unfair isolation that had been inflicted upon her by them. Deviant that I was, I knew that the numbing cruelty of family can be a tragedy of lifelong dimensions. To think that they had put their daughter at risk of death, and her child, over something as common and as understandable as pregnancy, I found hard to believe and totally despicable of them. In any case, she was the sickest patient since Maria, but she responded well to the antihypertensive therapy we gave her, though not completely.

Bonita had her baby the next day and had convulsions anyway.

The baby, a girl, was born around noon. After the delivery, Bonita's blood pressure fell all the way to normal. She was groggy but wanted to hold her baby and did, until it was sent to the nursery. It was the first time I had seen her when she wasn't in crisis or in pain, and she was grateful for what we had done for her. She was also still frightened, having entered that troublesome jurisdiction wherein the laws of the body yield to unseen felons, but she was very brave. I kept her in Labor and Delivery for the time being, her blood pressure monitored closely, and returned to the Obstetrics Ward to complete rounds.

A few minutes later the phone rang: she was convulsing. When I arrived back at her bedside, she was having a grand mal convulsion, the worst possible thing that could have happened to her, and fleetingly I thought, *Only at Memorial.*

I injected a quick-acting barbiturate to end the convulsion, whereupon Bonita regained consciousness and seemed okay. But in spite of drug therapy and magnesium sulfate, she had another seizure later that afternoon and still another that night after I had left the hospital. She had not regained consciousness after the second convulsion and was still in a coma when I saw her the next morning. By then she had been moved into a private room on Obstetrics, the same room Maria had been in when I spent the night at her bedside.

During the next couple of days Bonita remained in a coma and gradually, I observed, experienced paralysis of the right side of her body. Convulsions don't cause paralysis. Not unless a brain hemorrhage had occurred, a hemorrhage secondary to that jackhammer high blood pressure, which can pound the small vessels of the brain into morsels of roadkill. Immediately I sought consultation with the neurosurgeon rotating that month at Memorial. Informal to a fault, the neurosurgeon was an engaging man who stopped by and saw Bonita that same day. After his examination, he ordered frontal and lateral X-rays of her skull and told me to call him the results.

When I reported that the X-rays were normal, the neurosurgeon declined to do anything further. To be sure, skull X-rays were useful in diagnosing a skull fracture or something that pushed one side of the brain against the other, but what they most often told about the brain was nothing. Newer diagnostic tools were not available in Corpus in 1963. Computerized X-ray studies of the kind that would come to be known as CT scanning, and a later development, magnetic resonance imaging (MRI), were decades away. There was a procedure that could be done, however, called carotid arteriography, though it could only be done by someone trained in its use, such as a neurosurgeon. That it was laborious, time-consuming, and a form of diagnostic surgery requiring interaction with the OR, an anesthetist, and the Radiology Department made me suspicious of the doctor's motives in refusing to do the study.

The study was designed to delineate a space-occupying disease of the brain, including tumor or hemorrhage, but it was a formidable procedure, as already stated. The surgeon had to inject dye through the carotid arteries (in the neck) while a radiologist captured the flow of the dye through the brain on a series of instant X-rays. The patient had to be scheduled and taken to OR for the study. The neurosurgeon injected dye not once, but several times over a period of an hour or two. Each set of films had to be developed before the next injections, and "an hour or two" could melt into an entire morning or an entire afternoon. In the instance of Bonita Sanchez, the neurosurgeon would be paid nothing for his time. Was that the relevant fact in her not receiving carotid arteriography?

*   *   *

Neurosurgery is one of the most difficult of surgical specialties, and all doctors respect those who practice it. When lawmakers debate whether to require motorcyclists to wear helmets, for example, the single most adamant group pushing for the law consists of neurosurgeons. Think about that and remember that they must wake up and go to the ER to treat brain injuries while others of their peers are safely asleep.

I called the neurosurgeon again the next day to ask whether he would please reconsider doing the study, her physical examination definitely indicating a lesion on the left side of her brain (which controls movement on the right side of the body).

He again declined.

*   *   *

It was time to look elsewhere for help, and I had as one of my supervisors a general practitioner, a young family physician in Corpus. This was a Caucasian man in his thirties, engaging and not the least formal in our dealings. He was as thin as a stork with fluttering wings and proud of his motility. He had seen Maria a time or two on rounds in July. The only advice the young GP had for me was to get a postmortem examination when she "crossed the bar." I had never heard death put that way but learned later that it may have been from Tennyson's "Crossing the Bar." Lord Alfred, help us!

I enticed him out to see Bonita Sanchez that evening by telling him she was in danger of crossing the bar. He appeared, saw the patient, and agreed to contact the neurosurgeon on her behalf, soliciting carotid arteriography.

He called the following evening and informed me that the neurosurgeon did not think further studies were indicated. I argued that they were. I had been looking in on Bonita several times a day, if for no other reason than that she was my sickest patient, and I had done a careful neurological examination within the hour: she definitely had paralysis on the right side of her body. I relayed this to the family physician on the phone and added, "All you have to do is look at her."

In that instant it was as if I had broken the seal on a container of explosives, which detonated in my face. I had never met with such blistering anger from a doctor, other than the chief of surgery after Maria's death. The GP may or may not have known about that, but he took up where the surgeon left off. And he had seemed so mild! During the spanking he gave me, I held the phone at a safe distance from my person while he impersonated Genghis Kahn. I insulted everyone, he said. I did not know what I was talking about. And I knew nothing about being a doctor and getting along with other doctors, medicine being a collegial profession. I was a fool to second-guess a board-certified neurosurgeon, and it was possible that I wouldn't receive credit for my internship if I continued to pursue that behavior, and so forth. The supervisor ended on a highpoint, telling me to rethink my entire life, which may have been the best advice I ever received, seeing as how I had just done that very thing. He must have slammed the phone down but was yelling too loud for me to hear it.

*   *   *

At the patient's autopsy, Dr. Pilcher stood across from me, as he had with Maria. I watched the pathologist find a pocket of blood, the result of an intracranial hemorrhage, on the left side of Bonita's brain, where I had expected it to be. It was over an inch in diameter, the size of a golf ball. It was already in the process of being broken down by the body. I asked, and the pathologist indicated that by its appearance it had occurred the day she delivered her baby, coinciding with a convulsion.

John Pilcher raised his head to peer across the table.

He said, "Did you consult the neurosurgeons?"

*   *   *

It was a fair question deserving a fair answer. I thought of the family physician, who I certainly did not hate. I didn't have any feelings toward him one way or the other except that I would probably not use him as a reference. Beyond that, we can never really know one another and flatter ourselves to try. And he was right about me. I couldn't get along with other doctors. I was blasphemous, breaking every taboo, pestering the gods, and annoying the minions in a factory where shrinkage was in vogue and the stock kept coming up short.

It was a factory, this I knew. It was a plant hidden behind a lovely White Curtain, universally praised by the citizens where it existed. But in too many respects it was the same as any other industrial unit, the difference being that its product was people. People were produced there and died there, keeping it all in balance. The factory workers were many, but the bosses were canny administrators and confident doctors who oversaw production and quality control.

As the factory product was the stuff of life, certain attitudes were forged. For example, when people are your stock-in-trade, they may be dealt with as any other product off the line. For one of them to die was bad, but it was part and parcel of the business and to be expected in this factory, and not nearly so devastating to those who ran the factory as one might imagine. For everyone who died, you see, two or three might be saved to keep the ledger balanced, and who was to say that the ones saved were less worthy than the ones who were not? The most frightening thing about it was the ease with which the factory might make up its own rules, satisfy its darkest impulses, and carry out what seemed to me barbaric acts that went unquestioned by other doctors out of a mutual vulnerability—and fright. It was like, think of the good we do! Testify to the tremendous opportunities available on the other side of the White Curtain! This factory rewards patience even as it exploits its product!

I never knew for certain whether the neurosurgeon at Memorial could have drilled a burr hole through the left side of Bonita's skull and suctioned out that pocket of blood, saving her life. Perhaps I was naïve to think that people went to the hospital in the hope of getting better. It wasn't turning out that way. Perhaps I had been stupid to believe that all doctors fought hard to save every life, even those of young Hispanic mothers who could not afford to pay a surgeon's fee. But I will carry to my deathbed the presumption that for this young woman with a cerebral hemorrhage, neurosurgery was not only possible, but straightforward. I will forever believe that a carotid arteriogram would have delineated the pocket of bleeding, which was sizeable. The only specialist who could have saved the patient refused to do the only workup that could have led to her salvation. Had she been a private patient, I was certain, she would have had the correct diagnosis made and, following surgery, most likely would have recovered. But then I was only an intern who knew nothing about getting along with other doctors by way of endorsing their choices.

*   *   *

I could have said all of this and more to Dr. Pilcher, but I didn't. I held myself in the immensity of nothing, reeling in a personal apocalypse. He was a normal, speaking to me as though I were a normal, little did he know.

Bonita Sanchez had a relative, a younger sister who worked in the Memorial cafeteria. I had seen her many times at bedside, crying for her sister and beseeching me to do the best I could for her by way of treatment. What bit of history I had on the patient had come from her. For the rest of the year our eyes met each time I ate in the cafeteria, and we grieved together for the terrible thing done to that young woman by her parents. OB/Gyn was turning out to be filled with women who gave their lives to produce life. Then again, what was new about that?

*   *   *

One day in late-August they brought to the ER a woman who was huge and howling in pain from her stomach. *"Me duele mi estomago!"*

Everyone was fussing over her as though she were dying, but she seemed, except for her screaming, to be in pretty good shape for what she had. Her heart was racing a bit, her blood pressure was up a little, but these were the things one saw in a woman in hard labor. We wheeled her down the long, dark corridor to a room I had gotten to know very well, and I delivered her baby. Her husband, neither of them professing to know that she had been pregnant, was absolutely astounded inasmuch as they already had a houseful of kids. He kept asking me how such a thing could have happened, and I was moved to give him a hug and tell him it was a miracle.

Birth is a miracle. That it begins with the union of two cells, each with half of their usual complement of chromosomes, and grows and transforms into an embryo and a fetus and an infant and a child and an adult, then repeats itself, is incomprehensible. As a physician, one sees the happy, normal outcomes and the outcomes that are not so normal. One evening, while relaxing at home, I received a call from ER.

Dr. Ramiro Peña had just delivered a small stillborn baby, but the placenta didn't come out afterward, and he thought she might need dilatation and curettage, or D&C. This was the surgery to ream out the interior lining of the uterus, allowing it to refurbish itself for normal function. I had been taught the procedure and offered my services to help prepare her for the surgery she might need later on, in the OR.

The ER treatment room was barely within walking distance of the ER, back in the vicinity of the entrance to Surgical Annex. It was about ten p.m. when I entered a room lit only by the glow of an examining lamp. A nurse stood and came forward, whispering that the patient had drifted off after saying that the overhead light hurt her eyes.

The nurse was young and anxious and probably not a nurse but a nurse's aide, a jittery person who was frightened to have been left in charge of this patient. She wiggled her finger at me and pointed surreptitiously to an aluminum stand that rose like a pod on a stalk. There, wrapped in a green surgical towel that she parted, was the tiny body of a stillborn fetus. It was the size of a four- or five-month pregnancy, held easily in one hand, far less than a pound in weight.

The patient was still in the stirrups of the examining table, and I turned on the overhead light. Upon awakening, the patient noticed my presence and I introduced myself and took my place at the foot of the table. Sterile gloves were obtained, and the nurse lifted the sheet. I saw that the speculum, the silvery examining instrument for the vagina, was still in place, locked in the open position.

The goose-necked lamp was positioned. The nurse handed me a ring forceps, and I folded and clinched between its teeth a four-by-four gauze. I employed it to blot the blood from the dilated cervix, whereupon I saw that from the cervical os—the opening in the cervix—extended what looked like a thick, brown string: the umbilical cord of the very premature infant. Not knowing what to do about that, I did nothing, except to take a history.

The patient said she thought she was about halfway through her pregnancy. Labor had begun abruptly, and as soon as she reached the ER, they had brought her around here. That was an hour or two ago.

While we were talking, she grimaced from pain. The nurse said something, and I turned away. The patient groaned. Her body underwent a contortion. Out of her, with the banging of the speculum to the floor, came a fetus that I just managed to catch with one hand. It was a little girl with eyes like raisins, attached by that brown string to a placenta the size of a sand dollar, which had two strings attached to it. Twins! Even though the nurse and I wore sterile examining gloves, the field itself was not sterile because we hadn't expected this. The nurse took the second stillborn fetus while I stood and went around and told the mother. She understood and began to cry, and I offered what comfort I could.

The nurse tugged at my sleeve. "Doctor," she whispered, "it's breathing."

Sure enough, the stillborn—wasn't. The tiny newborn was sucking air, its respiratory center giving it every chance to take up that oxygen addiction that lasts a lifetime and is the organ-grinder of life's melody. Its force was insufficient for her to cry, but breathe she did. Suddenly I was racing down that long, dark tunnel of Memorial Hospital juggling a miracle in the form of a shivering newborn swaddled in a green towel. My yells alerted people on duty in the nursery, and speedily the infant—instantly dubbed "Treatment Room"—was ensconced in an incubator. At a birth weight of ten ounces and with only a very remote chance of survival, the preemie was an instant phenomenon in the hospital. Through the nursery passed a disbelieving group of hospital personnel for the rest of the night.

Since I had ER duty the next day, I didn't stick around. But an hour or so after I arrived in ER the next morning, Treatment Room died, and I was summoned to pronounce the preemie. I also wrote a death note on the chart before returning to the ER. At lunch I crossed the hallway to the interns' lounge to use the bathroom.

Or I attempted to do so.

The woman from the Record Room who handled birth certificates and death certificates (not my fancied lover) saw me and stopped me. She was evidently there to see me. Hispanic and well-dressed, she had always been perfectly courteous to me. Now she informed me that one of the twins had been turned over to Pathology. Treatment Room, by contrast, having survived for a time, required a birth certificate and a death certificate and, as well, funeral arrangements by the parents. (The parents could also count her as an income tax deduction for that year.) These cold, hard facts of law weren't as baffling as they seemed. The medic, no less than any other professional, was and is bound by law.

That was why what happened next seemed so incredible. As I wheeled around and grasped the doorknob to the lounge, I noticed that she was upset with me. I knew her to be, to a tiny extent, a martinet, officious and self-important, the kind of person one encounters too often in a hospital, ambitious as the olive in a martini headed to hell. The parents, she said to me, could have been spared the expense of a funeral had I "taken care of things" in the treatment room. I thought I had heard wrong.

She said it again, for emphasis, placing the blame on me for my ignorance of such things. Mix hurt with pain and heap it upon my person, or whatever was left of it, and the next layer is the soul, or its masquerade. Already a feckless caricature of the doctor I had expected to be—chastened, impeached, and convicted of malfeasance; harassed, threatened, and betrayed by the factory bullies instructing me in the art of medicine—I was as off-balance as a man in an earthquake. Catching myself, I trembled before a precarious fault line, an abyss on another level of deepness from the first time I had encountered an undeliverable lie.

Bullies ruled the world, but what about the one inside each of us? Bullies existed there just as surely as those on the outside, allowing the intimidation that incarcerates the soul. That must be why we beat ourselves up, again and again, until the hero or heroine vanishes like a rainbow. Maybe it takes getting down to the soul to know that. Then, those who conquer their own bullies will learn something. On this occasion I accepted the challenge and made a decision. No one, ever again, would put me in that position. Get out of my kingdom, you aren't welcome here. Purchase air elsewhere. Flavor it with your own bullshit, and eat well. Live your crummy tyranny, concoct as scintillating a hell as you wish for yourself, but count me out. Inside my unfettered soul I found exactly what I was looking for, what was awaiting me there, and I let the woman from the Record Room know exactly what I thought of her suggestion and where she might place it, in a tone commensurate with the towering ugliness of it.

*   *   *

That sycamore tree in front of the Raymond Anderson place in Cooper's Chapel had been planted by my aunt Randie Anderson (once removed), when the family had returned from their five-year sojourn in the oil fields of Oklahoma. Short of stature but not of ability, Bernice Randie Vaught had been born in Cooper's Chapel in 1905. In 1920 she married Raymond Anderson, eighteen and a local boy, and they had six surviving children, three boys and three girls—actually three young men and three young women, as growing up in hard times bludgeoned one's pilgrimage to maturity into a headlong plunge, straight as the rows in a cornfield. Some of her children were born in that tent in Oklahoma, but some had been born right there in that farmhouse in Cooper's Chapel. She was perfectly capable of having her own babies, should help not be available.

Their farmhouse, set back from the road, was as modest as it was unapologetic. The front yard started beyond the barbed-wire gate and was smoothly mowed by its bovine employee. There was a stump or two sticking out of the ground near the lip of the front porch—footholds to it in lieu of actual front steps. The unpainted house had two front entrances, a long front porch, a tin roof, and a rain barrel beside the front porch. The well was in back. So, too, a big black pot for washing clothes with hot water after a weekly fire was built beneath it. The house was constructed as a plank-and-strip house. That is, planks formed the exterior walls all around, running vertically, with a smaller board—a vertical "strip"—serving to cover the cracks between planks, somewhat as how those who built log cabins chinked the spaces between logs with whatever was available. (Logs ran horizontally, of course, as opposed to the vertical planks in the five-room Anderson house.)

The planks were about eight inches wide and the strips a little less than half that. It had no sheetrock on the interior and no insulation. A wallpapering of the interior, however, had been done. It was the kind of wallpaper made to resemble newspaper, and it was so genuine in appearance that one could almost not tell the difference. The house did have a finished ceiling. It did have some linoleum in the kitchen and in the living room, where the fireplace was located. Still, cold weather found its way inside, and Choc remembered one time during a winter storm when his father was so sick with the flu that neighbors came and nailed big pieces of tarpaulin to the interior walls of the house to ward off that penetrating wind. Parts of the tarp would bulge and snap as wind blew through the icy cracks, and for days they went to sleep with the slapping sounds of that tarpaulin providing a temporary respite from the piercing elements of nature. (In the room at the back, where I shared a bed with Lula Faye, the water in the slop jar would freeze overnight during a cold snap.)

One might call this house drafty.

One might testify that it had cracks in the floor that the wind whistled through, the house having sagged on its piers like a hen in its nest. One might say that it was as out-of-date as a log cabin, but it had warmth, if any house ever did, the startling warmth of a working family raising kids, one of whom would fight in the Army with the Allied forces after the Normandy Invasion in World War II, one of whom would earn a doctorate in education, and another—as already mentioned—who would become a schoolteacher, school principal, and serve as president of the school board in Snyder, Texas. It was a Texas rural family whose kids learned to work hard and live frugally. They spent a couple of hours a day on a school bus into Mount Pleasant and back, for high school, and they were an asset to the United States of America. In that warm house dwelt the essence of America, its foundation and its durability, its patriotism and its reverence. Much later, with eyes blurred by sentiment, I was ever so proud to be able to say that I had spent a year with them.

*   *   *

At the time, however, I felt abandoned to a quaint people who might just as well have lived in Europe. I was important! I had lived in Houston, the twentieth century. The farmhouse was a nineteenth-century relic, and what was more, they were a strange lot, with the gall to claim that they were my relatives, and who had the nerve to chide me for being soft. Soft? I was *normal*. I had lived beside paved roads and roomy sidewalks. I had used a flush toilet and taken that for granted.

To start first grade in Houston and second out there in Cooper's Chapel, in 1946, seemed to me the equivalent of having stepped aboard *The Time Machine*, as recorded by old H.G. Wells in the previous century, and gone backwards. Even Mount Pleasant, by artful comparison, was as modern as could be. At least the streets were paved, the houses lit.

And as for the kitchen! In Mount Pleasant it was a wide room with a drainage counter and built-in cabinets and a sink and a stove and an electric refrigerator and other appliances, and even then it remained spacious. Food was made there and, as anyone knew, was eaten in the dining room. In the Anderson place, food was prepared and eaten in a kitchen that was a miniature of the one in town. They crowded around a cramped table covered by an oilcloth, elbow to elbow, close enough that eruptions of that southern volcano could not be localized, not that it would have mattered to the jubilation of the feisty, wisecracking family.

After each meal Randie brought out another oilcloth to cover the leftovers against the buzzing of flies, a constant in warm weather. They had no icebox—no one delivered ice out there—but a glassed cupboard served as a temporary storage for food. No need to store milk: the cow delivered it daily, raw and yellowish and with a taste like soured ice cream. Indeed, it was an unrefined product that drowned butterflies and paralyzed gnats. I had seen these people, milking, flick an occasional bit of dung from the top surface of the bucket, the way one flicked boogers.

That wasn't near all. Each breakfast had an excellent chance to turn into a seminar on the cow's palate. That strange, tainted flavor, of unnamed weeds in overgrown fields, or of a humongous mushroom happened upon behind the barn, its juices squeezed into that tall glass that everyone else sipped with pleasure might become—for the same percentage of city people who did not exit the shower with a full bladder—a treatise on the various factors influencing said taste. The conversation revolved around whether the cow had been eating bitterweed and ought to be changed to another pasture, or whether it had been dining on those funny-shaped flowers at the edge of the cow pond, or whether it had gotten into the clover that grew in the valley of the theatrical district in Manhattan, New York City, a vignette invented here but absolutely faithful to the cow's inspiration by way of dominating table conversation. Flannery O'Conner would have clicked her heels in glee. But in a kitchen the size of theirs, the cow's product was always the latest news, part of the festivities, and perhaps that is why the kitchen was the beating heart of the farmhouse. No judgment in hindsight could lessen that. Put feathers on a walrus and wings on an alligator and boots on a giraffe, and you still couldn't muffle those resonating memories.

It was located at the east end of the farmhouse, the kitchen, all the way to the right as you entered from the front. The adjacent living room, which had a separate front door, also led to the kitchen, and each morning after my hygiene on the back porch, I passed through our bedroom and another one and into the living room, the fireplace on my left, and thence the kitchen. I was usually the last one there, squeezing into my cramped place, except cramped did not exist in the country.

What existed in the country were make-do, elbow grease, and get-after-it. Country people grew up differently from town people, who grew up differently from city people. To the make-doers, every action was backed by long practice and held as sacred. Raymond Anderson sat at the head of the table, his back to whatever was there, and amid an unending passing of biscuits, I was to his immediate left.

People who have studied anatomy know that children up to the age of ten or twelve have an extra set of taste buds on either side of the tongue, serving whatever purpose that serves. It makes the young more sensitive to tastes than the adults who provide and prepare their food, for one thing. Years later, a lecturer at UT–Austin, I would have students each semester fill out a little questionnaire on one of two topics: *I hate this food so much that ...*, or, *I love this food so much that ...* It was a hilarious exchange enabling teacher and students to talk about food aversions and the techniques they had employed to avoid certain foods at the table. To be sure, people also had funny ways of getting food they loved, such as one woman promising sexual favors to her husband should he care to go out and pick up a certain flavor of ice cream. But by a wide margin, far more students spoke of how they had avoided a hated food that their parents expected them to eat.

It happened to me at Cooper's Chapel, but not for a vegetable. I even managed to acclimatize myself to raw milk, to an extent. But I had an instant aversion to the family's sweet of choice, ribbon cane syrup. It was the thickest of syrups, black like the inside of the smokehouse and thick to be cut with scissors. It came in a gleaming syrup bucket, a gallon in quantity and with a flat, round top, like a bucket of paint. It was made from the stalks of ribbon cane (sugarcane) or sorghum grown in the community. The juice was squeezed out by feeding the stalks into a contraption that was powered by driving a mule around and around in a well-trod circle, and the juice was then subjected to a huge furnace that heated it in sprawling pans designed for the job. Uncle Raymond grew some of the cane and helped the man who made it, who was his father-in-law, Denford Vaught. For this he was paid in bright gallon buckets of syrup. Raymond sold some of the buckets but kept enough of the product of the syrup mill to feed his family for the year.

The point being that, to me, the syrup was raw, onerous, and worse than medicine. It gave me chills on my back and neck to mouth it aboard, as though it represented a great vast endless frontier of wild things untamed, the birds of the air and the beasts of the field and the sea inside their veins. The syrup was from a past that held a stranglehold on rural palates, but not mine. I was certain about that. One sip of awful was enough for me.

But I was the only one who felt that way. I wasn't required to eat it, but I was force-fed my daily draught of ribbon cane by proxy, seated next to Raymond Anderson as he prepared his breakfast. Watching this became a daily rite of passage for me.

Each day the head of the household slid into his deep ceramic plate two or three eggs that had been served once-over easy. With his fork he stirred them into a confluence of white and yolk. There would be sausage and bacon as well, and these went into the mix. Add biscuits and country gravy. Real country gravy made from bacon drip and lard and any other holy thing. Thoroughly enjoying my reaction, he poured an indecent dosage of ketchup upon this primitive painting and, last, covered everything in a dark layer of ribbon cane syrup, served in a quart jar for his convenience and doled out by the pint. That it went on top of the ketchup, the gravy, the biscuits, the eggs, the bacon, and anything else that had survived, including when peaches or pears were offered from a Mason jar of same that had been "put up" last year and kept for just such special moments, seemed satisfying to him. Stirring all the while, and happy as a child, he appeared to have killed and burnt whatever it was on his plate, and he dug into it with a delicious pleasure.

"It's all going to get mixed up anyway," he explained.

*　　*　　*

A night with a severe thunderstorm found us marching into the front yard to take shelter in a hole in the ground. It was near the front fence, maybe twenty-five feet east of the gate. To me, this tactic was onerous and unnecessary. But I wasn't there to give advice, and many was the night when we passed an hour or two sleepily in the rain, seated as we were in a *U* on planks arranged around three sides of a storm cellar that was already several inches deep in rainwater by the time we got there. With a lantern to light our grief, our feet soaked from the torrent streaming in from above, we remained there until the storm slackened and there was no longer a danger of a tornado. It sure made the bed feel better afterward.

*　　*　　*

Saturdays we went into town and I got to see my mother. I thought about her all week, as I was sure she was thinking about me. She would soon realize the enormity of her error in sending me into exile among the unwashed and remove me to Pleasant and my life beside her: oh, joy! Mine was the eternal ache: *I want my mommy!* It was the driving theme of my life during those first desperate weeks. And, like the others, I looked forward to climbing into the bed of that clunky old Ford pickup on Saturday morning.

The ten-mile trip into town in the back of the pickup was fun in warm weather, less so in cold or rain. Anna Beth and Lula Faye were there in the back, usually with something to keep them warm. The best position was directly behind the cab of the truck, which cut a swath through the wind, though we had to leave enough space for Raymond to use the rearview mirror. Choc sat back there some and got the best place, though he sat up front more often, unless his mother went, because it was too crowded in the cab for both his parents and him. There was always someone else along, too, big or small, but from Cooper's Chapel and "family," and the more people in the back, the warmer it was on days when shared blankets converted the bed of the truck into a makeshift storm cellar. As it was, we had to shout to one another to be heard, our faces pinched against the elements, and what I learned about women in those trips into Pleasant was that they were amazingly like boys and men, watchful of their comforts.

Mother was working that year in a beauty shop on the north side of the Square, having earned her beautician's license in Houston, and my heart leapt with joy the nearer I came to that wonderful shop. The Andersons let me off at the Kimberlin house across the street from the hospital, and I would sometimes surprise Big Mama by sneaking in through the trapdoor. Then again, I only did that once. Having ascertained that she, Grandmother Alma Kimberlin, did not like me, I checked in with her and told her I was going to see my mother. She seemed to be as happy about that as I, and off I sped.

It was five blocks to the Square, a pleasant walk in a pleasant town, and the massive Titus County Courthouse rose like a mountain to guide me. It was white, four stories tall, and had been built in 1895 and remodeled in 1940. The first Titus County Courthouse had been built in 1846, when the county was organized and when its county seat was named for the pleasant wooded hills in the area.[18] What I knew from being told: they used to hang people on the lawn of that Titus County Courthouse, and that scared me sufficiently that I recoiled upon the sight of it and kept to the sidewalk that took me to the stairs to the basement, where restrooms were located. As to that, the smell! It had that public antiseptic stench, as if those who relieved themselves there had better watch out. It was a part of the package of strange repugnancies emanating from that beautiful courthouse, fascinating me with how a place can conceal things in the same way that people do. I wondered how people were able to go there every day and do whatever people who went there every day did. For one thing it was always crowded, this centerpiece of downtown Mount Pleasant, and for another, people slinked around it as though the building were more important than they were and they would beat the shit out of anyone who disagreed.

---

18   Mavis P. Kelsey, Sr., and Donald H. Dyal, *The Courthouses of Texas: A Guide*, 2nd ed. (College Station: Texas A&M University Press, 2007) 255.

The beauty shop, directly across the street, gleamed like a diamond ring but was as scary as a jack-in-the-box. It reminded me how far I had fallen, living in a farmhouse. With its glassy but narrow front, the shop extended backward a distance to accommodate six operators and a crowd of customers. The beauty chairs, resembling those in a barbershop, took up the wall to the left, lined as straight as kickstands on bicycles. My mother worked at the one in the middle or just beyond, and like everyone else, she looked up when the door opened. The metal handle on the shop's glass door was as thick as a monkey wrench and offered strong resistance before exploding like the kick of a mule. You had to backpedal to keep it from knocking you down. (I figured that was why they had put a rubber mat in front of the door.) The puff of cold air from air-conditioning was nice, but I dreaded the upturned faces of every employee and also of all of the customers including those using the hair driers lining the right side of the shop.

The beehive-shaped hair driers, mounted on arcing silver stands, hummed like insects above the chatter in the shop, each person exhilarated to share her life. It was hard for me to equate the smells in there with beauty, but I was only a kid. The women seemed satisfied enough, though suspicious of my credentials.

Who the hell is he?

I always wanted to retreat. I thought of how the women who taught first and second grade were always slanted against boys in favor of little girls. I was a second-class citizen in a world controlled by women, and the shop proved it. By the time I reached my mother's chair, where she was tending a customer or in the act of leading her to one of those buzzing hair driers, the element of joy was gone, and I felt like I had done something wrong. I had come there out of love, seeking love. I wanted my mother's love. It was not that I wanted my love returned, not that at all. I wanted her love as a birthright, not a privilege. I wanted her love as a young man needs his hunger satiated. I wished my mother the star of my boyhood. I wanted cookies and milk, hugs and kisses, fun and more fun. I wanted love.

But poke meatloaf through an hourglass and the part that is left is what I got. From that first time to every other time I visited my mother at the beauty salon, the only time in the week that I saw her, I was keenly aware of interrupting her at something important.

She stopped whatever she was doing for the briefest of instants, sometimes a quick hug, very occasionally, and just as quickly turned me away. Released, not having been given any money, not having been given any anything but the most perfunctory of brush-offs, I retreated outside. It was awful. Each week I expected better; each week it was the same. No! It couldn't be. Except it was, and I came to see that the occasional hug was for observers' benefit, not mine, since it never occurred in private, and that penniless hug was the most lavish affection I ever received from Mother. The mind of the person who would one day think of that reputed doorknob in Houston at the top of the stairs would not have known to ask, politely, whether there was such a thing as a postpartum abortion.

Back outside on the street again with a morning and an afternoon to kill, no money to spend, no nothing to do, no thoughts to consume me, I searched for meaning: I was seven years old and on my own. My assurance from an early age was that no one would or could help me but myself. First, I must learn to take it—lesson in progress—and then learn whatever else it took. Someday, maybe, I'd make of myself what I could. But Cooper's and the unpleasantness in an otherwise pleasant city taught me lessons no schoolroom could, a credo that did not quibble or exaggerate. Life was its own gift, voluptuous as a watermelon and as close as the fingertips, but everything else was at risk, including it itself. I could always go back to Alma's at noon for a sandwich or a nap. Mostly, I waited. I waited in the coolest place I could find in the heat or in the sun in the winter, sheltered behind a fence that shielded me from winds that seemed to blow especially brisk that year.

*   *   *

The explosion occurred at the Coastal States Petrochemical Corporation on the morning of October 23, 1963. By virtue of its deepwater port, sheltered by barrier islands from the Gulf of Mexico, Corpus was a shipping center. That, and an oil field in the region, had driven the development of petroleum and petrochemical industries in Corpus, and industrial accidents were a feared possibility in working with such volatile materials. The flash fire from this detonation killed three people instantly, injured thirty others, six of them critically, and stunned many more workers than that. The blast shattered plate glass in the surrounding buildings and hurled pieces of equipment and building material up to several hundred yards.

As Memorial was the region's designated Trauma Center, a dozen ambulances were soon screaming toward its ER. The *Corpus Christi Caller*, the local newspaper, described how the corridor of the old hospital soon resembled a freeway, with gurney stretchers stacked three high in some places and with people packed so tightly into Memorial's dark boulevard that movement was difficult.[19]

---

19 *Corpus Christi Caller*, Thursday, October 24, 1963, p. 1B. (Kindly supplied by Patricia L. Herrera of the Corpus Christi Public Libraries, May 28, 1999.)

The crowd included several dozen doctors who had dropped everything and rushed to Memorial. It included administrators and staff, police officers (who had brought some of the injured in their cruisers), priests, nurses, relatives, friends, and those who had come to the hospital out of curiosity or to volunteer to give blood for the victims. It was the biggest emergency that had ever occurred in Corpus, and it made the national news and brought reporters, photographers, safety engineers, and various government officials to Corpus with the swiftness that goes with such tragedies.

I was at first unaware of the news as word began to race through the hospital that morning. While the various and many victims of the explosion were en route to Memorial Hospital, I was in Operating Room 4, scrubbed in with my staff surgeon on a difficult and lengthy operation involving the biliary tract of a middle-aged woman. The accident did not improve my ability to respond to large-scale emergencies, but because of it I learned something about being a doctor.

*   *   *

Having rotated to Surgery in September, I had been on the service almost two months that day in late October when the explosion occurred. One day in September I had learned from Ramiro—who had rotated to OB/Gyn—that they had delivered Rosa Ramos's baby by cesarean section: a healthy baby boy. I had planned to go by and see her and the baby, for they had transferred the postpartum Rosa to a private room on Obstetrics, her cancer deemed inoperable. But somehow I never found the time. A few weeks later I learned that she had died, surrendering to a cancer that had riddled her body but spared her infant. Would that kid—or any of us—ever know what our parents went through to have us?

Rosa's death had given me time to reflect on how the two months on OB/Gyn had been the most pivotal of my life. I had seen life and death in all its hues in the *Eroica* of human endeavor. I had partaken of the sacrament. It came in a tumbler one drank to survive, and its solace was just that. I had delivered most of the hundred babies I would brag about delivering for the rest of my life. I had learned to use low forceps and an episiotomy when necessary and by practice was able to suture the latter so that the patient recovered with minimal pain. It amounted to learning to play doctor for real. I had experienced the heartbreaking loss of patients, had made the dreadful walk from the nursery back to the ward to inform a new mother that her baby hadn't survived. Had *I* survived? Not really. But what was left of the person I had been wobbled into the daunting arena of the surgeon.

I have spoken of the hospital as a factory, a people mill, its product life—and death. I included surgery in this figure of speech, surgery most of all, but keeping surgery in that metaphor puts description at risk. The difference between OB/Gyn and General Surgery is night and day, and the difference between Internal Medicine and General Surgery is that of the Earth to the cosmos. In point of fact, to slip on the garb, enter the OR, and view the world from behind a mask is like stepping onto another planet.

I would learn that there were different moons in this world and some surgeons behaved like lunatics. And although the sun was the same, surgeons owned it to the exclusion of all others, who dwelled in the darkness of lesser orbits. The galaxies consisted of stars, gas, and dust, and each person fit into one or the other of these categories and was constantly being reassigned by the star. That went for nurses, too, who became interplanetary luminaries by affixing themselves to a given star and dying for a constellation. This had been going on for so long before I entered it as a student that the rules were set like forces of nature, a universe daring intrusion by the would-be stargazer.

*   *   *

Nowhere in one's training can insecurity be greater than upon entering the operating room as an assistant for the first time. It's like picking the teeth with a machete, playing tennis with basketballs, employing a grandfather clock as a wristwatch. The old trick of the disgraced Roman running on his sword applies. Imponderables do not matter. The rapier tongue of the knowing is wielded like a lance.

The first lesson of a medical student rotating onto the Surgery Service at UTMB was that nurses ran the OR and considered themselves a cut above the ward nurses and having no equivalence to a lowly medical student. Nurses supervised the setting up of surgery and brooked no disagreement, invited no questions. They lent by their presence an air of importance to the proceedings and by their efforts let it be known that this was famous stuff, lifesaving, why they were there and why you had better be there for the same.

The first time I scrubbed in at Galveston Medical was on a cold fall morning in 1962, approximately a year ago. I wasn't sure which room or which resident I was assigned to, and I scrubbed my hands until they were rubbed red, watching for the guy I was supposed to follow. Then, extending my wet hands before me, I proceeded into the zodiac, where a nurse in a gown and a mask saw me and came forward and with her gloved hands offered me a towel to dry on. I thought how nice that was and used it and helpfully returned the towel to her.

She leapt backward as if I had struck her. *"Drop it!"* she hissed and with a dip of her head motioned frantically, her eyes wide with shock at my ignorance.

Having spent a lifetime learning not to drop things on the floor, suddenly I had to comprehend that in surgery, all rules are dropped. The floor was dirty. Ergo, anything dirty, such as a used towel, went to the floor. The strobe light, being dirty, was adjusted by a circulating nurse. One's glasses and face and facemask were dirty and could not be touched by their owner, no matter how much the nose itched or the eyes stung. The operating table itself, after the patient was installed, was covered with sterile items so that the operating field was clean, as was, of course, what every surgeon called the "wound," the cut itself and its contents, whatever they might be.

My first time, I was so overwhelmed by the efficiency of the place that I was moved to compare it to those famous first times that occur in any life, including flight, learning to read, and such other irregularities as rubbing destinies with another, dividing happiness in two, and, of course, adding the sun to the moon. Nurses, other nurses, raced about setting up the table, unwrapping green-clad packs of instruments. It had the quality of warfare, of people scrambling for cover and possibly dodging UFOs. I felt miniscule in the face of it, and perhaps that was one of its purposes. A nurse held a gown for me, and I wanted to fall to my knees and thank her from the bottom of my heart. It was the first time a woman had dressed me since Irvington Courts in Houston, when I darted next door for a teenage girl to tie my shoelaces. I found it sexy.

Arms forward, I stepped into the gown, and she applied gloves to my hands and snapped the elastic ends up over the sleeves of the sterile gown. That felt good. It felt very good. It felt like the click when you cocked that double-barreled shotgun for the first time. Meanwhile, someone else tied the thing in back. That also felt good, an amazingly sexual experience, it being fun to be dressed by a masked woman, eyes dark and thrilling and serious as a woman drawing on her stockings. In fact, this minor planet was the sexiest place in the Milky Way. It was a secret every surgeon learned, and no OR nurse was willing to have him or her forget.

Nurses continued scuttling in and out the door, bringing in celestial things, and I was guided to a position on the left of the starry host, where I would hold the spatula for the experiment—but which was called a retractor—once the wound was fully exposed. Finally, the scrub nurse who had handed me the towel mounted a push stool beside the surgeon, giving herself the proper elevation, and shortly began passing instruments with such a rhythmic force that when they hit the pocket of a gloved hand, they made a *pop!* The surgeon loved this and complimented it. "Now there's a nurse who knows how to hand an instrument!" We all felt the better for it, took pride in this high praise from our momentary deity, and began working still harder to earn still more praise. It seemed, somehow in that setting, the most important thing in the universe, and we bathed in it with the casual intimacy of naked strangers.

*   *   *

Surgery itself, should I have left the wrong impression, was not all bad. One wrote with a sharp quill that libretto, to a melody that was new with each performance, the work itself having scales and octaves and brass and so forth. It was physically demanding, as well. It almost required an athlete to withstand that pitch of orchestral effort, that stultifying concertmaster insisting on unending hours of intensive work. A good surgeon became a great surgeon not so much by surviving it as by coming to see that the tool of most importance was not his skill or his stamina or his age or his personality or his judgment. It was in that most intimate of harmonies, the tenor of his heart.

*   *   *

The morning of the 1963 explosion in Corpus, Dr. George McGraw* and I were removing a woman's gallstones in Memorial's OR 4 when the first news of the tragedy reached the hospital. Initially it'was thought that there might be hundreds of casualties headed our way. Everything went into crisis mode. A feeling of impending doom pervaded the hospital. People and their actions became unpredictable.

I liked George McGraw. He had won my heart to the extent that I recognized a truth. Had he been the surgeon rotating at Memorial Hospital in July and August, Maria would still be alive. That in itself was enough to ravage the soul—that a person's life depended on such randomness, but in medicine random events were like summer storms: they followed no rules except seeming to test the boundaries of human endurance.

Gallbladder surgery is in the right-upper quadrant of the abdomen, and I was holding a retractor and assisting in such other ways as was required when someone dipped into the room, holding the door open, and tasked us with immediately vacating the OR because of the impending emergency.

The surgery was tedious and intricate, and we had just reached the critical stage. Besides removing the diseased organ, we had to open and explore the bile ducts to remove any stones that had wriggled their way into it. As the finishing touch, the main bile duct was closed around a T-tube, a length of

– 202 –

rubber tubing in that shape, the two ends of the *T* serving as an artificial conduit, or reinforcement, of that part of the patient's main bile duct. The top of the *T* was sutured in place and the bile duct was closed around it, then the free end of the *T* was brought out through the wound, which was closed around it. Covered by a gauze dressing, the tube remained in place for six months before it was withdrawn during an office visit, with the small residual opening left to heal on its own.

George McGraw was an athletic man of thirty-eight, whose training at the Baylor School of Medicine, in Houston, included two years of cardiovascular surgery. Perhaps that was why his hands moved at blur speed during an operation: the man was teeming with an energy I admired. McGraw taught dexterity, to the extent that it can be taught, and he taught how the surgeon functions in his dealings with doctors. He had also demonstrated one morning how to talk to the relatives of a patient.

After an exploratory operation we had performed on his private patient, wherein the finding was cancer, Dr. McGraw closed the wound and sent the patient to the recovery room. Still in scrubs, we entered the waiting room, where he spoke to the patient's wife, daughter, and sister. Upon hearing cancer, one of the women threw up her arms and began flinging them about in wild gyrations while yelling to the top of her lungs. Quietly Dr. McGraw said, "I'm not going to talk to you if you act that way."

Instantly the woman stopped wailing, ceased all activity, and stood respectfully and silently while the surgeon finished telling them about the cancer and its prognosis.

To require this of a patient's family, of course, reflected the control the man exercised over his own emotions. During surgery he exuded the concentration of a man building a ship in a bottle. He did not rant like an infant and fling surgical instruments in a fit of rage. He did not speak rudely to nurses or assistants. He never lost his equanimity. The one time he did seem a bit perturbed during surgery, and did raise his voice, had absolutely nothing to do with the surgery itself. It was on that October morning of the explosion at the petrochemical plant, during surgery on the woman with gallstones.

*   *   *

A crisis, if it does anything, clears the mental slate. Patent as the free end of that T-tube coursing from inside the abdomen to the exterior, a crisis is a tunnel one must squirm through by whatever means are available, allowing one to explore his capacity for control. Mine wasn't very good.

As the crisis hurled itself toward us, and hit, I felt like I was in one of those states described by those who have had a near-death experience and recovered. I seemed to see myself apart from myself, even while I was assessing what had happened and what was happening and worrying about what to do. That George McGraw would have saved Maria was only as it should have been, yet the certitude of that conviction had become a thorn in the thistle of my evolving education, because why should a patient's life hinge on whether one doctor or another happened to be on duty, except for the inconvenient and universal truth that all of life happened exactly that way? Why had certain individuals gotten up the morning of Wednesday, October 23, 1963, driven to work, willingly taken their places on the line, and died instantly? As to that, in retrospect, why would President John F. Kennedy come to Texas for assassination within a month, an event of such overwhelming tragedy that it changed world history?

"Deaton, you have pretty good hands."

George McGraw said it abruptly and startlingly that October morning, and I was surprised and flattered. I had probably just tied a passable square knot around a vessel he had clamped, no mean feat when you consider that I was wearing rubber gloves, slick and bloody, while holding three or four palmed clamps and a scissors in my right hand, plus a couple of clamps in the palm of my left hand. Of course, a knot of surgical nylon doesn't count unless it holds on a wet surface while its ends are being cut, a surface moving with the respiratory motions of the patient, which have caused many a knot to slip uselessly asunder.

"Ever thought of going into surgery?"

I suppressed the obvious—that I had spent a lot of time thinking about not going into surgery, not going into anything but another field. Actually, I didn't enjoy surgery. I did not like the mask, which was uncomfortable; I did not like the gowns, which were hot and had no pockets; I did not like the surgical cap that was tied around one's head as though he were going swimming. And I didn't like that all of your best work—or worst—occurred in a public arena arranged by others for conditions yet to be determined, eternal tussle with an irregular irregularity of spittle and idiom and dialect, a parody of catechism and the ardent fearsome, an improvisation upon the glamorous and the burlesque. No, I did not intend to go into surgery even though I had cut flesh, or probably most of all because I had cut flesh and found it unsuited to my temperament.

It had also not escaped my notice that to become a surgeon, extending care to everyone regardless of payment, would honor Maria. But I did not have the bold air of confidence required for it, the physical strength and stamina, the ostentatious precision that the surgeon expends years and years perfecting and can make into an art. Another intern had told me that he wanted to be a surgeon because when they needed you, they really needed you. There was a lot of truth in that, Maria being Exhibit A. I had not shared her story with George McGraw. I wasn't sure how he would take it and could not risk alienating my supervisor. It would have been suicide to tell him that I no longer wished to be a doctor.

"Probably go into internal medicine," I said.

"Then you will be one of the enemy."

But the surgeon quickly laughed, as I did, for the surgeon and internist complement one another, one relying upon the skills of the other.

At this point, as I said, we had reached a critical point in the surgery. The most tedious part, to check the patency of the biliary tract before instilling the T-tube, included injecting dye into the bile duct and taking an X-ray of the area. Known as a cholangiogram, it was both necessary and further lengthened the procedure. By then, the crisis having struck, it was impossible to ignore the racket in the hallway outside the operating room.

Suddenly the door burst open again, only this time the nurse was yelling hysterically at us. It was all about the news of the explosion. It had been mandated that all operations in progress were to cease, including ours. All of the operating rooms were to be vacated to provide room to treat the countless casualties headed our way.

Following Dr. McGraw's lead, who said nothing, I ignored her.

The nurse left, slamming the door that connected to the hallway, her contortions visible from OR 4, visible because the wall on that side contained a bay window of plate glass. The way we were situated, Dr. McGraw's back was to the glass, but I was on the opposite side of the table and could sneak glances and see the commotion taking place out there. The thwarted nurse stood fuming in that glass hallway, her hands on her hips, then turned and carved in the air a gesture of utter futility toward us and stalked away. Muffled voices reached us from elsewhere, smacking of irreverence from still other surgeons who would not stop what they were doing.

An emergency wakes up a part of you that you hadn't known was asleep. Were I in charge, what would I do? A lot of my training taught me to yield in deference to higher authority. Follow wisdom or else.

We were taking up space in an elective operation on a woman who might not die were we forced to stop. But it would be dangerous to her, putting her at risk of bile peritonitis should we stop at this stage of the surgery. Still, the patient hadn't asked to be operated upon the same day as a tragedy that broke the threshold of human nerves. It wasn't her fault, and George McGraw had no intention of stopping.

Boom! The nurse again. "Dr. McGraw, you have to leave. Clear out! Emergency!"

George McGraw did not so much as acknowledge her. It was as though he were locked into a time zone that she couldn't reach, and Dr. McGraw not only did not recoil in a fear of the unknown, he failed to heed ungodly gods that buzzed like a bluebottle fly.

Odd how appropriate the image. Odd that the operating room was insular from the world, at once a haven and a bastion of controlled theater, where every actor had a part and a place in the ritual offering to the silent gods that take blood and give it back in pain and misery and death. Odd how the pleasures of civilization so often came down to this: the yielding of one's will to another. Odd how every suture was a filament tracing back to barber poles and trepanation and divination and all of the healing in all of the temples of Aesculepius, humankind's defiance of the assorted intrigues that laid waste to red bile, yellow bile, black bile, and phlegm, the repudiation of which brought medics in a whirligig, a dizziness not lost on a history that was permeated with the struggles of Hippocrates and Aristotle and Claudius Galen, physician to Marcus Aurelius—Galen, whose name meant *calm*. His calming effect via copious writings on the Hippocratic teachings ruled medicine and surgery for a millennium and a half, even though Galen had taught, among other fallacies, that the uterus had two compartments, the right side for the male fetus (of course), and the left for the female. The guy had placed a bone in the heart, coaxed air into the bloodstream. Yet of him it was said, "Better to err with Galen than to be right with someone else." Indeed, in 1559, fourteen hundred years after Galen's death, a member of England's Royal College of Physicians was asked to retract his statement that Galen had erred in some of his conclusions. The penalty for refusal was expulsion from the Royal College: the doctor hastily retracted. Did doctors always retract?

It was all I did. I had spent hours, days, and years at it. But the great ones did not retract, physician or no—not Copernicus, who died in the same year that Andreas Vesalius published his great anatomy book, 1543, and not even Galileo a century later, not really, who was kept under house arrest by the authorities of the church and made to publicly retract, but he mumbled and muttered the truth until he died. The sun did not orbit the Earth—the other way around—and patients did not exist to serve doctors, but vice versa.

The nurse again. "Dr. McGraw, you *must* leave!"

OR 4 was a chestnut brown in color, as opposed to the confluent green of everything operative in Galveston. We were in Memorial brown, that part of the spectrum that exists for no other reason than to add dissonance to human endeavor. It was a spacious room, the size of a delivery room, the kind of operating room built for modern times, with room in there for a dozen and a half people, should they have wished to intervene. The room was dominated by that long-assed light, supported above the table. The room had three solid walls and a brown floor that slanted down to a grate of metal forming a drain in the exact center of the room, shiny as the grill of an automobile, for cleaning up with liquid soap and hosed water the bad stuff that might be spilled onto an operating room floor. And it had that glass wall facing a corridor that was changing by the second, with people beginning to shout and to jostle one another out there, the brusque nurse above all, setting up her docket. A giddy something else was in the air, explosive in nature.

The OR smelled good. Before it was dressed, the sutured wound and the surrounding area were sprayed with a brown, sticky something to heighten the adhesiveness of the tape used to hold the dressing in place. The smell lingered, begetting an exotic aroma. Oil of wintergreen cut by essence of clove, say, or good old sarsaparilla, a fragrance equivalent to poking a new stick of gum into the smacking jaws of the exalted beast.

The nurse seized the door and flung herself into the room, yelling at us to the top of her lungs. It was hard not to hear.

"Dr. McGraw!" she screamed in earsplitting invective.

In attendance were an anesthetist, a scrub nurse, and a deadhead intern, as well as a circulating nurse already bringing in what would be needed for the immense number of casualties headed our way.

The surgeon stopped the operation with a motion of his hands. He straightened his shoulders and rotated around from the waist so he could see the source of our harassment without breaking scrub. His voice had an edge to it I had never heard. He told the nurse, who after all was only doing her job, that we were going to finish even if it was World War III, and she was to leave us alone starting *right now*, or he would take it up with her supervisor. It grew very quiet. The nurse went silent. And then she went.

And did not bother us again.

We finished in another forty-five minutes, and the two of us pushed the patient's gurney to the recovery room. By then, crowding the hallway of the surgical suite, doctors were lined up to be matched with patients injured in the explosion. They made snide remarks to George McGraw that he did not dignify with a response. There were twice as many doctors as needed, and after changing into street clothes, Dr. McGraw and I attended Surgery Clinic.

Yes, I admired the guy. I respected him. He was like so many doctors in Corpus, first-rate, well trained, intense in commitment to the patients, be they private patients or staff patients. The essence of writing is to employ that long-armed light at will, a spotlight descending from the ceiling, and to twist it here and there limitlessly to probe what can cause the eye to recoil in horror or what can guide it to rejoice in the kaleidoscopic beauty of human kindness. Doctors, while imperfect, are from the part of society that christens education and service and, yes, devotion. How unfair it seems to speak of the shortcomings of certain surgeons who, after all, were well loved and thoroughly competent, who just happened to commit neglicide on those who could not pay a fee or didn't measure up in some other way. Medicine, in all its palatial invincibility, permitted certain doctors to treat human life as a commodity, value-based, as though life itself were there for them to render a service unto themselves.

*   *   *

The events that day in surgery, during a crisis, fit the dynamics of Authority vs. Responsibility, AVR in DoctorSpeak:

AVR = AUTHORITY vs. RESPONSIBILITY

AVR exists in the interactions of every doctor–patient relationship. There is always someone who takes Authority for a patient's care, as there is always someone who takes the Responsibility for it. The patient has the right to expect that the attending physician, or any specialists summoned to help, will assume both Responsibility and Authority for his or her medical care.

But what happened the day of the explosion in Corpus, when trauma patients and chaos descended on us in the OR, was a chilling example of the danger lurking behind the White Curtain when Authority is split from Responsibility. In trying to stop the surgery on a patient who had every right to have her surgery completed, and certainly as much right as the patients injured in that explosion had a right to emergency care (and who had not yet arrived at Memorial), that nurse had attempted to wrest from Dr. George McGraw his Authority over the surgical treatment of his patient, while leaving him to accept the Responsibility for the outcome. The surgeon, Dr. McGraw, didn't explain it to me, but he didn't have to. The math—actually postulates—was easy:

$$AVR \div 1 = 1.$$
$$AVR \div 2 = 0.$$

Most frightening of all, and appalling in its implications, was how often Authority was split from Responsibility in the setting of medical training. It always put patients in danger. An example of attempted splitting of AVR occurred that day in the corridor when the fussy woman from the Record Room said that I could have "taken care of things" instead of admitting Treatment Room to the hospital. She may not have known how it worked, but I did, although incompletely at the time. Had I followed her suggestion in that instance or in a future instance of same, I would in the instant that I killed a newborn have allowed her to become the Authority sanctioning it, while leaving me with the Responsibility for taking a human life. It was that simple and that ugly. Is a physician the subject of a sovereign Authority or the poet laureate of his own integrity?

*   *   *

The heartbreak of being powerless to stop the splitting of AVR enables the Authority to commit neglicide on medical or surgical patients and to do so with impunity. It's a scientific lynching done not by rowdies but by an enterprising practitioner applying his or her set of values. Have you survived your personality? Have you become your character? Have you lived your fate? Have you done more than take in oxygen and return carbon dioxide to the air? Have you justified yourself to the world? Have you existed in such a way that you leave the world better than it was when you entered it? Did you/have you/ can you pass Doctor's muster? Are you a worthy person to Doctor, dedicated and true, or do you happen to be a person of lesser worth in Doctor's eyes, one who might—sad as it is!— be counted by race or revelations to be worthless? Is your skin the right color, your aspect admirable, your attitude refreshing? Quite possibly you are being graded on these standards even as we speak. I know this not because I never did it but because I have looked inside my own heart and found it there.

*   *   *

In 1969, when I was in the Air Force serving at a base in California, I was an internist who both worked in the Air Force Clinic and saw people sick enough to require a stay in our small hospital. The year itself was a hard one. Because health care was part of the payment package provided to them by the service, active duty and retired personnel—and their dependents—sometimes looked on doctors and nurses as their employees.

For instance, I saw on rounds one Sunday morning a retired officer admitted overnight, having suffered a myocardial infarction, or heart attack. The proper tests had been ordered, including the EKG and blood work, and these were diagnostic. According to the chart, which a doctor always reviews before seeing the patient, his chest pain was gone and his vital signs normal. The patient was on the open ward and eating breakfast when I saw him. In fact, he was presiding. It was as though a busy potentate had stopped by to honor us with his presence.

One of the things I knew to order for the victim of a heart attack was a diet that included nothing hot or cold since, when swallowed, such foods may stimulate the heart as they pass adjacent to it down the esophagus. For some reason the patient had been given a regular diet and was enjoying a piping-hot cup of coffee, its caffeine yet another reason for excluding it from the diet, as caffeine stimulates the heart rate. I wrote the order to change his diet to nothing hot or cold and no caffeine. I have a fuzzy memory of the nurse or myself mentioning to the patient his current nourishment, though I am not sure. At any rate, he did not surrender the cup. He may have toasted us with it, offering a mischievous smile.

Our conversation went elsewhere. Our facilities were inadequate, he said, and he demanded from me that he be transferred to a civilian hospital immediately where, as he put it, "the doctors know what they are doing." (In a sense, having been put on the wrong diet, he was correct in this; we did the best we could.) In his surprising diatribe against me that morning—this from a man I had never seen before—I heard my abilities reduced to a new low, while I nevertheless accepted responsibility for his care. Marilyn Monroe once reportedly said people came up to her and talked to her as though they were speaking to her clothes. I know the concept. After rounds, I filled out the necessary paperwork for the transfer before leaving the hospital. Meanwhile, in my trips back and forth to his bed, the other patients on the ward did that thing with their eyebrows showing that to marvel at an asshole is a universal thing.

An hour or two later, after I returned home, the nurse called to report that the patient with the heart attack had just suffered a cardiac arrest. The hospital's equivalent of a Crash Team saw him but could not resuscitate him. By the time I got back to the hospital, he was in the morgue, and mine was the task of notifying his next of kin. And I've always wondered whether that hot cup of coffee I did not take or he did not surrender figured in his cardiac arrest. I think it probably did, but he may have already had a couple of cups before I even saw him.

My point is that I harbored the feeling of not particularly caring that he had died, it seemed an affirmation of his error in ridiculing my abilities. Pardon my French, but he had pissed me off. My reaction was one of those things you wish you hadn't almost as much as you were glad you did. A doctor who tells you he or she has not had similar feelings toward patients is lying. But having the feelings is one thing, acting on them another. Professional conduct calls for a physician to award the patient with the best of one's training and experience, no matter how belligerent or abusive the patient may be. Or so I thought.

*   *   *

Death by neglicide can occur in much larger teaching centers than Memorial Hospital in Corpus. It is always Doctor's Choice, but in big hospitals politics may enter the equation. As a resident in Internal Medicine in Galveston, I watched another resident admit a woman diagnosed with meningitis. He took a history from a family member and did a physical examination and a spinal tap, confirming the diagnosis. He then made the mistake of asking consultation from the Infectious Diseases service before he started treatment. The specialists saw the patient and wanted her treated with only one drug, ampicillin, rather than the standard three-drug approach then offering the best chances of a cure for this critical disease. The dynamics then existing in training meant that the resident in Internal Medicine took a very big risk by refusing to follow the recommendations of specialists.

It was Doctor's Choice as a power play. The resident, having Responsibility for the patient, appealed to the chief of internal medicine, Dr. Raymond L. Gregory, who sided with the Infectious Diseases service and its doctors. They were, as he said, "trying to get enough patients for a paper to be published showing that ampicillin alone was sufficient to save a patient's life." In this instance, the chief of internal medicine, having Authority over the specifics of what drugs the patient received, was risking nothing because should the patient fail to respond to the ampicillin, that burden would fall to the Infectious Diseases doctors and/or the resident who, by the way, knew there was a three-drug regimen for meningitis and intended to give it and told me that he had consulted the Infectious Diseases service only because he wasn't sure about the third of the three drugs, one or the other of a couple of choices. This middle-aged woman did receive treatment for meningitis, but not the best treatment, not the standard treatment, and she died a few days later.

AVR ÷ 2 (or more) = 0.

Academic neglicide, different from individual neglicide, has probably accounted for more patient deaths than all of the individual instances combined. As for this woman, I don't know whether the Infectious Diseases physicians lost any sleep over it, but it was devastating to the resident who held the Responsibility for her, and I saw in it the same undulating tenets of indifference that I had found in the chief of staff and the chief of surgery after Maria died. In fact, I shared my friend's feelings of having been betrayed. In a prestigious hospital, despite the availability of excellence, the patient was lost forever to her family, her friends, her place in the world by a selfish entitlement to publish a paper in a journal by those who had Authority without Responsibility. Each time a patient dies from a splitting of AVR, those nearest the patient, doctors in training, can do no more than offer a compassionate hand extended in Responsibility, while behind them stands an Authority tugging backward with just enough force on that hand to keep it from pulling the patient from the throes of death. It was wrong but it was how a blithe surgeon committed neglicide on Maria Chavarria, the fruition of Doctor's Choice.

Some years ago, doctors employed by certain HMOs made complaints that were taken up by the national media. Doctors took Responsibility for their patients. But the Authority, vested in the HMO executives who were in charge, denied them certain tests and treatments they required for appropriate therapy. Why? Because the HMO made more money that way and the doctors took the fall—not to mention their patients.

This has been at least partially corrected, there being no expendable patients, but when you separate Authority from Responsibility behind the White Curtain, the death of patients becomes not only possible, but predictable. Unknowing patients are placed at risk of their lives, families of losing their loved ones, and the doctors who have been victimized alongside their patients carry the cruelty and pain of it for the rest of their lives, which adds to the tragedy. Doctors live through others, but that is not a small subset. It includes doctors, patients, nurses, and those in training. Hippocrates had it that life is short, the art long, opportunity fleeting, but know this: the choice is yours.

To my knowledge, mine is the first attempt at using AVR to model the dynamics of neglicide by Doctor's Choice. The definitions below are offered with the understanding that these are in no way the final say on the subject. They are the best I can offer for now and therefore must be considered tentative.

- *Responsibility.* In the sense of a doctor for a patient, *responsibility* means nothing less than the role of a physician in taking on an obligation to the person by way of caring for the patient's well-being. It encompasses diagnosing and treating the patient in the best possible way and by the best possible means, involving timeliness and the best choice of drugs, surgery, and so forth for that patient and that illness, also including consulting other physicians when necessary and, finally, the dutiful monitoring of the patient during treatment, whether in the hospital or as an outpatient in follow-up visits that continue as long as mutually agreed upon by doctor and patient.

- *Authority.* In the sense of a doctor for a patient, *authority* means nothing less than having and exercising to the highest capability of authority, and in a timely and caring manner—the means by which the patient receives the best possible outcome by way of prompt curative surgery or its attempt and the unencumbered choice of any and all other materia medica and/or medical or surgical procedures needed for the patient's diagnosis and treatment, including referral, if needed; admission to the hospital or any other care facility, should that be indicated; and the various other duties incumbent upon one's simultaneous exercising of responsibility for the patient.

- *Neglicide.* Not being a lawyer, I coin *neglicide* as a combining form between *negligence* and *homicide*, but I do not mean "negligent homicide" or "criminal gross negligence," legal terms having to do with the statutes on criminal behavior. Whether neglicide is criminal or not is beyond my capability of determining, though I have an opinion. Neglicide consists of negligence by way of a doctor's willful behavior in delaying treatment or in deliberately giving too little treatment, too much treatment, or the wrong treatment, each situation recognizable only by another doctor or a qualified nurse. At the core of its ugliness, it is the taking of one person's life by another, even should that other be a physician sworn to help the patient and to rebuke all such dangerous behavior, which leads to the incalculable harm and loss of life I witnessed during my decade in medicine.

I have chosen *CARE* as an acronym for the four items every doctor owes every patient:

C for *Commitment* to the patient, which every doctor or team member must have or none of the rest matters.

A for *Authority.*

R for *Responsibility.*

E for *Equality.* Earlier I spoke of this complicated matter. A doctor has a certain ownership of his or her own patients, but all patients look alike. To one holding Authority over a patient, Responsibility must be undertaken simultaneously, no matter the patient's differences from the physician. From the outset, the healer recognizes and praises each person's humanity. From the outset the practitioner honors their life. From the outset every doctor celebrates the commonality of all in a community that happens to include everyone in the world. And by the way, CARE means absolute devotion to saving the patient by the best possible means.

- *Doctor's Choice.* This occurs when a physician willfully bypasses the guidelines of CARE. The most common method is by a physician Authority failing to assume simultaneous and compassionate Responsibility for the patient, as that doctor might treat his or her own family. Doctor's Choice is the wrongful or negligent application of medical or surgical treatment so that a patient is put at risk of becoming a victim of neglicide. By definition, Doctor's Choice is always wrong, absolutely fraudulent, and possibly criminal. It resides starkly outside the boundaries of the benevolent medical, surgical, emotional, or educational treatment doctors owe their patients.

*   *   *

Although I had nothing to do with the medical response to the explosion at the petrochemical plant in Corpus, I was not exactly idle during the last days of October, 1963. Dr. McGraw, having been trained in vascular surgery, offered his services to two patients we evaluated in Surgery Clinic. Both had a severe reduction in blood supply to the lower limbs. The workup consisted of studies similar to carotid arteriography, only the dye injections were made from the back, into the abdominal aorta, while X-rays delineated the patency—or lack thereof—of the major vessels to the lower limbs.

Mary Itz* was in her midfifties, a white woman with limp blonde hair and an air of faded gentility, as though she had just stepped out of a play by Tennessee Williams. Perhaps it was *The Glass Menagerie*. Or maybe she was Blanche Dubois from *Streetcar*, but without the unflattering pretensions. One thing was certain. She had all but given up walking normally again because it was so painful to her, and she could no longer work as a secretary to support herself. She had been referred by her doctor to the Surgery Clinic.

Homer Epps* was a white man in his forties, rail thin, who had probably been raised on a farm peering between plow handles at the statuesque hindquarters of a mule, scratching a living from the earth. He grew up on raw milk and running boards and had learned not to depend on the kindness of strangers but on the strangeness of kindness. He held a job as a long-distance truck driver but was incapacitated by intermittent claudication.

That was the diagnosis in both patients. It meant, literally, an intermittent limp, but it referred to a person unable to function because of a reduced blood supply to the lower limbs and in particular the part of the leg from the knee to the sole of the foot. A month or so previously we had done an amputation of the leg in a patient whose circulatory problems were much worse. That man's right femoral artery, which courses through the thigh, was so diseased from atherosclerosis that it literally did not bleed a drop when it was severed and the clamps on either side of the cut were removed. That was the end result of a disease not yet that severe in Mary Itz or Homer Epps.

We operated on her first, Thursday, October 24, the day after the explosion occurred, and on him the next day, installing in each a DeBakey-style nylon graft to replace the lower abdominal aorta and its two main branches. The latter were the common iliac arteries. (A bit lower down, the iliac arteries continue as the femoral arteries.) In each patient the Y-shaped graft we used was as white as house paint and as elastic as a girdle. The main section of the graft was as wide as a garden hose, corresponding to the lower aorta.

Each surgery took hours. Each graft was the better part of a foot long and had to be matched up with vessels that branched to either side of the aorta, as well as sewn onto the proximal ends of the two iliac arteries conveying blood supply to the legs. Clamp after clamp had to be applied and loosened and reapplied. Those who haven't done it have no idea how physically draining that can be. I was exhausted when we were through and very glad that my surgical rotation was almost over. Surprisingly—for I hadn't expected it—I was informed by Dr. McGraw that he was leaving for a surgical conference in another city the last few days in October, beginning Sunday the twenty-seventh. He announced his plans to both patients, assuring them that I was perfectly capable of handling postoperative problems, should these occur. The patients agreed to accept me as their sole physician, and both patients had postoperative problems.

Mary Itz experienced kidney failure. Her blood pressure had fallen precipitously during surgery from a spurt of bleeding we were unable to stop; the bleeding was massive but for only a few seconds, though it was enough to send her into hemorrhagic shock, a plummeting of the blood pressure secondary to bleeding. The shock stressed her kidneys to the point that they temporarily ceased functioning.

She had received a blood transfusion while still in the OR and had definitely come out of shock. Ideally, a patient with temporary kidney failure was treated with the artificial kidney until the patient's own kidneys healed. Memorial did not have an artificial kidney. But Galveston did, and I remembered the names of the two professors at UTMB who ran the Renal Service. I called one of them, explaining the problem, and the specialist agreed to accept Mrs. Itz on transfer. After informing Mary Itz of this development, I asked whether she had the money for a plane trip to Galveston. Yes. I wrote the order to alert the nurses and began calling airlines. Shortly an ambulance arrived to pick her up and convey her to the airline terminal in Corpus. The airline had made special arrangements to accommodate her stretcher. That same Monday, October 28, she arrived in Galveston and was admitted to John Sealy Hospital, where she underwent dialysis treatment until her own kidneys recovered. After a week or two she returned to Corpus and was still doing well when I left after finishing internship the following year.

I thought it a bold move and was proud of myself in a place where I had not that often felt proud. I was so absorbed in Mary's transfer Monday afternoon, however, that I missed something. Homer Epps had begun vomiting.

Epps was a likeable man, blunderbuss of speech. During his workup in the clinic, I had asked where his pain was located. "Right chere," he'd said, grabbing his calves and pulling them up onto the examining table beside him like sticks of wood. On his ankles were ulcers the size of half-dollars, endowment of that shrinking blood supply.

"Stays there?" I asked.

He pointed. "Naw, it ain't. Maybe run up chere, run up chere right by your buttrick. Sometimes all the do-ee to your ann-us."

His answer may have been funny, and certainly different, but I felt a fierce sense of loyalty to Homer Epps, a man neither begging nor absent pride. Homer Epps was of my clan, that bucolic descent. I had been with him in the watermelon patch and in the cotton field and in the smokehouse, and I knew how badly he wanted to get well so that he could get back to his job and make the money that it took to "raise them kids he had had" with that sweetheart he finally wed. A job was a rare and sacred thing to the forgotten. To them, life was a series of miseries cut by the occasional rapture of satiety. I have neither described him completely nor given all of his history, which I remember well, for I had met Homer Epps many times before.

*   *   *

Once, in the sixth grade, he was a boy named T .O. Roth* of Pittsburg, Texas. T. O. was in my homeroom. T. O. didn't smell very good. He wore stalactites of snot hanging from both nostrils, day after day. He may not have owned a toothbrush or a comb, and he wore the same striped unionalls every day. He also came to school barefooted except in the coldest of winter. Once, to her everlasting shame, our sixth-grade teacher had the gall to have the janitor take T. O. aside during recess and give him a bath with Lysol or one of those milky cleaning solutions that smelled like two-day urine. That it occurred during recess in front of all was horrible, my classmates remembering always the kid's embarrassment.

One day I skipped lunch in the cafeteria because Mother had given me a sack lunch when she couldn't scrape up lunch money. With a sack lunch, you remained in your room, seated at your desk in one of the rows of wooden desks, windows to the left, blackboards front, right, and posterior, and teacher's desk presiding.

I had opened my sack lunch and begun to eat before I noticed that T. O., over to my left by the window, did not have one. He was a skinny kid anyway, and he did not have a lunch of any kind. We were the only two kids, and T. O. was swinging his legs back and forth beneath his seat and desk, looking straight ahead, seemingly without a care. A teacher had come in to sit with us during lunch, our homeroom teacher having that time off.

The teacher looked and said, "T. O., don't you have a lunch?"

He said, "No'um, but we havin' good old beans and taters tonight for supper!"

When I was a few years older, I met another Homer Epps on a bus to Arizona, where I spent the summer of 1954 with kinfolks. He had befriended me and I'd sat, hour after hour, enveloped in secondary smoke, listening to him and his stories, until finally I worked up the courage to ask him his goal in life.

"I live for a better day," he said.

To city folk, Homer Epps was a rube, but so what? Woody Guthrie loved him. Homer had stepped out of the pages of *The Grapes of Wrath*. He was Walker Evans plus the internal combustion engine, Upton Sinclair after Collective Bargaining. He was the American version of Frank McCourt's childhood but without the alcoholism, Flannery O'Connor without the idiosyncratic mind-set. In Appalachia, Homer Epps lived out on a "point" somewhere in an old house surrounded by decrepit cars. It was not a monetary society. There was no TV or radio. He did not know the name of the president or care and did not serve in the military—not that he could, due to too many missing parts: teeth, fingers, toes, eyes, limbs, education. He did not pay income tax except when he couldn't help it, he would figure an Eagle Scout was some kind of a goddanged bird dog, and if you missed a meal or two, why, *by golly!* you took up your belt a notch and kept right on agoing.

I needn't have asked where Homer Epps was from. He was from America. He was one of our own. He did not attend school reunions because he did not graduate. He lived as he could—on the fringes, and medical academia spotted him in a heartbeat and used him without conscience, as had occurred when I was a medical student and watched him die from treatable lobar pneumonia on Ward 4-A, without receiving a single dose of curative penicillin. The resident had not seemed concerned about the man, but that was typical. Homer was the one who always had the worst cancer, the biggest hernia, the "interesting" instance of tertiary syphilis with that fluttering, broad-based gait of tabes dorsalis, a man in tattered clothing hobbling along as though astraddle of a bobbed-wire fence, flinching along maybe to avoid the sticker burrs and the goddanged bull nettle that began at the fencerow and went all the way right out smart to the middle of the goddanged plowed field that he had managed to escape so long ago, but never really had. Homer was the backbone of the beast of civilization.

*   *   *

Atherosclerosis is a chronic disease of the body's large highways and can strike women as well as men, depending on genetics and body type and such variables as tend to modify health. I expected Homer Epps had eaten whatever he could get without thought of saturated fats and cholesterol, and he may have had the worst case of atherosclerosis in history. Diet aside, he had smoked heavily since grade school, which he had not finished. His teeth were long and curved and bore several colors other than white, almost as though a rainbow was waiting to be discovered by his smile. His skin was the texture of rotten leaves, and speech, for him, brought on a cough that sounded like stones tossed into a millpond, the succussion *splash* of clogged airways and frail lungs reeling from the effects of those four packs a day. Appearing ten or twenty years older than he was, Epps was everything he had inherited and every blessing he had managed beyond that. Epps was perversity personified.

Postoperative from the vascular surgery, he had good pulses in his legs and feet. The ulcers on his ankles were better, but he had become sick, and it had to be addressed.

All I could think to say to the nurse who had informed me of his vomiting was that Homer had been okay on Sunday.

"Yes, but look."

We were in the nurses' station and the nurse opened his chart. It was that same nurses' station on Med/Surg, though unlike Maria, Homer was out on the open ward. Other things were different as well. The nurses' station had the same cabinets and lavatory and counter as when Maria had been there, but it was lighter than it had been. Perhaps not all of the windows were closed, as had been the case last summer. Things seemed quieter, as well, as I sat on a cushioned stool beside the new nurse—new to me—whose name was *Sister*.

Though from Germany, Sister was a naturalized US citizen and may have been of the Schonsted Order of nuns. The part of her face revealed by her nun's habit was so white she might never have seen the sun, but she was an RN with excellent skills and a warm way. Stupidly I had asked her the meaning of the wedding band she wore on the ring finger of her left hand, and with forgiveness she had explained that she was married to the church. I liked her better than any nurse I had met so far at Memorial, other than Hulsey in the ER.

Sister found the place in Homer's chart.

The vomiting had begun Sunday night and persisted all day Monday. Homer Epps was vomiting as badly and as unexpectedly as had Maria Chavarria. Sister and I rose in unison, without speaking, and soon approached the bed in the two rows of beds that held the patient. Epps was seated on the side of his bed, staring at a fixed point in the near distance, his face stiffly contracted in the manner of a man looking all the way down that pike and stricken by what he saw. The items on his bedside table were awry, and he held a metal emesis basin in his hand. I asked how he felt.

"Natigated [nauseated]," was the answer to my question. As if to prove it, he arched his back and vomited like a sick dog. Without wiping his mouth he went back to frowning at a spot that only he could see.

I examined him, paying particular attention to the abdominal examination, while Sister waited. Early vomiting after surgery, my training taught, was due to the anesthetic, but Epps was three days out from surgery. Stomach flu was possible but unlikely. The most common condition to be ruled out was postoperative ileus, a cessation of bowel function from the roughhousing the intestines took incidental to abdominal surgery. Ileus, an insolent condition, meant the stricken bowel might sulk for several days or a week by refusing to bestow its rhythmic contractions. Treatment was to put down a nasogastric tube by way of anticipating it. The tube was both preventive and proactive, but I had removed Epps's nasogastric tube the day before because his bowel sounds were completely normal.

Now, at his bedside on Monday, October 28, I put the tube back in. I gave verbal orders to Sister for continuous suctioning of the gastric contents. I kept Homer on the IV fluids he was already receiving but increased the amounts, including electrolytes. I also ordered blood tests to check various bodily functions.

By the next afternoon, Epps was much worse. He was vomiting frequently in spite of the tube and had the thunderous bowel sounds that ruled out postoperative ileus. Epps did not complain of pain except for his sore "belly." Nothing about him made sense.

"Why don't you get an X-ray?" Sister asked.

I was in Surgery Clinic when the call with the X-ray results came from the radiologist. The news was quietly riveting, the kind of news that bypasses the ears and lands squat in the middle of the *ann-us*.

"Your man Epps," the radiologist said, "has a high-grade small bowel obstruction."

I begged to disagree. I told the radiologist that it was not possible and presented the patient to the surprised radiologist over the phone, in the callow fervor of a student begging a point in a debate.

"Come look at the films," the radiologist said.

Epps's small intestine was blown up like a balloon, to the point of perforation. It was exactly the X-ray findings I had seen in Maria Chavarria. "He needs surgery," the radiologist said as if this had not already occurred to me, and I continued staring in silence at the overwhelming evidence of what could not possibly be. After a due interval, the radiologist spoke again.

"Who is your staff man?"

I mentioned Dr. George McGraw, explaining that he had left town.

"Didn't he check out to somebody?"

That was just it. But instead of answering the radiologist, I fled the radiology suite and found myself once again lodged in that long, intestinal corridor, dark and bulging now with the volume of my uncontrollable emotions, the sheer horror of the terrified. George McGraw, the way it worked, had checked out to the previous surgeon on the rotation list. Dr. Carl Broderick.

*   *   *

Bracing myself, I made the call from the interns' lounge so I could speak in privacy. My teeth were chattering. I felt chills. I expected to be stricken dead. When that didn't happen, I became aware of my surroundings. I was seated with my back to the corridor on that imitation-leather couch the intern-on-call used as a bed, beside a coffee table strewn with old notes from phone calls and the odd plastic coffee cup and the ever-present torn magazines. I had logged plenty of time in this small room off the corridor, with access to the medical library. I thought of Maria Chavarria, held the thought. Carl Broderick shared an office near Memorial with another surgeon, and I reached a female voice.

He wasn't there, and a huge surge of happiness passed through me.

The surgeon, she thought, was still in surgery at Spohn Hospital, the other side of town. I called Spohn and was told that he had left to return to his office. His office was some distance from Spohn, and I waited five or ten minutes and called his office again; I was not surprised when Broderick's nurse again said that he was not there. Her suggestion was to try paging him at Memorial. I did that by calling the operator. Then, having spent half an hour on the phone, most of it on hold, I raced back to the clinic to see a few patients.

The doctor did not answer his page at Memorial, and I asked the clinic nurse to try reaching him in the new part of Memorial. She came back to say that he had just left. Finally his office said that he was there, and I flew back to the lounge to make the call.

The surgeon came on the line sounding warm and engaging, a busy physician kindly offering his services to those who might need him.

"Yes?" Carl Broderick said, and he waited.

I had never spoken to this man before. My voice faltered. I had the elocution of a sixth-grader stricken with stage fright. Somehow I managed to convey to him that I had a surgical problem at Memorial and was seeking his help. I added the reason and then waited for him to respond.

He chuckled as though it was news to him that Dr. McGraw had checked out to him before leaving town.

"Didn't he tell you?"

"Well, one supposes he must have mentioned it."

I spoke. I managed the strength to describe the problem. But I was confused. Carl Broderick sounded so nice, so goddamned nice. He listened without comment while I presented Homer Epps. I ended by quoting the radiologist, emphasizing that the intestinal obstruction was high-grade, a strong risk for perforation. I thought of Maria but did not mention her. When I was through, he spoke.

"Put down a Miller-Abbott tube."

It was the same thing he had ordered after Maria was transferred to the Surgery Service that Sunday afternoon, July 21, over three months ago.

"Sir, I'm not sure that—"

"Put down the tube and I'll try and get by tomorrow."

He hung up before I could say more.

With the help of Sister, I obtained and put down the Miller-Abbott tube as a replacement for Homer's nasogastric tube. I told Homer that this might help and the patient offered no objection. The nausea, the vomiting, the soreness in his abdomen were as before. I spent the rest of that Tuesday afternoon, October 29, seeing patients who had been waiting in the clinic while I ran back and forth to the interns' lounge. Before leaving that evening, I stopped by the ER to tell the intern on call about Homer Epps.

That night, sleep did not come. Next morning, I had Mimi drop me off early at the hospital. I changed into scrubs but refused the invitations of other doctors to assist them in surgery. After rounds, I camped on the Med/

Surg Ward writing progress notes and waiting. Carl Broderick arrived just before noon.

It was the second time I had seen him but the first time up close, and he did not speak to banality. Instead, he spoke to the courtly demeanor of self-importance. Perhaps, like an older physician in Galveston, he had a wife he still called "the bride," a doctor's bag the size of a suitcase, and at an instant's notice could whip out a diatribe against the government for its plans to seize control of health care. In the pocket of his suit coat were coiled the jaunty loops of that stethoscope, its bright, metallic lips pursed in the smile of a willingness to accept deference, that ambrosia that tastes as good as brown sugar but is far more fattening. He shook my hand warmly, courteous to a fault, spoke to the nurses by name, and led the entourage to Homer Epps's bedside.

I waited while he spoke to the patient about the air hose down his throat. The tube commanded more of his attention than did Epps, for the surgeon did not so much as examine him. Taking the chart from a nurse, he wrote a short progress note and on the order sheet gave instructions to advance the Miller-Abbott tube at more frequent intervals.

He returned the chart to Sister, who voiced no disagreement, and left the ward forthwith without another word to me or anyone else.

I caught up to him across the hallway of Memorial Hospital, near the sumptuous entrance to that gleaming theater. Gurney stretchers gleamed there because it was lighter there, as from a skylight in an auditorium, but I have already said that too many times. It was where I had last seen Maria alive, lost in the coma of intestinal perforation three months ago. I was shaking so bad my teeth chattered.

I said, "Aren't we going to operate to relieve his bowel obstruction?"

"No, we'll give the tube a few more days. I think it will work just fine."

All of my life, all of my life I had come up against it, this thing that got me in trouble. I saw differently and I had been tattled on, spat upon, shat upon, sent to the principal again and again, paddled and spanked and whatnot and it didn't take. I had learned that the boss was the person installed by life to make sure you did not enjoy your job, the principal to make sure you had no fun, and leaders were power seekers who loved themselves as much as they hated unbelievers. Was it possible for me to live without their punishment? No. And it was no fun, fighting always, scared shit but no good at sucking up; obsequiousness in all its fawning varieties gave me the ass ache. But the dynamic had changed.

It was different and it made all the difference: it wasn't my life in jeopardy, but another's life, and I must take the responsibility for it. Maria's death taught me that. Maria's death had taught me that any doctor who is worth his license must be equivalent to any and every other doctor throughout the universe or the system will not work. It was like taking a swing at a complete stranger, one who might be armed with nuclear weapons, who might be a black belt in karate or a muscleman beneath the surface or a rare species of Martian bullshit. But a young doctor must equilibrate himself for the good of the patient, and those who tell him otherwise are no more and no less than his enemies. Send Hippocrates to hell, Galen to a roadside commode. Attain what you already have or you will lose it and then they will laugh at you, withered as you are in all the furies and futilities of what might have been. Lawyers dealt in conflict, but so did doctors, by god, and out of me it sprang.

"May I speak to you in *private*, sir?"

Suddenly the surgeon began watching me very closely. "You had best say what you wish right here, Doctor."

People continued to pass. The gurneys were horizontal as were the tables as were the graves on a distant hill, the vertical surgeon facing me from a bit farther out in the corridor, as though he were keeping all of his options open. *Do not talk back. Do not remove under penalty of law. Do not fold, spindle, or mutilate.* What did it matter except for the life of a patient who had come to me for help? What did it matter except for the future of the world, the odiousness of existence, and the contemptible exploits of physicians like this one, index case of an unknown and unknowable number but not less than the nameless hordes who practiced their barbarity with doctorly indifference, like philanderers on the prowl, who had the honor of ape shit and the integrity of a fluted asshole? Still, it was not easy. Later, I wouldn't be able to recall my exact words to the man; anger can do that.

But I plunged ahead, telling the surprised surgeon that Homer Epps was going to have surgery if it required me to bring his bed into the hallway of Memorial and beg every passing surgeon to do the obvious. (It was what I wished I had done for Maria after she was transferred to Med/Surg.) And if no one in Corpus would operate on Homer Epps then I, by god, would drive him to Galveston for surgery or anywhere else in the world, if it took it.

The point I drove home to the man, this board-certified surgeon and Fellow of the American College of Surgeons, whom I have referred to by a pseudonym, was that I was going to write up a full account of his method of caring for staff patients at Memorial, particularly of one Maria Chavarria, whom he might remember, and post same on every hospital wall in every hospital ward in Corpus, with the hope that he would sue me for libel or slander or both and in that way allow me in open court to broadcast his methods of treating a person who had just happened to be my patient, seventeen-year-old Maria Chavarria, two weeks postpartum and dying of intestinal perforation because he had refused to *operate her.*

For his part, the surgeon of course raised the subject of the approval of my year of training—they always did that; oh, how they loved to trot that out, misers hoarding a jewel more valuable than Harvard Med or even Johns Hopkins except, were they to happen to look, they'd find a faceted coprolite gleaming like the hovel that housed their values and by the way, I would spend the rest of my life wishing I had never heard of Memorial Hospital, much less spent a year there, and I welcomed from this individual an open review before the forum of his choice.

My face was as taut as the skin of a football and my head was hammering like a bass drum, but I had finally stood up to the bastard, and now what happened was up to him.

An OR nurse happened to pass and speak to him. He turned and told her that he had decided to have lunch at Memorial and do Homer Epps that afternoon. Would she please put the patient on the schedule?

It was as simple as that. As horribly horrible as that, in what it meant to me.

I scrubbed as first assistant and we quickly located the problem. A lengthy laceration had occurred in the posterior peritoneum covering the Teflon graft; a loop of small bowel had slipped beneath, and been pinched shut by, the graft that Dr. McGraw and I had sutured into Homer Epps's abdomen the previous Friday. I suspected that the patient's stentorian cough was the culprit. At any rate, it was easy to reach and free the intestine and to close that peritoneal gash to prevent the problem from recurring. In half an hour, we were closing.

Whatever else I may have said about Dr. Broderick, he was a fine technician. He spoke while suturing the skin.

"The Miller-Abbott tube would have taken care of this."

He didn't mention how the Miller-Abbott tube would have sewn up that long-assed tear in the posterior peritoneum, but never mind. He didn't mention that, to him, Homer Epps and Maria Chavarria weren't worthy of his services, but never mind. He didn't mention that his patients and his Responsibility were in the nice hospital and he had no obligation at all to these "charity cases," but never mind. His strength was not in truth but in the grandeur of himself. In the OR were myself, the scrub nurse, the nurse anesthetist, and a circulating nurse who had just walked in. Also, the ghost of every patient who ever died by Doctor's Choice, the Doctor *of* Choice being a self-appointed soloist who takes a life as he sees fit. I didn't kill *you*, so why should *you* care? I found his eyes.

"I know one patient where it didn't."

He took the hit, said nothing in reply. If he had, I would have spent the night in jail.

A few minutes later I walked out of the OR and followed the patient to the recovery room. I finished my time on the Surgery Service a day or so later and never again saw the man who had killed Maria Chavarria. I did not exult in this small victory, did not gloat. But I had stood up to a bully and looked evil down. It was not the first time in my life that I had done that, but it was the first time as a physician, and I would learn soon enough that there are just as many bullies among doctors as there are among the adolescent assholes who rule junior high.

I realized later that the surgeon would have known that I reported him after Maria's death. Perhaps there had been some behind-the-scenes pressure applied by his surgical colleagues. Maybe he was skittish about Maria, a guilty conscience? In that sense, Maria's death had helped to save Homer Epps. That is good but it is not enough. It does not eradicate the bad. The devastating thing it proved to me was that had I stood up to the surgeon, gone to the brink as I had just done, Maria would have had her surgery and been saved. She died because, a few weeks into internship, I had cowered before the might of a physician experienced in neglicide. It was the ultimate proof of my shame.

Why must a patient die to teach me life? Why did I let it happen when I knew it was going to happen? Why was I so timid? Where does strength come from in the face of all that? I did not know. But I knew that not all eternity would bring back that lost opportunity and I would have to live with that for the rest of my life. But I had made a promise to her and would expend my life in the effort to tell her story, a story that became my own, my only wish that it would survive me and stand as a tribute to her life while its reckoning was in the everlasting shame heaped upon those doctors who committed neglicide or participated in its cover-up.

*   *   *

I saw Homer Epps leave the hospital, even though I was by then on another service. The bypass relieved his claudication, and he felt like a new man. His ankle ulcers healed and he was most appreciative to Memorial Hospital. I had done my best for him, which was only right.

But there, the story turns ugly. For far too many years I had begged Providence to have let Maria Chavarria be the one who was saved, because of her youth and her son and her future. I had wished this because I wished release from the guilt I have carried all these years. I wished for Maria the life she did not live, to raise her son and have other children in that happy future we all envision. But along the way I learned something. I was a doctor, and those shouldered with that curse must not judge. Homer Epps had as much right to live as she. I had spent all of those years valuating people just like the surgeon I condemn, but when that happens, the person who dies is not the patient, or the patient is not the only one. The person who dies is the doctor who should have been.

PART III.

Behind the White Curtain

One day that fall, shortly before President Kennedy's visit to Dallas, I was in the living room of the house on Seventeenth Street rejoicing in the first cool weather to push its way south to the Gulf Coast. It was Saturday and it was fine. It was a time to leave the front door open, the back, and the windows as well, to behold the swirling leaves chasing one another in a swooping frolic as old as the pox and as new as a smile, overture to the enthralling possibility that happiness still existed, the exquisite possibility that it still existed for me.

We had purchased on time a wooden cathedral that played records, and I was seated on the sofa and listening to Richard Burton's "How to Handle a Woman" and to Julie Andrews's "I Loved You Once in Silence." These treasures from *Camelot* seemed perfect to my grazing soul.

The woman from the Record Room visited—my recordess, to whom I had devoted far too much attention since last summer—and eagerly I sought her rounded perfection, bartering fate to reveal whether her fetching beauty was real or only a lollipop extended through the bars to a hungry gorilla. I had thought the distant past retrievable. One had merely to turn and lift it to one's breast and instantly take communion, forever and ever, embracing in all its loveliness the bounce of boyhood, the zest of youth, the quest for rapture. She, every time I saw her, proved me wrong. She represented the unopened door, now closed to me, and locked. I had been anointed and acclaimed, *doctor* stuck to me like the insignia of rank on a soldier. I appeared in lists, compilations, certifications. I was like a man forced to project himself into the idea someone had of him, like a knight pulling on a suit of armor and tilting with the forces that would do him in, when the real enemy was already inside and thrusting away.

I thought I had lost my innocence that time in high school when Judge Acker had incarcerated me for the morning, but innocence, I had learned, can be severed from one's person any number of times, daily or even more frequently than that: hourly? Innocence was the price of admission for one who dared slip behind the White Curtain.

I had not learned this from those who were forever reminding me that I was still in training, but from Maria Chavarria and Homer Epps. Maria, in her waking hours the last week of her life, knew that she was not being given the care I had promised, the care she so desperately needed, yet all she could do—all that was within her power—was to ask her question. To her it was the most important question of her life. To me it was an item of anger and frustration that did her no good at all. Her death was my bad day. Can the hurt of a needless death be dismissed by a pretty song? No. Realization of same left me worse off than before. Realization of same ruined me and went on ruining me.

Mimi knew, of course. Hobnob with monsters and they will follow you home. But we had not shared it. How can you share a death only one of you has experienced? How can a brisk autumn day replace the withering winter rain that is still to come and has already been and always will? I teetered on the altar of existence, seeking to answer my unending scream.

*   *   *

The First Baptist Church in Corpus was a nice-looking suitor wearing a bright-red corsage and a clean suit of clothes and a tall white hat guiding people to its spacious organs of reproduction. The people were courteous and happy, and Mimi and I were placed in the Young Married Adults class and attended church every Sunday except when I was on call, when she and Roger went without me.

My attendance had been erratic, but earlier that fall of 1963 we took Roger and attended the evening service. He stayed with the other kids, and Mimi and I went to our class. Someone had come up with an idea that was both shameless and harmless. We, the men in the class, a few more than a dozen, were ushered to a stage that formed part of the room where we met, which was probably the auditorium of the church's educational center. At any rate, we were led up beyond the proscenium and the thick velvet curtain was drawn, separating us from what was now the audience, consisting of wives and assorted others. We were told to mix up our positions from how we had last been seen and to remove our shoes and socks.

We hoisted our pants above the ankles and each of us lifted the curtain sufficiently to show only our feet. Soon, a bunch of women who were rollicking with laughter were passing down the waist-high row of feet, each person trying to identify her husband. It was high school stuff, really, and embarrassing should a woman not be able to tell her husband by his feet. I heard various names shrieked from women amid guffaws of laughter following a blunder. Embarrassment would be mine, for being the last one identified from the group.

But Mimi walked down the row, stopped at my feet, and said, "Oh, this is Johnny."

Instead of being the last, I was the first, and how keen was that?

In retrospect, in our make-believe world, I could probably have identified her by her feet. She obligingly let them partake of the floor, and I knew them to be small and perfectly shaped, feminine rudders in a pink-toed ocean. The calluses on her heels were an item conferred upon American women by people in Europe who held an enduring grudge (and also charged for it) against American couture. High heels, of course, caused bunions and all sorts of other problems, including what was then the male chauvinist physician's definition of a woman: *a constipated animal with a backache.* But not her! If there were scars from earlier—the audacity of ingrown toenails!—that was okay. Hers was a soft grandeur. Beauty must be natural or it does not count, and even then the magic hides just beyond the seen.

Marriage itself, to me, was proving to be a mystery. The curtain opens immediately but participants in this pas de deux are so blinded by love that they may as well have missed Act One. Ditto Act Two. Again and again the curtain rises to a standing ovation, but hidden backstage and abruptly introduced is a revue accompanied by tears of hurt, sudden drama for those who haven't learned that the lines in this production require a bit more of grace and a bit less limelight than either of them might have imagined. Why? Because to hold a right to the other's physical self was more of a task than anticipated, as it included not only the fun part but the in-between—all of the in-betweens, including the act where she doffed makeup and disappeared offstage only to lead back a tiny new member of the cast, with encores, whereupon all illusions ended. The majesty was in the creation—by amateurs—of an acclaimed drama, sex being the part that kept them stealing extra bows, the applause reminding them of their good fortune in following signposts placed by angels upon the boulevard to the unassailable.

Love was an art form, really, though would-be artists roamed the world in droves searching not for art but its fakery. Maybe what children did was not so much to save the production as to instill integrity into it. Didn't they become the parents of adults, teaching us lessons we never knew? Like doctors, children saw beneath the surface. But unlike that innocent childhood pastime, playing "doctor" for real was an unwritten script acted by professionals, based on time and custom, a theater played to its audience one at a time.

*   *   *

In high school I had bragged of becoming a doctor and doing as many pelvic examinations on beautiful women as I could cram into my day. It turned out otherwise, for a good reason. Doing a pelvic examination is the least sexy thing a doctor does. The explanation works best without accompanying detail, other than that the human body is designed and functions as a unit, and in the practice of medicine one never sees a thing in isolation, as in fantasy. One instead sees something that is his responsibility to examine as a part of a patient, and that is what is done. I didn't defraud myself into thinking that I was any good at it, but for that matter I wasn't all that horrible at it, either. I knew that women dreaded having pelvic examinations, and we were taught to try and minimize the pain.

The surprising thing to me was that men were as embarrassed at exposing themselves in the setting of a doctor's office as were women. The difference is that in performing a pelvic examination on a woman, there is always an attendant present, a female chaperone. The examination of a man's privates or the male rectal examination occurs, when the doctor is a male, as something going on just between guys. Doctors, male doctors as well as female physicians, have had to undergo physical examinations themselves along the way and may take their personal feelings about these into the examining room. Don't embarrass the patient, is the idea, without slighting the examination. And watch out for surprises.

I had been taught to examine the prostate during a rectal examination on a man. The examiner puts on a pair of latex gloves and lubricates the examining finger to make the examination easier. The urology professor plainly stated that palpation of the prostate would express secretions from the penis, a passive ejaculate, if you will. The idea was to pass the man a piece of tissue paper afterward, as a courtesy, so that he could blot the secretions to prevent a stain in his clothing. But it never happened that way. Instead, the man invariably used the Kleenex to wipe the examining jelly off of his anus.

Wiped it and said, "Hey, Doc, where's the trash can?"

With women, a male examiner was never unaware that she was of a different sex, which conferred a richness to her physical presence that was lacking in men: she had more to examine by way of privates. The first criterion was to invest the moment with the respect and dignity owed the patient, a construction calling for one's awareness that here was a patient seeking your help. My surprise was that women undergoing a breast examination, having nothing else to do, stare at you like someone who has just taken a bite and is not sure whether to swallow. If your thoughts are easy to read on your face, you may be the one who ends up embarrassed.

*   *   *

We're walking, we're walking, going back a year or more to my time as a student on the Medicine Service at John Sealy Hospital. I was assigned a healthy woman of about thirty who had been admitted to the hospital for tests. She was in the bed nearest the window of a double room on a private ward. This person owned a flawless face and the long, dark tresses of a leading lady in Jane Austen's novels. She was married and had a couple of kids back home and was none the worse for having had them. She had the savvy to understand that I was a student and that was fine; we were both in uncharted territory.

I had hoped, for my start on the clinical rotation, to have a less spectacular patient. I wished to consummate the doctor–patient affair upon one of my own, a skinny gal from the country with a quick laugh and a willing way, someone raised on chicken and dumplings. Instead, this patient: urbane, intelligent, and accompanied by her own chaperone, none other than her husband, who planted himself beside her at the head of the bed and with a look of withering intensity seemed disinclined to move, no matter what I told him to do. It was as if the two men in the equation had met on a field of honor—the husband having caught his wife and I flagrante delicto—and the older and more experienced of the two was not about to grant his opponent even the slightest mercy.

Had I been experienced enough to take on that particular swagger, I would have compelled the husband to step outside until the examination was completed (which might have been the patient's preference, come to think of it). In a double room in that scenario, theoretically, the person in the other bed, unseen because of a curtain around each bed, would serve as the chaperone. But that didn't happen. That I was not in the least sexually attracted to her, on reflection, came as a surprise, though maybe it was that beefeater standing in the sawdust beside the block. His steely gaze remained riveted on the object of his intensity, the one who had stopped by to cop a feel, as it were, and on second thought he would probably not have removed himself no matter who did the examination.

What saved it was the woman herself, who treated me with kindness. That she was not sick at all and had been referred to a former professor by one of his former students as a favor to him was something that went on commonly at John Sealy Hospital during the sixties, among other felicities. Very often it seemed to be the young of the female sex whose hospitalization was bestowed upon a former (male) professor.

*   *   *

Chief of Medicine Raymond L. Gregory presided over the Medicine Service and its functions in teaching students, interns, and residents, but he also had his private patients and maintained them from a separate office in John Sealy Hospital. The man's reputation made him a legend in his time, and he was so powerful in the medical school that he could kick somebody out or make them repeat the year of training, if he desired.

I remember another "sweetheart" referral from a former JSH resident. The patient was in her late twenties, a picture of health. She had been sent to the chief for a workup of her thyroid function. She stayed in the hospital for a week before Gregory even got around to seeing her. Some people tire of waiting after an hour in a doctor's office. Gregory used the hospital as his waiting room and sometimes kept a new inpatient for two weeks before deigning to see them. Of course they were being seen daily. The student, intern, and resident, on this particular patient, had to think up every test of thyroid function known to science, performing at least one a day on this healthy young woman, who saw pretty quickly that it was a waste of her time. Upon discharge, the chief of medicine wrote "euthyroidism" (normal thyroid) and seborrheic dermatitis (dandruff) on her chart. Then he dictated a letter to the referring physician inviting him to stop by for a visit next time he was in Galveston.

Dr. Gregory admitted patients to the hospital for a complete fast as a method of weight loss. (All of them regained the weight upon discharge, and some were in the hospital for a second or third course of a "complete fast." They loved it because "it worked so well," in a logic that bordered on delusion.) He also admitted normal women to the hospital to help them stop smoking. One patient comes to mind. She was in her thirties and in a private room. The method she used to stop smoking was to keep her smokes in a cigar box that Gregory had given her. Opening the box, she saw her several packages of cigarettes, and on the inside lid she had taped a mirror above this message: *Do you really want this cigarette?* Evidently, yes. Her room was ever befouled by cigarette smoke, and Gregory was not above having a cigar with her. The picture of my chief of medicine, seated with a cigar, smoking it in the hospital room of a patient who was also smoking and whom he had admitted to the hospital for the express purpose of her stopping smoking, is a vision that lingers.

This patient, not being sick and having no intention to stop smoking, began showing up downstairs in the hospital cafeteria—which had a convenient cigarette-vending machine—to join the staff during what we called "coffee rounds." She and another female patient on the loose began chasing various male doctors at the hospital and leaving with them on passes from the hospital. Told of her exploits, Dr. Gregory took a long pull on his cigar, smiled, and said, "Well, has she had a cigarette today?"

For that matter, I learned quickly enough on the Psychiatry Service that a ward known as Unit D, which seemed to have formerly been a two-story, L-shaped motel, sometimes admitted adventurous patients from Houston for the weekend. I'd arrive at a room to do a history and physical examination on the "patients" and find them gone, husband and wife having donned bathing suits and driven themselves to the beach for a day of sun and surf. Worst of all was going back and finding them just back from the beach. The two were often cross and tired and ordered me to come back some other time. They didn't want to be bothered. I believe their holiday weekends were paid for by medical insurance.

That is why I was not surprised to find myself summoned to a private medicine ward, 5-A, to do the admitting examination on another young woman who seemed the picture of health. I introduced myself to the patient, who was so recently arrived that they had not yet found a bed for her. A new chart had been made up, and I glanced at the front sheet, saw that she was married but with no children—though she said she could be pregnant—and noted that she was twenty-five years old. Her symptom was a vague abdominal pain and Dr. Marcel Patterson, one of my favorite professors at the medical school, had requested that the student on the service do the admitting workup.

It was nearing nightfall of a lazy summer evening in Galveston, 1962, a towering evening wherein the Gulf Coast mated with the sun and offered as its offspring the muted twilight. I had been at the hospital since seven o'clock that morning, not having stopped to eat. Ward 5-A's food carts were still there and rich with the aroma of buttered rolls. The ward itself pointed phallus-like toward the Gulf of Mexico a mile away, and the patient commented on the view. The treatment room was just past the nurses' station on the left, and we opened the door and went inside to cover her history and do the physical examination. The room was unusually cluttered with equipment, such as Bird respirators, oxygen tents, bedpans, linens, and packs for various purposes that had been sent to the ward by Central Sterile Supply. Most of these items occupied the adjustable shelves of three tall, metal bookcases made of what seemed like steel Tinkertoys. In the middle of the treatment room, instead of a regular examining table, a sturdy operating table offered itself for our convenience, and the patient took a seat while I remained standing. After I finished taking her medical history, I stepped out of the room while she removed her clothing and covered herself with the sheet.

So far as I could tell, only two nurses were staffing the ward, and they had far too many duties to stop and chaperone a physical examination by a medical student. I did not mind. The patient was sexy. To even think such thoughts about a patient was wrong, but back of the White Curtain I had made my own share of mistakes, and in this instance I drew perilously close to disaster. Stepping inside again, I found myself alone with this buxom young woman only three years older than myself, who would have been a senior while I was a freshman in high school.

The treatment room, I had decided by then, was a storage room. But it had a metal folding chair next to the table, and the patient had neatly folded her blouse and slacks and placed these on the chair, with her black, low-heeled shoes carefully in front of the chair, as though she had just slipped into bed for a night's sleep—though with only a single white sheet covering her.

My thought was of what need not be conveyed, but she snapped me out of it with a question about her symptoms. Unlike the first brunette with the mean husband, this young woman had graduated high school and let it go at that. Why was it, I remember asking myself, that having a blonde beauty for my own made brunettes that much more attractive?

I had her sit up, keeping herself covered, and she made a cape out of the sheet and the examination began. I noticed that she had not removed her underwear—worry about that later. I listened to heart and lungs, peered into ears and mouth, poked her in the neck searching for an enlarged desire or a reduced will. She knew this, knew the drill, and while I fiddled in my doctor's bag for a reflex hammer, I asked her to remove the bra and again assume the recumbent position. To this she complied, keeping the sheet up to her neck. Drawing the sheet down on one side, I saw that her bra strap, undone in back, allowed the cups of the bra to stay in place but off a bit, like two carelessly worn baseball caps. Softball caps? Anyone want to play ball? *Let us go then, you and I/When the evening is spread out against the sky ...* She was endowed in the way one might come and go, *Talking of Michelangelo.*

Prudence, and not J. Alfred Prufrock, cautioned me to think no more such thoughts. She was endowed, and I will say no more. I must say more. I was experienced enough by then to examine breasts in a rational state of mind, but was that even possible with a strange beauty alone with me in a crowded storeroom? And why were hers so exquisite?

To divert my attention from her explored parts, I thought of home, of dear wife, of the doctor I heard being paged in the distance beyond the door, of the doctor I wished to be. This while paying homage to what she had brought, twin pets, alert after a good nap. I was dazzled, wished to genuflect before sovereignty, wished to circumnavigate those globes. A few moments later, accomplices in a masquerade, the patient and I began the campaign to unmask her abdomen. I held the sheet against my vision, leaving her to hook and scoot and heft in choreography aimed at relieving sheer material from biting into soft flesh, answered dreams posing as piquant schemes. She was comfortable with this. I wasn't. She had pulled the hem of the garment even with the base of her triangle, its elastic sufficient that it did not touch flesh in every inch of its expanse.

How to Stuff a Wild Bikini.

Without answers, I fled toward known questions. All the while I felt her eyes on me, burning into my thoughts. Things on the veranda stood and waved, signaling events at the edge of the night, and my face blazed like a campfire. Blinded but sighted, lashed but mobile, scrambling to keep ahead of the scorching ferocity, I dashed to a region that was puffy-pouty no more, a leisurely expanse erected between house and field, brook and meadow, can and can't. I crashed into her right groin and an unexpected savior: a tattoo. Throbbing in certitude, it graced that swell of kissing flesh beside Venus. It was a bright-red Cupid's bow, drawn and ready, the crimson arrow curling through the air toward the thick dark forest. The patient tensed at my reaction in discovering it, held her breath for a long count of three, and burst into hysterics, bucking for the two of us in ripples of squirmy laughter.

"That," she screamed, "don't tell anybody about *that!*"

Not in half a century, and presently I wrote up the patient and spoke to Dr. Patterson about her, who had happened by and was in the nurses' station. What if he had entered the room and caught me at it? It was all I could do to keep from blurting out the obvious—that she was maddeningly sexy, examine at your own risk. Maybe professional control is as thin as sheer silk; as soon as I could, I flew home to wife and safety, to exorcise demons.

The idea of clinical training, to acquaint young doctors with examples of each disease, enables one to turn back through memory and compare this with that, and that person in the treatment room became my example of a would-be physician on the verge of losing professional control. That Cupid's arrow, that guffaw, had rescued me.

*   *   *

We're walking, we're walking, going from before internship to after, when I was a resident physician in 1965. A sylphlike sixteen-year-old was admitted to Ward 4-B of the John Sealy Hospital while it was still the staff ward for white females.[20] This one was sick. She was very sick; she required treatment for an aggressive hemolytic anemia, and I eventually gave her blood transfusions and corticosteroid therapy. Yet her illness was mononucleosis, "kissing disease," a vulnerability of the heart that in no way disqualified her body from devouring itself.

Students on the service had previously compromised an appealing young woman of twenty or twenty-one, who had signs suggesting infectious hepatitis (hepatitis A). I had noted that her breasts, reaching their appointed time, had barely been touched by gravity. They were serious breasts, hers, perhaps in the way that breasts can be the most serious part of the body when a woman is of a certain age—and she was of that age. I had done an admitting examination on her and never taken another look, but one day she motioned to me and drew me aside after rounds. She had a question.

"Is there something wrong with my heart?"

The crowd at rounds included several nurses, half a dozen students, and an intern, and the swarm had moved away and planted itself by the nurses' station just there. The patient's bed was offset around a corner from the nurses' station and unseen from there. It awarded her a degree of privacy. Yet she was troubled about her heart.

"No, I don't think so."

"Then why do they keep coming to my bed and examining it?"

Oh. I assured her that her heart was fine and afterward assigned the randy male medical students on my service to do something other than to palpate her chest, listen to her breasts. As students, they didn't know any better, but were they that different from me?

The patient with mononucleosis, who was in the last bed to the left in the back corner of the open ward, required a thorough abdominal examination with careful attention to her enlarged spleen. But the thing I remember with chivalrous indifference was the instant the sheet dipped sufficiently to permit a pubic peep. There it was, waiting, as I had expected it to be, and at a youthful sixteen it was perfectly formed and overly ambitious and sent me reeling through time and space to that laboratory known as adolescence, where one

---

20   Medicare having passed in 1965, integration of the wards at John Sealy
      Hospital began the following year.

lived or died by experiments far short of a pubic peep. I was embarrassed, deeply so.

The patient, watching my every twitch with the keen alertness of every lithesome brunette who ever lived, saw it and *knew*. And smiled like a centerfold, truth from the mouths of babes. She had caught me out. I was happily married, we had kids, but what the hell difference did that ever make? They see you seeing it, see how you see it, and they see more than seeing it could possibly yield: guilty as charged. Women are never too sick to notice a notice.

In my defense as to her peep, I was merely trolling for signs of disease. I could tell at a glance whether she had lice (just kidding), hypertrichosis, dermatomyositis, or alopecia areata. One glance wreaked the possibility of femoral hernia, femoral aneurysm, tinea pubis, chloasma gravidarum, trichotillomania pubis, neurodermatitis, the hyperpigmentation of Addison's disease, hypervitaminosis A, granuloma inguinale, and a few less common entities. I also knew from it and from my reaction to it that she kept it covered because of the strength of the statement it made. Where a face-to-face pelvic examination was without sexual allure, the pelvic peep was light-years ahead of it by way of its effect on the neutral observer. The statement it made was made by nature and stayed by a maiden's hand. Modesty commanded her to be immodest, as it were, in times like these. I could not explain this beyond common sense and evolution and what her mother had told her fifteen minutes ago. I could not explain it other than to remark that the spacious expanse of her smooth belly pursued the Equator in all its gallant felicity.

This was no imaginary line! It was where one encountered the rainforest, the last vestige of the jungle she left behind, the slinky pinky of wild things, claws and paws and jaws in a savannah teeming with primitive impulses amidst the growls of furry predators. The pubic peep was the end of civilization as we know it. Merely to see it was to be changed forever. Take it in and pass from Before to After, to things that go on in the dark, to things that belonged to the monkeys before us and the fowl of the air and the fish of our sea (piscis peep) and the poof! marking the spot. It was there to get its comeuppance by way of celebrating the only colossus sought by all, that gleaming crustacean that arrives lustily, crying out in its selfsame importance, hence the position of its nursery in the proximate vicinity of the maw of life, that cloverleaf of multiple dimensions.

Did this explain why this young woman, then seventeen or eighteen, had sought me out one day outside the hospital? The small post office that served good old UTMB was located in Old Red, in its basement, a few steps down from the exterior. Old Red was the hoary old original building of UTMB, beloved by all, a Wailing Wall for megalomaniacs of the doctorly set—though all it reminded me of was pigeon shit and a place to get my mail. It was separate from the hospital itself and in distance a couple of hundred feet into a sunlit plaza once removed from sickness and disease, a way of seeking out a refreshing few minutes from what had been wrought by the peccadilloes of nature.

And there she was.

Healed, she should have been in her classes at Galveston's Ball High School, which seemed a perfect moniker for Galveston's testicular merchants and the stretched scrotum of its double-dribble beaches. Yet there she was, with a girlfriend, and it was quite possible that she had arrived outside John Sealy Hospital that afternoon to look up the doctor responsible for her care a year or two earlier. Having seen me and found him, she took up where the centerfold had left off. How was I? Fine. She smiled and introduced her friend, who also smiled, and there we were, exchanging smiles as wide as possibilities. What was I doing? None of your business. Of course I was not rude to her, but I had discovered why she was there in a couple of milliseconds, and she knew that I knew why she was there because she had not forgotten that roving intake of the pubic peep in all its storied contours. The friend knew it, too, having been told, and out of desperation I barely slowed.

Actually I was rude to them. But I wasn't running from them; I was running from myself.

*   *   *

The thing about the staff Psychiatry Service at John Sealy Hospital was that half of the inpatients were in a horribly misnamed building, Psycho 2, which had been a nurses' dormitory in earlier years. The second floor of Psycho 2 was a locked ward. It was a locked ward for females. For whatever reason, these patients had lost their freedom. Nikki Richards* was an eye-catching young patient on the floor, and I met her one morning in the spring of 1962, having gone there to see a different patient, one assigned to me. I had no interest in Nikki Richards—or at least I thought not.

She was prettier than the rest and younger, too, Nikki, a victim of that hoped-for condition among unknowing males, nymphomania. For this psychosexual disorder she required treatment as an inpatient to save her from herself, as it were, for at age eighteen Nikki Richards thought she had found her niche in life. She lit the world with a stunning deliciousness, her manner that of a savvy seeker of what drove her to excess. It was as though she had just awakened to all the bright possibilities of the world, a Sunday school teacher become pole dancer. That particular morning she had packed herself into some skintight shorts. She wore a simple white blouse tied so that belly dipped beneath it, but her clothing was not so limiting as that. Her attire extended to the reaches of her vision, the milieu of her person, the bedlam of which she was the exemplar. She sidled up to the nurses' station, put her hands on her hips, looked me in the eye, and said, "Do you think my shorts are too tight?"

By about half a mile.

With thirty-five patients on Psycho 2, the nurses were racing around elsewhere on the ward, rendering treatment for psychosis and neurosis and such. Basically it was just me, protected by the locked lower half of the Dutch door that was the entrance to the nurses' station, clinging by a thread to my self-control.

"Are my shorts too tight?" she asked again.

The shorts were pink—no, more red than pink—and when I looked up again from my patient's chart, she was fiddling with the zipper on the left side of said item. I supposed this was my punishment for having spoken to her. Her fingers traced teasingly along the white buttons of her blouse. A voice sounded from the corridor, the nurse. I was more aware of the tone and amplitude than of the words, and when I looked again, Nikki Richards had disappeared, her footsteps following her down the hallway to her room. With a key the nurse opened the door, and then she bent and wrote something on a chart.

"Some patients," she said to me in a tone asking for mutual condemnation. I left the nurses' station with her a few minutes later, and the nurse locked the Dutch door behind us.

A young man's adolescence brings an admixture of feelings, and two young women twirlers on an August night in the year of Our Lord took me to that place and showed me what it was about unexpectedly one night early in high school, in the dark outside the band hall as we left the building for the field. The field was distant, its lights also missing, and darkness swallowed us. That I knew. What I did not know, what I had not expected, was the advent of a young woman's life intersecting with mine, possibly on a collision course with that crossroads that is waiting at the end of every path, just as it is the beginning of every path. In the shivery darkness of a very warm night, from an unscripted play that was still in rehearsal, I passed the Pathfinder Merit Badge, which every Scout covets most of all.

There on Psycho 2, hardly ten years later, I was the same person, and what had really changed? I had a beautiful, sexy wife who told me later that the first night in our marriage on which we didn't have sex, she cried herself to sleep, thinking the marriage over. But 1962 brought the two-year itch, a dominating theme in my dealings with sexy young things. I had been amazed to discover in marriage something I never thought would happen. As a child, eating the occasionally offered pie, I thought how wonderful it would be should the entire thing be the delicious filling. The crust seemed to me unnecessary. It was a mere formality. All it did was support the nice things inside. One went at things, it seemed to me, backward. Then one day, years later, I woke up to something that had been there all along, unnoticed by me. And it was that the crust offered delights of its own. In some instances it could be even better than the filling. It had the advantage of proximity, it did not seem to mind second billing, and everything about it was quieter and less imperious than the filling.

And suddenly that morning in Galveston in 1962 I found Nikki Richards to be the most desirable female I had ever seen, and when she had asked me that question about her shorts being too tight, I was moved to think, *Well, no.* But I have not described it sufficiently. She stood beyond the Dutch door that was the locked entrance to the nurses' station on this locked ward and unlocked herself radiantly, wiggling and wriggling just so, posing to me a question that was as unspoken as it was outspoken.

One part of me wants to tell how I had leapt to my feet and followed her like a frisky puppy down the hallway to her room. I knew the room. There were some contraptions on the windows, bars and locks, beyond the second twin bed, so that the filtered light was as thick as dust. And there she was, naked as a thought, swaying in the corner by the closet, arms upthrust as if to seize her cross and mount it in all its glory. But it didn't happen. I did not follow her to her room because the nurse chased her away, though a fellow medical student a day or two later told of entering the room to see the roommate and there was Nikki without a stitch, calling to him in that siren song that sailors know all too well.

The thing is, of the patients I've just described, Nikki is the one who has stayed most vividly in my mind. I never examined her, never even touched her. I never saw her again after that morning, that I remember, but in my fantasies she and her forthright manner remain as astounding as the first time I experienced them. *Let's begin here and we shall go on from there,* she seemed to be saying, ready to make that happen. Certainly the sensations she aroused in me would have ended quickly enough, because she was sick, and yet her unhealthy ghost has pursued me all these years. Maybe the reason was that the pubic peep unseen was sexiest of all.

*   *   *

Male sexuality can seem strange. About the same age that young women begin to menstruate, or a year or so later, young men suddenly discover an emission from the penis following an orgasm. The emission, of course, is ejaculation. The fluid is semen, consisting of sperm cells and accompanying effluvium, the sperm having traveled from the testes to the exterior through the sperm duct, a tube—one on either side—that is the required length to climb from the testicle, up over the pelvic bone, and then to descend to deeper structures before finally reaching the penis itself. Ejaculation, like erection, occurs by reflex. A man can will himself to an erection by thinking sexy thoughts, staring at sexy pictures, or by self-stimulation, but ejaculation only occurs after the male orgasm. Several things about this are better known to men than to women. A sustained erection, for example, produces a few drops of a clear solution that exits the penis but is not ejaculate. It is not semen. It lubricates the chassis, as it were, oiling the pathway of the ejaculate at orgasm, helping it make its bold, pulsating appearance exterior to the body, like a fountain celebrating its spout.

The volume of the semen has been closely studied not only by scientists but by those whose organs produce and release this viscous fluid. The volume varies from man to man and in the same man depending on the frequency of ejaculation, his age, and his health. Peak production occurs in the teens and twenties; after forty, it begins to decline. Young boys have been known to exaggerate the amount, as when a youth a couple of years older confided to an awed group of us that he could produce "a handful" of semen. Scientists are much pickier than that about data, but as a safe assumption, the volume is anything from about a spoonful to "a handful" of ejaculate.

One ejaculation contains up to half a billion sperm cells. To put this into perspective, each male orgasm releases enough sperm cells to theoretically replenish the entire population of the United States, with enough overflow to reconstitute the citizens of several other banana republics, were each sperm cell to fertilize an ovum, or egg. But all of those unused sperm cells emitted each time actually do help the one cell that manages to unite with an egg and achieve a pregnancy. Fertilization is a collective endeavor.

In a sense, fertilization is the culmination of everything else in life. We are here for it, we live for it, and we live from it. It may be why sex is at its keenest when reproduction is in the offing. *Speak for yourself,* some men may say—and they have a point—but every dissenter should first count to half a billion.

To an extent, as every man learns, the more frequent the ejaculation, the less the amount. Then again, the more infrequent is the ejaculation, the greater the thrill. Sperm and seminal fluid production is a continuous process. It doesn't include cramps and men do not have a menopause. The menstrual cycle and sperm production also differ in that the cycle is much less affected by sexual activity (except for pregnancy and nursing) than is the case for ejaculation. Sperm production eventually requires release. At some point the male must clear out old sperm cells by way of orgasm so newer and fresher sperm cells can take their place. The interval for this cycle varies among men and with age, but it is on the order of four to eight weeks. In men who do not masturbate for whatever reason, or who do not have an orgasm during that interval of time, a sexual explosion known as a wet dream occurs, the so-called nocturnal emission, an orgasm subsequent to a sexual fantasy happening during sleep.

> And in his sleeping as in his waking dreams, the river ran. ...The river shimmered on its mudded floors. Sometimes, he would find a young woman in the reeds. He wanted to look directly into her green eyes, and persuade her to become again the goddess of the river. But in the climax of the dream, as he sought her skin under a green dress, he would find himself entangled in rushes, her slippery body writhed whitebellied and flaggyfooted, escaping in the yellow reeds, and then the spasmed jet of his desire would stream off his body in the night, finding no place for its delicious anguish except the river.[21]

It also may happen that one awakens during said fantasy and applauds its theatrics, so to speak. Penile emissions and also urine are propelled by the same mechanism one may employ in watering the yard with a garden hose. By placing a finger to partly occlude the nozzle, one makes the water squirt farther. The penis is built that way. The smallest point in a man's reproductive and urinary anatomy occurs at the tip of the penis, just inside the opening. As illustrative example, instances have occurred of kidney stones passing their way painfully down from the kidneys and into the bladder and urethra, finally lodging just inside the tip of the penis, where they must be removed surgically.

In women, the reproductive and urinary pathways are separate. In men they are combined, and this explains why the passages cannot open simultaneously. Sphincters below the bladder act to occlude the urinary tract during sexual excitement, which explains why it takes a bit of time before a man can urinate after having sex. Rising sexual tension creates this change. Then, as pressure in the sperm ducts rises, the man begins to realize that he can ejaculate, knows it a few seconds before it actually transpires, and allows

---

21   Ross Lockridge Jr., *Raintree County* (Boston: Houghton Mifflin Company), 1948, 115.

it to occur by relaxing a voluntary sphincter that, in human history, has dutifully never not been opened at the asking.

Everyone has heard truisms about the sexual organs, the size of a man's penis being this or that, and possibly the less said about it, the better. The hair of his beard does not always approximate the color of a man's pubic hair, especially when the beard or the hair on his head turns white or gray prematurely, the pubic hair maintaining its natural color longer than might be predicted. Probably the best estimate of the color of his pubic hair is the color of a man's arm or leg hair. The head of the penis, scientifically called the glans penis, is the triangular part with the slit, and its color varies from a bluish-red to a deeper purple or much darker than that. Its suppleness—even during erection—serves its use in gaining entrance to its intended site, and in exploring same.

Normal testicles in an adult vary in size, but surgeons replacing an absent one use a Ping-Pong ball. That is about right in size though wrong in consistency. The normal testicles are the most tender part of a man's anatomy and probably should not be grasped by his partner without fair warning or unless he guides the hand to them. A growth of either is a strong indication of cancer, its most surprising feature residing in how it picks an otherwise healthy man who may still be in his twenties or late teens. Such a growth is painless, and the cancerous testicle has a firm consistency. The testicles lie one above the other for a reason easily explained by any man who ever sat down and crossed his legs.

A "missing" testicle does not make a man infertile, but this requires comment. It has often been said of Adolf Hitler that he had only one testicle, which led to a jingle about him used in the UK during World War II. The thing is, other than surgical removal or an exceedingly rare agenesis, no male has only one testicle. The "missing" testicle is present in the inguinal region or higher up in its path of descent from below the kidney, having failed to peregrinate into the scrotum during fetal development, a condition called cryptorchism. For that matter, both testicles may be undescended, and in these young men a surgical correction is needed, because such testicles are more likely to turn cancerous than are those that have descended to their intended destination.

*   *   *

Women have their own variability in feminine features, as any doctor soon learns. Not in most, but in quite a few persons, is my memory, one breast is a bit larger than the other. Were I to wager a guess, most often it is the left, where anatomy grants it a better blood supply, though sometimes the right is larger than the left. Breast implants can be used to even the appearance. These days, many women have breast implants to add to the size of both by way of their image of themselves as well as their presumed attractiveness to others. No doubt this occurs with excellent results. But the telltale difference is in the appearance of the upper part of the expanded breasts. The natural breast has a benign softness and a pendulous appearance difficult to achieve with implants, surgery often leaving a taut, balloon-like enlargement in the upper half, noticeable above the brassiere.

Women with naturally red or blonde hair tend to have a more reddish color to the nipples than the chestnut-brown or olive-brown nipples in brunettes—with exceptions—or in women of color. The nipples darken during pregnancy no matter the person's skin color, unless further darkening is not possible. These changes serve to increase the visibility of the milk-giving parts to the baby that feeds at the breast. The nipples lighten again later.

The anatomy of the uterus, or womb, consists of an upper and a lower part. Pregnancy distends the upper one into a spacious hideout for the fetus, a roominess only fully appreciated when the baby is born. This part cannot be seen directly because of other structures, and after emptying itself at childbirth, it retreats to its former size like a faithful tenant awaiting another summons. The lower part of the womb, the cervix, has its own role in reproduction. Where it is accessible to sperm cells and can be viewed during a pelvic examination, it commands the back third of the vagina like a doorman beneath a canopy guarding the entrance to the building.

In a woman who isn't pregnant and hasn't been, the normal cervix appears as a short, red cylinder, smoothly domed on its surface, and endowed with a small, perfectly rounded opening. In thickness or consistency, when a woman is not pregnant, to palpate the cervix is somewhat the same as touching the tip of the nose. Fairly early during pregnancy, the cervix begins to soften, and by the time a woman misses her second menstrual period—about six weeks along—it has the soft consistency of the cheek on either side of the nose. By that stage of pregnancy, the blood supply to the womb having increased dramatically, the cervix has become bluish in color. Its softening and color change are so specific for early pregnancy that physicians of yore used these signs, along with the enlargement of the womb, to confirm the diagnosis of pregnancy. Modern tests are easier and quicker, but an early appointment with a health care provider is still advisable.

A cervix that has gone through the changes of childbirth—well, I'll give an example.

Once, at a clinic where I worked, a woman and her fiancé came in for premarital physical examinations. They were both about thirty, he the younger of the two. I examined him first, while the woman entered another room for a pelvic examination. Before checking her, while she was seated on the examining table, I took a brief history. The standard questions included problems with the menses and any history of pregnancy. She responded that things were fine and that she had never had any children.

But when I checked her a few minutes later, I did not find the small and perfectly rounded cervical opening mentioned above. I saw at a glance that her cervix had an enlarged, "fish-mouthed" opening of the kind seen in women who have delivered a baby through it. After the exam I stepped to her side and asked again about children.

"I have two," she said quickly, "but don't you dare tell him!" I wouldn't think of it, and I hope they lived happily ever after.

*   *   *

People may wonder whether a doctor thinks about all of the niceties of the anatomy lab when engaged in lovemaking. It is a question I can answer only for myself. No. That stays behind like an accountant's ledger, a policeman's cruiser, or a lecturer's notes, stashed harmlessly out of sight.

In the fall of 1961, well into our second year of marriage, Mimi began holding me tightly and whispering, "Babies, babies, babies!" She had learned that babies born to medical students were given free baby formula by one of the companies that made it. Was that the motivation? As an additional incentive, obstetrical care was free. Babies have been born for lesser reasons than that.

Christmas of 1961 we attended a party at the Nu Sig house and listened to a mysterious priest sing "Scarlet Ribbons." He was a handsome man in his twenties and accompanied himself on the guitar in a magical, captivating rendition, as though he had lost a love never to be reclaimed and was hoping to spare us same. The man did not sing the song, he sculptured himself inside it and drew us with him; we saw her face in all its loveliness, we wove ourselves into her lovely curls, shared the blush of that lovely radiance, did pirouettes to her dancing beauty—as if we had escaped Earth's boundaries, because it took that to fully appreciate its gravity, love as life, its loss as death, feelings as future, intimacies the ribbons untied again and again, unleashing a force inaccessible except to those who believe, those who would worship it with all their hearts, those lucky enough to kneel before its crowning magnificence. Serves two.

There must have been something about that night, because we were pregnant and Mimi loved it. She loved the anticipation, the suspense of not knowing whether it was a boy or a girl. Her obstetrician, Dr. Leslie C. Powell Jr., a professor at UTMB, encouraged her to remain active. She continued her teaching job in Texas City until the summer and then found a job as a secretary to a physician whose office was in downtown Galveston. She continued, in other words, as the main source of the money in the marriage, though I had managed to swing a $750 fellowship the previous summer.

As she shopped for groceries and brought them in herself, for the most part, I had pointed out to me that at the very gravid eighth month of her pregnancy, she still did this, and each trip in with another sack of groceries, up those front stairs and onto the landing and then through the screen and the door, she had to pass my carcass on the bed, where I had paused to take a nap and instead fallen into that deep coma known to every medical student as the point where the physical simply severs itself from the functional. (It was the equivalent of what marathoners call a "brick wall.") I had no excuse otherwise, and am happy to report that it only happened once.

Somewhere along the way a baby bed had materialized, a mobile, clothing, a bassinet, a few rattles, and a couple dozen cloth diapers. Each addition to our small rent house at 320 Tenth Street in Galveston, built as a garage apartment in a row of others, brought the exhilarating notion of change. I did not wish to deflect the unassailable fact that not only her life but mine was changing forever, but what left me agog was that this person I had married had caused to bring into the world (with very little help from me) a new individual. It was as startling as if the US Treasury had allowed us, at our own pace, to mint what was more precious than any currency, more valuable than any gold. We received the gift with due reverence, feeling as special as orchard dwellers have always felt. It put one in mind that the idea was to pass along the splendor. Create incandescence, share the spectacle. Pay homage to the ventriloquist. Feed at the table of the exquisite. Lovely was the time when, as vintage novels put it, "She felt new life stirring within her."

Years later, teaching at UT–Austin, I would guide nursing students through the astonishing repertoire of happy feelings experienced by a woman during pregnancy, having accumulated them by hearsay. It was fun to open the discussion to those who were mothers and ask them for their own experiences at the time of what is known in obstetrics as *quickening*, the first sensations of fetal activity. Some of them likened it to a not entirely comfortable sensation, rather like gas on the stomach. Others put it differently. But they all laughed when I told them Mimi's experience.

"It feels," she said, "like there is a little person in there kicking around."

To be sure, some of the mothers pointed out that the patchwork pattern of it could keep them awake at night, when the activity—basically a fetal exercise session—coincided with bedtime and the hope of a much-needed night's sleep.

Then, we had the matter of naming the baby. The father, it seemed, could not take this assignment with any degree of certainty that the privilege of naming a kid rested with anyone other than the new mother herself, who would provide it at the appropriate time, probably when he was not around. But it was our first and I submitted that, were it a boy, I ought to get to pick a name. After some period of discussion, this was agreed to. For a boy who got his start late in 1961, the very year that Roger Maris had hit those record-shattering sixty-one homers, why not name him Roger? Mimi warmed to the idea, choosing Stuart as a middle name that she got I know not where. She also selected two very nice names for the little girl we weren't going to have, and I thought them pretty names.

*   *   *

The day Mimi went into labor was a terribly hot and humid September day in Galveston. That afternoon she had walked home from her job downtown at the doctor's office because she had been told by one of her friends that walking late in pregnancy might bring on labor. She took Market Street, or Avenue D, from downtown to our house, a distance of a mile or so. I arrived home from the hospital and she made supper, as always. After supper she went into the bathroom and then came back out. She had begun to experience what she thought might be labor pains. She refused to be taken to the hospital yet.

It was Thursday, September 27, 1962. Not until ten o'clock or so that evening did she begin to agree that her time had come. By then the pains were regular, and hard, and very uncomfortable. I helped her down the stairs and into the Plymouth then drove the half a block distance to John Sealy Hospital. Leaving the car in the ER parking lot, I accompanied her to the third-floor delivery suite and stood by while they were getting her a bed, doing admitting lab work, and notifying Dr. Powell. Somewhere in there, Mimi informed me that she did not want me to see her during labor. Could she actually think it would change my love for her? She never said, and I returned home to sleep the rest of the night but was up early enough to check on her first thing at the hospital.

The first surprise was that one of my classmates, a man that I did not know well, and who was from Kansas in either the actual town or the adjacent one where the 1955 movie *Picnic* was filmed, was following Mimi through labor. I accepted this. I didn't like it. The stipulation was that "free" obstetrical service meant submission to the staff and students in the teaching hospital, including also interns and residents. It meant that Dr. Powell would bring the vast experience of a board-certified specialist in Obstetrics and Gynecology to the event. It meant that a medical student would most likely perform the delivery.

*   *   *

I had become an alternate student the previous spring and was ending my rotation on the Medicine Service, my assignment being to the Ziegler Hospital, a TB hospital run by Dr. John Middleton, a well-respected professor of medicine. Mornings were the busiest times at Ziegler, and at eleven a.m. on Friday, September 28, 1962, we had a meeting in the conference room during which we spent an hour examining interesting chest X-rays. It was a time dearly loved by Dr. Middleton and the others, and I did not have the guts to approach the doctor and ask for the hour off to attend the birth of our first child. Not being in the delivery room would not keep me from the vicinity, I thought. I wanted to see the new baby as soon as it was born. I wished to be there. But my cowardice in admitting that I had personal needs and my fright in having my reputation suffer kept me from asking off, and I remained in that crippling conference room in Ziegler until twelve o'clock finally came, instead of being present in the only place in the universe that I wished to be.

Roger Stuart Deaton, weighing eight and a half pounds, was born at 11:05 a.m., meaning that had I skipped the conference I would have been there in time for the event. As it was, racing down hallways and leaping the elevator, I had missed the birth by an hour. It was nothing on the order of the disappointments I would accumulate, but doing somersaults by way of the weighing of regrets had its price. For the rest of his life, the father of that child would berate himself for putting school ahead of family.

I was willing even as a student, it seemed, to sacrifice everything in my plunge to succeed. I would exceed every barrier put before me, be it health, family, or future, in the pretense of an excellence that mattered more to me than the reality of what I was doing to myself. A well-ingrained habit, coaxed from fear of failure, crept around my future, its tightening coils strangling my ideals and, eventually, what was left of the idealist. But that was later, much later, and at the time I could not be contaminated by such dribble.

Mimi, for her part, had not missed me, and that made me feel better. First I visited the nursery and saw through the glass our amazing new son. It made me so happy that I was willing to forgive the world and myself of everything—the tortured past, the blind rage, the incorrigible impulse—all of it, every bit of it, every last morsel, redemption being the Rosetta stone of understanding. It was an event, and not only in my life. I felt that some great fault had shifted somewhere to realign the forces of nature. The noise occurred offstage, but the event was real. On one level it was like the feeling that persists after one has seen a terribly good movie: one doesn't wish to leave the theater, having entered a make-believe world that was yours for oh so brief a time, the loveliest part of this being that not only wouldn't it end, it would grow, and in its inspiration, so would we.

Mimi was in a double room on the second floor of the east end of John Sealy. That part of the hospital was known as Randall Pavilion, where each floor had a solarium looking to the east end of the island and whatever beauty was lent by way of the hulking ships, one after the other, clumping into the Houston Ship Channel. She was in the first bed and saw me enter the room. I was wearing a smile as wide as the boats out there in the estuary, but she had been through an ordeal and was not in a particularly good mood. She had been given something for pain and it helped, but not quite enough.

"We've got a beautiful son," I said.

"I'm never going through that again!" she said.

To reassure her that her efforts were appreciated, I went around to the head of the bed and gave her the kiss that answers for words but turns awkward in its effect, and I told her once again how proud I was of her.

"That's good," she said, "because we have an only child."

In time we would differ on whether or not that was humorous, because Roger was the first of four. Still, that day and for a couple of years we had an only child, and I slipped home to the garage apartment to call relatives. While working at the grocery store she and husband Gilbert were managing in Crystal City, a two-hour drive south of San Antonio, Helen Garrett was anything but joyous to hear the news. It was as if she had been told that mother and child had died at delivery—she was that stunningly unresponsive. After a quick lunch I returned to my hospital duties, though I went by to see Mimi as often as possible and made a longer visit that evening. When I reached home after dark, I spoke to Helen again, she and Gilbert both. Apparently Helen was so numb at being a new grandmother, she had been dumbstruck. What Helen did, which was to prove so crucial, was to make arrangements in Crystal and present herself in Galveston a few days later at 320 Tenth Street, Gilbert remaining behind to attend the store.

Bringing Mimi home with the new baby was a joy. She stood holding Roger in her arms at the foot of the stairs, a mother struck by the rapture of giving birth, that enthralling event, and were we given to spend eternity in that moment, both of us, along with Roger, we would have gladly accepted the barter and taken our places in that picture of forever.

*   *   *

A few days later, the dates fuzzy but not the events, I awoke in the middle of the night with Helen at the foot of my bed saying, "Johnny, Mimi's bleeding. Johnny, Mimi's bleeding."

Gaining my feet, I saw in the light from the kitchen the vast pool of blood puddled on the double bed Mimi and Helen were sharing. Mimi was absent the bed, and the trail of blood led through the tiny kitchen to the open door of the bathroom where, in total silence, seated on the commode, my wife was bleeding to death.

Events thereafter dissolved time but not effort: the rapid dressing, the two of us getting Mimi down the stairs and to the dirt floor of the garage and into the front seat of the '54 Plymouth, Helen remaining behind because Roger's crib was in that same bedroom and someone had to stay with him, and what might have happened had she not been there?

The night air was cool, too cool. I was shivering in fright; Mimi was shivering from shock, despite the blanket I had wrapped her in. I asked of her and kept asking of her during the five-minute drive, or the one-minute drive, and she only whispered unintelligibly. Then she didn't whisper at all, didn't say anything.

She had fainted.

Hemorrhagic shock is a silent killer.

It is as though a bloodthirsty monster has sneaked aboard, a glutton dealing its deathblow in the silence of internal suffocation, a strangler hiding in all the parts of the body that can't be seen. I had no vocabulary for it as I had no explanation for it as I had nothing for it except my sheer, devastating fright.

The parking lot for the ER was empty.

I left Mimi in the car and went roaring into the hospital, bawling for help. A medical student, a friend from Nu Sigma Nu, raced toward me with a wheelchair. Together we got Mimi into it and rushed her inside to the ER, which was about twice the size of the one in Corpus. But first we had to get her there, and she kept falling out of the chair. Finally I lifted her in my arms and kicked the goddamned wheelchair out of the way, as it was only a short distance to ER, but it was the longest trip of my life.

The hallway had the green wainscoting of the rest of John Sealy Hospital and the same hard-as-marble tiles on the floor. But what I noticed for some insane reason were the veins of gold radiantly streaking through the tiles like a million golden sunsets, or like gilded spiders come alive from the age of hieroglyphics and Egyptian tombs—things as frightening as the trail of blood we were leaving on the floor. I was struck by how terribly pretty things must seem when you are dying, and those precious images are all you have to take with you. I saw the blood and slipped on it as people dashed out and joined us and as I surrendered her unconscious form to them. The part of me becoming a doctor saw again the horror of the bright-red arterial tree, toppled by trespassers, bedlam of one's lifeblood being siphoned away, and a shudder like the kiss of a glacier shot through me.

The friend who was on duty in the ER had spent our brief time together warning me not to let the intern on duty touch Mimi. The intern was a man from another state who had come to Galveston for internship for whatever reason and who may or may not have been an idiot. But he was a trained physician on duty in the ER, and he saw to Mimi being placed on an examining table in one of the private rooms and got a drip of normal saline going.

Then he turned and bluntly asked me whether he could examine Mimi and try and stop the bleeding. It was my first life-and-death emergency, and I found it hard to answer questions. Everything seemed so obvious to me that I could not understand their need to catch up to me. I wished to be alone with my thoughts and my horror so I could think things through and give the right answer so Mimi would be okay. But people kept asking me questions as though I had come there to recount a narrative they wished to hear. More than one asked whether Mimi and I had been having "relations." (With Helen in the bed with her?) It begged sanity that I would begin what I had been taught should be omitted for at least six weeks after delivery, and Mimi was sore down there. The nurse asked it, and then the intern, who threw up his hands and walked away in the manner of a man who had been unjustly convicted of a crime that didn't exist, then he pivoted and came back to ask again whether he could have permission to try and stop the bleeding and save Mimi's life. And was refused. Refused by a confused young man twenty-two years of age who stupidly said no, a horrible mistake, because I was unwilling to upset my friend by going against his advice.

*   *   *

Dr. Powell reached the ER in about half an hour. Mimi was stabilized by then and had regained consciousness. The obstetrician determined that she was bleeding from her episiotomy incision. He inserted a vaginal pack then called and made arrangements and took her upstairs to OR to repair the wound. That was somewhere around three a.m. Before leaving the ER, he began the first of several blood transfusions she would receive.

The wait while she was undergoing surgery in the OR was endless. Seated outside, on the floor of the second-story corridor, I examined in unforgettable detail those granite tiles containing the hieroglyphics of the narrative of every transgression that had ever occurred in the life-and-death horror of the human species. Improvise. Copulate. Populate!

The idea of an episiotomy was to substitute a surgical incision of the introitus for a possible serrated, unkempt laceration resulting from delivery, a laceration that might include all or part of the anal sphincter and impair the new mother needlessly. The cut itself was routine. We were taught that it was most important in a primipara, her birth tract not having previously adjusted to the size necessary for vaginal delivery. I would learn to do it, not having yet rotated to OB/Gyn, and would find it surprisingly easy. The incision was made with surgical scissors on an anesthetized patient, and the same person who had made the incision also sutured it shut, beginning at its innermost borders and proceeding outward.

It was rather like sewing up a hole in a sock but from the interior of the sock, the sock being large enough at its opening to see the two halves of flesh created by the incision. In fact, it was much different from darning a sock. It was done with surgical instruments that required training in their use. One, basically an elongated tweezers, was used to hold the flesh from slipping. The other, a needle holder, permitted the needle to be woven through one side and the other, allowing the suture itself to be drawn after it and gently tightened. It began with a crown stitch at the back of the incision, tied as an anchor, with the rest of the closure consisting of a continuous running suture that was tied only at the end. The suture material, a thick catgut—000 chromic catgut, to be specific—was an absorbable thread made from the lining tissues of certain animal species. That the catgut was absorbable meant that the sutures would not have to be taken out later on, like silk or cotton sutures, avoiding a painful experience. Ordinary catgut would not be absorbed by the body for weeks. When the catgut was reinforced with chromium salts, both its tensile strength and its lifetime in the recipient's body were increased. This meant that natural healing of the surgical wound, in the expected outcome, was finished well before the absorption of the suture material.

That being the case, the cause of Mimi's hemorrhage remained unknown, at least to me. While it is possible that my fellow student had erred, Dr. Powell was both her doctor and a teacher in the medical school, and I was not concerned about causes. I thanked him lavishly for his services that night and spent the rest of the night and the next day beside her bed or just outside in the corridor while she was in the recovery room. (I don't remember whether I called Dr. Middleton or my resident, but I was excused from time lost during this critical event.) That day or the next, I was informed by the UTMB blood bank that I was in arrears, and by making phone calls to my mother in Pittsburg and to Gilbert in Crystal City, I secured an ample number of commitments to make up the deficit, and more—another thing I was unspeakably grateful for, as was Mimi upon learning of it.

Helen, of course, remained during the week of Mimi's hospitalization, looking after Roger. Once while she was changing his diaper, he let loose, hosing down the wall and the bed and part of her and sending her, whose two girls had given her very different experiences because of very different plumbing, into hysterics of laughter that also recurred to the point of asphyxia whenever she told the story.

On its surface, the day that I brought Mimi home from the hospital was without peer by way of anticipated events and the happiness that would be ours. That very day, however, I got Mimi settled with Helen and Roger—it was about noon—and the mail was delivered. I stood with it in my hands a moment. I had received an official letter from Dr. Raymond Gregory, Professor and Chairman, Department of Internal Medicine at UTMB. By then I had served on Dr. Gregory's private service and had done library research for him, for money, and I had thought we had a good relationship. I decided as I opened it that Gregory was writing in sympathy for the problems Mimi had had.

Not quite. By then we were in mid-October of 1962. I was on a new rotation, the Surgery Service, and the grades for my rotation on Medicine had been turned in. The letter was blunt. It stated in dry, official prose that at least one evaluator of me during my time on the Medicine Service had recorded a grade of "Inadequate but Passing." The letter further commanded me to report to the office of the chief of medicine at my earliest convenience.

It turned out to be a defining moment in my nascent medical career. It frightened me to death, and it obliterated the image I had of myself—the one I had thought to project to others at the medical school—and with it came a conviction of my abject failure, crushed as I was that I had made not an F, but a grade close enough to it to require a reprimand.

*   *   *

I knew I had trouble with people. What I learned, because I had sincerely not known, was that in rotating through the clinical services in medical school, you are graded by everyone who has power over you, whether intern or resident or staff physician and possibly by the nurses and ward clerks. Each turned in a grade sheet on you. Each was required to do so. All of the confidence in a lifetime of study, a college degree, and the certain knowledge that one's bold manner was a merit rather than a deficit, were turned topsy-turvy by the idea that brownnosing was alive and well and one had better be as skilled in its practice as any other first-grader. The cathedral was built by those who build cathedrals, to honor the sacrosanct, and from that divinity came the ritualism of worship: offend at your own risk.

It reminds me of a story. Dr. Raymond Rigdon of UTMB, a professor of pathology, might as well have confined himself to Keiller Hall, where the students learned the basic sciences of medicine and pathology. He performed autopsies. He taught students and was well loved, not least for his inimitable drawl, a man proud of being raised in *Jaw-ja*. Y'all know how to get to *Jaw-ja*, don't you? Now you go to Alabama and you keep, ah, straight ahead!

One day several years later, Dr. Rigdon appeared unexpectedly on my ward. It seemed that an elderly woman had died and been sent to him, and he was searching for her false teeth. Finally these were located in a glass used for bedside water in a cabinet in the nurses' station. Taking the set of teeth, the pathologist gathered the white shirts around him and said, "Now, gent-men, need understand this. When she dies, you need get those teeth right back into that mouth. You don't, like with this lady, that mouth goes shut and you need you a brace and a mule to get 'em in! So remember, gent-men, it's a, ah, look here, important part, you know, in taking care of dead folks."

It had struck me as so funny, because right up until then I had only thought of taking care of live folks.

Medical training was like modern art. The parts were all there. The partaker, to remain unscathed, had merely to assemble and reassemble them constantly, with the temerity of a slithering earthworm. In fact, I knew how to brownnose with the best of them, those I respected, and I had learned how to do this with Dr. Gregory to an extent that he had complimented me on my skills. Learning he liked the write-ups I did on his patients, I learned to make a rough draft in the patient's room and then to rewrite it once or twice elsewhere in the hospital or at home. Then, when the great man got around to seeing his patient, he liked to find my workup and read it to the patient, making emendations where indicated, then signing it at the bottom, making it his workup. I had a head for figures and began memorizing the latest electrolyte numbers on his patients so that, should the great man ask what a patient's electrolytes were, I could reel them off from memory. This type of thing went back to what Don Shell of Pittsburg had told me about college. I had asked how to make As and Don said, "Figure out what the professor wants and give it to him."

When I appeared in Dr. Gregory's office that afternoon about the "Inadequate but Passing" grade I had received, it became apparent to me that Dr. Gregory had signed a form letter written by a secretary. He seemed surprised to see me. He looked up the specific grade given by the specific doctor. We both knew he was a doctor in the clinic who was pissed because

I had forgotten to go see him a couple of times, as my mentor on medicine, because I was too busy running around the hospital seeing to Dr. Gregory's patients. That wasn't all.

This doctor, whose office was in the clinic, a building across the street from John Sealy, and up on the fourth floor, had been inadequate to me, as long as we're talking grades. He seemed the one who needed a mentor. He kept his feet up on the desk and in my face while we spoke, and he smoked cigarettes constantly. He did not seem to mind that I brought up the subject one day while he was puffing away. Remember that this was back in 1962. It was in the early days of the accumulating evidence that, among other things, cigarettes caused lung cancer. He didn't buy it. He allowed that cigarettes did not impair the health in any way, more of less defying me to disagree. I went to the library and found an article showing that premalignant changes in the lungs could be correlated with the length of time that a person had smoked cigarettes. These results did not faze him; probably it was because of the adage that one will never find what one has concluded beforehand does not exist.

Dr. Raymond Gregory assured me that afternoon I went to his office that I should not worry. I was going to make an A in medicine, he said, which, as an alternate student, meant for both the junior and senior years. That was huge.

*　　*　　*

I am an intern again. It is 1963. I read somewhere that Marilyn Monroe was twenty-three years old when she began taking the sedatives that would kill her a decade and a half later. Lord Byron held that age twenty-three, not forty, was when life began to slip away. Certainly twenty-three was an age of reckoning, and it was my age when I began regularly using the diet pill Preludin, which worked like Dexedrine, to summon the stamina I needed to get through that twenty-four-hour ER rotation that came once in a week plus a day. By the time I turned twenty-four in August of 1963, I needed them to the extent that they had become a part of my life at the hospital.

Why? That is as easy to answer as it is impossible to explain. I did it because I needed them. I did it because that is what it took. Being a physician doesn't change the stuff inside your head, only its alignment, and not even that very much. I felt inadequate in everything I did. I went through life in fear of failure. I was terrified of being found out as the fraud I was, found out by those older and better, including most of the other interns at Memorial Hospital—so went my thinking. The excuse for my self-medication resided in meeting the expectations I had for myself and thought that others had of me. Taking them, of course, only worsened that hiatus because it implied, and was, a weakness that I didn't dare to admit. I knew, of course, that some of the other interns used drugs to get through their time on call and am reminded of what Mother used to say when my defense was that everybody else was doing it: "Just because they stick their heads in the fire," she yelled, "you want to do the same?"

At any rate, taking pep pills became maintenance therapy. I am not sure, even now, that I could have made it the year, or at least the first six months, without them. Taking them when you are tired has been likened to whipping a dead mule, but the mule stopped feeling dead with peppers onboard. The mule could kick again and that was all that mattered. Very few people whom I treated in the ER stopped to ask what I had been taking or how I felt or inquired after my health and happiness. I played a role and saw to it that I was dressed for the part. It had nothing to do with marriage and responsibility other than that it had everything to do with them. The end not only justified the means, it multiplied them. I played doctor on myself with pep pills the way an athlete learns to go beyond endurance so that, in time of need, that extra strength is there. Pep pills helped me find it. They not only fed me during the night, they got me through what would otherwise have been a zombie-like eight-hour shift of agony the next day after a twenty-four-hour call, such existence spent among normal people who lived normal lives and arrived at work enviously fresh and refreshingly envied. To my way of thinking, stimulating the otherwise zombie meant joining them at their level, and I considered that heroic. I was doing nothing less than sacrificing myself for others, those who required my services.

It seemed to make sense at the time.

And was a choice not lightly taken—except that was exactly how I took it. I did no soul-searching. I didn't give it another thought. To use the vernacular, I didn't give a shit. Speed was the "pucker factor" allowing me to submit to authority and do as told, knowing all the while, should problems occur, that these would be as important to them as last month's bowel movement. They look for results. Children are to be seen and not heard! The pucker factor was a trip down the gut of that concrete aircraft in Corpus, a passageway hidden inside everyone and astounding only as to its vulnerability to bursting.

Besides, using pills was as American as apple pie. The sixties were the heady days—daze?—of modern medicine: pills, pills, pills! As a medical student, I had finally arrived when I could sit down with a patient, take a history, do a physical examination, put down a list of possible causes of each symptom, and prescribe a drug as treatment. It was all such a nice, neat package. Constipation? Okay. Arthritis? All right. Sleep? I can do that. You name it and I fix it. It was the modern way. It was my training and it worked.

It was what I did. And since my patients depended on the very medicines I supplied, I would be the most callous of all charlatans to refuse taking them myself.

In medical school we saw a film promoted with this fanfare: "No medical student who has seen this film has ever gotten hooked on dope." The film featured a general practitioner who gave in one night to fatigue and stress and took an injection of Demerol. The injections became a habit, and the addicted doctor lost his practice, his family, and his freedom. The film's point was, *Don't ever take that first injection*. Well, I didn't, but the film said nothing at all about restricting oral drugs. It said nothing at all about stamina or being in shape or staying awake beyond human endurance. It said nothing at all about working while you are sick as a dog but afraid to call in sick. It said nothing at all about the time you have to spend inside your own head at the end of the day or the week or the month or the year. And by the way, it was rollicking fun, at least at first. Whoring oneself was as exciting as breaking the law and as much fun as going to prison.

Across the hallway from ER was the interns' lounge. We used it even when we weren't on call. You could use the bathroom there or take a nap. Along with the phone, the sofa, and the medical library, the interns' lounge contained a drug locker stocked by drug detail men—drug salesmen to doctors—who were as anxious to ingratiate themselves to young doctors as we were to have their acquaintance.

The drug locker was in the bathroom, providing an excuse to lock the door while you picked and chose among the pills stacked on wooden shelves, a smorgasbord of the noxious offering relief to the ravenous. I remember the first time. Every whore is a virgin until the first time, and it was my first tour of ER, that Fourth of July already described. It was after midnight and so July 5, actually, and not only was I tired, I was drained: mentally, physically, and emotionally. I had never felt so exhausted.

Hulsey and Cordova—the day shift—were long gone, and the evening shift, with Reyes and a nurse, left at eleven p.m. I was on duty another eight hours, and the graveyard shift can be the most frenzied time in ER. With more work arriving by the minute, I desired help. The decision was easy. I had actually tasted speed before. During the last few months of medical school and studying for the National Boards, I had occasionally taken something to stay awake. It seemed harmless enough.

Preludin, a product of Geigy Pharmaceuticals, was widely available in the drug lockers of the outpatient clinics at UTMB. Geigy was a well-known and respected drug company. It was based in New York but had branch offices in Hollywood, California, at 6331 Hollywood Boulevard, phone number Hollywood 5-7267.[22] Good place for an assignation! Preludin, a non-amphetamine stimulant, was being marketed by Geigy to reduce appetite in a weight-loss program. It came in a square, pink tablet of twenty-five milligrams that was conveniently scored so that it could be broken in two. It was the one I had taken previously: half a tablet a few times that spring to keep from falling asleep at my desk during the grueling hours of study.

But there was a difference in taking the drug in a small dosage to study an extra couple of hours before bedtime and in using it in the heroic dosages required to stimulate human stamina beyond its natural limits. I was a doctor and well-equipped with that arrogance of person that plays god to the senses. Smitten by the lesson I had learned, that when you give a medicine you must give enough of it, I took a twenty-five-milligram tablet for the first dose, and it felt so good that an hour later, I took another hit. What I learned without noticing it was that the only thing one who feels that good wants is to feel even better.

I filled my belly sufficiently with them that first night that I felt invincible. I loved everyone in a pinnacle of excitement that made me want to pee in the sink, shit at the moon, dash outside and throw rocks at cars. Returning from a trip or two across the hallway from ER, fresh from the crucible of a dominion where quiet corruption hides in plain sight and calls itself wonderful, I was dead and gone, hooked by serendipity to the seahorses that galloped straight out of Corpus Christi Bay so fast that no stopwatch could catch them.

In time, I'd learn to duck into the interns' lounge and leave like Clark Kent become Superman. The world was a phone booth and I its impassioned caller. Hell, sometimes the peppers kicked in before I was out of the bathroom, and I felt as fresh as a twelve-year-old awakening from a night of sleep that had felt like the blink of an eye. The hairs on my arms emitted pleasant sensations, as if Marilyn Monroe were rubbing her titties against them. My clothing, instead of the chaotic crumpling that occurred when I was dead tired, underwent a realignment that felt crisp and straight and right and good, as though Liz had done for me what she did for Monty. I already knew it felt good, washing the grease from my face when I was tired, but washing my face plus putting something on board was jolly good fun, like crowding into a car beside Sandra Dee and setting out to find someone to marry us. I didn't clean my mouth, I cleansed it, and I combed my hair and genuflected to the privileges of a life unbounded. The peppers made me glad of life and everything in it. They

22 *Physicians' Desk Reference to Pharmaceutical Specialties and Biologicals*, 14th ed. (Oradell, NJ: Medical Economics, Inc., 1959), VII and 678.

removed doubts, convinced me that I had rather be right there doing what I was doing than anyplace else in the world, and to the extent that it lasted, it was true. I was trustworthy, loyal, helpful, friendly, courteous, kind, obedient, cheerful, thrifty, brave, clean, and reverent. I was sensational.

With speed on board, I could not do enough for other people; to serve them was my pleasure. I engaged everyone in conversation and was the life of the party and they loved me for it. I expected a call from the governor any moment, I was that deserving. My words brought smiles to the faces of my reassured patients, smiles of gratitude that they were, after all, going to get what they had come there to get: balm. I had plenty of balm, and I was the biggest balm of all.

I should have stopped taking the pills the first time I needed two instead of one, three instead of two, four instead of three. Why I did not heed such obvious warning signs could be summarized in that old copout: I had no choice. Heroes need not skulk. Taking them had already been decided. With the Rubicon behind me, the surrender of my person to an incalculable fate required an adequate dosage for replenishment, or why the hell was I taking the goddamned little bloodsuckers that I hated as much, and on every level, as I also loved them? The thrill, the thrill! Somewhere out there, I imagined, Diane Varsi from *Peyton Place* was contorting in spasms of desire for me that left me tingling; I conjured up ways of satisfying her. I was doing it for *them*, my fun secondary. The rest was arithmetic. As it happened, math being a dry science, I wetted it away with a handful of pills and slaked my thirst with a scoop of water from the lavatory. I was asked medicine and gave same. Needed it and took it. It was my commitment to *them*. Call me anything but a quitter. I was holding up my end of the bargain, see? See the newsreels? How perfect I looked? We were headed to the moon and I took peppers to achieve the trajectory that shot me past the suppressed ravages of my own silent martyrdom.

The bad time was the following day. The sun brought to the bumbling fool a teeming reprisal for every sin committed during his lamplight charade. That night and the next morning I was an alien to the bright, new world of the freshly awake, a visitor from *The Night of the Living Dead*. Too tired to sleep, too wired to eat, too numb to make good decisions, and facing another grueling day on OB/Gyn or another rotation, I was a mountain climber in need of oxygen, a runner in need of calories, a hunter in need of a weapon. Glimpsed in the mirror in the interns' lounge, my burning eyes were signal fires from the Land of Hammered Shit, I its sole inhabitant. Soon my intestines became blocked like a deadbolt on a door from the drug-induced constipation that went with speed, and that wasn't all. My urine turned a deep, dark yellow from my low intake of food and fluids, and the dehydration came with a written guarantee of a post-stimulatory depression at no extra charge. It was a hangover in hell except not as luxurious.

Like any other addict, I craved the hair of the dog. The drug cabinet came to my rescue. To take the pills again the following day was necessary because I had to be alert, had to go on—the show's star had to be his bright, charming self. And did and was. Pretending hero, I became its opposite. Do you see me in a different light from how I see myself? Things become possible that you may not see; I'm in every second person you meet, as every first person is a second person to the *thee* thou greets.

*　　*　　*

Preludin became my life. I wasn't taking it, it was taking me. Even so, it did work. It did underpin my success as an intern. There were other advantages as well. For one thing, speed made me a hell of a lot happier when my in-laws visited. I had always been a bit grumpy around them, as one will around in-laws, but Preludin turned me into their obedient servant wishing to do whatever was in my power to prove to them that their daughter had snatched the best husband in the world. (The drawback, of course, was that it encouraged them to visit more often.)

The bathroom in the interns' lounge became my second home. Occasionally, wracked by guilt and the self-loathing of the addict, I dealt severely with myself. *Why are you so unhappy with your life that you have to take pills? What is to become of you?* I found no easy answer but something must have clicked, because I eventually managed to quit the Preludin, in the spring of 1964.

*　　*　　*

Life at the hospital and at home skipped past weeks, months, seasons, with Mimi pregnant again that fall of 1963 and destined to have our second son late in June of 1964, as internship ended. Finding strength in the receding saga of Preludin, I was eventually able to do the twenty-four-hour ER calls, plus the piecemeal bedlam of the following day, without the drug. My break wasn't complete, however, because I would now and again use it, but only on occasion, and finally not at all. Getting over one addiction blinded me to the next. Well, not quite. It sounds better to say it than it was in reality. I'm dumb, but I'm awfully cognizant. Quit a drug, as an addict, and you are cured of addiction? Glance in the mirror.

Uppers, after all, require downers. Having no previous experience with sleeping pills, I turned to them for the well-deserved rest accruing to me from my selfless labors on behalf of mankind. The first time I took a sleeping pill was one night late in 1963, and it worked beautifully. I slept and awoke as fresh as that first day of being in love. Speed was my problem, barbiturates ancillary. And the drug detail men in luminous generosity provided each intern that fall a gift box of dozens and dozens of barbiturates. It was like a Whitman's Sampler. In it were shiny yellow capsules, bright blue-and-red capsules, and the strawberry-red Seconal capsules that I liked best. The pills were as shiny and festive as the Christmas season. I had parked my box on the shelf in our bedroom closet, convenient to all, and there it remained, unused, until that first time. Unused, those pills were nevertheless in my mind and consequently, and subsequently, my body.

It turned out that Maria Chavarria and the woman who died after the convulsions of eclampsia weren't the only troubling patients I saw at the hospital. In all of history, I was probably the least likely person to withstand the vicissitudes of disagreements with others, that agony that brings on the dull, deep cut of a grinning saber. I continued to have run-ins, the kind of thing that causes a frisson of fear upon encountering the person again and that escalates from there. It wasn't just doctors and nurses: I was an equal-opportunity offender.

The hospital had devolved into a delirium of problems that followed me around during the day and slithered up beside me at night in the form of a telephone. Let it be silent and I worried about patients. Let it be mute and I worried about doctors. I fretted about the day just ended. For patient after patient, I retraced my treatment and its effects. The worst thing was to finally fall asleep and then be awakened by a frantic call from the hospital. Someone's blood pressure was down. Or a fever was up. Or his pain was worse. Or her mother or daughter or aunt or friend, or his neighbor or acquaintance or son or father, was worried about him and had just one *teensy-weensy* question to ask. Any of a colossal, mind-boggling number of potential problems, including deaths and near-deaths and emergencies that orbited around death, chased me through my searing existence. Even when I did not have to leave the house, it stayed, and I became its unintended casualty for the remainder of the night. Call it neurosis—my nerves!—but there it was.

I did not just toss and turn; I revolved on a spit erected above the blazing flames of that dread dimension, gift of my obsessive-compulsive personality. A sleeping pill was a natural antidote, though I soon learned that if I took the Seconal late at night, I faced the next day with a barbiturate hangover that required Preludin to remedy. Better to take the sleeping pill at bedtime on a regular basis, don't you see, like a toddy. *One at bedtime, PRN sleep.* The kid doesn't smoke or drink, never tasted marijuana or LSD, lives clean, works hard, needs something, no, deserves something, to unwind. And will stop tomorrow, next week at the latest.

I had always made good habits and stuck to them. Bad habits were just as easy to make. And keep. I should have stopped taking them the first time I took two instead of one, three instead of two—here we go again. Tolerance is the natural enemy of the addict. Always, always, one requires more to get the same effect, and the biggest step of all is that first time you take one extra pill or injection or inhalation. This is not the Rubicon passed, it is the Armageddon arrived. It is as elegant as hell and as nice as the chilling repulsion of everything normality calls its own, such as the ability to live life commemorating the small joys that make existence possible, even delightful. And I actually did pause the first night I found myself reaching for a second sleeping pill.

I remember it well. I took the bottle of Seconal down from the shelf and examined it in the closet light, Mimi sleeping blissfully just there. The bottle was labeled *Seconal, 100 mg. caps.* I knew the little red capsule I held in my palm was one hundred milligrams, but surely there had been some mistake. It looked so small, so tiny. Could it be only fifty milligrams? Yes! That was it, of course! In shipping or packaging the drugs, a mix-up had occurred. These were only fifty milligrams and you had to take two to get the same effect as the hundred-milligram size! Relieved, I took the second capsule. Tossed it off without another thought, because all I was doing was making up for someone else's mistake!

*　　　*　　　*

After my altercation with Dr. Broderick over Homer Epps at the end of October, I began my rotation onto the Medicine Service on November 1. The staff doctor was everything one would want in a supervisor: gentle, kind, and excellent. We had a wonderful relationship, which was a relief. I began looking forward to learning from the man, and did.

One of my patients later that month was a woman in her forties, on the Med/Surg Ward, which was closer than the Internal Medicine Ward to Obstetrics and to the cafeteria opposite it. The patient had polycystic kidneys. Her BUN (blood urea nitrogen level), as I recall, was 78 mg%, (i.e., per 100 mL of blood). The BUN should normally be less than 20 mg%, result of healthy kidneys removing nitrogen, in the form of urea, that had been ingested in food. Polycystic kidneys slowly fail in doing this, but the immediate problem was that she had a urinary tract infection that aggravated her kidney failure. I had admitted her the previous day and started her on antibiotics. She was a nice person, with a husband and a family, and the idea was to clear the infection and then to see where we stood with the chronic renal failure. One day I stopped in to see her as the hour approached noon. Med/Surg was an open ward, of course, and she happened to be in the first bed on the left, the one nearest the corridor.

Having just checked to see whether anything had grown out of the urine culture submitted on admission, I told her that so far, no growth. Therefore, her treatment remained the same. In the meantime, I had read about the management of polycystic kidneys, including dietary restriction of nitrogen, and I promised to answer her questions when I saw her again after lunch. I knew she wanted information about her long-term prognosis, and I hadn't decided what to tell her. I wasn't sure myself. But the carts for the noon meal rolled onto the ward and we broke for lunch.

I saw Dale Brannom and another intern headed into the cafeteria and joined them.

Past the serving line, the hospital cafeteria was the same as a school cafeteria. The tables and chairs were made of dark wood, the kind of furniture that never wears out, the kind that glows in happiness at the approach of its regulars. It was not a large cafeteria, but I rarely saw it as crowded as it was that day. We sat at a table halfway back and talked about patients and how our fellow interns were doing, that sort of thing. It was fun to talk to Dale because of his war stories. He had been a pharmacist before entering medical school and before that had been in the Marine reserves in Houston. His unit had been activated in 1950 for the Korean War, and in the tumult as the North Koreans overran the South, they were thrown into the pitched combat that took place up and down the Korean peninsula late that year, culminating in a retreat from the Chosin Reservoir deep in North Korea.

Dale said it was so cold there he could spit and it would freeze before it hit the ground. American combat troops carried (in their mouths, to keep it from freezing) a syrette of morphine—a collapsible tube and its attached needle—to use for pain relief in case they were hit. The then-young Marine corporal won the Purple Heart on a day when their patrol met a Chinese patrol and exchanged gunfire. After the skirmish, while the Marines were assessing themselves, Dale had experienced a lovely, warm sensation in his right foot—literally the first time that he had been able to feel his toes in weeks. When he looked down, he saw that his boot was filled with blood, his first jittery inkling that he had been hit.

Dale, who is gone now, carried his war lightly, but he was the unofficial leader of the interns, if for no other reason than he was bigger, older, and more experienced. I liked and trusted the man. After the three of us had finished eating, we carried our trays to the place where these and any leftovers were deposited, standing in line to do that, and exited the cafeteria.

The November days were short and often cloudy, but the sun was bright outside on this particular day, and without the sweltering heat, Corpus had become a nice place to live. Over lunch the subject of football came up. It usually did. The other two were also Texas fans, and since it was Friday that meant high school football. The Texas Longhorns, though, had an off day on Saturday but would play A&M the following Thursday, Thanksgiving.

I told my two colleagues good-bye when I came even with Med/Surg and my patient with the kidney problems. But as I turned away, Dale said something strange that caught my attention, not in what he said but in the way he said it, and I stepped back into the corridor beside the other two interns, who were watching Jean Oliver hurrying toward us from the direction of her office way back down the hallway in the region of the ER and the interns' lounge.

I had never seen Jean upset, but she was terribly so at something, stopping in each ward for a moment and then hastily continuing toward us. Reaching us, she drew up and stopped. Looking from one to the other, she caught her breath.

Jean Oliver was a pretty woman, a delight to see. She dressed well and, unlike some beauties, was both courteous and not in any way full of herself. Every intern was secretly in love with her, but she had a husband and a family; she was Mrs. Benson G. Oliver, and we treated her with the respect she deserved. But it was frightening to see her that upset. I glanced at my wristwatch and noted that it was a little before one o'clock of that Friday, November 22, 1963.

Her eyes flashed and she said, "President Kennedy," and the rest came from a great distance as I made out the words *shot* and *Dallas* and the weight of it began to fall into that dispirited outrage that hurts first of all its punctured owner: I had not voted for the man, had been told he was the enemy, had listened perhaps too closely as one doctor after another badmouthed him, had tried to glean without opposing them the reasons for their detestation of a man I had increasingly found charismatic and courageous. He had made mistakes but he'd stood up to the Russians and made America glad. Yet all did not love him for it, especially those who loved Richard Nixon instead. Maybe it was that the most beloved are also the most hated. Mainly it was in the magnitude of the irony that a historical figure of that importance might be slain in public before the world's counterfeit pageantry, and how this person then became public property to be photographed and probed and fought over, to be badgered back and forth and have his every bodily enclave made a point of contention in one way or another until he became an outcast to the very people he had given his life to serve, his life and his early death a new continent everyone avowed to explore by proxy, his death a vast field where any furrow must be followed, where any seed might take root, any growth as malignant as a cult, each book outselling the one before it because the world was so ravenous to digest and regurgitate the young president.

His young widow would be hounded for the rest of her life by those who considered her public property. She could not sneak out to see a movie without having it ballyhooed and held against her. She could try all she might to live an unfettered existence but would never again have it. Her children would have the bad luck to live in his shadow for the rest of their lives, a thing one intuits the man would gladly have skipped the presidency to avoid. Great risk exacts a fierce, terrible price, and that was the lot of President Kennedy. Maybe the saddest thing about the events that weekend of the assassination was the discovery that everyone was an assassin, Oswald only the most egregious. It took that tragedy to remind us of it, whereupon we turned quickly away, so as not to be discovered treating the event as an exercise in fascination: what lovely repugnance will happen next? The revolting became the absorbing, and America hid its face in shame. That patient with polycystic kidneys: did I ever see her again?

*   *   *

In a photograph taken by Cecil Stoughton in the first photo section of *Reclaiming History*, by Vincent Bugliosi—the best book ever written about the assassination and likely the definitive one[23]—the president and his wife are deplaning from Air Force One at Love Field in Dallas that Friday. She is dressed in a pink wool suit and a matching pillbox hat, attire forever fixed in the images of that day. He is modestly dressed and seems fetchingly happy at life and its promises. It is impossible to comprehend that this man, the most powerful in the world, will within twenty-four hours be murdered, flown back to Washington DC on the same plane that contains his widow and the new president, autopsied upon arrival there by a team of Navy doctors, embalmed, and dressed before lying in state. It just can't be. To this day, the very idea is infuriating. The tragedy spoke to how good things do not last and the very best things are always the most fleeting. And yet somehow, someway, the assassination begins to seem inevitable. Kennedy had been having premonitions about it for weeks.

---

23   Vincent Bugliosi, *Reclaiming History, the Assassination of President John F. Kennedy* (New York: W. W. Norton, 2007), after 434.

He had remarked that very morning, apropos a full-page funereal ad in the *Dallas Morning News*, "Oh, you know, we're heading into nut country today ..."[24] He meant of the rightwing variety, whose hatred of Kennedy was well-known. But nuts can come from both extremes of the political spectrum, and one of those from the left was a Communist-loving insouciant pathologic narcissist named Lee Harvey Oswald. It is Oswald's role as the lone assassin that undercuts the tragedy with a macabre, inexorable irony. The assassination could not have happened had Lee Harvey Oswald not taken a job at the Texas School Book Depository only a few weeks before. It would not have happened had an open presidential motorcade not passed through Dallas, Texas, that day and turned from Houston Street onto Elm Street in front of the Texas School Book Depository. It would not have happened had President Kennedy not forbidden the Secret Service agents from riding on the two standing posts either side of the back bumper of the presidential limousine. (He had thought it would obscure him from the onlookers but instead it had made him visible to the assassin.) The fatal bullet would not have happened had not the president been wearing a back brace that prevented him from bending forward at the waist—as Governor Connally did—after the second shot, which passed through both of them.

And it would not have happened had Lee Harvey Oswald been able to contain the narcissistic rage that had been building in him for his twenty-four years of existence. I was born on August 19, 1939, the day the unborn Lee Harvey Oswald's father died. The assassin himself was born on October 18, 1939, elsewhere than Texas, making him just two months younger than I.

As to Dallas, I had been invited to consider an internship at Parkland Hospital, where the mortally wounded president had been taken. But Oswald is not the subject; this is not about the death of the thirty-fifth president of the United States, John Fitzgerald Kennedy, 1917–1963. It is about how life is a room in a world not of your own choosing, to do work not of your own liking, and subsequently to live not of your own desiring.

I did not think myself a pathologic narcissist, but I was no stranger to a rage hidden within my persona, a weapon loaded long ago and ever ready to be triggered, a rage against unrelenting things that had been done to me back when, and more recently, the things done to my patients through the outrage of Responsibility without Authority. Instead of having Authority, I became its tool and I hated it. An unwitting young doctor is made into a killer in the slaughterhouse hidden beyond the White Curtain. He is made into a killer because killing goes hand in hand with healing. The rich get well and the

24 Sarah Bradford, *America's Queen: The Life of Jacqueline Kennedy Onassis* (New York: Viking Press, 2000), 266.

poor fend for themselves, killed not for sport but by their unworthiness to doctors and their for-profit employers, virtuosos who sing to the top of their lungs about how compassionate they are while *First, Do No Harm*, is replaced by *First, Do Nothing*. It was perfectly legal, perfectly lethal. Knowledge of it turned me into a doctor who hated the practice of medicine. It went beyond that. I didn't know whether we were all assassins, though I just said it, but at the age of twenty-four, I was. I assassinated the person I was going to be. It didn't start out that way, but then again, what does?

I was sickened by internship without understanding that sickness is the price one pays for health—when one is very lucky—and death is the price one pays for life. I had met the great principle behind the White Curtain. You must learn to protect yourself from the nastiness hidden in the sump that is right there waiting for you. I didn't, or couldn't, or thought it unnecessary, and I died. The protection I speak of is not from lawsuits, necessary as that protection might be. One must learn to protect oneself from patients, their families, the pathos, the marathon days and stifling nights, the salesmen, the nurses, the aides, the administrators, the pain, the bleakness, the doctors who are your enemies whether you call them that or not, the effrontery of a society in failing to concede that the rules don't apply to you, and the long luminous pestering pinnacle of the illness that is medicine and the needless deaths that are its symptoms. You must protect yourself or you will die. The only choice is by your hand or theirs. Because the mess of it will spill and it will stain you on the outside and make of you what you do not wish to be on the inside. And that is that.

For my part, it was already too late, or so I thought. There weren't enough pills in all the pharmacopoeias of the world to eradicate the ugliness in me. Addiction is a stranger you meet once or twice a day, while living your unblemished life. The beauty of it is in how untroubled you may be by the secret that sustains you. That is also its heartbreak, for the one must find the other, and honor can be as elusive as a pinprick in a swordfight. More than anything else, I knew that.

*   *   *

Those weekly Saturday mornings and afternoons in Mount Pleasant were the worst part of my year in the country, 1946–47. The trip was anticipated and fun for the Andersons, who might see a movie or visit a place that offered a rip-snorting bowl of chili and beans for not that much, to kick up their heels, as it were. They had shopping to do, friends to see, places to go. But my Saturday was utter dread, and that fall of 1946 I hit on the idea of simply staying at the farm in Cooper's Chapel in lieu of whiling away those endless, boring hours in Mount Pleasant every Saturday. Upon my own authority, but to Aunt Randie's concern, I quit going into town on Saturdays.

Behind the farmhouse was a trail that paralleled the road and led to the schoolhouse. It went past a lazy old tree-shaded cow pond with yellow water and the occasional gliding snake and with rotting logs forming sunning places for the lines of shiny turtles taking in the sun and blissfully unbothered by their proximity to others of their kind. I could wander in the country back there and be alone with my thoughts, looking for huckleberries and hickory nuts, the way the Anderson children had taught me, and mainly filling a day so much more easily than I could in Mount Pleasant. The feeling one has on a farm is of the individual self. One is not dwarfed by buildings and pavement and poles. The farm is something you don't have to own to possess. Cities aren't like that. They shrivel the people and inflate the rage.

Beyond that, Aunt Randie was a kind person. She usually stayed home Saturdays anyway and I had her to myself for the day. She fed me and, if I wished, talked to me. She seemed not to mind listening to me and in her actions cared more for me than did anyone in Mount Pleasant. I had one weekend of freedom like that, and another or two. Then word came that I was not allowed to skip the visit—perhaps it looked bad—and back to the wagon yard I went.

Every enticing Saturday.

In time, I became a veteran of the Mount Pleasant streets. I knew nothing of those elsewhere who had a street life and lived it every day, knew only of myself. I knew nothing of conditions like depression, neurosis, or obsessive-compulsive disorder. I just knew that it was bad. It was bad enough that I created another world from it.

I began this after a deep revelation one day in Mount Pleasant; to wit, I neither understood nor especially liked being alive, if that is what it was—and it was overrated—but I could with effort find something to do, boredom being the biggest punishment of all. I did not begin with a fantasy such as, "When I Used to be a Man"; in fact, "When I Never Was a Man" played better in my fancy. In that disavowed world I did whatever I could to pass the time in the space between the Kimberlins and the Courthouse Square. Certain games, being free, became my pastimes: don't step, look up, look down, and kick-a-rock were favorites. I made of the five blocks of North Madison that I inhabited a supermarket, the sidewalks its aisles, and busied myself passing down aisle after aisle selecting items to purchase—what fun! I gorged on candy and ice cream. I took cigarettes and whiskey to excess, staggered drunkenly through the store, its shiny offerings as bright as stained glass.

Don't step, my favorite game next to kick-a-rock, was ever a challenge. I must negotiate every bit of the five blocks of North Madison, Kimberlin house to the Square, without stepping on a single line, which turned out to be a challenge in a northeast Texas town that prided itself on being hilly and pleasant, with its streets lined with sidewalks that ran beneath tall, shady trees. There were numerous lines other than those separating the etched parts of the concrete sidewalk. A few places, faded lines of chalk marked the perimeters of ancient games of hopscotch. (Where were those kids now that I needed them?) In many places tree roots burgeoned beneath the sidewalk leaving lines that looked like spider webs frozen in concrete; it took real skill to avoid stepping on them. Sometimes I had to leap great distances to remain pure.

Look up and look down were opposite parts of the same game. I must walk all the way to the Square while looking up, or I must do the opposite and interest myself in every item I came across, while looking down. I found cigarette packages and greedily stripped them for the tinfoil inside; wasn't that worth good money? People saved it during the war. I found odd bits of cardboard and the wrappers from candy, which sometimes had a golden lick or two of residual sweet. Also, the ever-present leaves of trees and bushes, and even a penny that had spilled from near where grease spots marked a parking place for an automobile.

Kick-a-rock, my favorite of these pastimes, first required selection of the rock. That was important. You didn't want one too big, but it had to be big enough that you could see it to kick it. Generally, flat rocks of the kind one found in gravel were the best. Round ones went too far out into the street and made people mad who were driving by. Occasionally I would fall in love with a particular rock, flat and sassy in a deep tone of shiny brown, and try and keep it for future games, my most important possession, my favorite thing in the entire world, but I never kept it for very long. Back in Cooper's Chapel it just looked like a rock you could sail through the air and I did, and then I had to find a new rock next Saturday, but rocks were plentiful. There were always rocks and kids to kick them.

Kick-a-rock only engaged my attention when I reached the rock I had kicked and gave it another blow, so that in between kicks, thoughts sought me out. These were echoes of people talking, of conversations I'd overheard or mean things people had said to me and that hurt so much my neck ached in front and I didn't know why. Sometimes the voices were my own demons, summoning me from the depths of wanting out. I knew nothing of art, of the Minimalists who had replaced the Impressionists, or of the songs I'd heard and that stayed with me, music being the flavor in the feast of memory. All songs were either waltzes or love songs, except for the hymns in church, metaphors in search of a willing simile. Music was special because it was made by those who didn't necessarily sing any better than others but who could and did surrender themselves to others in the music; they spread their arms and sang from the heart, without affectation or embarrassment or pride, except of the best kind. It was a sharing that went inside and stayed, of artists expressing themselves in their work, bringing to it their take on the things that had dogged them through their lives. They must have had the same ruinous doubts but released them in the music, and maybe that was what it took to create something out of nothing, incredible as that attempt might be. Maybe they did it to keep from dying.

*   *   *

Occasionally I would encounter a girl or a boy I knew from first grade at the West Ward School. He or she would usually be with a parent on North Jefferson Street near the Square, in a row where businesses were located, and I always tagged along for a while, until they went into a store, and sometimes I went with them because it was something to do and also in the hope that they might buy me something or give me some money—a few precious pennies or a nickel. (I never hoped for a dime, which was very big money.) When the woman would pause to ask where my mother was, I'd lie that she was also shopping and I was waiting to meet her. Or I would tell the nice lady that my mother was busy at work but would soon be through, and then we'd go home together and be very happy. In considering my statement, the well-dressed woman would take in my overalls, hover over a scuffed brown pair of work shoes, and politely continue on her way, making sure to separate her child from the likes of me. The woman and her child, in other words, were normal, that lucky species. Normal people living normal lives in normal ways. It wasn't a function of how much they had or didn't have, it was a function of how well they lived together.

In desperation, I became a thief. Early, before foot traffic grew heavy, I sneaked into a five-and-dime at the northeast corner of the Square on North Jefferson, the courthouse facing east. The candy was in convenient glass bins up at the front, and shrewdly I'd case the joint like a pro, merely walking past and sizing up the piles of candy to be had. Then, furtively, I'd select one or two items—criminal I was—and quickly check to see whether the clerk was watching. He, studiously, was not. I might purloin a nickel's worth or so of the little wax figures that were filled with a sweet syrup the color and flavor of grapes, strawberries, or oranges. The juiciest part of it was the best, but I could chew on the residual wax for up to an hour before it began sticking to my teeth so badly that I had to spit it out, in chunks.

That dear man, the clerk! My more mature self came to understand exactly what he was doing. He was allowing the theft out of the goodness of his heart and in that sense was offering a strange boy in overalls a bit of merchandise out of sympathy and consideration. I owe him!

Outside again while it was still cool, I sometimes sauntered up North Jefferson to the block where the Kimberlins lived, crossed to North Madison with an occasional nod to Van Buren along the way, or found my way to Washington Street, the backside of downtown Mount Pleasant, where one could kick plenty of rocks and watch the trains go by. An icehouse two or three blocks south of the Kimberlins on Madison was always of interest. At certain times, when the sun was just right, I made a gazebo of the cool shadows that clung to the icehouse. Grass grew greener there, from the constant fountain of cool spray that emanated from it, and on a hot day it was so nice to squat there that I found myself rather enjoying life than dreading it, and the hours would magically fly away. That was in the afternoons, though, because I never stopped at the icehouse in the mornings, and it was probably in the spring of 1947.

In fact, afternoons in Mount Pleasant were easier to fill than mornings. For one thing, half of the day was gone and I was sliding downhill to four o'clock, when I met the Anderson pickup in front of the Kimberlin house for the windy ride back to Cooper's.

One afternoon I saw a boy who was a friend of mine from first grade. He was by himself and had that strong sense of purpose that I clearly lacked, wherein he was bent perpetually forward, like a runner at the starting gate, only he stayed bent, his feet underneath him, and did not mind when an old acquaintance took up with him. He was in a great mood, besides, a catching contagion, and then it occurred. I was astounded when he asked whether I wanted to go to the picture show with him. Wow! Of course I did!

The Texas Theater was on the west side of the Square directly behind the courthouse, and it lit up the entire block. Besides its neon lights and smart exterior, it had enormous advertising windows for "Coming Features." The bright posters invited one to partake of cowboys and Indians or of soldiering with the Foreign Legion. There were cocoons in which to snuggle, havens transporting one to the timeless depths of the unknown. I knew nothing of William Boyd (Hopalong Cassidy) or of Johnny Mack Brown, but I had memorized them on the posters outside the Texas Theater. It owned the magnetism bestowed upon it by every kid who ever lived. It smelled like fun, it was fun. There were snacks by the gunnysack and, beyond the lights, a glorious darkness celebrating the iconic mystique. I had been there to the movies with a cousin when I was in first grade. On this particular day, however, I admitted to my friend that I had no money.

The generous boy said, "My dad will give you the money!"

It excited me not least because it was what I had dreamed of. I was practically skipping in joy when we reached the auto shop where his dad worked. The dad came outside with us. A freeloader, I stood watching while he greeted his son and squatted to talk to him. His dad wanted him to spend the afternoon at the movie, seeing it twice if necessary, and then to return to the shop at five o'clock. He removed a dime from his pocket and gave it to the kid. The kid said something, and his father turned and looked at the sponge and changed his expression and took back the dime and gave his son a quarter. The kid mentioned me again.

Having sized up the situation, his father said, "Let him go his way, you go yours."

Nothing was said about how it had been my friend's idea, not mine. Still, dutifully, I followed the kid on his merry path. It was early of a hot Saturday afternoon, and we passed the courthouse on the same side of the Square as where my mother worked. We walked past her shop. The streets were busy with people who were happy that it was Saturday, the day to go to town. They were talking energetically among themselves and laughing, and it was infectious. We passed other stores with customers in them, people shopping and spending their money in Mount Pleasant.

I kept thinking about that quarter my friend had clenched in his fist. The movie only cost a dime, and he could pay his way and mine and still have a nickel left over for a soft drink. But with a quarter he could also get in, buy a bag of buttered popcorn for a dime, and wash it down with a big soft drink in a stiff paper cup with crushed ice in it, delicious, for the other nickel. And do this in the luxury of the air-conditioned Texas Theater. If you handled it right, the popcorn and drink could last you maybe the entire picture, and you could keep the paper cup as a souvenir of your largesse and take it home with you afterward and show it around by way of bragging about what you had done. Hell, keep it and be buried with it at the end of your long and happy life, to remind you of a magical Saturday afternoon at the picture show.

The kid stood in line, paid, and without looking behind him hurried past the line of others waiting to buy a ticket and entered the double doors of the picture show. Trailing him, I shrugged with nonchalance and hurried in behind him. A guy in a uniform was taking tickets. He was probably only a teenager, but he was as big as a football player and wore that impeccable gray-and-purple uniform, trimmed in gold, like a decorated soldier.

The boy gave him his ticket and started for the concession stand. I braced myself and tried to follow him, knowing full well that it was a bluff, and was stopped by the young man whose job it was to stop the likes of me.

"He's got my ticket," I lied, pointing to my erstwhile friend.

The authority shook his head and said something I don't remember. Firm hands on both shoulders guided me toward the door, and that was the worst part—being escorted in embarrassment as far as the double-glass doors, where the lovely smell of popcorn and elegance ended and the outside reality blistered me with its stinging rebuke. The kids with their mothers, serene and safe, with money for attendance and refreshments, stared with reproach at one so brazen as to think that the rules did not apply to him. Reaching the sidewalk, I turned quickly away to get out of sight, feeling the most awful shame of my life.

Grasping frantically for some way to restore my feeble sense of self-worth, I spotted a piece of chewing gum stuck to the sidewalk in the sunlight. I reached and peeled it off and popped it into my mouth, hoping that it still had some of the sweet left in it. It did! It tasted like honeysuckle! It was far better than some old, greasy popcorn probably two days stale. And that movie was no good! I could watch a better one in my mind anytime! In fact, I knew that there was to be a hanging in front of the Titus County Courthouse that very day. She was a beautiful young girl who was my age, of course, maybe a year or two older, who had been condemned to death for the crime of love. She was so pretty and so vulnerable as they led her up those twelve steps of the gallows.

Suddenly, from nowhere, I appeared and whisked her to safety with the ease of an Errol Flynn, and she beseeched me, telling me how she would be eternally grateful to me and offering her hand in marriage. An episodic coquette, she illuminated the dark places in my life during times when I was so desperate for what I did not have, could not have, and would never have, that I lost hope.

Throughout the rest of my life I have revisited that day and shuddered at the aching wretchedness of being out of sync and not knowing what to do about it. In a part of me it is always there, I return endlessly to that blistering sidewalk in downtown Mount Pleasant, feeling deserted and worthless and hopeless in my wanderings, until happy relatives picked me up in front of the house across the street from the hospital at four o'clock and drove me ten miles out into the country on a dirt road leading to their warm house and my chilly future. People growing older speak of time passing more quickly, and that is because each day or year is a lesser percentage of your life as you grow older. Children are not so fortunate and a day, a single afternoon, can seem endless. And possibly the saddest thing about the event was that I was half a block from my own dear mother, working in the beauty shop, but such were the two of us that I never once thought of dashing in there and excitedly asking her for a dime to go to the movie. I had my pride and could not have taken the further humiliation of being refused twice. I have never liked to beg.

*   *   *

A new century brings time for reflection on the past, including those timeless images of small children dead, having starved to death in one ghetto or another, in the European abomination known as Nazism. The children are humiliatingly thin, their clothes in tatters, sores visible on their limbs and heads. One grasps that their parents are gone and they have been left to make it on their own at too early an age, outside in the streets, under a heartless sky. An older boy may appear and offer to help. They follow him down the street, where he drags them into an alley and steals any valuables they may have left, something sewn into the lining of a garment and cherished as a last resort, and leaves them there, bruised, hurt beyond tears, abject in their hopelessness. Steel yourself, or it will break your heart. What must they have thought of the world, to let them die in misery and hunger?

I was not starved. I was not being beaten regularly during that year in the country, and I still had my health. But relativity is unknown to children. Just because children are starving somewhere in the world does not make broccoli or cooked squash taste any better to a child who discovers it on his plate. What did happen from that time I spent on the streets of Mount Pleasant that year was that I found the story of my life. Whatever story people make of their lives, and it may be clarified throughout one's years, determines the narrative they look for and luckily may find in books, movies, songs, and any other form of art—or trickery, for that matter—from ballet to billiards to baseball. We start with our own story and define it by what we find along the way. Story is the skeleton of a life we flesh out as we go, and the favored grow into theirs with no understanding of why others cannot do the same, while the latter either shed their story as unacceptable or continue to relive it for the rest of their lives.

Much later, years by the score from those meanderings in Mount Pleasant, I came to understand why I liked *David Copperfield* so much and *Jane Eyre* especially. In the popular term it is known as identifying with a character in a book. It happens in every book, should the book succeed, but I find in these two stories such a striking similarity to my own childhood that I periodically go back and revisit them—and a few others—by way of finding myself in an acknowledgment that the hurt of childhood cannot be removed but it can be stepped around. It can be risen above. It is always there, like a lurking monster, but time erases most of the pain, and wisdom shrinks the remaining hurt to an appropriate size. Somewhere along the way I learned that if you do not get the blessing, you must learn to give it and, giving it, receive it. This is one of the great secret sources of happiness on Earth. They can take everything from you but your happiness; do not let them have that—keeping it is the subject of all art that counts—for if you stand fast in your grasp of the unassailable, you are the richest person on Earth.

*   *   *

Love is our most important goblet, its stem a oneness with others, its glass the emptying of which brings untold quantities of love into one's life. We love that we may be loved, and there is nothing wrong with that. Love to love and you'll always be happy. Love is the shelter we seek during childhood, the flamethrower that strikes us in adolescence, the magic we savor for always, perhaps the adulation we seek from the beyond. What is life but the reshuffling of a few chemicals and the rededication of a bit of real estate? Should there be one element of most importance in the admixture, however, surely we should be able to find it in that terrarium of quenched dreams known as a cemetery. More than anything else, cemeteries are about love.

I am eleven miles out of Mount Pleasant and in another century. I'm well north of the interstate, whatever its number, and there is only one house, just yonder over there, with no one about. Texas can sting in September, doubly so because the supposedly worst of the heat occurred in the preceding two months, July and August, the latter in which, in this year, I had my sixty-eighth birthday. Cemeteries are about birthdays. In a sense, that is the most naked thing about them, the reduction of your life to dates.

It is Sunday, September 16, 2007, in the churchyard at Cooper's Chapel.

I am by myself in a rented car parked on the other side of the church. I have come through a passageway in the chain-link fence. The gate—always one of those—is a few steps from, and south of, the church building. The fence is only waist high, and standing near it one can will it away. Why fence it at all? Because that is the way things are done. It protects the gravesites from canines and their brethren, it adds order to the enclosure by limiting foot traffic from those who might wish to take a casual shortcut through solemn grounds, and it sizes the extent of the resting place, like framed art, a needed enclosure of this from the rest of the world. Yet the fence itself is not unmovable. Since my time here in the 1946–47 school year, the cemetery has tripled in size, extending north all the way past the former site of the Cooper's Chapel Overland School.

Something else must be remarked, and that is the unsettling thing about a cemetery. We all know it but do not voice it because to do so might be conceived as in poor taste. What's unsettling is not *memento mori*—remember that you die—so much as it is that here is the visible proof. We draw comfort from having that proof safely fenced and separate from the rest of us, the bereaved living.

*   *   *

Here is Lula Faye. I know now that she was the namesake of my great-grandmother, Lula E. McCauley Anderson, who is also here among the better part of seven hundred others. Her numbers were 1869–1919. She lived fifty years, not unusual for Cooper's Chapel at that time. Lula Faye Anderson was born on December 7, 1937. She was the first young woman I ever slept with, in the days when the term was used much differently than now, and we did it the year I was here, every night. I slept on the side nearest whatever was there by way of a walkway to the back porch, and she on the colder side next to the wall. These were board walls with matching floors of the color that wood takes when it is left to age quietly, the color of the tanned hides that were still employed then for the seats and backs of straight chairs. I don't remember a headboard to that bed, which was a gilded item anyway, prideful and hogging more space that it was worth, but the mattress sat on box springs and a bed frame, complete with a few pleasant squeaks that could make a child giggle, and topped by ample bedding.

As well as I can remember, I don't think I ever exchanged a word of conversation with Lula Faye after we had gone to bed. Did we not giggle over the giggly? Did we not snuggle on cold nights? That is possible, but not that I remember. It was a big bed and we were small people and I let it go at that. I was too young to know that sex existed. I thought pee-pees came in two sizes because they got it messed up somewhere back along the line and would eventually get it straightened out. I thought the things I did in the bathroom—rather, in those times, at the outhouse or the chamber pot—were my personal curse, and I had no idea of their universality. And I thought school itself a form of punishment, serving no other purpose than to free the adults of the kids by way of making them into slaves for a sizeable chunk of each day, liberating parents from their needy, whining voices.

And as to that, that raw affliction—existence—that sudden wallop of awareness of finally waking up to be fully awake and fully engaged in what was defined as life, painful and cruel and disappointing as it was, seemed to me a dubious honor, like seeing yourself in the mirror for the first time and being forced to accept *that*, the ludicrous responsibility of being no more and no less than yourself, to reconcile indignity with the incoherent and to bear the constant comments on it by others, the way one's life is most clearly enunciated by his fellow creatures, who seem to think that task their duty and your privilege.

*   *   *

Pauline Anderson Slovak, Lula Faye's eldest sister, has written eloquently of the grounding of Cooper's Chapel in history[25] and helped in the processes that led up to the events in 1993, when the Texas Historical Commission saw fit to bestow upon Cooper's Chapel Church and Cemetery the honor appertaining to a Recorded Texas Historic Landmark. The engraving to that effect is on an official sign held by a metal post that is anchored to the firmament just to the left of the locked front door of the church.

Through a window on this broiling summer afternoon, I have certified to myself that this Church of Christ—no piano or organ permitted—is unchanged, except for shrinking a good bit during the last sixty years. Its wooden pews, curved as the back of a man lifting a heavy load, or as of a woman in the pain of childbirth, were finished, but barely, and as hard as the plates on an ironclad. Choc told me once how they draped sheets from the ceiling, giving privacy for separate Sunday school classes. I had none of that, probably because the year I was here, the service was at two o'clock on Sunday afternoon, after the pastor had held services somewhere else that Sunday morning. But oh, those dinners on the grounds! We had them every month or so when it was warm: life in Cooper's did have its pleasures.

In the Depression of the thirties, the government handed out the things required to make a mattress or two for each family, and the people of the community gathered at the church or out under the trees there in front, where it was cooler, and helped one another to stitch together the new mattresses. Did Lula Faye and I sleep on one of those? I suppose so. Impossible to ask her now, though I did see her once, in September of 1979, when I came to this place to participate in the burial of my grandfather, Jim Kimberlin.

I knew him as Daddy Jim, though I never liked that name very much, in spite of liking him in every way that it is possible to like someone else, especially one with power over you—though the thing was, he never claimed anything over me except fellowship. Part of the problem with "Daddy Jim" was that in that part of my life I had two Daddy Jims, the one sullying the name of the other. Nevertheless I saw Lula Faye that September afternoon almost thirty years ago when we buried Jim Kimberlin, saw her not here at

---

25   Pauline Anderson Slovak, "In Remembrance." *East Texas Historical Association* (no. 1), 1992, 58–65.

the cemetery but up by the road west of here, in front of the Anderson house, that same old farmhouse, then still standing on its wobbly legs.

Lula Faye had remained country, lived in the country, made it her life. I saw this at a glance. She had moved but not far. She had married and had children. She was happy, so far as I know. She died, Lula Faye, on June 7, 1988. That's only a few years beyond the lifespan of her namesake.

Suddenly, beside her grave, I wish very much that I had known of her death, dropped everything and returned for the funeral, or even seen her again before she died, which is probably a stretch. The way it worked in our family, Mother the conduit of information, was that I found out what she cared to impart to me at the time of the event or, rather more likely, afterward. So when Lula Faye died, Jim Kimberlin was gone and incommunicative anyway, and his wife, Alma, "Big Mama," *Magna Mater*, incommunicative but in a different way and given to blunderbuss opinions at close range, would see no reason why a telephone call to Austin should be billed to her phone.

She kept up fiercely with all of her relatives, Alma, and once flew into a rage with ten-year-old me when she discovered that I couldn't recite the names Vie, Beulah, and Delta, among others, of her siblings, as if my lack of knowledge were very close to genealogic treason on my part and might merit the death penalty from her. It might have been her lack of subtlety and her staggering indifference to the waltz to which we are all summoned, but Alma Anderson Kimberlin lived for a century. Jim was three years older but lived sixteen years fewer, and his was a good lifespan. His numbers are 1894–1979. Hers are 1898–1998. Her missing the actual count of a full hundred years by six months and fifteen days is of no import. Complain about it and she will come back and excoriate you.

I came not to like her, but I can say something good about her: she made a hell of a banana pudding, which is still my favorite dessert. She also made a fine pecan pie and, before she entered the nursing home for the last chapter of her life, made pecan pies for my sons Roger and Steve, regularly, and that alone ensures her a place in my heaven (though possibly on the second row). In all seriousness, she never whipped me. She never disowned me, even when I had done that to her. Mother said that she visited her one day in the nursing home in Mount Pleasant and the next day she was dead.

As Mother put it, about a person who all of her life she had called Mama, and meant it, "She never said anything about dying. She may have thought she wouldn't."

So I can vow that, here in the midst of the Texas heat of this September afternoon, I did not know Lula Faye had perished until some months or a year or more after. About her I can say this. She was a decent person. She was a good person. She was never stuck-up or selfish, that I saw, and to me she was the most important member of the Anderson family because closest to my age. I loved her without understanding the concept, which no one ever explained to me. At the time, I wasn't familiar with the term. I'm not sure I had ever heard it spoken. I'm not sure even now that I can explain its workings, perhaps the affection for self extended to another, with irrevocable intensity. It is the undergirding of a kind of ecstasy given off in its vicinity, and reproducible, a celebration of the ability to live in peace with another, the happiness of shared time and a communal spirit, the freedom to be one's self without worry or regret.

As for Faye, as she came to be called, I am immodestly and immensely drawn into the eternity of now, wherein we all meet concurrently to discuss everything, but getting in touch with eternity doesn't happen every day. It only happens in cemeteries or when they impossibly play your song at just exactly the right moment, but the view is nice, and I will say, simply, I loved you, Lula Faye. You died too young and I am sorry for that. For you I will add that the flame went out but not the glow. Perhaps that's as much as anyone could wish.

*   *   *

Cemeteries are about love but they do not bury love. The only love that cemeteries bury is the love you allow them to bury, and if you are like me, that is very little. Love, unlike so many things, cannot be undone. If it can, it wasn't. And if it wasn't, it doesn't qualify, love being the bedrock through which shovels and the like cannot cut, ever. And if happiness is the negotiation between the self and all of the cogwheels and tarpaper of life, the bandages and the clustered inflictions, the dearness of loved people and the infallible strength of that undying love, couldn't it be that nothing ever really ends, not even ourselves?

These people here haven't ended anymore than did Jim Kimberlin in 1979. I am Jim Kimberlin. I realized this a year or two after he died, while in San Antonio attending an American Medical Association convention. I left the River Walk near the entrance to the Alamo and briefly visited this palette and paintbrush of the Texas tableau. It was gripping, as always. Still, I had been there before, but I knew that Jim Kimberlin had not, and after I returned to the River Walk I found myself just this side of an epiphany, wishing that this man I had loved with all my heart might have been given to see and experience the Alamo and suddenly realizing that he had seen it—through me! There had been no end for him or for any other person here in what remains of old Cooper's Chapel; I am the living proof.

For a time they will go on living as I go on living. Then they will go on living because of my children and the others descended from them, and if we are very fortunate and very lucky, as they were and will be, we will all live forever and never be dead of what cannot die so long as others do their part in continuing it. Eternity is not a hollow promise. It is the unobstructed view. It's tomorrow plus a day in the bedrock of a love so prodigious you cannot see it or hear it and maybe not even feel it to the heights of its unlimited power—not until you are here in the cemetery, among your people, and then it stuns you, blinds you with its strength and immensity, and everything is good, and everything is one, and you a part of it and of them in the transcendent moment. And if you listen closely in a cemetery, nestled inside its expanses, alone beside its headstones, quilted into the woven fabric of its solemn mounds and its floral wreaths and its unfinished conversations, you may find your own voice, and maybe that is why cemeteries are so quiet. You have to come by yourself, of course. A funeral is a noisy thing; so is a memorial service, wherein we raise our voices in joined grief and shared love, as kindred. Yet the real treasures exist here, in the quiet. And they remain here, immersed in silence, waiting for your visit, awaiting your heart.

* * *

Move ahead two years: another cemetery, another visit.

It is Monday, August 3, 2009, and I am at the Macedonia Cemetery, that ancient kingdom. In location, it is north of Pittsburg. It is morning and cool and nice despite the month of the year. I have driven down County Road 2110, which leaves US 271 north of Pittsburg and continues north, parallel to the highway, to the Macedonia Missionary Baptist Church. As at Cooper's Chapel, the cemetery is behind the church. Only this time I have driven around an encircling road in these spacious grounds, glanced on the way to see a marker offering the words *Till We Meet Again* and found myself touched to tears.

I am here because my mother is here, beside her last husband (and by far the best), Willis A. Rose. His dates are 1912–1989. Hers are 1915–2000. It is fitting that she is buried here, halfway between Pittsburg and Mount Pleasant, the two main cities of her life, the one always tugging at the other, and she crossed that sputtering Cypress Creek causeway—bisecting not twin cities but the Mutt and Jeff of northeast Texas—so often that in her mind they probably fused into one. I am here to make peace with her, but that is a private matter, not to be shared. I will say only that seeing her here back in 2007 left me more shaken than I had thought it would. Now it is two years later and my demeanor is in keeping with what I flatter myself that I have learned. In making it better than it was, do not make it worse than it might have been. I did not attend her funeral, but that was no reason for keeping the rest of my immediate family from attending.

*　　*　　*

Macedonia Cemetery is dominated by a large tree in its center, perhaps a copse of trees, and in a bricked enclosure nearby rests our high school principal, Mr. Acker. His is a lonely vigil for now, but the marker is sizeable and good and the proximity of trees counts in his favor. For that matter, a book is like a tree: grown thought by thought, page by page, memory by memory, so that its spine is strong, its gutters clean, its arms uplifted, wrapped in a package that meets the eye without surrendering its details. Students love trees, and all of us learned at least a few lines of "Trees", by Joyce Kilmer:

> I think that I shall never see
> A poem lovely as a tree ...
>
> A tree that may in summer wear
> A nest of robins in her hair; ...
>
> Poems are made by fools like me,
> But only God can make a tree.

High school is where you learn poems like that. It is where you come into a certain confidence from having studied all those years and learned all that stuff. We know, for example, that the brothers Wright made the first heavier-than-air flight at Kitty Hawk, North Carolina. A famous gun battle occurred at the OK Corral, and *Alice in Wonderland* is the title of a famous book. But the Wrights actually made their flight at Kill Devil Hills, four miles distant from Kitty Hawk, which had the nearest telegraph line. The gun battle did not take place at the heralded corral, but between a rooming house and another building a few blocks away. The title of the famous book is *Alice's Adventures in Wonderland*, and by the way, Joyce Kilmer was not the name of the young lady who wrote "Trees", as I had thought was the case well into old age. Joyce Kilmer was a man.

At that, and despite his large family, Kilmer enlisted in the Army during World War I and was killed in 1918 at the age of thirty-one. He rests in the

Aisne-Marne American Cemetery and Memorial, having died in the Second Battle of Marne.

Elton Acker was not the person he seemed to be, to me, during high school. To me, he was the stern disciplinarian whose penetrating gaze I tried to avoid. His daughter Martha spoke of him as a boy from Newsome. It was a small town west of Pittsburg, with which it had once contended to have the railroad crossing. Pittsburg having won, that metropolis grew while Newsome shrank. The Elton Acker invisible to me, the striving student, had worked tables for what he could make and had cut grass for twenty-five cents—the entire lawn mowed with a push mower—working his way to and through a teacher's college before his service in World War II. I wish so much now that I might sit down and have a conversation with him, to apologize and to admit my debt. The thing is, I have.

As for poems, I've a poet friend at UT–Austin, retired now, who thinks that Keats's "Ode to a Nightingale" is the best poem in the language, and I have read how Keats went out back of where he was living, taking a chair, and sat beneath a tree to enter into a rapt conversation with the source of the music, which he happened to set down. We hear bird music and listen without always being able to see the source. One might speak of it as cleverness in a coloration that escapes notice. But cleverness is not the cause. The bird, like its ancestors, came to us evolving by way of coloring and behavior over time, allowing it to melt into invisibility for its safety, both in living and in reproducing.

Elton Acker was the product of his time and place. That he rose above poverty counts like a nightingale in his favor. He was a decent man, a family man, and he and his wife and two daughters lived on their farm north of Pittsburg, where he was said to retreat to his tractor as a way of relieving the stress of trying to maintain discipline and demeanor at Pittsburg High School.

As if I were some kind of expert, I was fond of saying that the truly great teachers I had along the way could be counted on the fingers of one hand, with the thumb left over. I never counted Mr. Acker, because he never taught a class that I took. But I did remember his way of maintaining control—not in breaking the pointer, which was a bit much, but in quietly demanding the respect of the class. The way Mr. Hardaway did. The way Mrs. Spearman did. And Mr. England. The way Mrs. Hargrove did, who once sent a student back to study hall in such a quiet tone of dismissal that it seemed as if he were doing her a favor.

Again and again through the years, I have been told of special things that Elton Acker did for students during their time in school. I was told by Dr. Pendergrass that Mr. Acker loved me. I thought that a bit much. But I was surprised, at our 2007 fifty-year reunion, at what happened when Mimi showed a video of class pictures set to music. Near the end, a picture of Mr. Acker flashed into view. The class broke into applause.

The hardest part of the medical education was to get into and through college. Then you learned that the hardest part was getting into medical school. It took grades and it took determination, and it took letters of recommendation—five is my memory—and one of these had to be from your high school principal. How sneaky is that? They wanted to find out how you did at the level of the adolescent fraud that is a high school student. They wished to know whether, safely graduated, you had turned around and sent an unflattering message to the principal. They cared how you handled stress. In short, they wished to know whether your high school principal thought you a gentleman.

So, thank you, Mr. Acker, for doing as much as anyone else by way of recommending me. Without you, I would not have achieved my goal of becoming a doctor. Thank you for teaching me the imperfection of people, which finally matters less than the perfection of the shared past, where edges are rounded and people are fleshed out, and Elton Acker would write this to our class in Pittsburg High's yearbook (the *1957 Treasure Chest*), as though he were speaking directly to me: "If you fall, do not stay down. Greatness does not consist in never falling but [in] rising every time you fall. Never give up …"

I'm in mind of a noontime at PHS in 1957, springtime and a few weeks before graduation, when all of this might very well have been negated by one simple act of retaliation on my part, for what I had perceived as a slight on his part, that of Mr. Acker, to a young woman I was seated with on a blanket on the grounds of the school. Oh so briefly, oh so agonizingly, that sliver of an instant that would have ripped my Charles Favor Deaton future to shreds, and I wouldn't have met Maria Chavarria, and she wouldn't have changed my life, and none of the rest of this would have occurred, at least in the way that it did. Of such perilous instants are lives made—or lost. And, as Fitzgerald put it, we are borne back ceaselessly into the past.

Part IV.

Medicine's Golden Days

I started the paper route each morning at the City Café, near the (almost always) empty jail and the classical revival Camp County Courthouse behind it. It was still dark at four thirty a.m., in that springtime of 1957, in sharp contrast to Pittsburg at noon.

The City of Pittsburg offices and the fire station were hidden in the dark, directly across the street from City Café, like forgotten items on a playground. Since the café was at the back of the block, it did not front on Jefferson Street as did the city offices and, directly across the street from them, the red-brick post office. Every parking place beside the café and over by the city offices and in front of the post office was empty. You could not buy a parking place there later on, when you really needed it. As for the post office, I almost never passed it without remembering that day I was in the lower grades and on the way home from school. By habit, I cut between the post office and the rest of the block on Jefferson Street, and on that particular day noticed that the yard in front of the post office was full of clover and as green as the jungles I had seen in *National Geographic*.

It was a compact yard elevated from the adjacent sidewalk by a concrete parapet and a low fence consisting of a single strand of wire stretched between posts. But there were no signs on it saying *Keep Off*, and I sat down that day in the lush shade and spent a pleasant and wistful hour looking for a four-leaf clover. I felt as if I had parachuted into that verdant land, in a city a third the size of Mount Pleasant and ten miles south of it, and was happy beyond measure.[26] "Roll Me Over in the Clover" would one day suit me better, but

---

26 Among other changes, Mother gave me money to go to the picture show every week, and much more.

I never forgot that lovely day. Funny, growing up, how memories eke out an existence all their own, cranky or pleasant or cataclysmic in their power to jolt one awake like a bump in the road. Maybe memories bite hardest in the dark.

I didn't know whether Fred Bevel had opened his café that early to accommodate me, but I was usually the only customer, and Fred's shiny, bald head was bent over the bar stacking pies into a glass container and setting out the cream-colored coffee cups, ladling each of them into a matching saucer. It was almost musical, the sounds they made, like Grecian urns banging around in the hold of a ship. But it was the smell of coffee first thing in the morning that was enrapturing. That first sip of hot coffee was divine. Or was it the cup itself? We hadn't anything like it at home, an ageless ceramic cup as heavy as porcelain and as warm as rainwater on fresh concrete of a summer day. Drinking coffee from this apparatus transformed me into a long-haul truck driver or a bleary-eyed collier coming up for air after the night shift belowground. It was the type of thing, men in Pittsburg said, to put hair on your chest. The coffee came equipped with a slice of cherry pie, the best in town. The tab, a dime, meant five cents for each, though to be totally accurate, his price for pie could have gone up to ten or fifteen cents since it was getting to where, by 1956, all of the stores were doubling what they used to charge for nickel items. Leave a quarter on the bar, call it even. It would make no difference to him, and Fred would never say anything about his prices.

*   *   *

The two brothers, Princeton and Fred Bevel, had at one time owned the Owl Café. Approached from Jefferson, it was on the right at the corner by the stoplight, where four highways intersected. Rusk Street went south, Mount Pleasant Street went north, and just to make things interesting, Jefferson Street, from the east, stopped at the light. The same thoroughfare continued west beyond the light as Quitman Street, pointing as it did toward Winnsboro and then Quitman, where the actress Sissy Spacek had been born on Christmas Day of 1949.

The Owl Café no longer existed, but I knew it well. Like every café in Pittsburg, it had a bar. The city was dry and the bar, finished in a dark wood that gleamed like a lodestar, was a convenient place to sit and eat if you were alone or were a kid too timid to take a seat at a table. I had eaten a hamburger for lunch at the Owl Café many times, and in 1947 they cost only a dime. I was so enamored of the Owl Café back then that I thought it the model for all of the cafés in the world. It had an enormously tall ceiling, like saloons in the Old West, as though you were eating beneath a night sky. And it was sinful. It had a wicked pinball machine or two that you passed going in the front door and that were played by men who left their shirts open to show the tattoos on their bellies, matching the ones on their arms and shoulders. The ten-cent hamburger—add a nickel for a Coke—smelled like food should smell, naughty with grease and spicy with onions and squishy with tomato slices and lettuce, the delicious meat thick and moist and grilled to perfection. The hamburger was wrapped in a thin butcher's paper, really wrapped, so that you always had control of it and would not lose anything to your plate as you peeled the crackling paper back from the diminishing remains of the hamburger.

I knew the Owl from my first year in Pittsburg because Mother worked next door in Doris Riggins's beauty shop. The bottom floor next door held a barbershop, Lloyd Langdon and George Rumsey. The ceiling in there was as high as the Owl Café's, the walls were as yellow as sunshine, and there were facing mirrors on facing walls by the barber chairs, making one person into a populace of reflections extending past the edges of the mind. To the left from the door, and halfway to the back, was a long, narrow stairway leading up to the beauty shop, tucked under that tall ceiling and, once you reached it, dark and cramped and tinted with the odor given off when women had their hair set in a permanent, the essence of ammonia cut with rotten eggs.

In the spring of 1950, Mrs. W. C. Hargrove, whose husband had helped start the First National Bank, and who lived with him in the Hargrove mansion on Quitman Street, and who was known to the youth of Pittsburg as Old Lady Hargrove, fell and broke her hip coming down that high stairway from the beauty shop. As was usually the case in those days, she was bedridden thereafter, and she died in May of 1950, a couple of months before her husband also died.

A year later, in April of 1951, the Owl Café burned down.

It was a calamity of major proportions in Pittsburg. It was as though a war had broken out, the city bombed by airplanes. The fire began in the kitchen of the Owl Café, quickly sprang out of control, jumped through the wall to the barbershop next door, and the next building, and the next. The fright was that it would reach a building in that block that sold nitrogen-based fertilizer—a lot of fertilizer. They let school out early that day and told the students to go straight home. I was finishing sixth grade at the time and the awful wail of clashing sirens drew me inexorably to the event, where I joined the huge crowd on Rusk Street south of the fire.

I was staggered by what I saw. People, grown men, were screaming above the roar of the fire, which leapt higher than any of the buildings. Men were yelling at one another and running back and forth and crashing into one another in their efforts to direct water on the fire. Fire trucks had come from Mount Pleasant, Winnsboro, Gilmer, and Daingerfield to join the one from Pittsburg. It was a vast conflagration, confusing and frightening, with thick, dark smoke billowing skyward in every direction and the flames licking at that fertilizer, which might explode at any instant. Surely people were injured in the fire, but I don't remember any fatalities, and the blaze was finally controlled well after dark, after eight businesses had been destroyed that April day.

As such, the Owl Café was never rebuilt. Instead, the Bevel brothers dissolved their partnership. Princeton rebuilt at the previous site and called the new restaurant by his first name. Fred went down the block of Jefferson Street and around the corner of Tapp Street and on the corner of Church Street built and opened his City Café.

*   *   *

The red light was blinking yellow that time of morning, Pittsburg's only light, and the two sets of railroad tracks crossed Quitman a couple of blocks west of downtown. Unlike Jefferson Street, Quitman Street did not run straight. There was a curve in it, downtown in the block past the light, supposedly because the initial road went around a big tree that had been cut down ages ago but too late to straighten the road. Quitman Street curved again, out beyond the hospital, as though the question mark it made in town were being answered by another question.

Having finished my coffee and pie, I sometimes brushed shoulders with men who drove a bread truck or some other vehicle, including one that dropped off newspapers such as the *Dallas Morning News*. The papers, in five or six bundles tied with yellow cord, were left by a courier each morning on the corner of Jefferson and Tapp Streets, just up from the café. The courier, J. D. West, brought the papers to Pittsburg from Mineola, where they had been taken from Dallas as soon as the final edition went to press. Pulling a trailer behind his vehicle, he left off papers in Quitman and in Winnsboro then turned south in Pittsburg to visit Gilmer. (My memory is that at one time, his route continued east to Texarkana.) Next to the papers I had parked Bullard's green '55 Chevy station wagon that I had picked up at his house shortly before.[27] I opened the back end to receive the bundles of papers, but the first item was to break a bundle and load the paper stand.

---

27   Bullard left it in his garage, the keys in it, and I parked my car and took his without awakening anyone.

Papers were not stacked inside a plastic dome that lifted with the right change. Instead, I put about fifteen of them into the open holder, which had its spot near a parking meter just up from City Café. When it was raining, they were left inside on the bar with Fred. The holder resembled a folding chair propped on its four stick-like feet, the papers upright and held in place in the lap of the chair. The holder was made of cast iron, painted black. An iron cylinder, like a length of pipe, ran down the right side of the holder beside the newspapers. It was large enough to accept a quarter, but the arithmetic favored a nickel for the daily, the Sunday for twenty cents. (The system did not lend itself to making change.) Indeed, there was a coin slot near the top of the pipe that was convenient for the customer to insert coins. The price was known, but when in doubt, people could consult the front page of the paper itself for the newsstand price.

Although the top of the cast-iron pipe was sealed shut above the coin slot, the bottom was not. It contained the apparatus that held money. A couple of inches from the bottom of the pipe were two small holes, opposite each other, holes of a size to admit baling wire or a section of a clothes hanger. The wire held in place a U-shaped wad of newspaper. Indeed, to get the money out I pulled on one side of the wire while straightening its opposite side to pull it through and then removed the wedge of newspaper, making sure I had my hand under the iron pipe to collect the pennies, nickels, dimes, and quarters left since the previous day. No one in Pittsburg—no one in America, at the time—would think to rob it by removing the wire and paper, any more than they would think to take a paper or an extra paper without paying for it. My last step in a process that took perhaps a minute and a half was to reinsert the wad of newspaper and the length of wire that held it in place. Then it was time to load the bundles, all except the opened one, into the back end of the Chevy wagon.

I was the paperboy for the *Dallas Morning News*, the daily, and in addition to that, a dozen or more customers took only the Sunday paper. That was about four hundred papers in a town of three and a half thousand. However, I also delivered another paper. The grand sum of three people took the *Fort Worth Star-Telegram*. This was a thin paper, less than half the size of the *Dallas Morning News*, and it was brought by the same courier. One of the Fort Worth papers I left downtown at the foot of a stairs leading to an apartment above the First State Bank. Another I threw in the white section of town. And one went to an elderly gentleman in Harlem Heights, which everyone in town called Happy Hollow, the part of Pittsburg, within lethal limits, that contained the black citizens, who were known to not a few of the white citizens by another name.

Bullard Johns, of the Cozart-Johns Insurance Agency, owned the paper route. He sometimes remarked to his family that it was his punishment for not attending college. A former neighbor and a friend for as long as I could remember, Bullard Johns was a man I loved. He did not talk down to me. He seemed genuinely fond of me. Bullard knew of my early milieu and had extended a hand to a kid who never had a legitimate father. He was the first trustworthy adult—outside of teachers—that I had ever known. Bullard was special. I loved about him his enthusiasm for life. The man could grow excited about things, and it was infectious. He was serious, he was an adult, but he enjoyed life for what it was, and not many of the adults I was around were like that. Bullard knew what it meant to be alive. He met you on that level of camaraderie that transcends description but was not less than loving friendship from a generous heart.

While it was true that he had skipped college after World War II, Bullard held a doctorate in life. He had helped any number of young men in Pittsburg, his "honor roll" of paperboys, and what he got out of it was the joy of being able to help. It was a community and every child a part of it, every one of their achievements shared by all. He asked me after my junior year, summer of 1956, to take over the route from Robert Spearman, who was leaving to become a cadet at the Naval Academy. The pay was $7.50 a week, to throw it five days, and I was allowed to select the days. I spent a week or two with Robert Spearman learning the route and also a week or two with Bullard, who had shown me how to roll and tie the papers, one by one, as I approached the next house.

It sounds harder than it was. To start, still in the dark, I loaded the rest of the opened bundle of papers into the front seat of the station wagon, to my right. White twine, a big roll of it, went onto the floor on the outside of my left foot as I sat behind the wheel of the green Chevy. The free end of the twine came up past my left knee, to be held in my mouth. Then, under way and bracing my thighs against the steering wheel to keep the car on the road, with my right hand I took a flat paper from the bundle. It was already folded once, and at the spine of that fold, using both hands, I quickly rolled it into a tight cylinder. In one continuous motion I grabbed the free end of the twine in my left hand and wrapped the paper in it with my right hand, weaving the paper back and forth so that two or three loops of twine went around it. Using both hands I tightened the string, and with my left hand I rolled the loops of twine into one tie and instantly broke off the string with my right hand. The paper now in position in my left hand, I let it fly, a beat or two of music sending it spinning out the window toward its target while my right hand returned the string to my smudged mouth and the cycle began again. The motions would remain with me always, like riding a bicycle, except one's face gets dirtier throwing newspapers, and the afterward bath was the high point of the morning.

I did it this way every morning and had no problems steering by my knees, at least down the wide, empty streets of white Pittsburg. But in Harlem Heights, all of that changed. In Harlem Heights, where I threw a few papers, including a couple to the red-brick school, the roads were narrower and the ditches deeper. This section of town, bordered by US 271 (Rusk Street) on the east, and by an ill-defined distance south of Quitman Street on the north, was new to me. The main road was paved, but many of the roads back there were not. Narrow streets of dirt led to what could only be described as hovels propped up with scrap lumber. Their segregated high school, Douglass High (for Frederick Douglass), would not be touched by integration until the midsixties, and meanwhile students at Douglass studied out of books that had been withdrawn from the school for whites—PHS. Their band always wore the previous set of uniforms of the white band members, as did their football players always wear the previous set of uniforms from PHS. That was Pittsburg; that was the South; that was my America at the time.

The topic was news, and the route headlined the story in the darkest of print. What had been there all along had never been seen by me. Failure to see negates its presence, of course. One does not have to deal with what isn't there. A journey through this shadow of Pittsburg was as wrenching as a crawl space through hell. Most Harlem Heights houses were served by outside toilets. Many were little more than lean-tos in a shantytown, shacks without electricity or paint, hovels with rusted tin roofs against the elements of a grinding racism that had existed for a century in the incalculable irony of their "freedom" from slavery.

My great-uncle Allen Deaton, sheriff in the forties, prevented those same people from walking Main Street. They had conducted their business by calling at the back door of a shop or a residence, to see whether someone would wait on them, and this had not totally ended by the fifties. Slavery had been a lesson in school, totally unrelated to me. Yet these were descendants of a people less than a century from being human property, bondsmen owned by other human beings. Before, they had been hated as necessary; now, they were hated as unnecessary. It was a slippage of valuation from institutionalized to individualized.

Virtually every scrap of land in Harlem Heights that did not have a building had a garden. In a grocery store that accepted black customers inside, I had seen them attempt to steal food. Caught, they were not arrested but were chastised. One could not condone theft! The First Baptist Church bestowed a Lottie Moon Christmas offering to offset feelings of guilt. Named for Charlotte "Lottie" Moon, longtime missionary to China, the collection was taken in Sunday school and, China now being Communist, aimed instead to benefit poor people in Africa. The Lottie Moon Christmas offering was vital. The way it worked, the Sunday school teacher spoke glowingly of how important the mission was and how much good it did for those poor Africans, who lacked the riches of Christianity. Lottie Moon would fix that! Since the offering was separate from the Sunday school offering, where I was lucky to have a nickel or a dime to put into the small white envelope that was sealed shut at the top, it was a double embarrassment to turn in two empty packets and squirm while the Sunday school teacher tested the weight of each packet and smiled forgivingly at me in an *As I expected* way, while the others in the class received the blessing.

One time, probably in 1950, I had saved up fifty cents and changed it into a fifty-cent piece, which I took to Sunday school that morning. It would be the best offering in the class! But while we were getting out of the car, my mother saw it in my eager fist, voiced surprise, and confiscated the coin for herself. I never did have much luck with fifty-cent pieces, and Lottie was down by that amount before I even went inside. Mother never mentioned what she did with it, but I expect that Lottie was also down by that amount before she went inside.

"Well, goddamn!" I said to myself on that stunning summer morning in Harlem Heights. "Goddamn!" By virtue of the paper route, I retroactively forgave myself for not supporting poor Lottie's missions and in the moment experienced the heady and profligate happiness of one seeing hypocrisy to its ugly core. I drove through the route in Harlem Heights that morning in a kind of splendor, beating my chest in exultation, and saying as many *goddamns* as it took to expunge poor Lottie from my heart forever.

*   *   *

The summer of my sophomore year, 1955, I had met the principal of Douglass High School, D. M. Smith, who picked me up as a hitchhiker several miles south of Pittsburg on the Gilmer Highway. Smith had been hired in 1946 by Fred Covin, Superintendant of Schools, and was thought by all to be a fine man. He drove a fairly new pickup and was successful in his job. He was instantly likeable the time I met him, even considering that some of his praise may have been insincere.

A young man from Harlem Heights worked with me on the paper route. I picked him up at his house Sunday morning by honking and waiting for him to come out, and he sat back there with the Sunday papers—too bulky to fold while I was driving—and folded them and readied them to throw while the two of us went through the route. We came to know each other warily. He did not even pretend to be well-mannered. One morning he said he had two children by a woman who lived in Mount Pleasant, yet they were not married. It was a troubling bit of news to me, but not to him, possibly because of the Aid to Dependent Children that supported them. (I truly don't know whether they received it.) I was not yet aware that the forced parting of families during the centuries of slavery in America had done irreparable harm, and I had no right to judge him. But I was seventeen.

My mouth went dry as he kept asking, "Are you hot? Are you hot?"

Ill-prepared for confrontation, I backed down to the extent of silence.

A year earlier, when Bullard was teaching me the route, I observed something that spoke to the perennial uneasiness between the races, as well as to the better qualities of that tense compromise. People in the black community also worked in the houses of white citizens, and one such woman, Ludie Johnson, worked in Bullard's home. Sometimes he picked Ludie up at the end of the run and delivered her to his house. Bullard and his wife, Nan, loved Ludie. One day she worked at their house and the next day, when Bullard and I were doing the route, we stopped to pick her up. There was a long lapse of time when we could rouse no one by honking the horn. Finally a young man came out and said that Ludie had died the night before.

"*Ludie Johnson?*" Bullard shouted at him.

The reply was affirmative. The young man said that she had only wanted to see her son again one more time and he had come home last night and she was ready to "pass."

Bullard was astounded, shocked to speechlessness by this thunderbolt. Nan burst into tears when we returned to the house and Bullard told her. Nan and Bullard loved Ludie as though she was family, and so did their children. Everyone who knew Ludie was shocked and aggrieved. Not the least of it was that she had never spoken of being ill or of having family problems of her own. Bullard and Nan attended her service, and as was the custom, he stood and spoke lovingly to the congregation about the role this woman had played in their lives and how deeply sorry they were at her passing.

The same was true for others in the white community, who loved as family the black persons who worked for them, and one cannot too easily dismiss this as irrelevant. I saw black people many times approach Bullard and put the touch on him for money, and he gave it. That doesn't undo anything. It doesn't brighten that ever-present shadow a bit. But the repellant obstinacy of white racism in the fifties, inherited by my generation from evil committed centuries earlier, was occasionally softened into fragments and shapes of a humanism one did not fail to note. When history can only contrast one thing against another, in stark tones of black and white, it may miss the dappled reality. That makes me sound like a racist, and at the time I was.

*   *   *

Seniors in the spring of 1957, we were driving in my car down Rusk Street one afternoon after school and turned right on Fulton Street, which took us into Harlem Heights a few blocks away. Shortly we came to a business on the south side of the road, a service station/grocery. It was unpainted and about the size of a double garage, with a tin roof and a few big bright signs urging one to drink this cola or to enjoy that flavor. The others, three or four of my classmates, went inside to make arrangements for what they swore were easy lays. I was above such. I was in love with a flaxen beauty and that was sufficient for me. But one of the guys came to the screen door and pointed me out, and presently a pretty young black woman came swaying out the door, eyes crinkled in the sunlight, and eased around the car and began talking to me.

The car was a blue '46 Chevy coupe with vacuum shift. It had forty-seven thousand miles on it. I had shaved the trunk, purchased fender skirts, and installed a high-speed camshaft. Its steering wheel shone like ivory, and it had a spotlight on the driver's side. The young woman stepped forward, even with the spotlight, and smiled down at me as though she were a carhop ready to take my order. It was distinctly odd.

It was literally the first time I had ever spoken a word to a black girl my age, and I wasn't quite sure how to conduct myself. Her speech was different from mine, a syrupy Southern drawl, yet she was absolutely attractive, another surprise. Her hair was short and, perhaps because it was the style, covered by a pink scarf. She wore lipstick, a blouse, and a skirt. A human being, and that was the biggest surprise of all. I had not thought we could meet as equals, yet here she was and there I sat. I did not ask whether this meeting of a white boy from the other side of town was a first for her. (Intelligence from a cohort, whose probity was on a par with Ponzi schemes, held that these were loose young women, if not professionals.) I did not inquire what grade she attended at Douglass High. I showed no interest in whether she played in the band, did not ask about her dreams or what she thought of the forces that had brought the two of us glancing against each other at this moment in time, on an afternoon when I owned the world.

Instead, point-blank, I asked her a question about what might be depicted as an intimate matter, a question I would never address to a white girl.

Both of her hands removed themselves from the car, where she had touched the spotlight and the sill of the open window. She stood there in disbelief, her eyes fixed as though she were an opera singer informed that she was singing off-key and the orchestra had abruptly stopped and everyone in the house was booing her. It was then that I said the most regrettable utterance of my life.

"You're just a nigger!"

Now she was stricken. I'd made her the repository of my odium, injected into the body of whatever existed between us, transmissible as any germ with its own incubation period, signs, symptoms, chief complaint, present illness, past illness, family illness, personal history, and review of systems—all of it in acute and chronic forms, and don't leave out the mental status examination. To her regret, she had initiated a polite conversation with a white boy who had seemed, for the moment, nice. She had not known where it was going but was courteously willing to make the effort at flirting. Perhaps she had been warned not to talk to white boys, ever, warned by those who knew. But she had done it and it got her this.

In that liquid instant the hurt I had inflicted upon her made me sick. I hadn't known I would feel that bad but I did, because of how she reacted—as though I had struck her in the soul. I had opened my own festering wound and flung the purulence at her, and she was unable to shield herself from it and the betrayal of what she had thought of me. I had been doing the paper route for almost a year, thinking how wonderful I was to feel sorry for the people in Harlem Heights. That, apparently, was a sham, and I hated myself for my hatred. I was seventeen years old. I was as reckless and stupid as only those in the last few teenage years can be, because when you feel that good about yourself, what does it matter what other people think? What I had not understood until then, that instant, was the fatality inherent in that word, the N-word, for it made of me a murderer. To dehumanize is to kill. It is the homicide of human dignity, the murder of being. It is the slaughter of character, the beheading of benevolence, the assassination of every aspect of humanity. Love is an art we may share. Hatred is a virulence that is just as deadly on its host as on its victims.

But that came later. All I knew at the time was how bad I felt for the pain I had inflicted. But I couldn't let that show, dared not admit a mistake. A few minutes after the event with those young women, we were speeding away and laughing like loons about the experience, which in my case followed me home. The young woman, standing just there with her hand on the spotlight, has been with me ever since.

She had said, "Oh, you white-un!" and spun and left.

How pitiful her comeback, I had thought, but maybe that was because she was not a murderer. Maybe that was because she was a better person than I. By nightfall I had resolved to do better, be better. I had been vaccinated, but they had missed the most important disease of all. Still, I had heard men say that the only person who hadn't made a mistake was the one who had never done anything. I had heard all sorts of witticisms.

*   *   *

I had moved in the spring of 1947 to Pittsburg with my mother and stepfather. I had survived Cooper's Chapel and Mount Pleasant. I was seven years old and going on eight and had finished the last six weeks of second grade there, learning that I was academically behind those in my class. It had been a chance to start afresh and love everyone. My life was much easier than it had been, prayers answered, so what had gone wrong by 1957? Was I the product of a milieu or its outcast? It had to be one or the other: a war had been fought over it and, it seemed, America was the beacon of hope.

The boys were back and there was a glorious feeling afoot, as if great things had been accomplished and everyone mattered and every dream would be answered. Plumbing had come indoors along with tap water and electricity, but those who had lived through the war years could recall when things had been different. An elderly woman was heard to complain, "Oh, I wish I had me a good old cob!" But she was in the minority. The Second World War was won, and America was "the Land of the Free and the Home of the Brave." People did not lock their doors at night—no reason to in the small towns of America, where three-fourths of the people still lived. Most people did dishes by hand, but even those who had a clothes washer hung the linens out to flap in the breeze. Sheets smelled fresh back then and gleamed like paint, stiff from dancing in a wind that blew only to change things for the better. God bless America! The lawns were green, the houses pretty. The boys were back and settled into careers, and they and their families were living the American dream. On a warm autumn noontime on a Saturday that same year, I had passed through the kitchen of our new house at 504 Elm Street, where Mother was cooking dinner—the term for the midday meal in those days—with the radio tuned to WFAA in Dallas:

> If the world would smile each day
> Helping someone on life's way,
> Bring the wandering in from the paths of sin
> To the Master's fold today …

The Stamps-Baxter quartet does the hymn perfectly for a Saturday noontime, likely sponsored by Gladiola Baking Powder. Through the screen of the open back door, the friendly tufts of Bermuda grass poke up in splendor, the yard itself only recently tamed from a corn patch and the conquering push mower preening in the sunshine just there, the clothesline with its silvery tendons just beyond. The one-car garage is to the left, unbearably plain in the same dull green of the house but beautiful to my eye beyond description; the steel-blue of the house next door and the lemony sheen of the one on the other side are as fine to me as heaven could possess. Straight back behind us, past what we call "the lot," is a two-story frame, tall and shaded, its exterior of chalk-white beginning to fade but its interior important, for it is the residence of no less than the local veterinarian, which imparts to us from living in his vicinity a sense of importance ("makes us proud"). Importance is important to us. Perhaps, if we are observant, important things will occur, and we will impart this about the veterinary doctor to others, making people stop and listen, proud to know important us.

It is 1947 (Maria is a year old), and the boys are back, and one goes to school in order to "grow up and be something." School begins to make sense. One day I hold up a page of hieroglyphics, really look at it for the first time, and decide that it might be neat to learn that language, see where one might go. Surely it is somehow related to being something, making something of myself. Is that possible? It is a ticklish thought, betterment, one that I keep to myself.

*   *   *

But I learned to read and in 1949 found, in the newspaper we took, the *Dallas Morning News*, the word *virtually*. I asked people what it meant. They didn't know. But sometimes a man would look at me with the amusement of having found a nickel on the ground, and then he would grin and shift his shoulders with that inviolable sense of responsibility for it and look off into the distance and come back to say, "Had it to do over again, I'd get me all that education I could. Not have work out here, this old, hot sun. No sirree, bub, get me all that and I could set on the front porch and drink ice water."

Pittsburg High School, 1955. PHS was the name of the building and it accommodated junior high and high school students. Junior high met on the first floor and shared with high school the second floor, which held the trophy case. The top floor was reserved for the high school students, each of whom had a desk in the long rows of them in study hall, which extended, except for two or three windows on either side, the length of the building. (It was later divided into a library and a hallway.) Each Monday until 1960, high school students assembled first thing at their seats in study hall, then stood respectfully as Mr. Acker took his place at the head of the study hall (the left side in the picture) and led them in prayer. Unless there was an announcement afterward, he then dismissed the students, who dispersed to their classes.

Superintendent Fred Covin (from *1957 Treasure Chest*): "While you are in high school ... you are a part of everything around you, and the experiences, desires, hopes, and sorrows of other students and teachers become a part of your life. ... If I might have one fond wish for your future, it would be [for you] to thumb through the pages of this yearbook ten years from now and know that each of you has used your experiences from Pittsburg High School to courageously face the exigencies of life which come to all and graciously accept the blessings which make life worthwhile." PHS was peacefully integrated a decade later.

The '46 Chevy Coupe, parked on Hess Street atop Stafford Hill. I shaved the tail, bought skirts (not shown), and let the engine idle a bit fast. The mileage was palpable. The thing purred like a kitten, the plugs gaped in awe, and those pistons turned like a plunger in a churn, making the buttery lubricant all good vehicles love. I left it beside a road outside Houston in the fall of 1957—but not the memories!

Janet Hargrove, 1954. She was the best of a great group of teachers at PHS in the fifties. No one who had her would thereafter ever be able to say that another teacher was better. Or even came close! Mrs. Hargrove was the talisman, to use one of her words, who endowed us with the notion that nothing in the world was beyond us.

I was fortunate to enjoy a correspondence with her some years after I left high school. She would read things I wrote about my Pittsburg days, and I once told her—gratuitously, I thought—to alert me to any mistakes I might have made, as she had once done on my homework. I called myself a professional writer and editor, but that was before Spell-Check, and when she returned the manuscript, and in the most tactful of ways, she suggested I spell "extemperaneous" the correct way: extemporaneous. At the time, she was in her nineties! [Photograph courtesy of *1954 Treasure Chest*.]

James Spence Beckham, 1955. [Photograph courtesy of *1955 Treasure Chest*.]

Elton Acker, in retirement. His home and the farmland around it were a fixture, a point of reference off US 271 north of Pittsburg. Seeing his picture in a video Mimi had done for our fifty-year reunion, the class broke into spontaneous applause. Mr. Acker died in 1991 at age eighty-four and is buried in Macedonia Cemetery. [Photograph courtesy of Martha Acker Lorenz.]

2009: Pittsburg, Texas. This is the Cypress Street crossing of the Cotton Belt route. It hadn't changed from 1948, when I climbed the hill, walking my bicycle, and saw how close I was to Quitman Street. An impulsive shortcut put me on the tracks, barefooted, pushing my bike. The freight train, heading south from Mount Pleasant, came from the right, behind me.

JGD, 1948–49. A class picture of me in fourth grade, the year after the accident.

Railroad tracks looking south from Cypress Street Crossing.

Farther south, railroad tracks from the Cotton Belt
line cross those from the east–west line.

Railroad tracks approaching Quitman Street. In the background,
an auto supply store still exists at the site of the service station
operated by Elmo Deaton almost a century earlier. (My mother and
father were pictured in front of Elmo's shop in a previous picture.)
I had oriented myself by it in 1948 and was heading toward it.

Quitman Street crossings in 2011. In the foreground, the east–west tracks, marked by the sign at the left. A pickup is approaching the other set of tracks, the north–south Cotton Belt route. Three miles south of town is where James Spence Beckham had his accident, with the train coming north. In my case, the freight train was headed south, and it hit me no more than a few hundred feet north of Quitman Street. No one ever told me where I was found, other than that "half of the train" had passed over me. Amnesia left me with no memory of the accident or any desire to revisit where it occurred, until I finally did so in 2009. [Photograph courtesy of Mayor Shawn Kennington of Pittsburg.]

Quitman Street in Pittsburg, 2011. View is from the curve in Quitman, looking west past the auto supply store, left, and the Quitman Street crossings (note the barriers). The street continues past the hill to the site of what was the old Medical & Surgical Hospital. [Photograph courtesy of Mayor Shawn Kennington of Pittsburg.]

Pittsburg in 2011, looking east from the curve in Quitman Street. Jefferson Street begins east of the light. In the distance is a prayer tower in a small park, a unique feature given the City of Pittsburg by Patty and Bo Pilgrim. [Photograph courtesy of Mayor Shawn Kennington of Pittsburg.]

The original Medical & Surgical Hospital in Pittsburg, Texas. It opened in 1941. That it resembles a residence is more typical than not of small hospitals in those days. It had expanded by 1948, when I was a patient there, but I remember being in the next-to-last room on the right, with a view out the window of Quitman Street in the near distance. I particularly remember one "get well" card: "Friend or Enema?" I was not given a choice! [Photograph courtesy of Barbara Johnson Brieger.]

Dr. Robert L. Johnson and wife, Ella Mae Johnson, at the opening of the clinic adjacent to the Medical & Surgical Hospital in Pittsburg, probably early fifties. The doctor and Ella Mae shared a strong Christian faith, and both were active at the First Baptist Church. Dr. Johnson took Thursday afternoons off and spent them with his wife at their farm, where he raised cattle and later grew peach trees. Inset: Dr. Robert L. Johnson in 1961. [Photographs courtesy of Barbara Johnson Brieger.]

Captain Percy Reitz, Medical Corps, US Army, 1942.
[Photograph courtesy of Ronald C. Reitz.]

Major Percy Reitz in Belgium, January of 1945, during his tour of active
duty in Europe. Comparing his expression with that in the previous picture,
one can see a difference. [Photograph courtesy of Ronald C. Reitz.]

Dr. Percy Reitz examining a child in the clinic in Pittsburg during medicine's golden days. The doctor enjoyed fishing and had Friday afternoons off to devote to that. He shared his love of fly-fishing with oldest son, Ron, and with his twins, Bob and Sharon. He used bamboo fly rods to fish for bass, and after they had fished, Ron remembers, they would stand by the boathouse and stretch the fly line between the two of them and shake it until it was dry. Inset: Mrs. Hazel Reitz at home. [Top photograph courtesy of Ronald C. Reitz, who also took the picture of his mother in the inset.]

Robert K. Pendergrass, MD, in retirement. The photo, supplied by him, was taken in 2005. The amazing thing about it, and him, is that his eyes hold as much light and wit and grace as they ever did, maybe more. "Come along grow old with me," Robert Browning wrote, "the best is yet to be." Whatever I may be on the positive side of life's ledger, I owe to this man.

Mary Pendergrass, Austin. Asked by me whether she liked being married to a doctor, she said, "I do this doctor." They built their home upon love, raised four children that way, and were always willing to spill the decanter of love in my direction—mine and so many others.

Cooper's Chapel Cemetery sign. One happens upon it suddenly, around a curve, like the mast of a ship that had run aground, coming to rest near the serrated landscape of the reef it had struck.

Cooper's Chapel Church. The historical marker and the pavilion to the left were added more recently, in acquiescence to the idea that history is historical, for the former, and for the latter to accommodate the large crowd that gathers for services and dinner-on-the-grounds each Decoration Day.

Cooper's Chapel Cemetery from behind the chapel at sundown.

The author, in 2009, with his former teachers in a Mount Pleasant care facility. To the right, Charlie Groom, age 84, who taught me second grade at Cooper's Chapel (1946–47) and was the "Miss Charlie" shown earlier.

To the left is Janet Hargrove, age 103, who taught me third grade in Pittsburg (1947–48). Charlie had a varied career in teaching, and married and raised a daughter. Mrs. Hargrove had just returned to teaching in 1947 after her husband died. The reason for that causes one to look at an earlier time. Janet Blair was born in Houston in 1906. Graduating from Rice Institute in 1928, she attended North Texas State Teacher's College for her teaching certificate, and was duly accepted for the position in Pittsburg, teaching high school Spanish and other subjects. Upon her marriage to Willie Hargrove, she lost her job. That was the policy of the school board then, though she was thereafter mindful of how unfair it was that she was replaced by a woman who said she was single but was secretly married. Janet's youngest of three daughters, Marie, was in third grade with me that year. Subsequently Mrs. Hargrove returned to high school, spending the rest of her career in Pittsburg and, for a few years, in Mount Pleasant.

I grew up loving these men. Some of them wore bib overalls, never mind. Some of them spoke in a high, whiny voice, and others barely spoke above a hoarse whisper, and still others were given to profanity in lieu of riches. But I never met a one I didn't like and respect. Their heavily calloused hands wore sun spots and scars as slick as corn silk, and to them the ultimate pleasure was "to set on the porch and drink ice water."

The boys were back and these were the boys. One of them said, "Some of them over there acted like they didn't care whether they never come back, but not old Guy. I got back and thankful for it!" They had gone to grade school, maybe tried high school, gotten married, gone to work, had a family. Some took jobs in town, but most still worked the land like those before them, a good life but a hard one. Some moved away, like Homer Epps, but that epic gesture was beyond most. Quit roots? Leave Mama? Give up opening the back door and taking you a good old country piss? Forsake the familiar ruts and roads; the trees, lakes, and land; the blazing sunups and the gentle sunsets; the hurried baling of hay in a chasing wind that tasted of rain? Give up the sweet smell of the red dust along a tree-channeled road, the symphony of frogs and critters by the crick at night, the people and soil and culture that had nourished them? No, by god! But their choice need not be repeated: "Yes sir, I'd get me all that education I could."

What they did not say because they could not know was that "all that education" did not come cheaply, ice water sipped on the front porch drinking better in vision than in reality, because dreams in crisp clarity are a painting cut to perfection, but life wields a scythe of its own.

*   *   *

The man in Harlem Heights who took the *Fort Worth Star-Telegram* lived in the first house on the left after I turned south off Quitman and went into the Heights on Mill Street, near the railroad tracks. The houses didn't start right away, but when they did, he was in the first house on the left. It was a white clapboard house built on piers with a swing on the front porch and a small yard enclosed by a white picket fence. The customer was an old man who carried his dignity well. His name may have been Chaney. Sitting in that porch swing most mornings, at least on warm days with an early sun, he waved his thanks. We came to know each other by gestures and I thought we became fond of each other. I hatched a plan to throw his *Star-Telegram* in a way that would have it land in his lap.

But it would not be easy.

The house had a dirt yard, which was more common in the country than in the city. With a dirt yard, one didn't have to mow. One just weeded and raked it like a batter's box, taking pride in its fresh appearance. This small, clean yard, inside its fence, was a blur. I concentrated on the old man, living with his daughter, whom I had glimpsed a time or two. The old gentleman had trouble with ambulation, and a brown, wooden cane was always propped beside him in the swing. I suspected that he had been helped outside and placed there as a part of his day. So I would throw his *Star-Telegram*, a slender mimic of the Dallas paper, and let it land in his lap.

What stood in my way was a massive oak tree in that front yard, guarding the customer from the vendor. It was nigh on an impossibility to get the paper through that tree. The tree was fearsome. The man himself was no more than five yards from the street. One had the idea of being able to lean out the window and hand it to him, but then again he was well above street level, with a steep staircase feeding the porch, and so the throw must find its way through a gap in that tree. The easy way to throw his paper—the requirement only to get it into his yard—was to pass his house, which reached to the corner, and toss the paper back to the left and over the fence, avoiding the rough, as it were. But that did him no good. And when the ground was wet, the paper landed in the first cousin to mud. Probably the old fellow did not walk well enough to descend those stairs, which meant he was beholden to his daughter or son-in-law to fetch the paper for him every day.

I began to notice, however, that as I passed the tree a V-shaped slit flashed open for a fraction of a second. Perhaps it was a fork in the trunk, I wasn't sure. The fork did not play fairly. It had tines aplenty. It was situated in such a way that the paper itself would have to be spinning perfectly: one end would have to go through before the other, and no other way would work. All I had to do was time the throw, because at twenty miles per hour I must make it before I reached the tree, a left-hander's curveball breaking to the right. Up and to the right, in fact, the opening being a few feet above the level of the driver's window on the Chevy wagon. I expended far too much time trying for one thing and achieving another. What I needed was a fool's version of a miracle.

The times I missed, time after time, I had to stop because the tree threw the paper back at me. And since I was up and out of the car, why not take two steps and toss it up onto the porch beside him? Okay, and I did that a time or two. But had I opened the gate, climbed the steps, and handed it to him, people being people, the man would come to expect that. And I didn't have the time. Didn't have the patience. Probably I didn't have the goodness for it, because it was more about me than about him.

My practice at shooting the paper through the oak began in the summer of 1956, continued through that autumn and winter, and warmed in the beautiful spring of 1957. By then I had measurements of the task. To reach him the *Star-Telegram*, ejected from a moving vehicle, must pass through an opening a foot and a half long and six inches wide, and the folded paper was itself a foot long, or a bit more. Solid geometry is solid.

Then one day it was different. I was proceeding through the route on a morning in May of '57 that was so irresistibly gorgeous that it was frightening. It was approaching seven a.m. as I eased the Chevy onto Mill Street, being at that point within half an hour of finishing the route. Four hundred papers a morning, five days a week for ten or eleven months meant I was approaching ninety thousand papers thrown, and maybe I had learned a thing or two. I had thrown his *Star-Telegram* over two hundred times, always in frustration or by giving up and just tossing it over the fence.

In fact, I was not doing anything any differently that morning from what I always did. I knew that I had to time the throw and release the paper well before the tree, like a pass from the quarterback that is thrown before the receiver makes his cut. And that morning, I went for it. Approaching, I could see the man seated in the porch swing, as always. With the skinny Fort Worth paper already rolled, I let fly. The paper sailed from my hand. I was so used to it hitting those tree limbs and then falling just inside the fence or just outside the fence that I listened for the noise of it, which sounded like the crack of a whip followed by the thud of its landing.

For once, that didn't happen. The old guy was still up there, and he was wearing the same khaki shirt and trousers and the old felt hat that he always wore. His cane was beside him, as always. He was sitting by himself, as always. The only difference was, he had a *Star-Telegram* in his lap.

The old gentleman was as surprised as the author of the throw. He was startled, but appreciative. I had one glimpse of his enormous smile and I was past, but I felt so good for making that one lucky throw that it carried me through the rest of the day—indeed, instilled in me the conviction I would carry forever, that should I go back and look closely enough, that old guy would still be seated on that front porch, riding that swing, waiting for his *Star-Telegram*, and I'd take a victory shot at getting it in his lap.

Came happening instead, a few minutes later, driving with my knees through Harlem Heights, an accident. Grabbing the wheel to prevent one thing, I achieved the other, sweeping out a ditch just down from the school. For an instant I thought the station wagon might roll over, but it righted itself after a glancing bump and regained the road. It put a couple of solid dents in the bumper and shook me to the point of talking severely to myself. But

Bullard, an insurance agent, never mentioned the dents, and I had only a scratch or two from where my forehead touched the rearview mirror.

*   *   *

Had I required medical care for that incident in Bullard's '55 Chevy wagon—pardon the awkward transition—I might have visited any of the three doctors of medicine or the osteopathic doctor living in Pittsburg. These were the most important men in town, a fact universally acknowledged. Their very names manifested awe, like news of the president. In their presence one was aware of deference, the need to keep a certain distance, reverence requiring no less. People go into medicine because of their experiences with doctors, and I had three to choose from: Percy A. Reitz, MD; Robert L. Johnson, MD; and Robert K. Pendergrass, MD. (James W. Coldsnow, DO, was a physician in Pittsburg and would have been held in as high an esteem, but I never met the man or interacted with him in any way.) The stories of these three medical doctors were inextricably tied to the Medical & Surgical (M&S) Hospital at 414 Quitman Street, several blocks west of downtown Pittsburg. This facility was built in 1940, but at least one hospital, much smaller than M&S, had been built some years earlier.

Martin Hospital, located at the corner of North Avenue and College Street, northeast of the courthouse in Pittsburg, was a single-story hospital operated by Russell L. Martin Sr., DO. It had two or three rooms for patients and a small apartment at the back, where the aforesaid Dr. Martin lived with his wife and two children (a daughter and a son named Russell L. Martin Jr., who would later become an MD).

The senior Dr. Martin subsequently moved to Mount Pleasant to practice, his hospital there being the one across the street from where Jim and Alma Kimberlin had lived. I could make a fairly strong case that it was that elder Dr. Russell Martin who had performed my tonsillectomy the year I spent at Cooper's Chapel. Of the illness leading up to it I have no memory. But galloping and catching up to me are the fear bordering on horror I felt after the surgery, that winter midnight spent riding between Cooper's Chapel and the hospital in Mount Pleasant while spitting up a steady stream of bright-red blood in the wild abandon of the dying, babbling in fear as the blood pooled frighteningly in a dull metal washbasin Aunt Randie had provided me for the purpose, bouncing with my uncle along that narrow corduroy dirt road with its jackrabbit stops and its shotgun twists on the way into town in his battered old pickup.

I thought the worst, but did not say it. Then: "I'm going to die," I said anyway.

"No you ain't," Uncle Raymond maintained.

I continued my claim, variations on a theme, until we reached the hospital, where the same Dr. Russell Martin or one of his associates sutured the bleeding vessels in the back of my throat. Postoperative hemorrhage was the most common complication of tonsillectomy in those days and probably related to how kids had a tendency to swallow the stitches before it was time for their removal. I don't blame the doctor for it. As well as I remember, he was a nice man beloved by his patients.

*   *   *

When Pittsburg became our home in 1947, M&S was thereafter our hospital. Pittsburg itself was a safe community of people who believed in history and lived life a day at a time. It was a grounded community, a community of place and past, of people proud to live in Pittsburg because their people had lived there and they saw no reason to move. It was sometimes held that people got rich in Mount Pleasant and then moved the ten miles south to Pittsburg. I don't know about that.

My stepfather had served in the Pacific Theater and worked at Lone Star Steel, located east of Pittsburg near the city of Daingerfield. He and my mother, possibly with his Veteran's Assistance, were able to purchase the $5,000 house we lived in on Elm Street (two bedrooms and a bath). That it was spanking new and in a neighborhood west of town that was dotted with other new houses meant so much. Indeed, the difference in my new surroundings, as opposed to the farmhouse in Cooper's Chapel, did put us in that category of having grown rich in Mount Pleasant and moving to Pittsburg, although I suspect we were on the bottom rung of that slippery ladder.

Looming as it does over Pittsburg, Mount Pleasant being so much larger, citizens of each community maintained a gentle repartee as to athletic competition. In the locker room of the gymnasium in Pittsburg, for example, was a handwritten note above the toilet:

Please Flush. Mt. Pleasant needs the water.

Pittsburg, smaller, was also neater and prettier than Mount Pleasant. Its people were less diverse, its layout more elegant. It held a certain appeal that was lacking in its neighbor. If they tended to glorify that, those in Pittsburg, it was understandable. It could be glorious. Everything about the lives of the people in Pittsburg could seem that way, year after year, and why not? Happiness is a habit built on goodwill and contentment. A community, to be successful, needs pride, passion, and perfection—or at least its attempt.

Pittsburg offered good schools as well as a high school marching band where the most popular majorette, of course, went steady with the star of the Pittsburg Pirates' football team. The school had a Homecoming, a Halloween Festival, a May Fete, and proms and graduations each May.

Christmas was a season of inestimable joy. It was as though it had taken the entire year to build up the proper amount of love to be expended in the festivities. It was real, though. And it was fun and that was its magic, its awaited excitement. People drove up and down the streets at Christmas enjoying an ambience that, like most good things, allowed one to derive from it what he or she put into it. It could seem divine, as it was meant to be. We were a family, the same as, and that was important, take a pride in it!

The town held the most pleasant seasonal smells imaginable—places like Otto Smith's grocery store, which smelled like Christmas year-round, and Taylor's Drugstore, which held the essence of new things well packaged and neatly priced in huge islands that were monuments to the new commerce. The drugstore offered ice cream and banana splits, fresh nuts and the clean, crisp renown of Whitman's candies. The main street itself was like a Christmas tree, with the glow in its doors and windows as bright as ornaments. The homes joined in, like shimmering jewels owned by all, in a hushed feeling of reverence for all good and loving things and a wistful urge to peek into every happy home and soak up its joy the way children did on Christmas morning.

Christmas carols lit the background, a joyous tinkling of bells and song, a chorus of music relished for its capacity to inspire. Everywhere there were pine boughs and poinsettias and pecan pies, and every house held the promise of chocolate cake and stuffing and fresh rolls. The weather turned deliciously cold, with shivery nights and glad hearts, and groups of teenagers clambered aboard a flatbed truck and were driven to certain houses to serenade with carols those who were "shut-ins," and it felt so good to do that, by way of proving that the most important part of the celebration was a granted permission to love one another openly, unconditionally, eternally. And we did and it went by so rapidly, though its joy lingered in anticipation of more, in the trajectory of one season yielding inexorably to the next.

In the summer, the young people had Baptist encampment, where "mixed bathing" was forbidden but where love nevertheless bloomed. We were "saved" in that consequence of having been "lost." We rededicated our lives, again and again, and volunteered for "special service," receiving the "right hand of Christian fellowship" by way of support. Children grew up watched over, but not pampered. People seemed happier then and maybe were. Love was more felt than spoken, but the town was full of it. And flowers! There were more florists per capita than anywhere else on Earth, with a special interest in dogwood and roses and those resplendent corsages purchased at that special time and worn upon the breast or upon the wrist of the sweetheart and meriting, always, a culminating kiss—the first for each—that in its every particular was imprinted upon the hearts of each forever. It was a place of gentle pine trees that grew just about everywhere and that dropped their scented needles again and again, silently, year upon year, creating an outdoor carpet that was as soft as a comforter on a bed and yielded to the person on foot an incredible bliss. Pittsburg held all of the treasures of a loving hometown. People knew and trusted one another, and women and sometimes men sent notes that mentioned a Bible verse at the bottom of the message by way of expressing their love in timeless words.

*   *   *

Yet there was another facet to the pride in the white community, a reminder of the underbelly of the sleeping beast. Now and again, with no warning at all, death sprouted unexpectedly, claiming the life of a young person in town, apparently at random. The Parker girl drowned one summer afternoon at the natatorium, for example, even though a lifeguard was on duty. Apparently she slid into the water and didn't come up, and no one noticed it until too late.

Every bit as tragic was the death in about 1950 of a young married man, Tommy Law. He'd had a spat with his wife and taken a .22-caliber rifle out behind his in-laws' house, leaned against one of the clothesline posts, and shot himself in the heart, his widow and young son deprived of himself by a fatalistic impulse fancied by poets and martyrs through the ages and which, were it revealed, was probably more common than not among young people in love. I would find, for example, that after an argument with my wife, I had a terrible impulse to do the same.

Tommy Law's suicide happened behind the house next door to ours, that of Bullard Johns and family. Later, I used to think of that when mowing that yard back there, especially around the clotheslines in the backyard, which I passed every day on my shortcut to the dirt road that led to Texas Street and Quitman Street and thence to town and school.

Other tragedies as well: Rex Culver was a handsome young member of FFA (the Future Farmers of America) and, fifteen years old, had just completed his freshman year in high school. He had been driving tractors and such for years and like most others in Pittsburg had gotten his driver's license at age fourteen. Rex was a friendly young man whom everyone liked. He had a girlfriend, a beautiful young woman who also lived on a farm west of the city. Life was rich. Certainly one's mind can feast at such times, blurring the more physical rudiments of ordinary life.

On the afternoon of June 12, 1956, he drove the family pickup into town on an errand. It accomplished, he started home, driving west on Quitman Street. A rain shower had left the streets wet, the pavement slick.

There was a curve on the outskirts of Pittsburg where Quitman Street turned into Highway 11 and where Broach Road intersected Quitman Street. A little farther west, the speed limits changed from city to highway. Anticipating that, Rex accelerated sooner than he should have and lost control of his pickup as it rounded the curve.

Westbound, he careened into the path of an oncoming car, collided with it, crossed the lawn of a house at the corner of Quitman and Broach, and struck a light pole. He suffered fractures of the skull, a concussion, and a broken leg. He died the next day. (There were no injuries to those in the other vehicle, but the car sustained damages.) Not only are such events tragedies for the family and the community, they cause everlasting changes in the lives of those affected, and that was certainly the case in Pittsburg. Suffice it that John Donne was right. *It tolls for thee.*

*   *   *

A tragedy of equal dimension occurred seven months earlier. On November 8, 1955, James Spence Beckham, who had graduated from PHS that year and who worked for his father, Jimmy Beckham, as a bricklayer, had hurried home after work to shower and attend an awaited event. The Beckhams lived on what is now County Road 1323, three miles south of Pittsburg. It ran east–west and crossed the Cotton Belt railroad tracks adjacent to current FM 3384 (then the Gilmer Highway). For those who still lived on acreage "down there," still worked the land, crossing railroad tracks was a valid part of their lives. The Beckhams, a well-loved family, knew this.

Jimmy was a deacon at the First Baptist Church. His wife and the boys' mother, Julia, had taught first grade for many years. Jimmy, after he returned from Army service in World War II, had helped to build many of the homes in Pittsburg. He had hired his sons (James and his younger brother, Bill, a senior that year) and trained them as bricklayers during summers out of high school. Both brothers were athletes and James Spence, who liked food and tended to gain weight easily, had played tackle on the Pirates' football team.

As was true of Rex Culver's accident, it was a Tuesday afternoon about five thirty. But in November, as contrasted to June, it was growing dark at that hour. Late autumn was a thrilling time of year, the days shorter, the wind with more bite. Leaves seemed to stir the trees, rather than the other way around, and it was fun to look forward to Friday night meetings, a nondenominational service attended by all and known as high school football.

James Spence had a fiancée, a future, a happy life. Having showered and dressed after work, and perhaps with a slice of pie on board, he was tearing his car eastward through the twilight toward the Gilmer Highway (then US 271). He drove fast because he was in a hurry. He was an impulsive young man, eighteen years old, who—like all eighteen-year-olds—thought himself immortal. As a close friend of James Spence told me, "We were both somewhat of daredevils at that time in our lives."

In other words, racing a train was nothing new to this larger-than-life character. James Spence did large things in a large way, his appetite for excitement and his zest for living being only two of his conspicuous qualities. He was oiling the hinges of life. He laughed loud and often and, if anything, the happier he was, the more likely he was to take risks. It was the best time of day. Work was over and fun was ahead and risks were a piquant part of the enjoyment.

The train kept a daily schedule that everyone south of Pittsburg was well aware of. There were no safety bars to guard the crossing and no flashing lights, but that was well-known. The crossing was marked by a sign, by its physical appearance, and by the knowledge of its existence to those who had crossed it thousands of times before. They also knew how long a wait was involved should they meet the train.

A line of trees between the tracks and the highway made little difference in the twilight of that November day—the train's lights were on. Here it came. Those in a hurry must make choices. How many fleeting impulses had gone by unanswered? How many had been acted out in safety, but secretly? James Spence elected to race the train. It was not that he didn't see it; it was that he miscalculated it.

He may have thought it farther away than it was: the sound of a train rushing toward you does not have the same level of intensity as when one is standing beside or behind the train. Or maybe he was listening to the radio, the windows closed against the autumn chill. Or he may have thought the train was going slower than it was, this Cotton Belt freight train that, like all trains, had horsepower measured in the thousands. Something else—the tracks were six or eight feet higher than the road itself, a steep distance from either direction. One literally climbed up a small hill before reaching the tracks. In the gloaming of that November day, the hill's size may have been teasingly eradicated.

The event itself overshadowed its details, but other than the train's engineer, there were no eyewitnesses beyond James Spence himself. At some point he increased his speed approaching the tracks, and at some point it was too late to stop. Risk is like that. That's what makes it risk, a favor to the gods of chance, and to a certain extent, the submission of one's life to their will. This time, the offering was accepted. James Spence had placed himself a split second too late to cross and with too short a distance to stop. Accelerator to the floor, perhaps surprising even him, he slung the car up that steep hill containing the tracks. Perhaps at the last second he braked. The car lurched into the air, the train striking it broadside from the right.

Life, the event seemed to imply, is as impudent as those who wish to challenge it. Monsters lie in wait. And the most horrifying thing about these monsters is that they come disguised as things we see and hear every day. Time is what makes them so dangerous. The monsters don't change; time increases one's exposure to them. Having crossed those tracks a seemingly infinite number of times, James never reduced the risk of an accident; for each time he crossed them, the risk remained exactly the same. What changed was his perception of that risk, the most poignant thing about it being how preventable it was.

The amount of force expended by the train in a car–train collision is almost incomprehensible. The extent of their knowledge of collisions, for most people, relates to those between cars or trucks, which can be deadly enough. Collision of a moving train with an automobile involves stratospherically greater forces. Physics tells the dynamics of force: mass times the speed of acceleration. The train, sliding on steel-flanged wheels along steel rails, had a mass infinitely greater than did James's automobile, and the train was clicking along at its usual rate of speed. Hitting the car broadside, the train's impact was as though a brick building several stories high and going forty-five or fifty miles an hour had crashed into an object made of tinfoil: a sledgehammer pounding a toy car.

*   *   *

The event was so sudden and shattering that November evening in Pittsburg that it defied possibility. People simply could not believe it. What made it more gruesome was that James Spence had been thrown beneath the train by the force of the collision, dying instantly. More was not said and time did not stop. The *Pittsburg Gazette* related that the car, wedged against the front of the engine, was carried a third of a mile past the scene before the train could stop. It also stated that James was alone in the car.

He was not.

James Spence's death put everyone in high school in the car with him, right there in the front seat, suffering the terrible thing that had happened to him. One sensed the panic at the last moment, the horrible fright, the scream escaping the throat at the exact instant of knowing. With his death, more than with Rex Culver's the following June, innocence was lost. It was as though the school building and its campus had been shaken to their foundation, put on alert in one merciless instant, death teaching the most important lesson of all: that it can stomp on dreams and render the future obliterated. To those already eking out an emotion-laden existence, it redirected them to look inward and to learn. A large funeral was held for James Spence at the First Baptist Church and the high school was let out to attend.

I did not go. I was terribly shaken by the first death of someone my age. I was devastated. It changed my grasp of life and its idyllic promise, obliterated my confidence in the predictable future. It sharpened the teeth of the beast, inserted fangs into that vigil. It was a hurt beyond my expectation or understanding, because James Spence had been my friend.

We had not always been friends. When we were in the same Sunday school class years before, James Spence, standing next to me, had reached down and placed an ordinary yellow pencil on my chair, pointed upward, as I sat down. The point passed through my trousers and into my body, embedding itself in a laceration caused by the pencil, which broke in two. The wound began to bleed, a sticky nuisance. It was also somewhat painful, yet everyone seemed to think it was funny, especially James Spence, who acted as though the punctured one, singled out for this honor, should be as tickled as he himself was. Well, the idea of it was funny. The actuality wasn't, and my mother took me to the doctor the next day. The way things worked in Pittsburg, nothing was ever said to Jimmy and Julia Beckham about it. Because of his family's lofty status in town, James Spence may have enjoyed a somewhat risk-free license to amuse himself.

It was easy to forgive James Spence and I did. In many ways we were exactly alike. It was in the compulsive recklessness we shared, an unpredictability that made life fun. James Spence, no matter what else, was not mean. He was loud and sometimes crude but always hardworking and easy to get along with. We wrestled a time or two, in fun, on the church lawn. I seem to remember getting the best of him, though maybe not. Neither left the encounter with any rancor. What passed was a good feeling between competitors. We became partners on Scout outings, sharing our shelter halves to button together in the formation of a pup tent. Once, when it rained, we spent the night giggling because we had pitched the tent on an incline and began rolling down the hill in the sopping downpour, trying to keep the tent over us, and we were thoroughly soaked by morning.

James Spence was a happy man whose prowess was measured in laughter. It could be said of him that he shared the waltz with others, rejoicing in the light. It made the pain of his loss personal, involving as it did the part of each of us that died with him.

*   *   *

There had been another train accident years earlier, involving an eight-year-old boy on his bicycle. He had been sent into town on a summer day to purchase tenpenny nails (three-inch carpenter's nails), his destination DeWoody's Western Auto. It sold hardware and was situated on Jefferson Street the other side of the traffic light from where he would be approaching. In fact, DeWoody's was several doors down from the Owl Café, then still in operation. The boy never made it to the store, but as was true of James Spence's accident, the series of events leading up to the misfortune can only be approximated.

The family lived about a mile west of downtown. The eight-year-old had been given his bike earlier that year and had learned to ride it on the sandy road in front of their house. To be sent on such an important errand was a big deal. Even nicer, he would be riding on pavement for the first time. Down from his house on Elm Street, he met the paved Texas Street at the bottom of a gentle incline and turned left. Here, the tall trees were dripping with cool shadiness in an older neighborhood, nice on a hot summer day. After a block or two on Texas Street, he turned right on Mattison Street. A block or so distant, he pushed the bike across the railroad tracks at the Mattison Street crossing.

By then he was halfway to town.

At the end of the block, riding again, he turned right onto the paved Cypress Street. It was a shady street also of older homes and it ran north and south. The latter led to town, and after a distance of about three blocks, Cypress met an abrupt, steep rise in the ground, graded for the same railroad tracks the boy had crossed a few minutes earlier. This Cypress Street crossing was as high as the one on James Spence's road, but the slope was much more gradual. These were tracks of the Southern Pacific line of the Cotton Belt route, that historic line.

Apparently the young man dismounted and walked his bicycle up the hill to the Cypress Street crossing. That is known for certain. Almost nothing else is. That he was barefooted probably figured in what happened. It was late morning and it was hot. It was Saturday, August 14, 1948, eleven a.m.

According to a report published in the *Pittsburg Gazette* the following Friday, August 20, he was struck from behind by the Cotton Belt freight train. "The accident occurred at the Cypress Street crossing and reports stated that he was thrown between the tracks and that more than half the entire train passed over him. He was taken to the hospital where it was learned he had suffered a fractured skull and a badly sprained leg. He remained unconscious until Tuesday morning. His condition had improved [by] Wednesday." Upon his awakening he complained, and they found and casted a fracture of the right leg.

*   *   *

It was the transformational event of my childhood. Mother told me that God was saving me for something; otherwise I would have been killed. Like Rex Culver in his truck accident some eight years later, I had sustained a skull fracture and a concussion and had a broken leg. Like James Spence in 1955, I was hit by a Cotton Belt freight train and thrown under it. That I'd lived and they had died was inexplicable, an enduring source of mystery. The train was going much slower as it neared the downtown Quitman Street crossing than had been the case in James Spence's tragedy, which had occurred three miles south of town. The lower speed reduced but did not obliterate its force.

My father drove up from Houston to see me, bringing a golden cocker spaniel I named Lucky. Friends and out-of-town relatives came to see me; I was stunned at how nice the community was to me. Apparently, the initial report went out that I had been killed by the train. That I had lived was everywhere deemed "a miracle," a conclusion I would deny only at risk of inviting heavenly retribution.

The sobering fact was that an engineer on a train, during a twenty-five-year career, could be expected to have an average of one of these collisions a year. That's twenty or twenty-five, though each incident would not necessarily be fatal. On the other hand, depending on how many people were in the vehicle or were walking along the railroad tracks, an accident might claim multiple lives at each occurrence. A train collision took James Spence's life— half of that pup tent, but not my own.

The railway line bought me another bicycle, paid for the hospitalization, and also covered yearly visits to a specialist in Longview for follow-up to the skull fracture. This doctor, in those years immediately beyond the war, was a "head, eyes, ears, nose, and throat" specialist. The skull fracture, on the right anterior frontal bone two inches above the eyebrow, did cause some residual brain damage.

It also helped me in a way that I did not then appreciate. I was very competitive and very much wanted to play high school football, its heroism a requirement to "get along with the beautiful girls." But Mother wouldn't let me. ("He said that if you ever got another blow there …") Ultimately, it was for the best. For one thing, slight as I was, slow as I was, I would have made a terrible football player and probably would have lost some teeth in the bargain. Grasping at the only other option, I entered the high school band in junior high, along with others in my class, and I treasured the time I spent in it, where those beautiful majorettes happened to be, and where the woman who would become my wife sat next to me. Those years in the band were the happiest times of my childhood.

*   *   *

I would, on an August noon six decades later, revisit the site of the accident for the first time, drive the route I had taken on my bicycle that day, examine the tracks at the Cypress Street crossing, unchanged in sixty years because they were well maintained by the company during that duration of time, and stumble onto a surprising revelation about an accident that was the faulty judgment of a child who could become so lost in thought that he missed things.

The physical evidence consisted of the heaps of smooth rocks piled between and lining either side of the rails. It consisted of the creosote crossties, so hot in the noonday sun they seemed to emit smoke. Finally the steel tracks in their brawny menace and manicured indifference spoke loudest of all. They were blazing hot and studded with combustible spikes the size of a child's wrist. The distance between the Cypress Street crossing and the point where that line intersects the east–west Kansas City Southern line measured at 250 yards. The intersection, not far from Quitman Street, my destination, proved that I was merely taking a shortcut. I had seen that by walking my bike along the Cotton Belt line I could avoid some distance of Quitman Street and its automobile traffic.

Memory returned, some of it. I remembered leaving Cypress Street at the crossing and walking the bike along the railroad tracks. I was certain of that. And I was barefooted. I still didn't know where I was hit, but somewhere along that 250 yards. Going barefooted, which is taken as a self-endowed pleasure in the summer, left me exposed to the obvious. I was in a lot of pain. (That also came back.) Bad luck put me there with feet tenderly exposed to the burning rocks, creosote crossties, and steel tracks, the searing pain! What had started as an exciting adventure became pain and misery. I reached a point of abandon, not knowing what to do. So I stopped, unable from pain to go forward or to go backward. It was the worst pain of my life. Blistering! Piercing! Miserable, and in a struggle with fate, I finally mounted the bike to ride on the rail bed itself, and at the edge of memory recall a horrible screeching noise. Was it the train or my own naked scream? Almost—almost—I managed in a fierce instant to glance back—say I did, but it was too late.

*   *   *

People told me things I did when they visited me in the hospital that I did not recall. People told me things from school that I did not recall. But memory was a dance card generous to all, and at the prom I did the bunny hop with the cast on my right leg. My head was okay. But stuff down there itched awfully, agonizingly, and I expended all my effort over the next six weeks in reconnoitering the itching places and devising various ingenious methods of satisfying my need, the least of my injuries being by far the most irritating. Finally, a straightened clothes hanger proved most adept of all, providing an aching joy that my older self would liken to sexual fulfillment, that visceral liberation.

My leg, liberated, bore longitudinal scars, decorations from a war I had won. Much later, in high school, I was informed that my IQ test had jumped smartly from those taken closer to the accident. Of the lower grades after the accident I recall very little except that I was often sent to the principal's office.

But the biggest part of this transformational event related to my interactions with the doctors and nurses at the M&S Hospital. My two weeks there gave me an insider's tour of that cottage with a mansion inside, a place where a room both contains everything needed for its sustenance and everything needed for everything else. It was a monument to human achievement, a hospital room. I saw among its riches a heritage of caring, its benevolence inherent in the summoned strength to slay dragons and revive hope. I tasted that confection and found it sweet. Afterward about the hospital I felt a sense of comfort just in knowing it was there, as though it were an annex to our common house, the sickroom everyone respected and tiptoed around, a place of awe and reverence and gratitude and pride. One sought its shelter after the mortar and pestle of adversity. As such, it fed on important events, nurses and doctors its illumined intermediaries. They may not have been the leaders in Pittsburg, either town or church, but elected officials yielded to them as was befitting that sanctuary and its luminaries, the inherent power of a worshiped goodness.

*　　*　　*

Dr. Johnson was my physician, though probably both he and Dr. Reitz took care of me that day—after, I supposed, I was conveyed to the ER of the sixty-eight-bed M&S Hospital, unconscious, bleeding, and probably swathed in dirt. I saw others—people popped in and out of my vision when I awakened—but Dr. Johnson was the one I remembered. He was a serious man, and I noted how others deferred to him. His was the grace of one entwined in the lives of others. He was in essence an extension of the self, granted the right to enter and make it all better.

Robert L. Johnson grew up in Tupelo, Mississippi, did his undergraduate work at Ole Miss, and received his medical degree from the Tulane University Medical Center. He did a year of internship at Southern Baptist Hospital in New Orleans, finishing in 1936. Was it through word-of-mouth or an advertisement he saw in a medical journal? At any rate, he came to Pittsburg that same year because of the opportunity to work with an older, established physician, Dr. James H. Mitchell.

Dr. Johnson had met the former Ella Mae Lattier at Southern Baptist Hospital, where she was finishing her RN degree, and they were married about the time of the move to Pittsburg. The young Dr. Johnson may well have made his decision to come to Pittsburg in part because another young doctor of his age group was already there: one Dr. Percy A. Reitz had moved with his wife to Pittsburg in 1935.

Dr. Reitz had done his undergraduate and medical training at the University of Nebraska and had completed internship and a year of residency at Parkland Hospital in Dallas from 1933 to 1935. Mrs. Reitz, the former Hazel A. Thomison, had earned her master's degree from the University of Kansas. College educated, the two young couples with similar backgrounds would come to be fast friends and socialize with one another over the years. In a manner similar to that of Dr. Johnson, Dr. Reitz had come to Pittsburg to begin practice with an established physician, Dr. Robert Y. Lacy, who had received his diploma from the Jefferson Medical College in Philadelphia, Pennsylvania, in 1901.[28]

---

28 A granddaughter of Dr. Lacy told me that he had been a student at the University of Texas Medical Branch until the "Great Storm of 1900" struck Galveston, killing thousands and delaying classes at UTMB, sending many of its junior and senior students scrambling to find places in other medical schools.

*   *   *

Dr. Reitz worked with Dr. Lacy until the latter's death in 1952. Although similar in age to Dr. Johnson, Dr. Reitz affected a somewhat different personality. Where Dr. Johnson was totally serious, Dr. Reitz was given to levity, and perhaps that made for an attractive dynamic between the two. Dr. Johnson's appearance bore the physical dimensions of what he did, as though he had just come from attending a patient, which he had. Dr. Reitz was more the stalwart collegian, once removed—but not much more than that—from the high jinks of an earlier time.

Two of my next-door neighbors on Elm Street were Hubert and Jean Smith. She was an RN and surgical nurse who worked with both doctors at the hospital. She proclaimed both as first-class raconteurs, sometimes competing with each other during surgery by way of stories and anecdotes, the yarns probably embellished for her listening ears. Dr. Reitz loved the annual outings to hunt deer; his group included various men in and around Pittsburg, including my uncle, Graydon Adkins. Graydon remembered a time in the early fifties when they were in a hunting shack, perhaps near Kerrville, Texas, and someone farted. "Goddamn it, don't anyone strike a match, blow us all to kingdom come!" observed Dr. Reitz. One cannot imagine Dr. Johnson having said that. Graydon thought it was kind of funny.

Dr. Reitz was called to active duty in the Army in 1942, after the United States entered World War II. In 1944, beginning at Fort Sam Houston in San Antonio, he went by train with the Fifth Auxiliary Hospital Group to New York or Delaware, where he shipped out to England to serve in the European Theater. That September they were in Cherbourg, France; in early November of 1944 they were in Belgium; and they were in Maastricht, the Netherlands, at Christmas. That is where he was during the surprise German attack that occurred that December, lasting into January of 1945, known as the Battle of the Bulge. His unit worked night and day treating casualties during this pivotal battle. His unit crossed the Rhine in March of 1945 and went as far as Hamm, Germany, before being moved back to France at the end of the fighting. From Paris he flew home, arriving back in Pittsburg that September, after more than a year of overseas duty. A genuine hero, Dr. Reitz was promoted from first lieutenant to major during the war. His last entry into his logbook, when he arrived back in San Antonio, was, "'Twas almost like a dream now that it's over, and I'm lost." Not until after his death did someone at the hospital mention that after the war, Dr. Percy Reitz never charged any serviceman or servicewoman a fee for their medical care.

Dr. Johnson did not go into the service during the war, receiving a deferment because he was the only young doctor remaining in the area. He was probably on call most nights during that time, which was no small effort, and he continued to make house calls in the evening after finishing rounds at the hospital. (Doctors in Pittsburg still made house calls into the fifties.) His was a different heroism; as it was said, *They also serve who stand and wait.* What Dr. Robert L. Johnson did during those war years was what all practicing physicians did back then, including Drs. Mitchell and Lacy: they literally gave themselves to their community. They were absorbed into its social fabric and sewn into the lives of their patients. In all but name they were public servants. Everyone kept up with their whereabouts and who had been sick and the outcome. They were prayed for, "kept in our thoughts," idolized by people ever thankful for the gods of that common house.

The prestige inherent to that was commensurate with the dreary—and wonderfully enriching—hours of toil they put in every day. It exacted a price. Patient to patient, sickbed to sickbed, delivery room to nursery, surgery to surgery, clinic to clinic, they expended themselves for others, and perhaps only another doctor can truly appreciate how physically draining that was. Day and night they burned like candlelight, the tallow time, the candlewick love. It was love because no other force in nature could arouse such commitment. Yes, it could sometimes be grouchy love. Sometimes it might be weary love, tiredness not of the love but of the behemoth physical demands placed upon a human being. And sometimes it might be sentimental love, those special times so poignant that joy itself was a form of stamina. It was the kind of love where money doesn't matter, people do, and every life has meaning, and every patient looks the same, and one is aware of doing exactly what he or she was put on Earth to do. Throw out all of the science, throw out all of the gadgets, toss aside the fads and the fancy machines and the finagling bureaucracy, and there was just that one doctor beside a patient, one at a time, year by year, doctor by doctor, to keep the flame going. Those were the golden days of medicine, when gods were gods and theirs the golden flame, wherein, willingly and lovingly, they were consumed by it.

*   *   *

That was the profession I thought I had entered. A decade and a half later—was it only fifteen years after my accident?—I presented myself at Memorial Hospital in Corpus, having finished the academic requirements to become a doctor and a licensed physician. And I came to know a different kind of medical god, the Antlered Godhead. Real gods did not know they were gods because they were too busy caring for the sick. It was their life, their joy, their legacy. Antlered Godheads went around boastfully displaying those same antlers for all to see, because they required no people to deify them, only the exercise of a power granted them by the hierarchy of their own self-importance. In time, an unknown number of them discovered Doctor's Choice, an almost invisible decision back of the White Curtain, where they were protected by their colleagues, even should the latter distance themselves from what they had seen happen.

The vast majority of physicians—the vast majority—were and are dedicated professionals serving as best they can and beloved by their patients and colleagues. I mean to say only that the doctor who has lost control, captive to an addiction the depths of which may never be known, may practice one type of medicine for some patients and a completely different kind for others. I offer that most of these lost souls die in anonymity at a respectable age, perhaps without anyone outside the White Curtain ever having been aware of their peculiar impediment. Thankfully, modern medicine has much better means of detecting them than was the case in 1963.

*   *   *

By 1957 I had come to know Pittsburg well, especially the west side of it. Just past downtown, Quitman climbed an abrupt hill and then, taking its lazy time, curved gently and coasted leisurely down the other side, past teeming flower beds and majestic oaks in the city's most gentrified neighborhood. Nestled in the pastel blue of shade trees, the wide, two-lane street was smoothly paved and accompanied on its route by root-twisted sidewalks. As well, perpendicular sidewalks leading to each house formed a ladder-like procession to the front steps of the dwellings that fronted Quitman Street, many of these edifices consisting of two- and three-story mansions built at or before the turn of the century. There was a graceful feeling of continuity about it. It was as though the plants, bushes, and the occasional sculptures, worn and quaint, were honored by the lush green carpet that ranged wall-to-wall from one house to the next, all of it catching the eye, all of it important, all of it seeming to proclaim that it didn't matter at all to those near the white-bricked hospital at 414 Quitman Street that it had been built in the prettiest part of town. That the hospital's location was there on the south side of Quitman Street, just as the street gained another rise, seemed to have been planned that way by eternity.

When Drs. Johnson and Reitz moved to Pittsburg to join Drs. Mitchell and Lacy, there was no hospital for medical doctors and their patients. In March of 1940 the four doctors—Johnson, Mitchell, Reitz, and Lacy—formed what would become the corporation that built the M&S Hospital.

The lot they bought cost $500, and each member put in $125 to pay for it. Each member put in $1,000 to incorporate the hospital, and the $4,000 sum amounted to forty shares of stock at $100 a share (each member taking ten shares). The original hospital was built for $10,200. Dr. Mitchell loaned the hospital $7,500 at 6 percent, to be paid back semiannually at $600 plus interest beginning in March of 1941. In June of 1940 the stockholders assessed themselves $1,000 each to complete the hospital and equip it, and it opened later that year or early the next. By comparison, it was in 1944 that Memorial Hospital in Corpus opened.

In February 1941 the building of a "Negro annex" was discussed. In July a check was written for $867.43 to pay for the annex in full. A "nurses' home" was built in July 1942 for $1,000, Dr. Mitchell again loaning the money at 6 percent interest. Miss Iva Boggs was hired as superintendent of the M&S Hospital in August of 1940 at a salary of $60 per month plus room and board.

The hospital annex for black people had six rooms that would hold a total of ten patients, with four rooms having double beds and two rooms being private. Operating rooms and delivery rooms were shared with white people. After their delivery, the black babies were kept in the rooms with their mothers. It did not take government coercion for the doctors to do this. Medical training in those days did not include lectures on how white doctors were to conduct themselves as health providers for those of another race in a segregated society. They did not have to be taught. Such actions were inherent in their credo, the noblesse oblige of physicians of an earlier generation, in a time when that quality seemed to go with the medical degree.

As to the hospital, many times the doctors assessed themselves to meet the deficits each month so that they might keep building and equipping it. In the beginning, private rooms were $5 a day, and a room with a double bed was $4 a day. Rooms on the obstetrics suite were $6 a day, the extra dollar being for baby care. In 1944, prices were raised: private, $6; double, $5; and obstetrics, $7.50.

*   *   *

Dr. J. H. Mitchell and Dr. R. Y. Lacy having died years earlier, Dr. R. L. Johnson died in an automobile accident in 1965. Of the four doctors who had founded and built the M&S Hospital nearly three decades earlier, Dr. Percy Reitz was the only survivor as of 1968, when he and wife, Hazel Reitz, donated the hospital to the City of Pittsburg and to Camp County. Dr. Reitz, who would die in 1978, stated that it was only proper, the community having made the hospital possible. The only stipulation was that the City of Pittsburg and the Commissions Court of Camp County operate it to the benefit of the people of these communities. The estimated value of the property in 1968 was on the order of $300,000, although it would have surely cost more than that to replace it.

Subsequently the M&S Hospital became the East Texas Medical Center–Pittsburg (rebuilt at a different site in 2009), part of a regional hospital network, a primary-care facility and a Level III (the lowest level) Trauma Center. The classification of hospital trauma centers allowed patients to reach, more rapidly than previously, the level of care required for their condition or injury. The ER of a modern hospital in Texas will assess such patients, treat those they can, and refer others to, for example, the East Texas Medical Center–Tyler, a Level I Trauma Center, which treated patients it was capable of treating and referred those it could not to the Parkland Hospital complex in Dallas. (Parkland might refer certain patients, such as those with severe burns or those with special needs, to hospitals elsewhere.)

*   *   *

The first medical doctor to move to Pittsburg after the four doctors had built the hospital was Robert K. Pendergrass, MD, who moved with his wife, Mary, to Pittsburg in 1953, at the age of twenty-nine. Bob and Mary were Republicans from Dallas before that was a common thing. I finished eighth grade that summer and, with various family and personal difficulties, paid little attention to the arrival of the charismatic young physician and his bubbly wife, well on her way to having their four children. The couple joined the First Baptist Church, where I was a member, and that is how I came to meet them.

Dr. Pendergrass had served during World War II in Chicago, a noncommissioned officer, after ROTC training at Dallas Technical High School, from which he had graduated as salutatorian of the Class of 1941. Completing premedical studies during the war, he entered the University of Michigan Medical School in 1945, graduating in 1949. After two years of surgical residency at Baylor University Medical Center in Dallas, and having transferred his commission to the Air Force, he was called back to duty during the Korean War as a captain in the Medical Corps and served as chief of surgery of Perrin Air Force Base Hospital and subsequently as base surgeon and commander of the 3645th Medical Group and Hospital at Laughlin Air Force Base, Del Rio, Texas.

Mary Smith Pendergrass, daughter of a Baptist minister, had finished her undergraduate degree in social work at Baylor. To one who was often bested by her wit, I found Mary the furthest thing from the adults I had known. She was much too filled with happiness for that, much too zealous in her pursuit of grace and ingenuity, an exciting combination. She held a unique distinction in my life. She showed me how a wife and mother could live in creative happiness, a trait both courageous and rare, at least to me. She and her spouse held that magical quality of good humor in making life fun.

The couple had begun looking for a place to locate during their time in Del Rio, had happened to drive through Pittsburg, which was only a couple of hours east of Dallas, and they liked it well enough to stay. Dr. Pendergrass went into solo practice—family medicine and surgery. But his practice extended several leagues beyond that. It extended to the lives of young people in Pittsburg, and he became my friend, mentor, employer, and advocate, the most important influence on my life. One day while we were talking, he asked whether I had thought of going into medicine. He was unaware of the train accident half a dozen years earlier and of my exposure to the profession.

He said, "I think you would be a good doctor."

On rare occasion I had allowed myself to wonder, but before that moment I had not allowed myself to believe. Those eight words changed my life. Were it true that I expended my life trying to catch up to what was no longer there, it was equally true that the search began at that exact instant. Such was my confidence, my naïveté, my peculiar ability to converge on a goal, that I never gave anything else a thought.

Reitz and Johnson were men I esteemed, gods in that faith. They had treated me many times through the years, always professionally and lovingly, and I liked them equally, honored them equally in my thoughts. Yet simultaneously they were once removed from me by way of my deference. How does one aspire to be a god? I felt such awe for Drs. Johnson and Reitz that I simply could not see myself becoming their peer. But a fierce something else had begun to tick inside me: more than anything else, I wanted their lives!

*   *   *

An incident will serve to explain. Having had a great school year from 1953 to 1954, I was surprised that Elton Acker, the principal, called me in that May and told me that mine was the highest grade average in our class. It was a warm, good feeling, possibly the man's apology for having so easily accused me earlier that year. He could turn on the charm, I will admit that. At any rate, after a trip to spend the summer in Ajo, Arizona, with Mae Lynn, Jack, and Sonny Kimberlin, I came home for the fall semester of the next school year in 1954 to meet my mother's latest adventure in husbandry.

By name, he was Bill Thomas. By position, number three. He was a big man physically, proud of his athletic build. Originally from the Midwest, he did not wear jeans or that sort of thing but dressed instead in a suit and tie or slacks and a white shirt. He cared about his appearance and person; he used cologne. But nothing eradicated the smell of alcohol on his breath. An itinerant baseball player with a group known as the House of David—they had those long-ass beards—he was a pitcher on the verge of being cut because he had lost his "stuff." But the local baseball team was in need of a pitcher and a deal was made. Bill Thomas quit the House of David, shaved off his beard—it made him feel like he didn't have a chin, he said—and a job was found for him at Lone Star Steel. He courted and won the first available female and moved into our house on Stafford Hill, meeting me at the door after my summer away. His first words were something like, "Come in, you are always welcome here."

Jesus! A chill shot through my adolescent self that all but knocked me down.

Having walked the few blocks from where the bus let me off, and carrying my suitcase, I was hesitant to go inside. Bill's smile was wrong. He made me feel like he was fixing to throw a baseball at me. He lacked cultivation, clean living, and noncriminal behavior. When he left Pittsburg that December, after eight months of residence, he had been fired from his job, dismissed from the local baseball team, and had made a few enemies. The owner of a local filling station, J. S. Hackler, had loaned Mother a snub-nosed .38 revolver to keep beneath her pillow in case she needed it for a man who had a warrant out for his arrest on various charges, including felonious assault, failure to heed a restraining order, DWI, and injury to a minor. Mother readily admitted her mistake, saying, "Bill must have thought we had a little money and he would drink it up."

*   *   *

Summer of 1953, before I entered high school, Mother had bought the old Hess house atop Stafford Hill. She had managed to buy it by way of hard work and frugality and it was a good house, said to have the best foundation in Pittsburg. But it had been let to slide by its previous occupants. It had rats. Uncle Graydon, responding to our cry for help, appeared one evening at the house. Graydon knew things and was fearless and I greatly admired him for that. He brought five or six bottle caps from the soft drinks then available, and into each he poured a small bit of red liquid, strychnine. He placed the caps at strategic places along the walls of the kitchen.

It was a nice kitchen with an alcove beside a window. The table overlooked the sunken backyard, deep as the one behind the Kimberlin house in Mount Pleasant. But rats were the problem, and the next morning after my uncle's visit, a dozen of them, fat and dead, were laid out on the kitchen floor, big as squirrels and twice as fast—but not anymore. Still, the problem wasn't over. Late that summer, after I had with good effort conquered the backyard of its knee-high goodies and dug the trash out of what had once been a concrete goldfish tank in the backyard, I passed by the bathroom—shared by both bedrooms—and at a glance beheld a dark shadow in the bowl, a blur of motion no faster than my shiver of fright at recognizing a big, long rat climbing out of the commode. It was both aware of and unimpressed by my presence.

What came next was hand-to-hand combat.

Mother appeared and stood behind me while, man of the house, I dealt with this intrusion. First, I grabbed something and forced it back into the bowl, then I flushed the potty. The rat treaded water. I recall the absurd juxtaposition of the radio, KLIF in Dallas, possibly "Cherry Pink and Apple Blossom White." I flushed again, same result. Wet, the wet that streamlines, the assailant continued trying to vault out of the bowl. I needed a weapon.

A newspaper and matches appeared in my hands. I lit the torch and tossed it at the rat. It batted it back like a baseball and dipped beneath the water for protection. I had to be careful of starting a fire.

The radio was playing "Three Coins in the Fountain," the rat one of them. It simply would not be denied.

As I tried again to immolate it, it turned vicious, snapping fiercely at my hand, its teeth flashing like machinery. To avoid being bitten, I dropped the charred newspaper into the bowl. It was exactly what the rat wanted. Using it as a ladder, it began climbing carefully along its wet contours.

I dashed away and found my baseball bat. Returning, I held the bat in my left hand while using my right to fend off the rat with another roll of newspaper. But I could not stop it. Teeth exposed, it gained the edge of the bowl. I am right-handed, and my left hand moved independently. With a swatting motion the bat came down, catching the rat in the head with a crunching sound, whereupon it quit the paper, quit the invasion, and bobbing like a cork on a line, quit the world, floating as peacefully as a knight in a moat. What was all the fuss about? In light of my mother's praise, I thought it maybe the best moment we had ever had together—we thought it the last of the rats.

*   *   *

But a bit over a year later, autumn of 1954, Bill Thomas was in residence. Bill liked to eat and was a good cook, probably from his years spent in temporary abodes. He was in a great mood that evening. It was that time in fall when an explosion of colors paints the world on sky-wide canvas. Clear evenings brought clear mornings and the days were precious. My best friend, my blood brother, was visiting for supper. He met Bill Thomas, who liked him, and my friend and I began playing basketball, using a hoop nailed to a post in the backyard.

Bill was the kind of man who brings dogs home, and they shared the backyard with us, five or six in number—not mean dogs but rambunctious. The meal he was preparing was of a stack of veal cutlets, sizzling on the stove, and mashed potatoes and rolls and another vegetable. Near the end of the preparation—which had been interrupted by Bill many times as he danced down the stairs and took the ball away from us and shot a few buckets himself and then went searching for his cigarette (he always had several going when he was drunk)—Mother came home from work and, without a word to me or my friend, took up residence in the back bedroom she and Bill shared, adjacent to the kitchen in this house she owned.

I was fifteen, a sophomore in high school, 115 pounds. I sensed trouble but was powerless to stop it. One time Bill ran up the stairs with the basketball and tripped, ending up bouncing the ball as high as the roof and giggling in the good spirits of any other boy.

Called to supper at deep twilight, we found the table set, the platter of chicken-fried steaks in the center. My friend and I took seats on opposite sides of the table. We helped ourselves to the steaks, potatoes, and cream gravy, took a luscious hot roll and a serving of green beans. We had iced tea in glasses. It was the first time I had ever had a friend over for supper and it was important to me, very important. It was such a beautiful fall day, all things right and good. The overhead light cast its reflection on the linoleum floor. The house radiated the warmth of the day. The world rewarded those who were deserving of it. It went through my mind that the secret bathroom things we did sponsored all of the rest: we pass through the world as it passes through us.

Having filled our plates, my friend and I did not start. We awaited the adults, but I became aware that Mother and Bill were arguing and that she wouldn't attend supper. Words passed between them, and I tried to reassure my friend. Trouble didn't always mean trouble. We were going to enjoy this meal.

Suddenly, and without a word to us, Bill stepped back into the kitchen.

He slammed the door to the bedroom. He looked around, as if just discovering our presence.

With an athletic arabesque, he reached and took the steaks off of our plates. He piled them onto the platter, which he lifted and carefully placed on the floor. Then he opened the screen door and whistled the dogs inside. They came readily up those stairs and, that quickly, began devouring the supper that was to have been such a nice occasion for my friend and myself. We got up and left in silence, leaving the lights behind, the adults to continue their warfare, the dogs to nourish themselves, and the event to be shuffled into other childhood memories convincing me that I did not want that life. (Before Bill left Pittsburg a month or so later, having already been turned out of the house, he ruined our '53 Chevy by pouring five pounds of sugar into the gas tank. I would not live that life!)

*　　*　　*

What life was there to live?

Abuse is accompanied by neglect, always, two for the price of one, and I was fresh out of taking their shit. I was fresh out of being the whipping boy, nose broken in a sucker punch, hit so often and so hard that it was an expected part of my life. I had no father to take my side and everyone knew it. My foundation was not the best in Pittsburg; arguably it was the worst in the hell of every dehumanizing hell that ever was, especially in never being acknowledged, much less given to an admission of regret. But one night in January, in the house on Stafford Hill, a month or two after Bill had left town, conventions in the ordinary body politic came to a screeching halt.

I did what I am proudest of doing in my whole life. My entire life! Goosebumps stinging, I added a roundhouse to my repertoire, stored so as to drive those engines that would henceforth sustain me.

Noli me tangere!

Do not touch me. Ever again.

Things changed on a seismic scale that Sunday night in January of 1955, a change that would never again leave me though it cost me friends and earned me enemies and sent me chafing in what was very nearly an overpowering rage when someone decided to teach me the fist. From that moment was fixed in me the eternity of *never again*. It fixed in me the inability to stay even one second where I was not wanted, the urge to destroy myself rather than be humiliated again. It frightened some because so unexpected from a "nice" boy. What they didn't get was that hell is a garment made out of scraps that never quite fit, a hair shirt the divestment of which is more important than can be put into words, but not less than a willingness to fight back, and heaven must be attained anew each and every day, and any future I might care to share with a wife and children was under these conditions: it will be devoid of such. And will be as good and happy as we can make it or not at all. Were that the case, were that attempt made, I would sleep in a ditch and starve on happy before I would again tolerate even a single second of it. *I wanted their lives.*

*   *   *

That spring semester of 1955, the change in me was something of a surprise. In class, one of a couple of guys who were seniors popped me on the back of the head for no reason at all except that I was a sophomore and they were seniors and I had just taken a seat in their row, a girl between me and them. Perhaps they were merely establishing pecking order. The school had its rules about that, but I surprised them. Rage is as rage does. I jumped up with both fists doubled and came menacing at these bullies with the intent to kill, before sense saved me. Luckily I did not hit them, merely reminding them that their thought was in error.

I was fifteen years old. The thing is so real that I wish from this distance I had one more chance at it. They were rocked back on their wooden chairs, and, were I to go back, I'd lift the front legs of each chair in one motion and send the two of them barreling into the row behind them. Then I'd meet them after school in a willingness to fight them to the death, if it took it. That impulse hasn't changed, but thankfully I have learned to control it. (Among other things, doing that would probably have kept me from becoming a doctor.)

Someone, maybe Dostoevsky, said that suffering is the origin of consciousness. Draw a line from that abuse and those bullies, the last in a line reaching back through eternity, and connect it to Maria Chavarria, and there I am beside her. And always will.

*   *   *

Was I dangerous? Read the statistics: the abused often are. Banish the abuse and empty the prisons! The problem is in knowing how to contain it. I thought a teacher that spring of 1955 incompetent, a man I came to despise, and my willingness to hit back got me in trouble. Occurred an afternoon of ten beats of a board in the high school woodshop, said board having been drilled to airstream it and finished with a shiny coat of dark lacquer, slick as the wood on the electric chair in Huntsville. I held that the punishment did the teacher more good than it did me. Afterward came an extended hand. "No hard feelings."

Hell no! I had been battered by better batterers than that. The guy had to maintain control of his class in some way other than by teaching, of which he was incapable. I saw myself as leader of the class, the only one with the guts to stand up to him, but that pseudo-gallantry went nether. And from this distance I would say this to that troubled youth: when you are a barn-butt, watch your step. Those at war with the world should first make peace with themselves. And if you are going to annoy an idiot, make sure you know who the idiot is, because we are less the sum of our actions than the product of our divisions. A shrill math is the handiwork of vitriol. My ill-gotten courage had earned me a place alongside Charles Favor Deaton in a willingness to fight anyone and everyone anywhere and everywhere and to the death, for that matter, CFD having sought and attained, a couple of years previously, his death by gunfire in a bar in Houston. Maybe it didn't count, but that board by that teacher was the last I was hit.

Trouble sought, one might conclude, will trouble find.

Lillie Mae Kelley, who had a master's of English and a minor in pedantry, taught sophomores that year and was a stickler for having students follow her instructions. It was not enough to write clearly and spell correctly; one must dot an i directly above the letter in handwritten themes or she would fail the entire paper. After stressing this to no end, she wrote out an assignment on the board and, sure enough, the dot she placed above the i in one of her sentences, as is usually the case when the mind is on content rather than cursive, landed like a shot put somewhere between ten and twelve feet away, well past the base of the i. I held up my hand and told her to practice what she preached: how stupid that? In the hour after school that I spent with her, she told me stinking things about myself by way of how I had failed to live up to her expectations. A standard had been set! A toll levied. But wait, there's more. The shop teacher, having sought her good heart, required assistance in providing the best in education to a certain sophomore student (who would, for dotting the i in the tutorial she lavished on me, forever thank her for portraying how the world works).

*   *   *

It did not help my case in the spring of 1955 that I was a competitor. I entered the Extemporaneous Speaking contest (along with my entry in Number Sense) sponsored by the University of Texas at Austin by way of the Interscholastic League. These academic contests were meant to promote excellence and, not incidentally, bring the brightest students to the state meet held on the campus of UT–Austin. One other student at PHS entered the speaking contest, in which one reads up on current events and is given any of a dozen or so topics to speak on at the contest itself. The idea is to arrange one's thoughts over the half hour that is granted to entrants and then present the speech to a panel of judges.

The other person was Buck Florence of Leesburg, just west of Pittsburg in Camp County. A senior and a leader, he was installed as the favorite. Buck was a likeable guy. Orphaned early, he had made a name for himself by dint of hard work and the ability to exhale on any subject. Some years later he became a lawyer and was elected to serve his district in the Texas State House of Representatives.

To compete at the first contest against other schools, one had to win the contest held at PHS. As Buck and I were the only entries, we cooperated in preparing for the event and then were given a test topic one afternoon after school. The three judges were Janet Hargrove, Lillie Mae Kelly, and Lockett Chambers. I respected both Kelly (whom I did not like) and Chambers, the teacher of English for seniors. I dearly loved Janet Hargrove, who taught freshman English and had become my friend. Speaking to the three of them was difficult, and I faltered. Buck won. The judges had split, Janet Hargrove choosing me as best and Lillie Mae Kelly choosing Buck. Lockett Chambers thought we tied and gave the nod to Buck because it was his last year. In turn, I was awarded alternate status; I might compete should Buck prove unable to do so.

The district meet was held at Commerce on the campus of what was then known as the East Texas State Teacher's College. I was fortunate to win in Number Sense. That contest was held early in the afternoon, and having nothing else to do, I sought out the building where the speaking contest was held. My idea was to support Buck in any way I could. Upon arrival, however, I was told by an official that very few schools had entered anyone in Extemporaneous Speaking and that, as an alternate, I was permitted to enter the contest should I choose to do so.

The ironic thing was that the topic I drew was the one Buck had wanted so badly. It had to do with whether the United States would go to war should Red China attack the islands of Quemoy and Matsu where, in addition to Formosa (Taiwan), the "free" Chinese lived after fleeing the mainland Communist armies of Mao Zedong. For some reason, perhaps because I had not had time to get nervous, I gave the best speech I had ever given and won. Buck came in second. He was gracious, and I wished he had won. He would have gone to State. I lost at Regional but did advance in Number Sense.

That fall of 1955, start of my junior year, the entire high school gathered in the auditorium to learn the names of those selected into the National Honor Society. The chosen would be mainly from our class and people really wanted this. The list was called out and the chosen students, one by one, rose from their seats and walked down the admiring aisles and ascended to the warm applause accorded those so honored.

I was academically near the top of my class but was not among those chosen. With each name called out that was past mine in the alphabet, I sank lower in my seat. It happened that Kelly was the faculty sponsor for the NHS, and I had a not-so-vague idea of her intervention by way of grudges from the previous semester. She no doubt also blamed me for taking Buck out of the speaking contest.

One gazes at them in the *1956 Treasure Chest* (that year's volume having been dedicated to "Miss Lillie Mae Kelly") and realizes that the main thing about NHS was not about being in it. The main thing about NHS was in being left out of it. Its prestige was measured in terms of those it excluded. Subtract honor and what is left?

*   *   *

Skip ahead thirty years, and I am a teacher at the University of Texas at Austin, and one of my endeavors is to write recommendations to help my students get into professional school by way of their applications to nursing school, physical therapy school, medical school, and so forth. I am seated in my office with a group of students who want me to write them recommendations, which I am honored to do. They also ask about the vitae they must present to the professional school along with the recommendation. Theirs is the intent, common to all students, to pad it. One of them asks about her selection to NHS in high school, saying, "Can I include this, Dr. Deaton, will it help?"

I manage, with a moment of deep thought, to tell her that "everyone" got into NHS in high school and it means nothing to the professional schools. Instead, they must pad their application with things they have done *since* high school, including good grades, lab work with a professor, volunteer work in a school or for a charity, and serving in various campus organizations. It was the truth.

Being me, I thought of going back to tell Kelly that I had missed her NHS but managed to squeak into Phi Beta Kappa at UT–Austin, but I never had the nerve. Or maybe I had the smarts to recognize the Chinese saying that, when a man starts out on a course of revenge, he should first dig two graves.

*   *   *

Success was not about hitting back so much as it was about knowing when to hit and when to be accepting of the world's imperfections. It wasn't the most important thing I learned in life, but certainly the most important thing I learned in high school. Quiet. And, by the way, my career in high school was not limited to Lillie Mae Kelly and exclusion from the NHS. I entered the Interscholastic League in "solo contests" for band members and won a few ribbons. Jack England trusted me. He called me into his office early in high school. It was one night after band practice when we had spent most of the practice session on our marching routine on the football field. I dreaded having to see him, being all too aware of the reaction I elicited from teachers.

He was seated at his desk, signing some papers, and asked me to be seated.

I allowed that I preferred to take it standing up. He seemed surprised. I took a seat and he began talking about what had happened on the field that night. What had happened on the field that night was the old "hurry up and wait" routine. When one part of the band was being taught by Mr. England, the rest of us stood in our lines and waited. But I had done something different. I had used the time to show some of the younger students in my rank how to stay in step, always a problem for new band members, and within a few minutes I had several of them practicing that. I didn't remember Mr. England being mad at me.

He said, "I was working with the horn section and looked over and saw you working with the new band members in the clarinet section."

I said, very hesitantly, knowing what was coming, "Yes?"

He smiled. "I wanted to thank you for doing that, son."

When I didn't respond, he said, "There's a name for what you were doing, Deaton, but you'll learn it soon enough. I just wanted to tell you how excellent you are in the band and how proud I am to have you. A lot depends on you as the right guide, and I couldn't be happier to have you where you are."

One who has known cruelty is ever on guard for kindness, but in this instance I felt like crying. It was the nicest thing anyone had ever said to me. I knew immediately that I'd have followed Jack England anywhere and that feeling never changed. He's gone now, but I kept up with him through the years after he moved to Longview. One time at Christmas Mimi and I went by his house and let him see our children, and he and his spouse were so pleased. As he grew older, he would occasionally call me in Austin to find out how I was doing, or I would call him just to talk. One time, hearing me call him "Mr. England," he said, "John, you can call me Jack; I've known you that long."

I said, "Mr. England, you will always be that out of my respect for you and my appreciation for the things I learned from you in the PHS marching band. I can never repay you except in love and respect." Perhaps we shared some emotion that night, having in that moment succeeded in beating back the forces of deviltry. I shall always love the guy.

*   *   *

By my senior year in high school, medical school had become my dream, so much so that my last year at PHS, I attended in body only. (And, to be truthful, Mr. Acker stopped me one day and told me I could get into the National Honor Society my senior year, if I wanted. But I had my pride.) Having heard how difficult it was to get into medical school unless one had pull, I began wondering whether it was even possible. Drs. Johnson and Reitz had opened for me the heart of medicine, deep and resonant and thrilling, but it would require much more than that for me to make medicine a reality as my future. One needed a miracle.

By happy coincidence my miracle had already arrived in the person of Dr. Bob Pendergrass. His extended hand was in kindness, and no matter how little deference I showed the man by way of my adolescent ignorance and arrogance, he continued to encourage me toward the tantalizing possibility that I could become a doctor.

His proffered hand was both figurative and literal. One day on the green lawn in front of the First Baptist Church, in spring of 1955, we had enjoyed a good handshake. Maybe grass grew greener back then, not in the sense of always being greener somewhere else but in the sense of having been greener right there where we were. Day was orange and yellow, ground green and mellow. Teenage boys, among everyone else, gathered to talk on that front lawn on a Sunday noontime after church let out. It was the best part of the day, the best part about going to church. It was a time of joy, the morning over and the afternoon deliciously ahead, and my group of boys had begun shaking hands in a way that became a squeezing contest, closing the opponent's hand as tightly as possible, gripping as the equivalent of arm wrestling, all in fun by way of expressive fellowship. I thought myself better at it than I was. I was certainly not the champion, but suddenly Dr. Pendergrass, openly and smilingly, was participating in the contest.

He looked like a doctor, whatever that means, but didn't act like one. Or let us say, he was unafraid of revealing the person inside. The bulging cheeks of a hamster, a smile big enough for everyone else to fit inside of, and soft, blue eyes purloined from the heavens were there in abundance. About him was an appealing quality of seeming to wrest joy from the ladled impulse, to demonstrate that fun is always there: not in what you can have, but in what you can get by without, and how big a joke was that? One had the idea that he never frowned or complained. One had the idea of possibilities unlimited, of the reassuring hope that we can make of life what we will. Here was another man I would have followed anywhere, and did.

One of the places I followed him was to his farm, or ranch, south of town. We sometimes worked together. It was not that different from being alone with a guy my age. He sang to himself out of happiness, a song gets on your mind, and I heard his rendition of the "Unchanged Melody" so often I thought they had made a misprint when I saw that it was actually "Unchained Melody." That was nothing. I had heard Ella Fitzgerald mention "Satin Island" so often that I was eager to see that silky place in New York, and I thought Dean Martin was singing about a "piece of pie" rather than a "pizza pie"—who ever heard of that? In Pittsburg it was sufficient to catch the spirit of such, happiness not in the lyrics or the tune but in the background of days that could seem genuinely perfect. I couldn't believe this man was so open and unassuming to me. Sensing a chance for self-improvement, I asked how to behave with a girl on a date.

"Just be yourself with a little polish," he advised.

That's still pretty good advice, though I did not always heed it. To me, an adult who was a friend was like those dreams where you are walking along and spot a nickel on the ground and begin digging and digging and more and more coinage turns up, and about then is when you wake up. I woke up to the reality.

He wasn't perfect. He offered to let me and another boy farm that summer of 1955 at that same cattle ranch off the Gilmer Highway. What I found most interesting was his offer "to underwrite your deficit." I didn't go into things to build a deficit and thought the doctor kidding. (He wasn't.) Then a week or two later when we were on the church lawn and again talking about farming, another boy, a year or two older, took me aside and said, "What are you going to fertilize it with, Pendergrass bullshit?"

I thought that was kind of funny, and so did Dr. Pendergrass, when I mentioned it to him. The doctor could laugh at himself in that way that amuses the gods and is possibly the only way of getting back at them. I worked some at his house, on Saturdays, weeding the iris beds. It was not courageous, interesting work, but it was work they had designed for me at seventy-five cents an hour and that made it worthwhile.

For a time I seemed to know Mary Pendergrass better than I did the breadwinner. Once, I worked up my nerve and braced myself to ask of her an important question. She was an attractive woman, a brunette, and already had a couple of kids, boys, towheads who ran around the house in their jockey shorts, like all young boys do, and she was a gentle and good mother. She was in her late twenties and had a joyous way of speaking, as though she were perched on a bubble that at any instant might pop, and she more than anyone else was aware of the humor of it.

She was in the iris bed, in fact, helping me by way of showing that she knew a bit about gardening. My memory is that she had donned a couple of cotton gloves to save her hands from the soil and that she enjoyed working out-of-doors.

"Do you like being married to a doctor?" I said to her.

She looked up. Her eyes were very bright. "I do this doctor."

Does God put angels in iris beds? I thought of Ella Mae Johnson, an elegant woman who had a dignity that was clear to all. She had once taught our Sunday school class. She was telling of people who were hungry, who were doing the best they could, and mentioned how they had so little by way of possessions that they employed a sardine can as a plate, when to others the can was merely to be gotten rid of as soon as possible because of its smell. In that instant I saw her humanity, her caring, her love for others. But I never had a conversation with her.

With Hazel Reitz it was different. The Johnsons were in the First Baptist but the Reitzes were Methodists. Even so, mostly because of their son, Ron, who was a friend of mine, I often bummed a ride with Mrs. Reitz in their car for various venues such as out-of-town trips related to solo contests for band members. The contests were held in Commerce or Nacogdoches and the thing was, she was looking out for me. I was the one who could never supply a car, yet she never made me feel obligated about that. She was pragmatic, tactful, and given to service. Not only that, I had the idea—and kids can tell—that she rather liked me, both as a friend for her son and a fellow citizen. Never anything but grace from Hazel Reitz, an offering a kid doesn't forget.

So I had Mary Pendergrass and Ella Mae Johnson and Hazel Reitz as models. Each was a doctor's wife but her own person. It wasn't that I wished to marry someone exactly like them. It was that each represented a human being so different and so superior to what I had known, so filled with the eminence that is there for the having, that I could not but dream the dream of having that.

*   *   *

Lazy afternoons at the Pendergrass ranch, after I had built fence or cleared land or mowed pasture, we knelt by the barn and with a tree branch in the sandy loam the doctor would outline the rudiments of the female pelvic parts, again and again, while his understudy stared, hungry cows shifted impatiently beside us, and clouds dawdled by as if indifferent to the possibilities that might devolve from a tortured anatomy lesson.

Those drawings in the sand stuck to my eyes like a daguerreotype of Eden. Had I been informed I would one day teach anatomy at the university level, I would have been surprised and mortally frightened—as I was in fact upon the occasion. School wears many faces. It was not so much that life was a learning experience, it was that for one who is driven, school never closes, and Bob Pendergrass knew this and lived it. I felt like a participant in a theater of the possible, the kind where one is not turned away.

Many times the man I came to call Doc took me and another boy to the Hotel Stephens Coffee Shop off the Square in Mount Pleasant and bought us big meals of chicken and potatoes and gravy or hamburgers as big as the Ritz. It was a long way from combing the streets of Mount Pleasant in the hope of finding a stray penny or even a nickel. I had not forgotten that, and it was partly why I was so grateful. Doc also took us to Dallas, paying our way, and we dined at the Hotel Adolphus, at one of the tables in a circle around a small ice rink upon which, while we ate, an amazing young woman of soaring beauty bedazzled us on ice with pirouettes and pureness and the fetching purposefulness of budding young womanhood. Mary was along, and to see them in their happy marriage meant everything to me. New and exciting, seizing me, a smorgasbord wherein I dined on much more than all I could eat. Adults living together need not hate each other. Did not have to fight constantly or blame their children for having been born.

*   *   *

I remember exactly where we were when I asked it, this follow-up to that erudition in the sand. It was a weekday afternoon, meaning that I was not in school and therefore it was probably summer, 1955. The sun beat down fiercely. Heat radiated just as fiercely from the pavement as we stood on the center line in the middle of Quitman Street marveling at the traffic in downtown Pittsburg. Doc and I had just come from his office and were crossing the street to Taylor's Drugstore, which still had its soda fountain and the loveliest air-conditioning in town, Doc having taken the time to have a soda with a friend. He wore a summer suit and tie. I was in blue jeans and a shirt.

"Why do women have such big butts?" I asked.

Doc's laughter was loud, natural, disarming. We were fellow travelers in pursuit of life's mysteries and I had never known anyone like this. He was a centurion sent to the outlying regions of the empire to rescue the callow youth in peril, such were the legions of the emperors in those halcyon days.

*   *   *

Early in 1957 I was hired to clean Dr. Pendergrass's office Sunday afternoons. The suite of rooms was in a one-level brick building that fronted on Quitman Street just west of where it curved and very near to where the block tapered to an angular junction with Church Street, which was known to all as "backstreet." The latter was north of Quitman Street in the same way that its twin, Marshall Street, formed the backstreet south of Quitman and Jefferson. The suite had a doctor's office, a nurses' reception area at the front, a laboratory, examining rooms, two restrooms, and two separate waiting rooms. The pay was the same three bits an hour I received for labor at the ranch or for weeding irises, and it took me about four hours to sweep and dust, to strip the old wax and apply new, and to service the restrooms. So I earned myself three bucks. As was the case for Drs. Johnson and Reitz, Dr. Pendergrass saw black patients. Waiting rooms consisted of the one at the front and one at the back. Whites entered from Quitman Street, black people from backstreet.

People with limited bathing and whose food is cooked over a wood-burning stove tend to smell of smoke and a bacon-like essence that I had encountered even among white schoolmates who lived on a farm, and it was ripe that way in that back waiting room. It was a trick of the Nazis to dehumanize people whereupon, however it left them—emaciated, disabled, humiliated—the Nazis could then hate them for what the Nazis themselves had caused to occur, and I must be careful not to blame those waiting there for things not of their own making. I understood the smell and placed no blame. I had worn that smell the year in Cooper's Chapel, notwithstanding a weekly bath in a number 3 washtub in the smokehouse.

But the smell clung to that back waiting room, and toilet paper in its restroom did not last. (No amount was ever enough.) The bathroom itself was dirtier by multiples than was the case for the one at the front. What gradually became apparent was that black people visiting downtown and learning of this bathroom's location just inside the door from Church Street availed themselves of the opportunity. Who could blame them? In their place I would have done the same. Inevitably, however, overuse created plumbing problems well beyond the abilities of a teenager with a plumber's helper, and plumbers began making weekly pilgrimages to that facility. Eventually a lock was installed on the door. The nurse unlocked the door for each patient who expressed a need, but it stopped being a community restroom.

Dr. Pendergrass was not a racist. (That was me.) Neither were Drs. Reitz and Johnson. They complied with the separate-but-equal emendations of Jim Crow but were limited in what they could do by way of the social customs of the place and time. I had never seen a sadder face than Doc's the day he told me that he had been forced to lock the bathroom at the back. What commends memory is that the three doctors in Pittsburg in the forties and fifties all provided black patients with medical, surgical, and obstetrical care. Equal to that of the whites? No, definitely not. What mattered in a time of an inordinate amount of inequality was to end one's role in it, and in a time of shameless invisibility of black people to the white community, doctors did not make that mistake. The only other thing of note is that a decade after I left Pittsburg, Doc was elected to the school board, and this Republican from Dallas led the peaceful integration of the schools in Camp County, though he and Mary received death threats from those who resisted the change.

*   *   *

Besides throwing the paper and working on Sundays at Doc's clinic, in the autumn of 1956 I began delivering clothes for Mr. G. W. Keeling at his dry cleaning establishment. It was directly across Quitman Street from Doc's clinic in the same block that contained the State Theater a bit farther west. The delivery vehicle was a green Chevrolet panel truck maybe a year older than the Chevy station wagon I drove on the paper route. The back end was one long compartment that was rigged with two longitudinal metal crossbars on which the freshly cleaned clothes could be hung. The idea in G. W.'s shop was that they would pick up clothes that were dirty and return them cleaned or, more often, receive them dirty at the front counter of the shop and return them after processing to the person's home or business that same afternoon or the following day.

I did the deliveries weekday afternoons after school and worked all day at the shop on Saturdays, eight a.m. to ten p.m., whereupon my pay for the week, a twenty-dollar bill, was steam-pressed by G. W. Keeling and extended to me in the manner of a father proud of his son. I liked Mr. Keeling and Mrs. Keeling, who often joined us in the shop. They had one child, a daughter named Marlene, who was a couple of years older than I and who was in college at the time. G. W. Keeling, in summary, was a nice man. In a city of mostly nice men, he was a prince.

Every Saturday morning, early, Dub Curtis passed by the open door between the glass windows at the front, the ones announcing, G. W. KEELING, CLEANERS. Dub always came to a stop and stood looking into the dry cleaners almost as though it were a livery stable and he had a question about Hobson's choice.

"Hey, G. W.," Dub would say.

G. W., a balding man of about forty-five, wore an expression of polite amusement. He'd look up from working a steam iron on a cloth table in the shape of a pommel horse. A man at the back, a black man who had been with G. W. forever, was busy back there doing the nitty-gritty of dry cleaning in a big, gleaming caldron of steel that rotated with the thwacking sounds of elephants inside a clothes dryer. Mr. Keeling and others, two or three women, were fed the clean but wrinkled items and had begun working those steam irons in a routine that continued throughout the day, the finishing touches on the clothing given them to process. And there stood Dub Curtis, first thing.

G. W. invariably responded to him. "Hello, Dub."

"Hey, G. W. How you doing, G. W.?"

"I'm fine, Dub. How are you?"

"Aw, I'm great, G. W. Doing great! How you doing?"

"Just fine, thank you."

To which: "Hey, G. W. How you doing?"

It went on like that for several minutes until G. W. would patiently leave his iron, weave his way to the front of the shop, dip into the cash register, and hand Dub some folding money. For all I knew, this happened daily, to the city's "marshal."

"Thank you, G. W. Thank you!"

"You're welcome, Dub."

"Thank you, G. W.!"

"You're very welcome, Dub."

"How you doing, G. W.?"

Dub, who had Down's syndrome, was in his late thirties, a ward of the city who slept on a bed kept for him at the jail, and on his rounds each day he visited the various merchants in Our Town. With infinite patience, each time I observed it—and that was every Saturday morning—G. W. answered Dub unfailingly, always with tolerance, always with courtesy, always with love.[29]

"Hey, G. W."

"Hello, Dub."

---

29   Only in medical school did I understand what Dub had, and how Pittsburg had been so accepting and supportive in his life. Our youngest daughter has this condition and brought the magic of her joy into our lives.

"Well! I'm getting on by!"
"Okay, Dub, thank you."
"So long, G. W.!"
"Good-bye, Dub!"
"So long!"
And on it went, a credit to both.

*　　　*　　　*

Mr. Keeling was so nice to me, firm but fair, that I was surprised one day when he asked me a personal question right there in the shop. It was in the spring of 1957, a couple of months before high school graduation. Mr. Keeling chewed gum and also, after lunch, took a big glass of seltzer and drank the fizz straight down, right there at the counter that greeted customers stepping into the front of the shop. "I just like to," he had answered upon my questioning. Dressed in slacks and shirt most days, with a sweater added in winter, G. W. Keeling was an enigma to me, in that he resembled a character in a book, a British book of manners. Were vocabulary peerage, and actions knights, he would have done well in the lorded ranks.

It might have been early afternoon. We were not alone in the shop, but at least there were no customers about. The cash register occupied a spot at the angle formed by the L-shaped counter, which had a section extending toward the street, beside a rack holding the most recent items of cleaning, each in its crisp paper bag with the customer's name stapled at the top, ready for pickup—or delivery. I was in that vicinity. Mr. Keeling stood at his iron.

He said, "The man who had your job got a piece."

I knew instantly what he meant, because it had been a mild scandal. Apparently at one of his deliveries in Harlem Heights, the previous deliverer of cleaned items had left more than clothing.

Presently, without looking at me, G. W. said, "Did you ever get a piece?"

It was more than surprising to be asked that. It was shocking. To begin with, I wasn't on that kind of terms with G. W. Keeling. What I did elsewhere was of no concern to him, I thought, unless it affected my job. Then again, he was my boss in a job that was fun, and a kind man, and the last thing I wanted was to upset him. What was strange was that no one else had ever asked me that. There had been no reason.

Dr. Pendergrass had never asked it, but I suddenly remembered an odd something I hadn't totally understood. One evening when only the two of us were left in the clinic, the Doc had lowered the lights and had me take a seat opposite him in one of those low-slung chairs where one's tail drags the floor. He began talking in sexual terms, as though to receive a confession from one who had nothing to confess.

At the high school, Mr. Acker had never asked me that, though at lunch one day, to my sharp anger, an incident had occurred. I have referred to it without explaining it, and here I am wondering what puritanical logic can run (ruin?) the deep rivers of adult concern?

Mr. Acker, in the full regalia of his office, had stalked out of the door on the east side of PHS, just up from the band hall. In a grassy spot near the sidewalk, the flaxen beauty and I were encamped on a blanket in full view of everyone. We had just come outdoors at noon after eating lunch in the cafeteria. We were not kissing. We were not touching. (Okay, maybe a little.) It was a bright, sunny day, and all about us were other couples doing exactly the same thing, sitting and talking, enjoying the immense pleasures of youth, and suddenly the high school principal—who could act the bully—decided that my sharing a blanket with that young woman was wrong.

The principal told us to "break it up" in a tone so ugly that my first impulse was to charge the man in nothing short of rage. It was as though, for that moment, he had invaded our home and cursed my woman. After venting his anger, he turned and marched straight back toward the east door of the high school, the entrance I had used that morning when I was summoned from the band hall and accused of theft. There was a way to sneak up behind somebody, use both hands to shove the back of the knees forward, and watch the person trip to the ground. As I have said, it would have ruined everything, because you must learn to take it and live it or it will take you and leave you.

I had done nothing other than to grow angry at the insult, the young woman's honor impugned. But at that moment in G. W.'s shop, I thought of that day and wondered whether it was connected to whatever had made my boss suspicious. One ventures that G. W. Keeling, Bob Pendergrass, and Elton Acker, adventurous as they may have been, were blind to the local economics.

The nipple economy of the fifties was a bare market that left most young men penniless but not bereft, and I counted it a blessing to have been born at a time when a kiss was still a kiss. The Pelvic Generation and its promiscuous ways were still a decade away and to me, that prodded market—and its taut topic—posed unacceptable risks. I was glad to play with margins, the only leverage then permitted. In fact, to my generation, kissing was an end in itself. In movies, a kiss ended in a fadeout before you-know-what, but to crafty investors, the market being what it was, kissing led to … more kissing. And that was not a bad thing. Kissing could go on for hours, and the young man did not fail to become aroused by it. It was even possible that the young woman became aroused by it. And markets were volatile! One could go bust. Every so often the stock market crashed. People spurted out of those windows on the way to ... life in Pittsburg (or elsewhere, but unplanned). And that was something I did not intend to happen. To an extent, I also flattered myself that I didn't seek the thrill without its authoress. I had talked to Doc about sex in marriage and was told that if you took care of everything else in a marriage, the sex would take care of itself. It sounded good to me, and why not?

Yet, stupidly, it took me several years to figure out what had happened to provoke that Inquisition. I have always been slow that way. I was home from college a few years later and came across an old pair of trousers from a suit I had owned in high school. It was a white suit with two sets of trousers, one white, one blue. I wore the blue on occasion but preferred the matching pants with the white coat. I wore it to church, the prom, and to various other functions on which I had a date. And there, inside the front waistband, flaunting itself at me, was a mosaic of dark-brown splotches, semen stains. *Old* semen stains resembling a pastel drawing of superimposed circles, brown as coffee stains on a tablecloth.

It was a cataclysmic moment. It was like being undressed in front of the world, but what made it worse was that it had occurred irretrievably some years earlier. Had I actually turned these trousers over to G. W. Keeling? To be cleaned? I worked there and yes, I had done that, more than once. And had a young man who knew how to drive with his thighs while throwing a paper spent a few moments taking care of excessive sexual tension after a date, on his way home? Possibly. There being little traffic at night, one shifted whatever stick. The next question, beyond that burning embarrassment in retrospect, was what difference should it have made to anyone but me? Well, such things did make a difference. Pittsburgites thrived on them, the goings-on of others their stock-in-trade. It was always open season on the sexual habits of teenagers and the juicer it was, the better.

I had worked in a cleaning establishment in a town that worshiped cleanliness, the cleansing of the soul from the Original Sin that might have left those same stains, were good old Adam similarly clad and similarly slapdash. One of the women who worked there had a daughter in high school, who was probably the source for what was subsequently said about me and erroneously reported to the young woman I had been dating as something I had bragged about. It was another hit to my honor. My final defense was inadequate to do any good, but it was that trousers with semen stains on them—think about it—were less risqué than those without. It also explained those knowing looks one of the women in the shop had given me, a tight smile of pious valuation, indictment of one who had been caught with his pants down on Main Street. I concluded that word had jumped from her to

G. W., then across the street to the doctor's, and then to the school and even to my employer for the paper route, Bullard Johns, always like a father to me who had, one day while we were having coffee downtown, mentioned (out of nowhere) that it only took a little bit to cause a pregnancy. Well, guess what? I knew that. Slipshod as I may have been, I knew where babies came from and that, in this one instance, one did not dot the *i* directly over its body. But on that particular day in the spring of 1957, not understanding the source of the question, I answered G. W. Keeling in the only way that a kid could, confronted with such a question.

*   *   *

I graduated high school. Following Doc's advice, inspired by him, I would attend Texas A&M in College Station for premedical studies. That only left how to pay for it. I was proud and didn't ask for help, but frankly, had someone offered me financial help against a promised return to practice medicine in Pittsburg, I would have gladly taken it. I figured I needed a thousand dollars to get through that first year. But a month into the summer of '57, I had not quite $300 in the bank, maybe $270, having squandered far too much in buying the '46 Chevrolet, customizing it, and on dates in it that were simply wonderful.

The day after graduation I went to work for a commercial ditchdigger. Bullard got me the job, as one of a crew of about half a dozen, the only white member. I did heavy, hard, backbreaking labor for one morning, a total of four hours. I went home for lunch and was so tired and discouraged that I sprawled onto the floor, a defeated heap of bad grammar. I quit by absentee (and gained respect for those who could not quit because it was all they had). Mother and one of her friends happened to be at the house that day and kept telling me I should go back and draw those half a day's wages. I did not go back. That job had already paid me far more than the fifty cents an hour I had earned. It had magnified like streaks of sunlight on a looking glass the idea of ice water on that front porch, and for me, that was sunbonnet enough.

I still had the paper route, the delivery job for G. W., the cleaning of the clinic on Sundays, and the occasional job for Dr. Pendergrass at his ranch. I was at the latter when it happened (and probably was not delivering clothes in the afternoons that week). I was building a cow feeder for Dr. Pendergrass. It was the second day of work on it, probably July 2, 1957, a Tuesday. A truck from the lumberyard had come out the day before, bringing boards and creosote posts and nails, everything going well. The selected position for the feeder was just past the deserted old farmhouse and not that far from its dirt driveway, and around noon I looked up to see a car coming my way from the direction of town, its diamond of dust visible for half a mile. In amazement I watched as my mother, in her red-and-white '56 Chevrolet two-door, turned into the driveway and stopped.

She had been canvassed at her shop that morning, she said, by a salesman who had college boys working for him on his crew, selling magazine subscriptions on a route through Texas, Oklahoma, and New Mexico. Just him and the college boys, and one could expect, in time, to save one hundred dollars a week. I did the math and decided in the instant. I finished the feeder that afternoon and that evening drove with Mother to a restaurant on the north side of Mount Pleasant, the Alps Café (recommended by Duncan Hines) to meet with the man, one John Bob Parks, for an interview.

*   *   *

John Bob Parks proved to be what the *Reader's Digest* called, in an ongoing series, "The Most Unforgettable Character I Ever Met." He was thirty-eight that summer of 1957, lived in San Antonio, but had grown up in the bottomlands east of Monroe, Louisiana, the son of people who made their way as best they could. He had served in the US Combat Engineers in Europe in World War II and had been in combat many times. Not until I had known him several years did he mention killing two Germans one time after a landing of the Army on some beachhead. He had climbed a tree for some reason and noticed the two Germans crawling through the tall grass back from the beach, having been missed by the US troops as they swept ashore and trying to get back to their own lines. Parks, armed with his rifle, shot them both dead, in the back. And it still bothered him fifteen years later.

Although I didn't know what to say to him about the two dead Nazis, he of course had done exactly what he was trained to do. Before the war, while still a schoolboy, Parks had been a champion in Golden Gloves—or so it was said, Parks being no braggart—and after high school he had taken a job as a salesman with Keystone Readers Service. After the war he had returned to the company. Its regional office was in Dallas, and KRS was a subsidiary of the Curtis Publishing Company (*Saturday Evening Post, Ladies' Home Journal*). I quickly learned that the magazines earned their keep by advertising, thereby the need for more subscriptions: the more of them, the more they made.

*   *   *

The morning after the interview with Parks, I saw Bullard and quit the paper route and then saw Mr. Keeling and quit the delivery job. I did not learn until many years later that G. W. Keeling had paid the Social Security tax on my wages that year, which counted in my favor for calculating Social Security benefits. Hardest of all was to tell Dr. Pendergrass. He approved of my choice but with reservations, based on some unsavory aspects of traveling salesmen that he had experienced in Dallas. And he was, of course, looking out for me.

His warning, in fact, proved prescient. John Bob Parks having returned with his crew to San Antonio for the Fourth of July weekend, I joined the crew of two young men from Corpus Christi and their crew manager, who drove a '53 Cadillac coupe and was named Dave Bledsoe.* We departed Mount Pleasant the morning of Wednesday, July 3, and proceeded in the direction of Dallas, our plans hazy. We may have stopped for lunch. We did not stop for supper. Instead, after long periods of waiting in the car with the two from Corpus, we reached a boat dock on Lake Dallas. My bed that first night was the scooped bottom of an aluminum rowboat, my fellow crew members likewise accommodated.

The following morning there was no breakfast, there being no place to eat, and I realized that one of the thugs from Corpus—that appellation having been awarded them by yours truly overnight—had stolen my wallet, which I never got back and in which I had twenty dollars to get me home should the job not work out. That money was precious to me. As were my driver's license and some pictures I carried in it.

I don't remember much else about the next couple of days. I think we spent the actual holiday of the Fourth milling around that boathouse, near where Dave Bledsoe was spending the holiday with his brother. We drove to Wichita Falls on Friday and checked into a motel. On Saturday we worked, and I sold my first magazine subscription to a woman in a house trailer in Archer City, Larry McMurtry's hometown. That afternoon I sold another subscription, a bigger one of $22.50, to a woman in Olney. The total for the day was a little over thirty bucks, and I got to keep 40 percent of it. I had earned twelve dollars, the equivalent of working three days digging ditches.

And that was the point. I had to take the job, were it the biggest risk of my life. In that life my mother, despite everything I have said about her, had done two divine things for me. The first was to walk away from that abortionist's clinic that day in Houston in 1939, after putting her hand on the doorknob to keep an appointment my father had made for her and insisted she keep. The other was to have the good sense to see that I was the perfect candidate for Parks's crew. Indeed, John Bob Parks had seen my picture beside the lavatory behind her in the beauty shop, asked of me, and that was how it had come about.

John Bob Parks, joining us in Wichita Falls on Sunday, learned of what we had done since Mount Pleasant and fired Dave Bledsoe on the spot, who departed with his crew, except for me. I went on the crew with Mr. Parks, who was the best natural leader I ever met. What I did not realize until much later was the momentous change it meant in my life. In a week or two I was saving that $100 a week. At summer's end I had $750 in the bank and plans. Although that room at the front of the house atop Stafford Hill was still mine as a safety net for a few more years, I no longer needed it. I could support myself, and I was on my own. I was going to college.

Epilogue

By 1974 we had moved to the Northwest Hills section of Austin. Mimi was teaching and I was a writer and contributing editor for *Consultant*, a medical journal.[30] I had never stopped thinking of Maria, never would. One day the injustice of her death seemed to overwhelm me. It was only a decade after internship, but Mimi had to physically restrain me from dropping everything and driving to Corpus and confronting the surgeon I have called Carl Broderick. I intended to charge him with murder and make a citizen's arrest. But I did not do it and in reality could not have done it. By then I had left clinical medicine for good but kept my license, and doctors do not engage in fisticuffs, or they pay for it by the sort of thing that gets into newspapers. I had overcome drug addiction but not the anger that had been seething inside me since July of 1963.

In 1995, I retired from a teaching position at UT–Austin and turned my full attention to Maria after a hiatus of three decades. In March of 1996, in a spur-of-the-moment decision, I drove to Temple, an hour's drive north of Austin, to meet with my old friend, Dr. Ramiro Peña. Having done his surgical residency at Scott & White Hospital in Temple, Dr. Peña was a board-certified general surgeon. I had made an appointment and was shown through the doors and down the hallway to his office.

Smiling and happy at our encounter, we exchanged pleasantries and coincidences; we both had a wife named Mimi, had both been in the Air Force, had both served in Vietnam. At the mention of Maria, however, tears filled the eyes of my fellow intern. He not only remembered her, he had also been haunted through the years by her needless death and was very supportive to me about that. As he put it in a letter written a couple of years later:

---

30   Once we ran into Ralph Smith, a neighbor, who was delighted when we again thanked him for marrying us.

You know, John, until you came along in 1996 to speak to me about the story, I had almost succeeded in forgetting many of the details. I had forgotten the name of the girl and your involvement in her care. I had even forgotten about the birth of the baby. But those last few days of her life and Dr. [Broderick's] involvement have haunted my surgical and professional career. I have related that story to my children on cold winter nights when we sat in front of a roaring fireplace and were baring our souls and I have used the experience to teach interns and residents about the potential seriousness of intestinal obstruction. Always, I have felt myself wince inwardly [in] embarrassment in telling of my involvement. I have also felt shame and pain for my profession. A profession that I have followed with a passion and dedication that few physicians feel.[31]

I must be quick to point out that Ramiro had reached a different conclusion about Maria's death than I. He knew it was negligence, and malpractice, and he had suffered the "tragic consequences" of her death. But he wondered whether Dr. Broderick was stretched too thin in his practice and had simply forgotten about Maria. And that is fine with me. Visiting with him that afternoon proved restorative to my depleted soul. I found in Ramiro Peña an ally, derived an unexpected strength in having seen him and heard him speak of Maria, and something else. He had not remembered her name, but I had not remembered the surgeon's name, which he supplied.

With that information, I returned to Corpus Christi in May of 1996. Mimi and I had been back once, in the eighties, when the old hospital was abandoned but still standing. By 1996, Memorial Medical Center had changed even more. It had a new name and a new ownership and a new look. The modern hospital had a state-of-the-art ER and a second tall building that had been completed in 1964. Old Memorial, meanwhile, had been replaced by a parking lot, which is like wrapping hell with cellophane to pretend it doesn't exist.

Alone and with a sense of walking through a graveyard, I attempted to locate the spot in the parking lot where Dr. Pilcher had performed Maria's autopsy. I wanted nothing less than a key opening that door and all of the doors that were locked and inaccessible to me, time being the greatest gap of all. I wished for the relief that comes in a coalescence of every thought you have ever had in your life, jillions of them, stacked one atop the others but separated from you by the barest thread of restraint. It must have been an epiphany, and

---

31   Ramiro A. Peña, MD. Personal letter to author. 15 October 1998.

I recollect another such, the summer of 1953 after we had moved into the house on Stafford Hill and conquered the lawn and the rat colony.

I had just turned fourteen and suddenly felt myself emerging into an unexpected joy. I was walking down that hill on Saturday afternoon on my way to the picture show. And it came to me as a thrilling surprise, such thoughts! *I am alive and I can have a life and it will be whatever I make of it!* Had that come true? It had. A decade later I had experienced the low-point of my life, at least until then, but I never tried to disown it. We need not concoct through the pane in that broken glass any but the portrait we've been given. In great swaths mine had been in shades of everything from the impossible to the ubiquitous, the tragic to the heartrending.

After thinking something like these thoughts, I found myself again in that parking lot beside a hospital on a bright spring day in Corpus Christi, Texas. But I couldn't find a thing. I tried for that foreboding walkway, that esplanade, that thoroughfare, that turnpike to hell. I tried for those two delivery rooms situated in the cockpit of that concrete airplane, but not even its outline could be found. I wished to visit all the places that no longer existed. Beyond that, and conveniently, the hospital had destroyed Maria's clinical record, its policy being to destroy old records after twenty years, or so I was told.

For all that, the new hospital had begun a residency training program in 1973 (Family Practice) and was a bustling medical center situated in a largely Hispanic neighborhood. Having obtained the address of Maria's son, whose name was listed on the birth certificate in my possession, I left a note at his home.

In September of 1996, with my son Steve, now an Austin policeman, I returned to Corpus and met Luis Chavarria, now thirty-three, and his wife, Connie. It was a poignant moment. We spoke for a couple of hours at a restaurant. We took pictures. Luis asked the details of his mother's death, and one of the doctors who had taken care of her told him. Luis grew very quiet, his grief both apparent and restrained. Later that day I met with Maria's mother and stepfather. That, too, was a poignant moment. Our pain shared, we wept the tears that change nothing but make it, possibly, more bearable. Before leaving Corpus, my son and I visited Maria's grave. Had she lived, she would have been fifty years old.

*   *   *

An eye-crinkling Sunday afternoon in Corpus Christi's Rose Hill Cemetery, September 8, 1996. A purple granite marker wedged between markers for Solis, Gonzales, Castaneda, and Jaime:

SYLVIA M. CHAVARRIA
Julio 12, 1946
Julio 27, 1963
Recuerdos de Esposo Hijo y Padres

Maria Sylvia Chavarria was her name, and she said it was okay for me to call her Maria, though her family knew her as Sylvia, and that is why it went on the marker. The *M* in the marker is for *Mares*, her maiden name.

The service was on the Monday following her death the previous Saturday, and attendance was estimated at between 100 and 150. Father Fernandez officiated at the Holy Family Catholic Church. Then they drove you out here in a long line of cars and stood while your casket was lowered into the ground right here at this spot. Your son was too young then but first remembered seeing your grave when he was about five years old, and he remembers a little sapling of a tree—the one that now, just over there, soars with its branches uplifted, its shade running along the ground in golden splendor and shielding you and those around you.

It is not like I expected, Maria, this visit to you. Of course I did not go to your funeral; I was too ashamed and upset. But today my son Stephen, born at Memorial on June 23, 1964, shortly before I left the internship for a residency program in Galveston, accompanied me. The directions were excellent and he, younger and more certain of himself, stalked right to your marker and shouted, "Here it is!" I believe I may have hoped somehow not to find it here, not to see it as the culmination of what happened to you so long ago. We took pictures, of course, then got back in the car and drove away. Then I thought of something, the only lie I could think of, and we returned, and I am here for a moment by myself. He thinks that I am very strange. But I had to be alone with you for a minute or two. Did I think you would say something, forgive me at last for letting you down?

For I do feel guilt; that will always be a part of your memory—the knowledge that had I stood up to that surgeon on the Monday when you should have had surgery, you would still be alive. Guilt and anger have fed my frustration ever since, but all of it seems separate now, a part of me no longer as vulnerable as it once was. Now I have learned some of the things about life that I did not know then, and maybe that is finally what I wanted to tell you. I wanted to tell you that I was sorry and I thought tears would grip me when I did. I was afraid I would fall weeping to my knees. No. It is not like that; I feel no urge to cry.

The tree is here, with its shade, and it does not accuse. On this Sunday afternoon others are here, visiting, and it is a sacred thing to be out here today.

The marker is here, and you are here, and I am told your grandchildren come with their parents and kneel to pray for you beside your marker. Isn't that nice?

Maria, I heard what you said to me and will try and help your son. The strange thing is—and you knew this, of course—he doesn't need my help so much as I need his. Thank you for letting me discover that. You did not get to give him a "happy always," but perhaps he has found it on his own. I promise to keep up with your grandchildren and will try and tell them how proud you would have been of them. They are two boys and a girl. She is the middle child, and one of her names is Maria. One day they will have children of their own, and each of those kids will carry forever a part of you, your spark, your bravery, your specialness. But I see with my son sitting in the car over there with the engine running so that he can have the air-conditioning, I see that probably I won't get back out here again, but at least I know why I have come.

I have come, at last, to say good-bye.

Vayas con Dios, Maria.

The End

Maria's marker in Rose Hill Cemetery in Corpus Christi, where she has lain since July 29, 1963. The inscription, *Recuerdos de Esposo Hijo y Padres*, means, "Regards from your husband, child, and parents."

The author, in 1996, with Luis Chavarria (Maria's son) and Luis's wife, Connie. We had spoken in a restaurant for a couple of hours. Afterward, we continued to keep in touch by correspondence for a number of years.

Acknowledgments

Many people in or from Pittsburg helped with this book. The current mayor, Mayor Shawn Kennington, graciously supplied several photographs for use in the book. Of those who read part of the book, Charles "Chuck" Johns of Cozart-Johns Insurance—Bullard's son—was first and foremost. Chuck was enormously helpful in vetting the last section, in correcting historical facts, and in providing valuable insights on many subjects on many occasions. The information about Dr. Percy Reitz, who died in 1978, was supplied by Ronald C. Reitz, PhD, about his father, some of it from a diary Dr. Percy Reitz kept during World War II. After receiving a doctorate in biochemistry from Tulane University, Ronald became a professor of biochemistry at the University of Nevada School of Medicine in Reno, where he authored over seventy research papers and was active in graduate and undergraduate education. He is now retired.

I am indebted to Barbara Johnson Brieger, an exact contemporary of mine, for the material on her father, Dr. Robert L. Johnson, who died in 1965. In addition, Barbara's mother, Ella Mae Johnson, had typed up the information about the M&S Hospital's formation, and Barbara found it when going through Ella Mae's things after her death and kindly supplied it to me for use here. Barbara received her degree in speech therapy from UT–Austin, later earned a master's degree, and retired after teaching many years in the Pittsburg Independent School District.

No less appreciated was the help of Vernon and Bette Holcomb, for reading part of the manuscript and providing details of the accidents mentioned in the last section. This involved work at the library in digging out published accounts from long ago. Like Chuck Johns, Vernon is a proud graduate of Texas A&M University, and both are sterling examples of the best that can be produced by any school. Vernon retired with the rank of lieutenant colonel from the Air Force. Bette, for her part, is a woman of whom I am proud to say that I have known none finer.

In 2009, Robert L. Turner of Pittsburg kindly helped with the information about the names of the railroad lines that pass through the city. Ola M. Stone of Pittsburg helped enormously in providing background material on O. E. Acker, including contact information for one of Mr. Acker's daughters, Martha Lorenz. Martha, with degrees in dramatic arts, taught same at the high school level and is now retired. She told of her father's service in World War II and offered valuable insights about the man himself.

The kind people at the *Pittsburg Gazette* helped by locating and supplying newspaper accounts of several events, including Mr. Acker's retirement and the write-up after his death. They also provided newspaper accounts of the accidents narrated in the last section of the book: those of Rex Culver, James Spence Beckham, and me. The Reverend Rodney Williams, a childhood friend of mine, was close friends with James Spence and confirmed my idea of what probably happened, the two of them being "daredevils at that time." (So were we all.)

Information on the Martin Hospital was supplied in 2009 by my aunt, Mae Lynn Kimberlin, who in 1938 had her only child there—my cousin Jack. Mae Lynn also helped with the Kimberlin genealogy and tolerated in her home in Ajo, Arizona, in the summer of 1954, an adolescent nephew who grew to love her for the caring and excellent person she has always been. Jack also tolerated me that summer, taught me how to climb the "A" mountain, and shared with me an ongoing case of the giggles, aimed at the absurdity of life.

Austinite Dr. Bob Pendergrass, by phone and letter and e-mail, supplied me with the requested information about his and Mary's background and time in Pittsburg.

My first cousin from the Kimberlin side Chuck Bice and wife, Linda Birdwell Bice, read and offered suggestions about the manuscript, and more importantly, gave their love and support. Linda is an award-winning poet and an excellent writer, and the book is better for her copyediting, insights, and encouragement. I can never repay her for that, despite her claim that reading it was reward enough. Chuck, no less an artist in restoring vintage automobiles, was for many years a flight paramedic for Air One, East Texas Medical Center, Tyler, Texas. He was kind to let me read his unpublished memoir, a riveting account of his life in the air—some two thousand flights—and I am so proud to count this gifted man as both a relative and a friend.

Charles G. "Choc" Anderson of Abilene, Texas, provided background material on his family and on Cooper's Chapel. In our separate lives, it is amazing how Choc and I shared so many interests, including the drive to be a writer and our mutual interest in Texas history. As well as his books, Choc also writes for the *Abilene Reporter News*. Many of his articles have been about World War II heroes, including survivors of Pearl Harbor, Iwo Jima, and Normandy. His sister, Pauline Anderson Slovak, who holds a doctorate of education and is now retired, was also extremely helpful.

Shelba Davis Spears of Port Arthur, Texas, provided valuable pictures of the students at the Cooper's Chapel Overland School and at the Argo school. She also provided information on our teachers that year of 1947–48. Shelba, who rode the bus into Mount Pleasant for high school and was valedictorian of the Class of 1957 at MPHS, earned her degree in education and later a master's of education and is now retired from her teaching career on the Texas Gulf Coast. Charlie Groom and Janet Hargrove, my second- and third-grade teachers, respectively, provided helpful information. Charlie died in 2010, and Janet Hargrove died in 2011, at 104 years of age.

Mimi's parents, the late Helen and Gilbert Garrett, helped me by way of oral history in the section that describes their early days. In particular, Helen gave me the book I used to write about Greenville, and also provided a personal biography I drew from in writing about her. Mimi's sister, Vicki, and her husband, Steve Bradley, read a part of the manuscript and offered helpful additions as well as their much-appreciated encouragement. Mimi, of course, was the center of the book. I could never have done any of it without her. She drew a wild card and stayed, and we played out every hand together. One is tempted to say that almost—almost—everything else was made trivial by love. But love doesn't solve everything. In the end, though, it is the hand that trumps all others. Without it, and perhaps in spite of it, the game itself is always at risk, a thing we learn—and just as quickly forget, which is just as well.

I am indebted to the librarians at the Corpus Christi Public Library for supplying photographs and background information on Memorial Hospital. Jean Oliver, who had been the secretary of the Nueces County Medical Society when I was in Corpus, with an office in the library adjacent to the interns' lounge, provided valuable facts about the hospital and its history. She, in turn, credited the secretary of Memorial Medical Center for help with newspaper clippings and facts. A married mother of three, Jean always had a smile of encouragement that was wonderfully appreciated by the 1963–64 class of interns. My friend the Reverend James Hernandez Sr. of Austin provided an approximation of the wedding vows taken by Mimi and me in 1960.

I have also benefitted from the technical expertise in scanning photographs and the wonderful restoration of the picture of the PHS school building by the Office Max ImPress Team #0478 (desktop publishing) of Austin, including Tim, Abbey, and Francisca, the supervisor at the time. A special thanks to Sam, Brandon, and Ace at StarTech PC in Austin, for all-purpose excellence and service above and beyond the call of duty on my computer.

Maria's mother, Duvelia La Torre, provided background information on Maria and pictures of Maria and herself. Rosie Rincon, Maria's half-sister, who loved her dearly, provided during several phone conversations the background on their family and on Maria's life before she was married. Maria's son, Luis Eduardo Chavarria, and his wife, Connie, graciously gave of themselves by way of opening their lives to a stranger from Austin, and they have given me a measure of peace from an event from which only Maria can grant absolution. Only death will stop the agony I still feel from hearing Maria beg for her life, when I did not do everything in my power to save her. That stain does not lessen. Let the word go out that you must commit your life to save the patient, because that is the only way you can save yourself.

About the Author

John G. Deaton, MD, graduated with high honors from the University of Texas Medical Branch in Galveston in 1963. He was board-certified in internal medicine in 1970. In 1971, he left clinical medicine to pursue other interests. He is a retired senior lecturer from the University of Texas at Austin and the author of seven previous books, including the novel *Two Hands Full of Sunshine*, also published by iUniverse. The present book is the first of a three-part memoir of his years in clinical medicine, including medical school, residency training, and a year of active duty as a physician in Vietnam spanning 1967 and 1968.

For book or author information, please visit us online at:
www.thedeathofmariachavarria.com